Aquinas's Moral Theory

ॐ

NORMAN KRETZMANN

AQUINAS'S
MORAL THEORY

ಇನ

*Essays in Honor of
Norman Kretzmann*

EDITED BY

SCOTT MACDONALD
AND ELEONORE STUMP

Cornell University Press

Ithaca and London

Photograph of Norman Kretzmann by Jean Anne Leuchtenburg,
National Humanities Center

"Thomas Aquinas on the Good: The Relation between Metaphysics and Ethics,"
by Jan A. Aertsen, originally appeared in his book *Medieval Philosophy and the
Transcendentals: The Case of Thomas Aquinas* (Leiden, The Netherlands: Brill, 1996).
Reprinted by permission.

Portions of "Aquinas on Aristotelian Happiness," by Anthony Kenny, appeared in
his essay "History of Philosophy: Historical and Rational Reconstruction," *Philosophica
Fennica* 61 (1996): 67–81. Reprinted by permission.

First published 1998 by Cornell University Press

Library of Congress Cataloging-in-Publication Data

Aquinas's moral theory : essays in honor of Norman Kretzmann /
edited by Scott MacDonald and Eleonore Stump.
p.   cm.
Includes bibliographical references and index.
ISBN 0-8014-3436-x (hardcover : alk. paper)
1. Thomas, Aquinas, Saint, 1225?–1274.   2. Ethics—History.
3. Kretzmann, Norman.   I. Kretzmann, Norman.   II. MacDonald, Scott
Charles.   III. Stump, Eleonore, b. 1947.
B765.T54 A69 1998
171'.2'092—dc21   98-38623

Printed in the United States of America

Cornell University Press strives to use environmentally responsible suppliers and
materials to the fullest extent possible in the publishing of its books. Such materials
include vegetable-based, low-VOC inks and acid-free papers that are recycled,
totally chlorine-free, or partly composed of nonwood fibers.

Cloth printing   10 9 8 7 6 5 4 3 2 1

FOR NORMAN

Mos enim amicorum est ut cum amicus ad
suam exaltationem vadit, de eius recessu
minus desolentur.

Thomas Aquinas
Lectura super evangelium Johannis c. 14, l. 8

Contents

III
MORAL THEORY IN PHILOSOPHY
OF LANGUAGE AND METAPHYSICS

Abbreviations

Aquinas's Works

CA	*Catena aurea*
DEE	*De ente et essentia*
DPN	*De principiis naturae*
DRP	*De regimine principum*
DUI	*De unitate intellectus contra Averroistas*
In BDH	*Expositio in librum Boethii De hebdomadibus*
In BDT	*Expositio super librum Boethii De trinitate*
In I Cor	*Super I ad Corinthios*
In DA	*Sententia super De anima*
In DSS	*In libros De sensu et sensato*
In Heb	*Super ad Hebraeos*
In Joh	*Lectura super evangelium Johannis*
In M	*Sententia super Metaphysicam*
In Matt	*Lectura super evangelium Matthaei*
In NE	*Sententia libri Ethicorum*
In PA	*Sententia super Posteriora analytica*
In PH	*Sententia super Peri hermeneias*
In Ph	*Sententia super Physicam*
In Phil	*Super ad Philippenses*
In Po	*Sententia libri Politicorum*
In Rom	*Super ad Romanos*
In Sent	*Scriptum super libros Sententiarum*
QDM	*Quaestiones disputatae de malo*
QDP	*Quaestiones disputatae de potentia*
QDSC	*Quaestiones disputatae de spiritualibus creaturis*
QDV	*Quaestiones disputatae de veritate*
QDVC	*Quaestiones disputatae de virtutibus in communi*
SCG	*Summa contra gentiles*
ST	*Summa theologiae*

Modern Editions of Aquinas's Works

Blackfriars		*Summa theologiae*, general editor, Thomas Gilby, (New York: McGraw-Hill, 1964–81).
Busa		*Sancti Thomae Aquinatis Opera omnia*, edited by Roberto Busa (Stuttgart–Bad Cannstatt: Frommann-Holzboog, 1980).
Decker		*Sancti Thomae de Aquino Expositio super librum Boetii De Trinitate*, edited by Bruno Decker, Studien und Texte 44 (Leiden: E. J. Brill, 1955).
Leonine		*Sancti Thomae de Aquino Opera omnia* (Rome, 1882–).
Mandonnet-Moos		*Scriptum super libros Sententiarum*, edited by Pierre Mandonnet and Maria Fabianus Moos (Paris: Lethielleux, 1929–33).
Marietti	*DUI*	edited by R. M. Spiazzi in *Divi Thomae Aquinatis Opuscula philosophica* (Turin-Rome: Marietti, 1954).
	In I Cor	edited by R. Cai in *Super Epistolas Sancti Pauli lectura* (Turin-Rome: Marietti, 1953).
	In Joh	*Sancti Thomae Aquinatis Evangelium Sancti Ioannis lectura*, edited by R. Cai (Turin-Rome: Marietti, 1952).
	In M	*Sancti Thomae Aquinatis In duodecim libros Metaphysicorum Aristotelis expositio*, edited by M.-R. Cathala, revised by R. M. Spiazzi (Turin-Rome: Marietti, 1950).
	In NE	*Sancti Thomae Aquinatis In decem libros Ethicorum Aristotelis ad Nicomachum expositio,*

edited by R. M. Spiazzi (Turin-Rome: Marietti, 1964).

In PA   *Sancti Thomae Aquinatis In Aristotelis libros Peri hermeneias et Posteriorum analyticorum expositio*, edited by R. M. Spiazzi (Turin-Rome: Marietti, 1964).

QDP   edited by P. M. Pession in *Sancti Thomae Aquinatis Quaestiones disputatae*, vol. 2 (Turin-Rome: Marietti, 1965).

QDSC   edited by M. Calcaterra and T. S. Centi in *Sancti Thomae Aquinatis Quaestiones disputatae*, vol. 2 (Turin-Rome: Marietti, 1965).

QDV   edited by R. M. Spiazzi in *Sancti Thomae Aquinatis Quaestiones disputatae*, vol. 1 (Turin-Rome: Marietti, 1964).

QDVC   edited by E. Odetto in *Sancti Thomae Aquinatis Quaestiones disputatae*, vol. 2 (Turin-Rome: Marietti, 1965).

SCG   *Sancti Thomae Aquinatis Summa contra gentiles*, edited by C. Pera, P. Marc, and P. Caramello (Turin-Rome: Marietti, 1961–67).

ST   *Sancti Thomae Aquinatis Summa theologiae*, edited by P. Caramello (Turin-Rome: Marietti, 1952–76).

Aquinas's Moral Theory

за

SCOTT MACDONALD AND ELEONORE STUMP

ક઼

Introduction

The greater part of the vast corpus left to us by philosophers of the later Middle Ages fell into scholarly neglect in the Renaissance and Enlightenment periods. There are only a few exceptions to this rule, and the work of Thomas Aquinas is one of them. Discussion and study of his philosophical and theological writings have been ongoing from his period to our own, and so the remarkable growth of interest in his work in recent years cannot be characterized as a recovery of his thought. It is therefore different from recent developments in the study of many other areas in medieval philosophy, where there has been a genuine recovery of philosophical sources that have not been understood or appreciated for centuries. Nonetheless, the scholarly activity now being devoted to understanding and interpreting Aquinas's thought is remarkable both in its quantity and in its approach. There remains, of course, a strong tradition of Aquinas scholarship in circles influenced by the Thomism that flourished earlier in this century. But representatives of that tradition are now being joined in the study of Aquinas by increasingly large numbers of philosophers who have no particular commitment to Thomism as a philosophical or religious movement. Philosophers from different backgrounds, including many from the mainstream of Anglo-American philosophy, have begun seriously to explore and explicate Aquinas's views on a wide variety of topics. Aquinas is consequently acquiring a recognized place in professional discussions of the English-speaking philosophical community as a whole.

The ten essays in this volume offer a glimpse of both the vitality of contemporary Aquinas scholarship and some of its varying interests. The essays cluster around issues in Aquinas's moral theory. But readers

1

who come with modern expectations about the sorts of topics and problems that are to be dealt with in moral philosophy may well be surprised by some of what they find here. Because Aquinas is a systematic thinker whose works constitute an attempt to understand all of philosophy as a coherent whole, his discussions of ethics are frequently embedded in the context of other philosophical discussions, and his theoretical reflections on moral issues range more widely than the narrowly defined set of issues we have inherited in the philosophical tradition stemming from thinkers such as Kant, Mill, and Sidgwick.

One manifestation of this is the fact that Aquinas's reflections on moral issues are not always isolated in special treatises devoted exclusively to ethics, and the issues that he takes to be essential to theoretical moral thinking are not always cordoned off from issues that we might think of as proper to other, distinct enterprises, including metaphysics, philosophy of mind, philosophical theology, and the theories of action and practical rationality. Of course, certain of his texts—the *Quaestiones disputatae de virtutibus,* for example, and the so-called treatises on happiness, the virtues, and law in the second part of *Summa theologiae*—focus on topics that are indisputably central to ethics. These texts and the issues considered in them deserve careful attention from anyone interested in Aquinas's moral thought, and recent work in virtue-based ethical theories and in natural-law morality, for example, has drawn considerable contemporary philosophical attention to these parts of his thought. It is to be expected, then, that a volume devoted to Aquinas's moral theory will contain essays examining important elements of his accounts of happiness, virtue, and natural law. But in attempting to explicate and learn from his moral theory it would be a mistake to focus too narrowly on texts of this kind because they neither exhaust Aquinas's theoretical work on moral issues nor stand on their own as independent treatments of the distinctively moral issues they raise.

In addition to the discussions of such standard ethical issues as happiness, moral virtue, and natural law, a large number of analyses and arguments that are clearly pivotal to Aquinas's moral thought can be found in contexts where the main concern is something other than ethics. So, for example, his detailed and fundamental analysis of the nature of goodness in general occurs not in the second part of *Summa theologiae* with the bulk of the topics on moral theology but in the opening questions of the *Summa's* first part, where the issues under discussion have to do with philosophical theology and metaphysics. Moreover, his illuminating analyses of morally significant mental states and of attitudes such as love and anger occur not as part of his discussion of virtue and vice but in his lengthy treatment of the passions, in a part of his work devoted primarily to issues in philosophical psychology. So we cannot capture all that belongs to Aquinas's moral theory, or even all that is crucial to it, without casting our net well beyond the boundaries of the treatises that we might be tempted to identify as constituting his ethical writings proper. For this reason, some of the essays presented here explore issues that arise from other parts of Aquinas's work and that manifest his moral theory as it is embedded in other parts of his monumental philosophical edifice.

Aquinas's discussions of standard ethical issues not only fail to exhaust his moral thought but also do not stand on their own as independent pieces of moral theory. The reason for this is that his analyses of the notions that are central to his moral thinking often depend conceptually on ideas developed in other parts of his system. For example, when he undertakes an analysis of morally right action (in the *Summa*'s second part—IaIIae.18), he begins with an oblique but clear reference to his analysis of the nature of goodness in general as articulated at the beginning of the *Summa*'s first part (Ia.5), and the analysis of moral rightness he goes on to develop is difficult to understand apart from that metaphysical foundation. In a similar way, his consideration of the moral virtues presupposes his account of the nature of the soul and its role in the production of human action and activity, topics that would now generally be classified under metaphysics and philosophy of mind. Seeing this relationship between his consideration of the virtues and his account of human psychology helps explain why he prefaces the treatise on the virtues in the second part of *Summa theologiae* with a lengthy account of the human passions and emotions; it also helps account for the fact that his discussion of moral virtue in general begins with a discussion of the ontological status, nature, and causal powers of habits and dispositions of mind. So Aquinas's treatments of what we would recognize as the main issues in ethics are intimately tied to and cannot be fully understood apart from his treatments of many issues in other areas of philosophy. The theoretical rootedness of Aquinas's moral reflections, their reliance on metaphysical and psychological foundations provided by other parts of his philosophical system, strengthens and deepens his moral theory; it is a distinctive and attractive feature of Aquinas's moral thought. Some of the essays in this volume therefore focus on such broader issues in his moral theory.

Furthermore, the relations of influence by which Aquinas's metaphysics, philosophical psychology, and other parts of his thought are connected to his moral theory do not run in only one direction; his interests in moral issues often flow into and inform and shape his work in other areas, just as his moral reflections are shaped or grounded by them. Perhaps the clearest example of this sort of creative interplay between what we would recognize as distinct disciplines within philosophy is in the intersection of his moral thought with his philosophical theology. Like most philosophers, Aquinas is interested in the moral conundrums arising from his general worldview. That worldview is, of course, Christian, and Christian tradition is a particularly rich repository of moral reflection and moral doctrine. Hence, Aquinas could be expected to and does extend his moral thinking to address and incorporate problems raised by Christianity. He provides, for example, accounts not only of moral virtue and vice but also of sin, grace, and religious merit. He is interested not only in the conditions of human goodness and badness, praiseworthiness and blameworthiness, but also in the special issues associated with divine goodness, divine moral responsibility, and divine providence. Aquinas's moral thinking greatly influences important elements of such work in his philosophical theology—and this is just one respect in which his ethics shapes the wider system of his thought.

For all these reasons, his moral theory cannot be easily extricated and made to stand by itself apart from other areas of his philosophy. Consequently, mirroring Aquinas's own work on moral issues, the essays in this volume raise and explore the ethical dimensions of a wide range of philosophical and theological topics in a variety of Aquinas's texts. We have organized the essays into three parts: Moral Theory and Moral Theology; Moral Psychology and Practical Reason; and Moral Theory in Philosophy of Language and Metaphysics.

Moral Theory and Moral Theology

In the book's first chapter, "Aquinas on Aristotelian Happiness," Anthony Kenny explores the way in which Aquinas interprets and uses Aristotle's doctrine of happiness in the *Nicomachean Ethics*. Kenny examines Aquinas's treatment of Aristotelian happiness in four different contexts. The first is in his commentary on Aristotle's understanding of happiness in the *Nicomachean Ethics*; there Aquinas's primary role is that of Aristotelian commentator. The next is in his attempted reconciliation (in *Summa theologiae* IaIIae.69) of the Aristotelian doctrine of happiness with the Christian view of happiness expressed in the Sermon on the Mount; in this context Aquinas's point of view is primarily that of a Christian philosopher and biblical theologian. Third is his application and extension (in *Summa theologiae* IaIIae.2–5) of the notion of Aristotelian happiness to the Christian doctrine that the goal of human existence is everlasting union with God; in this connection Aquinas's main task is the exposition and defense of developed Catholic doctrine. The last is his use (in *Summa theologiae* IIaIIae.179–88) of Aristotelian ideas about happiness as part of his justification of a religious life devoted to teaching and preaching; in this practical application of Aristotelian ethics, Aquinas might be read as offering an apologia for his own Dominican order.

In the second essay, "Wisdom: Will, Belief, and Moral Goodness," Eleonore Stump examines Aquinas's account of wisdom as the most important of the intellectual virtues. Stump connects this account of wisdom as a virtue with Aquinas's theory of the relationship between intellect and will and with his general presentation of virtue and vice. For Aquinas, Stump argues, wisdom is primarily a state of intellect, but it can be a genuine virtue because certain of our cognitive states (including those constitutive of wisdom) are subject to our voluntary control; she explains and defends Aquinas's view that the will can directly cause and sustain certain of our beliefs. She shows how on Aquinas's account, as a consequence of will's relation to intellect, it is possible for our good and bad moral choices to give rise to corresponding cognitive excellences or deficiencies which, in turn, play a role in other moral choices, creating a spiral toward moral goodness or evil. Because of this dynamic interplay between moral choices and cognitive states, Aquinas's account helps to explain the puzzling phenomenon that has been called "the banality of evil," when persons who commit monstrous moral evil feel no remorse or moral anguish, either during the commission of that evil or later when they are publicly confronted with their crimes. On Stump's view, the interactions between intellect and will and their profound effect on a person's moral state help us understand the great value Aquinas places on the virtue of wisdom.

In "Saint Thomas and the Principle of Double Effect," Gareth B. Matthews scrutinizes the attribution to Aquinas of an important normative principle associated with the Natural Law tradition in ethics. At least on one formulation of it, this is the principle that when the performance of an action will produce both good and bad effects, an agent is morally permitted to perform that action only if she intends to bring about the good effect, and the bad effect is an unintended or indirect consequence. After examining a formulation of the principle found in the recent literature and its application to well-known issues in medical ethics, Matthews turns to the question of whether the principle has its provenance in Aquinas, as is sometimes supposed. Following suggestions of Germain Grisez, Alan Donagan, Joseph Boyle, and Warren Quinn, Matthews presents three other formulations of the principle, finally concluding that Aquinas's famous justification of self-defense (in *Summa theologiae* IIaIIae.64.7) neither endorses nor presupposes a Principle of Double Effect of the sort found in recent literature in medical ethics. But Matthews allows that Aquinas's discussion of the moral permissibility of self-defense is fertile ground for reflection on the issues raised by the Principle of Double Effect, and that the principle might justifiably be viewed as broadly Thomistic in this sense.

In the final essay in Part I, "Ideals of *Scientia moralis* and the Invention of the *Summa theologiae*," Mark D. Jordan compares the nature of Aquinas's project in the second part of *Summa theologiae* with other medieval conceptions and executions of the project of theoretical moral inquiry. Jordan argues that the structure and composition of *Summa* IIa are innovative and that the nature of Aquinas's innovations are the key to understanding Aquinas's own conception of *scientia moralis* and his criticisms of alternative views available to him. Jordan's contention, then, is that the *Summa*'s second part constitutes Aquinas's criticism of the philosophical and theological ideals of moral science with which he was acquainted. According to Jordan, the moral part of the *Summa* is constructed to present a careful middle way between the pretentious ambitions of a moral philosophy which fails to acknowledge that it cannot know the ultimate end of human life and the confused mass of accumulated moral theology: an unsystematic collection of anecdotes, cases, and catalogues of virtues and vices. Jordan concludes that "the *Summa* is at once a clarifying simplification of Scripture . . . and a clarifying generalization of pastoral experience brought back under the science of Scripture."

Moral Psychology and Practical Reason

The essays in Part II of the book focus on some of the prominent strands in the account of practical reason and moral psychology which underlie Aquinas's moral theory. In "Aquinas on the Passions," Peter King undertakes an analysis of Aquinas's theory of the passions of the soul, the appetitive principles belonging to what Aquinas calls the sensory or sensitive soul. King is interested both in what we might think of as the psychological status of the passions—what the nature of the passions is, what varieties of passions there are, and how the different passions are related to one another—and in what we might call their moral status: to what extent and in what ways our being subject to passions is up to us and can be brought under the sway of our reason. Focusing on texts from *Summa theologiae* Ia and IaIIae, King pieces together a subtle and penetrating Thomistic account that deserves to be taken seriously, he argues, by anyone interested in the nature and moral significance of human passions and emotions.

In "Practical Reasoning and Reasons-Explanations: Aquinas's Account of Reason's Role in Action," Scott MacDonald argues that certain features of Aquinas's accounts of practical reasoning and the will's place in it can help resolve a long-standing puzzle about how explanations of a person's action by reference to the person's reasons for acting can be adequate when the reasons cited in the explanation in no way constrain the person to act in the way that is to be explained. According to MacDonald, Aquinas holds that practical reasoning is very often not fully determinate: that is, our actions are typically underdetermined by the reasons we have for acting. It follows that most explanations of our actions which correctly identify our reasons for acting will be logically defective; it will not be the case that our reasons commit us, on pain of irrationality, to performing just those actions. But, MacDonald claims, Aquinas's account of the role of the will in practical reasoning explains why this logical defect in reasons-explanations does not undermine their explanatory adequacy. Because the will is a natural inclination toward the good as it is conceived by intellect—a motive power pressing for the realization of what intellect presents as good—having a reason to act can be sufficient by itself to give rise to action, provided that no countervailing reasons occur to the agent. On MacDonald's view, reasons for action are typically defeasible, but defeasible reasons can be sufficient explanations of action when there is no potential defeater in the vicinity.

In "Aquinas on Exceptions in Natural Law," John Boler pursues further the theme, introduced in MacDonald's paper, that practical reasoning is non-determinate and can "go in different directions." He focuses on Aquinas's conception of natural law and on Aquinas's claim that the mutability inherent in practical reasoning entails that the derived or secondary precepts of natural law are not the same for all but hold only "for the most part." By probing Aquinas's analogy between practical reason and speculative reason and examining Aquinas's examples of cases in which a precept of practical reason is seen to fail, Boler identifies the different kinds of mutability that might be at stake in the claim that practical reason is mutable, and he isolates what he takes to be the kind of mutability that is relevant to understanding the relation of secondary to primary precepts. He concludes by suggesting why exceptionability of this sort in the secondary precepts of natural law needn't undermine the objectivity or rational assessibility of moral claims in Aquinas's system of morality.

Moral Theory in Philosophy of Language and Metaphysics

The essays in Part III expose some interesting connections between Aquinas's concerns in moral theory and his work in metaphysics and philosophy of language. In "Aquinas on Significant Utterance: Interjection, Blasphemy, Prayer," E. Jennifer Ashworth argues that Aquinas's interest in the moral significance of various kinds of speech led him to examine a broad spectrum of significative uses of language, and that his awareness of actual linguistic practice led him to views in the philosophy of language which diverge from the prevailing thirteenth-century accounts and from his own explicit account in the commentary on *De interpretatione*. By looking at Aquinas's discussions of such topics as the relation of animal noises to human utterances, the relevance of a speaker's emotional state or intentions to an utterance's moral and semantic significance, and the correct moral and semantic analysis of cases in which speakers deliberately appropriate and use words that they themselves do not understand, Ashworth shows how Aquinas recognizes and explicates features of language that do not fit with his own preferred intellectualist model of language. According to Ashworth, that model portrays language as a rational system whose nature does not depend on context or speaker intention and whose primary units are propositions that bear a truth-value and convey information by virtue of the fact that their components stand as signs for concepts. Ashworth contends that in order to account for the moral significance of certain kinds of utterance, Aquinas had to reject or modify the main tenets of his intellectualism in the philosophy of language.

In "Thomas Aquinas on the Good: The Relation between Metaphysics and Ethics," Jan A. Aertsen objects to what he perceives as a strong tendency among modern commentators on Aquinas's ethics to emphasize the autonomy of his moral philosophy from his metaphysics. Since Aquinas's explicit classification of the sciences leaves unclear the precise relation between metaphysics and ethics, Aertsen investigates Aquinas's view of that relation by looking closely at his remarks on the notion of the good as such in a variety of his works, including the commentary on the *Ethics*, lectio 1, and *Summa theologiae* Ia.5.1, IaIIae.18.1–5, and IaIIae.94.2. According to Aertsen, Aquinas's doctrine that the good is a transcendental is the key to understanding his view of the relation between metaphysics and ethics. As a transcendental, the good is common to the various kinds of goodness, including moral and metaphysical goodness, and is an appropriate object of metaphysical inquiry. Furthermore, as a transcendental, the good is also among the primary conceptions of the intellect, grounding the first principle of practical reason in the way that *being* grounds the first principle of theoretical reason. Theoretical thought and morality, therefore, have a common ground in the transcendentals, which are the same in reality despite being conceptually distinct. On Aertsen's view, then, the doctrine of the transcendentality of goodness is the link that connects practical reason, human action, and morality with theoretical thought about the fundamental nature of reality.

In the last essay, "Degrees of Being, Degrees of Goodness: Aquinas on Levels of Reality," Paul Vincent Spade takes the doctrine of the transcendentality of the good as the point of departure for an investigation of an important tenet of Aquinas's metaphysics. As Spade points out, good stands apart from the other transcendentals by virtue of the fact that it admits of degrees. Spade then raises the question whether Aquinas's metaphysical commitments require him to hold that other transcendentals, and in particular *being*, must also admit of degrees. On the basis of a close reading of chapters 2 and 3 of Aquinas's *De ente et essentia*, Spade argues that Aquinas wants to ascribe important theoretical and explanatory roles to metaphysical common natures. (A common nature is required to explain, for example, how *human being* can be correctly predicated of both Socrates and Plato.) But, according to Spade, Aquinas also wants to deny that common natures as such have any kind of existence. (*Human being* can exist in matter, in which case it is individual, or in mind, in which case it is a universal concept, but *human being* can have no existence as such.) Spade claims that this violates the principle of philosophical fair play, the principle that requires one to grant ontological status to anything that one requires to do real theoretical work. There is an even more serious problem, in Spade's view. Among the roles Aquinas assigns to common natures are unifying roles—the nature predicated of Socrates and the nature predicated of Plato must be one and the same nature—but his doctrine of the transcendentals commits him to the view that *one* and *being* are convertible, that whatever is one also has being. So Spade concludes that given the use Aquinas makes of common natures, he must either grant that they have being to some degree (though perhaps to a lesser degree than do concrete individuals such as Socrates and Plato) or deny a corollary of the doctrine of the transcendentals.

These ten essays cannot, of course, provide a complete picture of Aquinas's moral theory. But we think they shed new light on some well-known features of Aquinas's moral thinking and uncover other features that have hitherto received less attention than they merit. We hope that taken together they give a glimpse of the richness of Aquinas's moral theory.

This volume represents the confluence of two projects with a shared purpose. In 1991 Norman Kretzmann's friends and students were stricken to learn that he had been diagnosed with multiple myeloma.

Jan Aertsen quickly arranged a special session at the Ninth International Congress of Medieval Philosophy, held in Ottawa in 1992, honoring Kretzmann's contribution to the study of medieval philosophy. The papers published here by Jan Aertsen, Mark Jordan, and Scott Mac-Donald were first presented at that session. At about the same time, we—Scott MacDonald and Eleonore Stump—were making plans for a volume celebrating Kretzmann's work in medieval philosophy. (A volume honoring his work in philosophy of religion—*Reasoned Faith*, edited by Eleonore Stump—was nearly finished at that time and was published by Cornell University Press in 1993. Together we decided to assemble a collection of essays devoted to issues in Aquinas's moral theory, supplementing the original contributions to the 1992 special session of the International Congress of Medieval Philosophy with essays specially commissioned from a group of Kretzmann's colleagues, friends, and former students. The result is this book. We are very grateful to all the contributors for their generosity in this collaborative effort and also to John Ackerman at Cornell University Press for his unfailingly gracious help. We are sad only that Kretzmann did not live long enough to see the volume in print. He saw and was pleased by the typescript, but he died August 1, just months before the volume appeared.

Kretzmann's work in medieval philosophy spans the period from Augustine and Boethius to John Wyclif, and his studies, translations, and editorial projects range over virtually every area in medieval philosophy, including logic, philosophy of language, natural philosophy, metaphysics, philosophical theology, philosophy of mind and action, and ethics. Given the breadth of his philosophical and scholarly interests and the importance of his contributions to these many areas, we might have chosen for the focus of this volume any of a number of medieval philosophers or philosophical topics. Moreover, given Kretzmann's commitment to encouraging scholarship in all areas of medieval philosophy, we knew he would welcome the publication of a collection of new work in any area of the field. It seemed clear to us, however, that this book should be devoted to issues that he would count as among the most important in philosophy.

Beginning in the spring of 1983 when he taught a graduate seminar at Cornell based on a complete reading of *Summa contra gentiles*, Kretzmann devoted a steadily increasing portion of his philosophical energy to the study of Aquinas. Though his seminars and publications have covered a variety of topics, the kinds of issues identified in this volume as constitutive of and fundamental to Aquinas's moral theory were at the heart of his research. The concern he had with these issues and his conviction that there is profound philosophical truth to be found in

Aquinas's treatment of them is evident in his published work. We thought, therefore, that it would be especially appropriate to honor the contribution he made to the study of medieval philosophy with a volume of sustained critical reflection on the thought of Thomas Aquinas and, in particular, on Aquinas's moral theory.

Kretzmann's committed and outstanding work on Aquinas has had a powerful effect on the field, and he did much to demonstrate the rich variety, systematic interconnectedness, and wide-ranging ramifications of Aquinas's theoretical reflections on moral issues. By virtue of the clarity and philosophical insight that are hallmarks of his publications, his work has not only drawn new philosophical and scholarly attention to these issues but also stimulated better and deeper work from those now working on them. It is our hope, then, that this volume of essays reflects not just Kretzmann's interests but also something of the difference he made to the field.

What can be said about Kretzmann's contribution to the study of Aquinas can be said with equal justification about his contributions to the study of medieval philosophy generally. His research helped to establish what many of us now have the luxury of taking for granted: namely, that clear and careful philosophical scrutiny of the ideas and arguments of the best minds of the Middle Ages can be expected not only to yield insight into the history of philosophy but also to provide invaluable resources for discovering, refining, and resolving the philosophical puzzles and problems of our own day. He helped to make clear to many who would otherwise have been skeptical that medieval philosophy has not just antiquarian historical interest but much that contemporary philosophy can learn from.

Contemporary work in medieval philosophy and its standing in the philosophical profession at large has been profoundly influenced by Kretzmann's research, but his teaching must also be counted among his most significant contributions to the field. He was known for his openhanded, wholehearted commitment to his students, and he drew students to himself not only because of his intellectual excellence but also because of their recognition that he poured himself out to nurture them and to draw out the best in them. What he gave to the field of medieval philosophy will live on not only in his work but also in his many students. We are grateful to be able to count ourselves in their number.

For all these reasons, we remember him with this volume with deep admiration and affection.

I

&

MORAL THEORY
AND MORAL THEOLOGY

ANTHONY KENNY

ই◆

Aquinas on Aristotelian Happiness

Aristotle's treatment of happiness in books 1 and 10 of the *Nicomachean Ethics* has been in recent decades the subject of intense discussion by philosophers. It is perhaps surprising that contemporary writers should find so much to say about chapters that are in themselves tolerably clear and that have been carefully studied for centuries. Some recent readings of the texts are so perverse that they can be explained only by the desire to bring Aristotle's thought into line with contemporary fashion. It provides a useful antidote to any such temptation—as Norman Kretzmann has shown in many fields—to pay close attention to the Aristotle commentaries of medieval writers who had preoccupations very different from our own.[1]

Accordingly, in this essay I consider the treatment of these Nicomachean chapters by Saint Thomas Aquinas. Just as modern writers strive to make Aristotle relevant to contemporary secular moral concerns, so Aquinas is anxious to enroll the Philosopher in the service of Christian theology. Nonetheless, I argue, he has more respect than many of his modern counterparts have for the plain meaning of the texts. The actual use to which the texts are put varies considerably from context to context. I consider four different approaches which Aquinas adopts, depending on whether—to put it very crudely—he is at any given moment writing as an Aristotelian, a Christian, a Catholic, or a Dominican.

---

[1] The contemporary discussions are summarized in my book *Aristotle on the Perfect Life* (Oxford: Oxford University Press, 1992), where also I justify the interpretations of the Aristotelian texts assumed in this essay. All English translation here are mine.

1

In his commentary on the *Nicomachean Ethics* Aquinas writes as an Aristotelian in the sense that his primary aim is to present the teaching of Aristotle rather than to set forth his own opinion on the matters under discussion. From time to time he draws attention to places where, from a Christian point of view, Aristotle falls short of the truth, but overwhelmingly his concern is with exposition rather than criticism. Though he knows Aristotle only in Latin translation, his commentary is in general remarkably clear and accurate. On the topic of happiness in particular he often grasps Aristotle's meaning where twentieth-century commentators have missed it.

It is common ground among commentators on the *Nicomachean Ethics* (*NE*) that happiness is there defined as the exercise of virtue. Modern interpreters do not agree, however, whether to take it as the exercise of a single dominant virtue, or as the inclusive exercise of all the virtues of the rational soul. Probably a majority of writers in English at the present time favor the inclusive interpretation. When Aristotle says in book 1 (1098a17–18) that the good for man is "activity of soul in accordance with virtue, and if there are several virtues, in accordance with the best and most perfect," these commentators understand "the best and most perfect virtue" to be the totality of virtues, moral and intellectual.

Aquinas will have none of this. The human good, that is, happiness, is activity in accordance with virtue, such that "if there is only one human virtue, the activity which is in accordance with that will be happiness; but if there are several human virtues, happiness will be the activity which is in accordance with the best one of them."[2] It will turn out, in book 10 of the *Nicomachean Ethics*, that the best of the human virtues is *sophia* or understanding,[3] and that perfect happiness is the exercise of this virtue, namely, the activity of contemplation. But neither Aristotle nor Aquinas explicitly makes this identification in the context of book 1; because at this point no distinction has been made between moral and intellectual virtues, or, among intellectual virtues, between wisdom (*phronesis*) and understanding.

---

[2] "Sequitur quod humanum bonum, scilicet felicitas, sit operatio secundum virtutem: ita scilicet quod si est una tantum virtus hominis, operatio quae est secundum illam virtutem erit felicitas. Si autem sunt plures virtutes hominis, erit felicitas operatio quae est secundum illarum optimam" (*In NE* 1.11 [128]). (I have used the Marietti edition of *In NE*; numerals in brackets refer to paragraph numbers in that edition.)

[3] The Greek word is often translated "wisdom"; but this is an inappropriate word in modern English to describe the excellence of the speculative intellect, whereas it corresponds very well to the Greek word *phronesis*, which denotes the excellence of the practical reason.

In book 1 of the *Ethics* Aristotle gives it as a characteristic of happiness that it should be *teleion*. The Greek word can be rendered into English as "perfect" or "complete." Those who hold an inclusive interpretation of the notion of happiness naturally favor the translation "complete." The Latin text that Aquinas used had the translation *perfectum*, and Aquinas takes the key to the meaning of this to be given by Aristotle's explanation (at 1097a30–b6) of what it is for one good to be more perfect than another.

Some things, Aquinas says in commenting on this text, are desirable only because they are useful; his example is nauseous medicine. Other things are desirable both for their own sake and also for the sake of something else. His example here is "warm and tasty medicine": hot whiskey toddy, perhaps, taken to ward off a cold. The second kind of good, he says, is more perfect than the first. The most perfect good is one that is desired only for its own sake and never for the sake of anything else.

Following Aristotle, Aquinas says that an end such as wealth, which is always chosen for the sake of something else, is imperfect and therefore cannot be identified with happiness: "The best end, which is the ultimate end, must be perfect. If then there is one such end, this must be the ultimate end we are looking for. But if there are many perfect ends, then it is the most perfect of these which is the best and ultimate."[4] If "perfect" were equivalent to "complete," it would of course make no sense to suggest that there could be more than one perfect end. Aquinas takes Aristotle to be saying that there are several perfect ends: honor, pleasure, intelligence, and virtue. But these are not the most perfect, since they are chosen not only for their own sake but also for the sake of happiness. (Some people, for instance, seek their happiness in pleasure.) Happiness itself is the most perfect, because it alone is chosen only for its own sake and never for anything else.

Aristotle gives self-sufficiency as another characteristic of happiness (1097b14–15). This too has been taken to indicate that happiness must include many other goods in addition to the exercise of contemplation. Aristotle says, "We think [happiness] most choiceworthy of all things, without being counted along with other things—but if so counted, clearly made more choiceworthy by the addition of even the least of goods" (1097b16–20). Supporters of the inclusive notion of happiness have to take the "if so counted" as a counterfactual whose actualization would lead to an absurdity; they regard the words as meaning "If it were—*per impossibile*—so counted."

---

[4] "Optimus autem finis, qui est ultimus, oportet quod sit perfectus. Unde si unum solum sit tale, oportet hoc esse ultimum finem quem quaerimus. Si autem sint multi perfecti fines, oportet quod perfectissimus horum sit optimus et ultimus" (*In NE* 1.9 [110]).

Aquinas interprets the text quite differently:

> The happiness about which he is now talking is self-sufficient because it contains in itself everything which is necessary, but not everything which could come to someone. So it can become better with any other addition. This does not mean that the person's desire remains unsatisfied, since desire regulated by reason, such as the happy person's must be, is not troubled about things which are unnecessary, even if they can be acquired.[5]

This by itself does not, of course, rule out the possibility of happiness containing more than just contemplation, but it does rule out the idea— championed by some of the more extreme critics of the interpretation of happiness as a dominant good—that happiness is a good which is inclusive of all goods.

The seventh chapter of book 10 of the *Ethics* takes up the discussion of happiness where book 1 left it off. As Aquinas puts it, Aristotle, having shown in the first book that happiness was the exercise of virtue, now goes on to show which virtue it is the exercise of.[6] The best human virtue is the virtue of the best part of a human being, and that is the speculative intellect; hence, it is the activity of the speculative intellect in accordance with its own proper virtue which constitutes perfect happiness.

It is difficult for any commentator to deny that in book 10 Aristotle makes a very close link between perfect happiness and the exercise of the intellectual virtue of *sophia*. Those who favor an inclusive notion of happiness can point, however, to one passage that might be taken in their support. Aristotle (at 1178a6), having summed up his teaching on perfect happiness by saying that the life of the intellect is the best and pleasantest and happiest life for humans, since a human being is above all else an intellect, then goes on to say, at the beginning of chapter 8: "And secondly, the one in accordance with the other virtue; for activities in accordance with it are human too. For we display justice and courage and the other virtues in our dealings with one another." The meaning of "the one" here is not totally clear, and it is, perhaps, just possible to read the passage as meaning that whereas the principal component of perfect happiness is the activity of the intellect, a secondary component of perfect happiness is the exercise of the moral virtues. But it is more natural to take it as saying either that the life of the moral virtues is a sec-

---

[5] "Et sic felicitas de qua nunc loquitur habet de se sufficientiam, qua in se continet omne illud quod est in se necessarium, non autem omne illud quod potest homini advenire. Unde potest melior fieri aliquo alio addito. Non tamen remanet desiderium hominis inquietum, quia desiderium ratione regulatum, quale oportet esse felicis, non habet inquietudinem de his quae non sunt necessaria, licet sint possibilia adipisci" (*In NE* 1.9 [116]).

[6] *In NE* 10.10 (2080).

ondary kind of happiness or, what comes to the same thing, that the person who devotes his life to the display of moral virtue is happy in a secondary sense.

It is thus that Aquinas understands the passage in his commentary. He sums up the message of chapter 8 thus: "The person devoted to the contemplation of truth is the happiest of all; but happy in a secondary manner is the person who lives in accordance with the other virtue, namely wisdom, which is the guide of all the moral virtues."[7]

In all the passages we have considered in detail, Aquinas's interpretation is preferable, it seems to me, to the alternative interpretations which have been canvassed by modern commentators. It is not that the idea of happiness as the exercise of all the virtues is not to be found in Aristotle: it is, but in the *Eudemian*, not in the *Nicomachean Ethics*. Aquinas is correct in taking the Nicomachean view to be that perfect happiness consists in theoretical contemplation, and in it alone.

2

As a Christian, Aquinas was anxious to reconcile Aristotle's theory of happiness with the teaching of the Bible and the Church. The most authoritative Christian statement on the topic of happiness is of course the set of beatitudes recorded in Saint Matthew's Gospel as part of the Sermon on the Mount:

Blessed are the poor in spirit: for theirs is the kingdom of heaven.
Blessed are they that mourn: for they shall be comforted.
Blessed are the meek: for they shall inherit the earth.
Blessed are they which do hunger and thirst after righteousness:
    for they shall be filled.
Blessed are the merciful: for they shall obtain mercy.
Blessed are the pure in heart: for they shall see God.
Blessed are the peacemakers: for they shall be called the children of God.
Blessed are they which are persecuted for righteousness' sake:
    for theirs is the kingdom of heaven.

Matthew's Greek word here translated "blessed" is *makarios*; it is one of Aristotle's words for the happy person, which he often (though not always) uses interchangeably with his more usual word *eudaimon*.

---

[7] "Cum ille qui vacat speculationi veritatis sit felicissimus, secundario est felix ille qui vivit secundum aliam virtutem, scilicet secundum prudentiam, quae dirigit omnes morales virtutes" (*In NE* 10.12 [2111]).

Aquinas uses the Latin word *felix* as the equivalent of *eudaimon*, and *felicitas* as the equivalent of *eudaimonia* when discussing Aristotle; when discussing happiness on his own account, he commonly uses the word *beatitudo*, which he seems to treat as synonymous. It is the word *beatus*, of course, which occurs in the beatitudes and which relates their content to the Aristotelian discussion of happiness.

It is instructive to read Saint Thomas's discussion of the beatitudes in question 69 of the *prima secundae*. He offers to reveal their structure by reference to the third chapter of *Nicomachean Ethics*, book 1, where Aristotle lists three opinions about happiness. Some people, Aristotle there says, identify it with the life of pleasure, others with the active life, and others with the contemplative life. Taking his cue from this passage, Aquinas tells us that the life of pleasure is an impediment to true happiness; the active life is a preparation for it; and the contemplative life is what it essentially consists in.

The first three beatitudes, Aquinas says, show that happiness demands the rejection of the life of pleasure: the poor in spirit reject riches and honors; the meek suppress the passions of anger; those who mourn are those who abstain from the satisfaction of concupiscence.

The next two beatitudes are concerned with the active life: those who hunger and thirst after righteousness are those with a passion to carry out their duties to their neighbor; those who are merciful are those who in service to others go beyond the calls of duty and kinship and consider only the needs of their fellows.

Finally, the remaining beatitudes express the happiness of the contemplative life: the sixth speaks of the vision of God which is promised to the pure in heart, and the seventh is explained thus: "To make peace in oneself or among others shows that a person is an imitator of God who is the God of unity and peace, and so its reward is the glory of divine sonship."[8] This sonship is identified by Aquinas with the perfect union with God which is brought about by the supreme contemplative virtue.

The endeavor to bring together the evangelical and the Nicomachean texts can hardly be regarded as successful. Of the first three beatitudes, only the first can plausibly be represented as describing the renunciation of the life of pleasure; it is fanciful to take the word "mourn" to refer to the suppression of concupiscence, and the control of anger and the pursuit of honor are elements of the second life, the life of action.

---

[8] "Constituere vero pacem vel in seipso vel inter alios, manifestat hominem esse Dei imitatorem, qui est Deus unitatis et pacis. Et ideo pro praemio redditur ei gloria divinae filiationis, quae est in perfecta coniunctione ad Deum per sapientiam consummatam" (*ST* IaIIae.69.4).

The fourth and fifth beatitudes fare better: love of righteousness and mercy (or at least equity) are no doubt attributes of any worthy pursuer of the Aristotelian active life, and purity of heart, at any rate in the *Eudemian Ethics*, is a condition of the contemplation of God. But with the seventh and eighth beatitudes the thread is again lost. Peacemaking belongs to the active, not the contemplative, life; and when it comes to the suffering of persecution, Saint Thomas himself gives up the attempt to match the two systems. What is remarkable about this rapprochement is not that it is done successfully but that it is done at all. Moreover, it is noteworthy that the Christian texts are distorted to fit the Aristotelian context, rather than the other way around.

3

Aquinas, as a Catholic, had to reconcile Aristotle not only with the biblical texts but with the developed doctrines of the Church. By the time he wrote it was accepted doctrine that the ultimate goal of human beings was to be happy, after the ending of this life, in everlasting union with God. It is unclear how far Aristotle believed, when he wrote the *Nicomachean Ethics*, that any part of a human being could survive death—just as (as Aquinas admits) it is unclear how far the happiness described in the beatitudes belongs to the present life and how far it belongs to some other dispensation. It is in the *prima secundae* that we see Aquinas relating the Nicomachean texts to the Christian doctrine of the everlasting happiness of the blessed in heaven.

The second question of the *prima secundae* asks where happiness is to be found. Like Aristotle, and often for the same reasons as Aristotle, Aquinas begins by rejecting inadequate popular answers. Happiness is not to be found in riches, or in honors, or in fame, or in power; because all these are exterior things, dependent on chance, all can be used well or badly, and none are self-sufficient. Nor can we find happiness in any of the goods of the human body, such as health and strength. Since all goods are either external goods, or bodily goods, or goods of the soul, shall we then say that happiness is to be found among the goods of the soul? When Aristotle put this question to himself, he gave an affirmative answer: happiness is a good activity of the soul (1098b13–20). But Aquinas answers by making a distinction. No finite or created good, whether of soul or body, can be the ultimate end which perfectly satisfies our desire.

> But if by the ultimate end we mean the acquisition, or possession, or some kind of use of the thing which is desired as an end, in that case something

human within the soul belongs to our ultimate end; because it is by the soul that a human being achieves happiness. The thing which is desired as an end is where happiness is to be found, and what makes one happy; but the acquisition of this thing is what is called happiness.[9]

It is only in God, therefore, that happiness is to be found. But it remains to be explained in what precise relationship to God happiness consists. This is the topic of the eight articles of question 3. Once again, Aquinas takes as his text Aristotle's dictum that happiness is activity in accord with perfect virtue (IaIIae.3.2 sed contra). It is an activity not of our senses but of our intellectual part (art. 3), and within the intellectual part it is an acitivity of the intellect, not of the will (art. 4). The enjoyment of the activity is no doubt an activity of the will, but the enjoyment is subsequent to, but not constitutive of, the activity in which happiness consists (q. 2, art. 6; q. 3, art. 4). That activity is an activity of the intellect, and of the speculative rather than practical intellect (q. 3, art. 5).

Up to this point, Aquinas is in entire accord with the *Ethics*, and indeed the arguments he uses to establish that happiness is an activity of the speculative intellect are all drawn from book 10.

If human happiness is an activity, it must be the best human activity. But the best human activity is the activity of the best faculty in respect of the best object. But the best faculty is the intellect, and its best object is divine goodness, which is the object not of the practical but of the speculative intellect. Therefore it is in that activity, namely the contemplation of divine things, in which happiness principally consists [cf. 1177a12–21]. . . . Second, the same conclusion is drawn from the fact that contemplation is especially sought for its own sake. The activity of the practical intellect is sought not for itself but for the sake of action, and actions themselves are ordered to some end. Therefore it is clear that the ultimate end cannot be found in the active life, which belongs to the practical intellect [cf. 1177b1–4]. Third, the same conclusion is drawn from the fact that the contemplative life is something a human being shares with superhuman beings, namely God and angels, to which human beings are assimilated by happiness. But the things which belong to the active life are things in which other animals share, though imperfectly [cf. 1178b20–25].[10]

[9] "Sed si loquamur de ultimo fine hominis quantum ad ipsam adeptionem vel possessionem, seu quemcumque usum ipsius rei quae appetitur ut finis, sic ad ultimum finem pertinet aliquid hominis ex parte animae; quia homo per animam beatitudinem consequitur. Res ergo ipsa quae appetitur ut finis, est id in quo beatitudo consistit, et quod beatum facit: sed huius rei adeptio vocatur beatitudo" (*ST* IaIIae.2.7).

[10] "Si beatitudo hominis est operatio, oportet quod sit optima operatio hominis. Optima autem operatio hominis est quae est optimae potentiae respectu optimi obiecti. Optima autem potentia est intellectus, cuius optimum obiectum est bonum divinum, quod quidem non est obiectum practici intellectus, sed speculativi. Unde in tali operatione, scilicet

At this point Aquinas seeks to improve on Aristotle by making a distinction between the perfect happiness to be enjoyed in a future life, which consists in contemplation alone, and the imperfect happiness that is all we can hope for in the present life. It is only imperfect happiness, he says, which is the topic of Aristotle's book 10 (IaIIae.3.6 ad1). "The imperfect happiness which can be had in this life consists primarily and principally in contemplation; but secondarily in the operation of practical reason directing human actions and passions as is said in the tenth book of the *Ethics*."[11] In this passage, unlike the corresponding passage in his commentary, Aquinas seems to side with those who see in book 10 a comprehensive happiness that includes the activity of both speculative and practical intellect.

In article 6, Aquinas again distances himself from Aristotle, saying that perfect happiness cannot consist in the contemplation of the speculative sciences listed in the *Ethics*. These sciences, being based on empirical principles, cannot lead beyond the realm of the senses; but the objects of the senses are inferior to human beings. The ultimate perfection of human beings must consist in something which is above the human intellect, and ultimately in the vision of the divine essence (q. 3, arts. 6 and 8). The object of the intellect is truth; only God is truth by his own essence, and only the contemplation of God makes the intellect perfect and its possessor perfectly happy (q. 3, art. 7).

Aquinas does not claim the authority of Aristotle for the link he makes between the Nicomachean theory of contemplative happiness and the Christian doctrine of the beatific vision. But it is not an illegitimate development of Aristotelian theory. Aquinas says, candidly, that the account of happiness given by Aristotle in the *Ethics* concerns a happiness obtainable in the present, everyday, world. But he also draws attention to hints in book 10 that happiness is something superhuman, and that the intellect in which happiness primarily resides is something whose activity is separable from the body. He links these hints to the teaching of the *De anima* about the independence of the active intellect (1178a22; *In NE* 10.12 [2116]).

---

in contemplatione divinorum, maxime consistit beatitudo. . . . Secundo apparet idem ex hoc quod contemplatio maxime quaeritur propter seipsam. Actus autem intellectus practici non quaeritur propter seipsum, sed propter actionem. Ipsae etiam actiones ordinantur ad aliquem finem. Unde manifestum est quod ultimus finis non potest consistere in vita activa, quae pertinet ad intellectum practicum. Tertio idem apparet ex hoc quod in vita contemplativa homo communicat cum superioribus, scilicet cum Deo et angelis, quibus per beatitudinem assimilatur. Sed in his quae pertinent ad vitam activam, etiam alia animalia cum homine aliqualiter communicant, licet imperfecte" (*ST* IaIIae.3.5).

[11] "Beatitudo autem imperfecta, qualis hic haberi potest, primo quidem et principaliter consistit in contemplatione: secundario vero in operatione practici intellectus ordinantis actiones et passiones humanas, ut dicitur in X Ethic." (*ST* IaIIae.3.5).

The distinction Aquinas draws between the imperfect happiness of the present life and the perfect happiness of the divine vision corresponds to an ambiguity in book 10 itself. At one moment Aristotle will say that perfect human happiness consists in contemplation because that is the best activity of the most human thing in us (1178a6). At another time he will say that the life of contemplation is something superhuman (1177a26). He encourages us to "immortalize as much as possible," identifying ourselves not with our complex human nature but with its intellectual element. His clinching argument for identifying perfect happiness with contemplation is that this, of all human activities, is the one most akin to the activity of God (1178b21–23).

Readers of Aristotle may feel that there is an inconsistency between saying that the intellect is what is most human in us, and also saying that it is superhuman and divine. Aquinas's treatment of happiness in the *prima secundae* may be seen as an attempt to resolve this problem. A full understanding of human nature shows, he maintains, that humans' deepest needs and aspirations cannot be satisfied in the human activities—even the speculative activities—that are natural for a rational animal. Human beings can be perfectly happy only if they can share the superhuman activities of the divine, and for that they need the supernatural assistance of divine grace.

Thus, in article 5 of question 5 of the *prima secundae* he puts this question: can human beings, by natural means, acquire happiness? He replies: "The imperfect happiness which can be obtained in this life can be acquired by human beings by natural means, in the same way as the virtues in whose exercise it consists; but perfect human happiness consists in the vision of the divine essence, and to see God in his essence is above the nature not only of human beings but of all creatures." [12] But does this not fly in the face of the whole Aristotelian doctrine of nature, and of natural teleology? Aquinas puts the objection to himself: "Nature does not fail to provide what is necessary. But nothing is more necessary for human beings than the means of reaching their final end" (IaIIae.5.1). After all, nature gives irrational creatures all they need to achieve their ends; why not then to human beings also?

His reply is that nature has provided for the bodily necessities of human beings not by giving them fur and claws but by giving them reason to invent and hands to use artifacts. Similarly, nature has not given humans a natural capacity for supreme happiness but has instead given

---

[12] "Beatitudo imperfecta quae in hac vita haberi potest, potest ab homine acquiri per sua naturalia, eo modo quo et virtus, in cuius operatione consistit. . . . Sed beatitudo hominis perfecta . . . consistit in visione divinae essentiae. Videre autem Deum per essentiam est supra naturam non solum hominis, sed etiam omnis creaturae" (*ST* IaIIae.5.5).

them free will by which they can turn to God, who alone can make them happy. Humans are better off than animals, even though they need outside assistance to achieve their goal: "Just as A is in a better state with regard to health than B if A can reach perfect health, but only with the aid of medication, while B is capable only of imperfect health even though he can reach it without medical help."[13]

To give Aristotelian support to this view, Aquinas quotes a passage of the *De caelo* which is only doubtfully relevant.[14] But his development of the Nicomachean doctrine should not be regarded as a perverse assimilation to Christian dogma. Aristotle would no doubt have been surprised at some of the uses to which Aquinas put his treatise, but he could hardly complain that Aquinas was completely distorting its meaning. The tension between nature and supernature is there in Aristotle's book 10, chapter 7, for all to read.

4

Saint Thomas was a Dominican friar, a member of the begging ("mendicant") Order of Preachers. Mendicant orders were still a novelty in the Church and aroused the suspicion and hostility of many conservative churchmen. Members of older religious orders argued that begging was disgraceful for those who could work with their hands; secular clergy resented mendicant preachers' trespassing in their parishes. Uncomfortably, the rule of the mendicants seemed to blur the familiar boundaries between the active and contemplative religious orders.

Several times in his life Aquinas became embroiled in controversy with anti-mendicants. In describing and justifying the Dominican ideal he once again makes frequent use of Aristotelian texts from the first and last books of the *Nicomachean Ethics*. In particular, in his treatment of the active and contemplative life toward the end of the *secunda secundae*, he addresses questions which still preoccupy Aristotelian exegetes.

When Aristotle speaks of a perfect life, for example, what is meant by "life"? Is it only the chosen supreme activity of the happy person, or does it include all other vital activities as well? Aquinas, when he in-

---

[13] "Melius est dispositus ad sanitatem qui potest consequi perfectam sanitatem, licet hoc sit per auxilium medicinae; quam qui solum potest consequi quandam imperfectam sanitatem, sine medicinae auxilio" (*ST* IaIIae.5.5 ad2).

[14] "With men's bodies one is in good condition without exercise at all, another after a short walk, while another requires running and wrestling and hard training, and there are yet others who however hard they worked themselves could never secure this good, but only some substitute for it" (*De caelo* 292a25–27).

troduces the discussion of the active and contemplative life, notes the possible ambiguity, but he makes clear that in this context "life" means "what a person most enjoys and is most devoted to." The active life, then, is one devoted to external actions; the contemplative is one devoted to the contemplation of truth (IIaIIae.179.1).

Another question currently debated among commentators is this: does Aristotle's contemplative possess the moral virtues or not? The correct answer seems to be that the moral virtues must indeed be possessed by the contemplative but do not form part of the contemplative's happiness. This too is the answer given by Aquinas: the moral virtues are necessary for the contemplative, to prevent his contemplation's being disrupted by passion or tumult, but they are not an essential part of the contemplative life itself (IIaIIae.180.2).

When he comes to compare the worth of the two lives, Aquinas draws very heavily on Aristotle. To prove that the contemplative life is better than the active, he produces nine arguments. Eight of these are taken verbatim from book 10, chapter 7 of the *Nichomachean Ethics*: the contemplative life is the activity of the best in us; it is the most continuous activity; it is the pleasantest; it is the most self-sufficient; it is sought for its own sake; it is leisurely; it is godlike; it is most truly human. Each text from the *Ethics* is paired with a biblical or patristic text in which, say, Rachel and Leah or Mary and Martha are taken as representatives of the two lives. As in the treatment of the beatitudes, more respect is paid to the literal meaning of the Aristotelian texts than to that of the biblical ones.

Although Aquinas sides wholeheartedly with Aristotle's book 10 in valuing the contemplative life above the active life, he shifts perspective in an interesting manner when he comes to treat of the vocations of various religious orders. All religious orders, he says, are instituted for the sake of charity, but charity includes both love of God and love of neighbor. The contemplative orders seek to spend time on God alone (*soli Deo vacare*); the active orders seek to serve the needs of their fellows (IIaIIae.188.2). Now which are to be preferred, contemplative or active orders (IIaIIae.188.6)?

Instead of giving an immediate answer, in line with his general Nicomachean preference for contemplation, Aquinas draws a distinction between two kinds of active life. One kind of active life consists entirely in external actions, such as the giving of alms or the succor of wayfarers, but another kind of active life consists in teaching and preaching. In these activities the religious person is drawing on the fruits of previous contemplation, passing on to others the truths thus grasped. Although the purely contemplative life is to be preferred to the purely active life, the best life of all for a religious is the life that includes teaching and preaching. "Just as it is better to light up others than to shine alone, it is better to share the fruits of one's contemplation with others than to contemplate in solitude."[15] Saint Thomas does not specify what religious order he has in mind, but his phrase *contemplata aliis tradere* is fit to serve as a motto for the Dominican order.

In this final glorification of the ideals of his own order as superior to either of the Nicomachean lives, Aquinas very properly does not make any appeal to Aristotle. Even here, however, there is an instructive comparison to be drawn between the teachings of the two philosophers.

In the *Nicomachean Ethics* Aristotle presents two ideals of happiness: a first-class happiness consisting in pure contemplation, and a second-class happiness consisting in the exercise of wisdom and the moral virtues. In the *Eudemian Ethics* Aristotle presents a single ideal of a happiness which includes both a contemplative and an active element and which can be summarized as "the contemplation and service of God."

Aquinas, in effect, transposes the Nicomachean first-class happiness into a spiritualized afterlife where alone it is really at home. In the present life his own ideal—unknown to himself[16]—is much closer to that of the *Eudemian Ethics*, combining contemplation and action, and seeking to practice "the service of God" in the particular form of teaching and preaching.[17]

[15] "Sicut enim maius est illuminare quam lucere solum, ita maius est contemplata aliis tradere quam solum contemplari . . . sic ergo summum gradum in religionibus tenent quae ordinantur ad docendum et praedicandum" (*ST* IIaIIae.188.6).

[16] I can find no evidence that Aquinas had any firsthand knowledge of the *Eudemian Ethics*. He does frequently quote 1248a20–28 to show that God is the origin of our deliberations, but he seems to have known the text only through its occurrence in the anthology *De bona fortuna*.

[17] I am grateful to Scott MacDonald and Eleonore Stump for helpful comments on an earlier version of this paper.

ELEONORE STUMP

ࢶ

Wisdom: Will, Belief, and Moral Goodness

Aquinas thought that there are intellectual virtues as well as moral virtues, and he took wisdom to be chief among them. His account of wisdom seems to me to constitute a rich and intriguing contribution to ethics and philosophy of mind. His discussion, however, is set in a web of medieval lore about the gifts of the Holy Spirit, the beatitudes, the cardinal vices, and so on; and it also presupposes a theory of the relations between intellect and will that is likely to look counterintuitive to many contemporary philosophers. In order to capture what is appealingly plausible and explanatorily useful about Aquinas's account of wisdom, therefore, one must approach it with a wide-angle lens, digressing both to a detailed discussion of will and belief and to a consideration of the medieval context in which his account is lodged.

For Aquinas, wisdom is a virtue in the sense that the will plays a role in acquiring and maintaining it.[1] The idea of an intellectual virtue in this sense is not so common now.[2] In contemporary culture it is more customary to think in terms of excellences, rather than virtues, of the intellect; and the paradigm excellence of mind currently valued is intelligence or smartness. We say admiringly of some academic whose philo-

[1] When wisdom is a virtue in our sense of 'virtue,' Aquinas thinks of it as a gift of the Holy Spirit. The subsequent discussion will help clarify the terminology.

[2] Virtue epistemology, of course, is the subject of much contemporary discussion, but the cognitive virtues of virtue epistemology are not explicitly presented or discussed as involving both a cognitive excellence and an excellence of will. (The extent to which virtue epistemology may be *implicitly* committed to a role for will in believing is not clear.) A good discussion is John Greco, "Virtues and Vices of Virtue Epistemology," *Canadian Journal of Philosophy* 23 (1993): 413–32.

sophical positions strike us as utterly wrongheaded that although his views are widely agreed to be wildly mistaken, he himself is *so smart*.

Of course, it is not entirely clear, even by our lights today, what smartness or intelligence is supposed to be. Intelligence is generally taken to be an innate, genetically determined characteristic. On the other hand, psychologists carefully control the distribution of intelligence tests, on the grounds that scores go up significantly with each retaking of the test—which, of course, suggests that the tests measure a quality that can be acquired or at least increased through experience. Furthermore, although it used to be common among psychologists and is still widely held by others, the belief that intelligence is a unitary quality of the mind is almost surely false; psychologists now acknowledge that intelligence is composed of "many discrete [intellectual functions] that work together . . . smoothly when the brain is intact."[3] One widely used intelligence test is the revised Wechsler Adult Intelligence Scale, or WAIS-R. It turns out, however, that the IQ scores obtained from the WAIS-R do not adequately indicate even serious neurological deficits and disorders; it is possible to have significant neurological deficits and test normally on the WAIS-R.[4] In addition, part of what we measure in IQ tests is just the speed with which a person can use the intellectual abilities he has; there are time limits for various WAIS-R subtests. Finally, it is noteworthy that in split-brain patients whose brain hemispheres are disconnected, "isolating essentially half the cortex from the dominant left hemisphere causes no major changes in intellectual function."[5] This result leads one well-known neurobiologist, Michael Gazzaniga, to claim that "specialized circuits in the left brain are managing the complex task of human intelligence."[6] But another possibility, of course, is that what intelligence tests are measuring as smartness is simply a matter of the speedy use of solely left-brain skills.

By contrast, what Aquinas values in wisdom is not the speed of in-

---

[3] Muriel Deutsch Lezak, *Neuropsychological Assessment*, 2d ed. (Oxford: Oxford University Press, 1983), p. 21.

[4] Some psychologists point out the "inadvisability of drawing inferences about neuropsychological status" from a consideration of scores on these tests; see, e.g., Lezak, *Neuropsychological Assessment*, p. 242. The same author says, "Both Verbal and Performance Scale IQ scores . . . are based on the averages of some quite dissimilar functions that have relatively low intercorrelations and bear no regular neuroanatomical or neuropsychological relationship to one another," and "it is impossible to predict specific disabilities and areas of intellectual competency or dysfunction from the averaged ability test scores" (pp. 242, 243).

[5] Michael Gazzaniga, *Nature's Mind: The Biological Roots of Thinking, Emotions, Sexuality, Language, and Intelligence* (New York: Basic Books, 1992), pp. 98–99.

[6] Ibid., p. 104.

formation processing or, as far as that goes, any other feature of the processing itself; what is important for him is the product of that processing. Wisdom is knowledge (or *scientia*) of the most fundamental causes of things; it is a matter of having a certain understanding of reality. Furthermore, Aquinas thinks that wisdom is acquired, not innate, and he thinks that the will has a role in its acquisition. As we currently think about it, a person's intelligence is not under her control. Being smart is a matter of genetic good fortune, not a matter of effort or choice. But wisdom, on Aquinas's account, is a function both of intellect and of will. It is fundamental to his account that the will has a significant role in the production and maintenance of belief.

Because this claim about the effect of the will on belief seems false to many contemporary philosophers, I begin with a discussion of belief and will. First, I briefly present Aquinas's views on intellect and will; then I examine some current reasons for supposing that a view such as Aquinas's about the effect of will on belief is false, and I argue that these reasons do not undermine Aquinas's view. Next, I lay out the web of medieval ethical lore within which Aquinas's discussion of wisdom is set, and I attempt to explicate his view of wisdom by focusing on wisdom's opposed vice, namely, folly. I then argue that Aquinas's account of wisdom and folly gives a good explanation of a common but puzzling ethical phenomenon. I conclude by briefly relating Aquinas's account of wisdom to hierarchical theories of freedom of the will, and I show how on Aquinas's account wisdom is crucially connected to an agent's inner peace and harmony.

Aquinas on Intellect and Will

Contemporary philosophers tend to operate with a conception of the will as the steering wheel of the mind, neutral in its own right but able to direct other parts of the person. Aquinas's conception of the will is quite different. He takes the will to be not neutral but a bent or inclination. The will, he says, is a hunger, an appetite, for goodness.[7] By 'goodness' here Aquinas means goodness in general, and not this or that specific good thing; that is, the will wills what is good, where the phrase 'what is good' is used attributively and not referentially.[8] And by itself

---

[7] *ST* IaIIae.10.1 and Ia.82.1.

[8] The distinction between referential and attributive uses of linguistic expressions is easier to illustrate than to define. If we say "The president of the United States might have been the son of Chinese immigrants," we may be using the phrase 'the president of the United States' attributively, rather than referentially, to indicate that the position of president could have been filled by a person of Chinese ancestry. If, on the other hand, we are

the will makes no determinations of goodness; apprehending or judging things as good is the business of the intellect. The intellect presents to the will as good certain things under certain descriptions, and the will wills them because the will is an appetite for the good and they are apprehended as good. For this reason the intellect is said to move the will not as an efficient cause but as a final cause, because what is understood as good moves the will as an end.[9]

The will does will some things by necessity. Because God has created it as a hunger for the good, the will by nature desires the good; and whatever is good to such an extent and in such a way that a person cannot help but see it as good, the will of that person wills by natural necessity. One's own happiness is of this sort,[10] and so a person necessarily wills happiness.[11] But even things that have a necessary connection to happiness aren't willed necessarily unless the willer is cognizant of their necessary connection to happiness.[12] Except for happiness and those things so obviously connected with happiness that their connection is overwhelming and indubitable, the will is not determined to one thing because of its relation to the intellect. On Aquinas's view, the will is free.[13] It cannot be coerced or compelled, and it can move itself.[14]

What the intellect determines with respect to goodness is somewhat complicated because the intellect is itself moved by other things. In the first place, the will moves the intellect as an efficient cause, for example, by commanding it directly to adopt a belief[15] or by directing it to attend to some things and to neglect others.[16] Of course, the will does so only

---

using the phrase referentially, we would be trying to say that the current president (President Clinton, in this case) could have had different parents from the ones he had.

[9] *ST* Ia.82.4.

[10] Happiness is the ultimate good for human beings. The ultimate good simpliciter is God, on Aquinas's account. Hence, the sight of God in the beatific vision also moves the will necessarily.

[11] *ST* Ia.82.1.

[12] *ST* Ia.82.2.

[13] In this brief summary I cannot do justice to Aquinas's claim that the will is free, but I have elsewhere presented his theory of free will in detail and attempted to defend it as an account of genuine libertarian freedom: see my "Aquinas's Account of Freedom: Intellect and Will," *Monist* 80 (1997): 576–97; "Persons: Identification and Freedom," *Philosophical Topics* 24 (1996): 183–214; "Intellect, Will, and the Principle of Alternate Possibilities," in *Christian Theism and the Problems of Philosophy*, ed. Michael Beaty (Notre Dame, Ind.: University of Notre Dame Press, 1990), pp. 254–85; and "Libertarian Freedom and the Principle of Alternative Possibilities," in *Faith, Freedom, and Rationality*, ed. Daniel Howard-Snyder and Jeff Jordan (London: Rowman & Littlefield, 1996).

[14] ST IaIIae.6.4 ad1; Ia.82.1; and Ia.83.1.

[15] Aquinas seems to suppose that faith results from such an action of the will on the intellect. See, e.g., *Quaestiones disputatae de veritate*, where he talks of the will's commanding intellect to produce faith: *QDV* 14.3 reply, ad2 and ad10.

[16] See *ST* IaIIae.17.1 and 6.

in case the intellect represents doing so at that time, under some description, as good. Every act of willing is preceded by some apprehension on the part of the intellect, although not every apprehension on the part of the intellect need be preceded by an act of will.[17] In the second place, the passions—sorrow, fury, fear, and so on—can influence the intellect, because in the grip of a passion such as fury, something will seem good to a person which wouldn't seem good to her if she were calm.[18] The intellect, however, typically is not compelled by the passions in any way; it can resist them,[19] for example, by being aware of the passion and correcting for its effects on judgment, as one does when one leaves a letter written in anger until the next morning rather than mailing it right away.

The way the will is moved by the intellect is also complicated. The will can be moved to will as distinct from not willing; or it can be moved to will this rather than that particular thing.[20] Nothing in this life (apart from happiness) can move the will necessarily in the first way, to will as distinct from not willing, because it is always in a person's power to refuse to think of the thing at issue and consequently not to will it actually. In the second way, if the will is presented with an object which can be considered good under some descriptions and not good under others, then the will is not necessarily moved by that object either. So, for example, the further acquisition of money can be considered good under some descriptions (for example, the means of sending the children to school) and not good under others (for example, wages from an immoral and disgusting job). For these reasons, no matter what earthly object (other than happiness) intellect presents to the will, the will is not constrained to move in a particular way, since it is open to the will to command intellect to consider that object in a variety of ways.

It should be apparent, then, that on Aquinas's account of intellect and will, the will is part of a dynamic feedback system composed of the will, the intellect, and the passions.[21] Any willing is influenced in important ways, but not caused or compelled, by previous willings and is the result of an often complicated interaction of the intellect and the will. For that reason, although Aquinas's account of the will assigns a large role

---

[17] *ST* Ia.82.4.
[18] *ST* IaIIae.9.2.
[19] *ST* Ia.81.3 and IaIIae.10.3.
[20] Cf. *ST* IaIIae.9.1.
[21] So, e.g., pointing to the difficulty of extricating will and intellect from each other, Aquinas says "it happens sometimes that there is an act of the will in which something of the [preceding] act of reason remains . . . and, vice versa, there is [sometimes] an act of reason in which something of the [preceding] act of will remains" (*ST* IaIIae.17.1).

to intellect, Aquinas is not committed to seeing immoral actions simply as instances of mistakes in calculation.[22]

Finally, Aquinas not only holds that the will can command intellect but also makes some helpful remarks about the manner in which the will commands all the powers under its control. The will is ordered to the good in general, whereas all the other powers of the soul are ordered to particular goods, but there is order among active powers so that the power which regards a universal end (goodness in general, in this case) moves the powers which regard particular ends. Consequently, the will moves the other powers of the soul (with the exception of the vegetative powers, which aren't under its control) with efficient causation, just as the general who aims at the common good of the whole army moves by his command the captains of individual companies, each of whom aims at the good of his own company.[23] So, for example, the power of sight has a good toward which it is directed, namely, the apprehension of color; and the intellect has a good towards which it is directed, namely, the cognition of truth. Because the will is directed to the good in general, however, it governs those powers which are directed toward particular goods.[24]

In other words, Aquinas's idea is that the will works in accordance with the nature of the power of the soul it is commanding in order to help that power achieve the good it was created to achieve; as we might put it, will works in accordance with the design plan[25] of the faculties it governs, not against them.[26] It is a result of Aquinas's position here that

---

[22] In cases of incontinence, where the intellect seems to be representing as good something that the will is not willing, Aquinas would say that the intellect is in fact being moved by opposite motives to represent the thing in question as both good and not good, so that the intellect is double-minded, in some sense of that term. Cf., e.g., *ST* IaIIae.17.2 and 5 ad1.

[23] *ST* IaIIae.9.1. The relation between the will and the sensitive powers of the soul is outside the scope of this paper, but it is not hard to see that the will has at least some indirect control over the sensitive powers, since, e.g., one can will to direct one's gaze or will to close one's eyes and thereby control what one sees.

[24] *ST* Ia.82.4. See also *ST* IaIIae.9.1. There is no suggestion in Aquinas that the direction of the will toward the good in general somehow *naturally* results in the will's governance of the other powers; this line of his may just be intended to explain why God gave the will the governance it has.

[25] I take the notion of a design plan of cognitive faculties, and associated notions, from Alvin Plantinga's *Warrant and Proper Function* (Oxford: Oxford University Press, 1993).

[26] Of course, on Aquinas's account of the relations between intellect and will, an act of will is dependent on some act of intellect (whether tacit or explicit) apprehending something as good. What is not clear is whether Aquinas thinks that the intellect's apprehension is the only constraint on the will in its relations to the other powers it can command, or whether he recognizes as well what seems clearly to be the case: namely, that acts of will are also constrained by the nature of the power or faculty or body part being com-

we do not have voluntary control over belief in cases where our cognitive capacities, acting according to their nature, have been abundantly or sufficiently moved by their objects.[27] This idea will prove useful in following sections.

Will and Belief

For our purposes here, the part of Aquinas's account likely to strike contemporary philosophers as most objectionable is his view that the will can exercise direct control over the intellect.

Of course, not all postmedieval philosophers have supposed that the will has no role in the production and maintenance of belief. The deontological tradition in epistemology, for example, seems committed to the view that the will can significantly influence belief. For example, W. K. Clifford's famous dictum that it is wrong everywhere and for anyone to believe anything on insufficient evidence seems to presuppose that we have some voluntary control over our beliefs. There is no point in issuing proclamations to people about what it is wrong for them to do unless it is in some sense up to them whether or not they do the acts in question.[28] Roderick Chisholm also (at least at one point) built his epistemology on a strong commitment to the role of will in belief. According to Chisholm, "If self-control is what is essential to activity, some of our beliefs, our believings, would seem to be acts. When a man deliberates and comes finally to a conclusion, his decision is as much within his control as is any other deed we attribute to him."[29]

But this tradition in epistemology has come under attack in recent years by, among others, William Alston[30] and Alvin Plantinga.[31] One of

---

manded. Since the latter point is not only true but also commonsensical and reasonably obvious, I assume that it is part of what Aquinas has in mind here.

[27] *ST* IaIIae.17.6.

[28] In "What Ought We to Believe? or The Ethics of Belief Revisited," *American Philosophical Quarterly* 17 (1980): 15–24, Jack Meiland makes a similar point about this tradition in epistemology, although he assigns a slightly different reason for it.

[29] Roderick M. Chisholm, "Lewis' Ethics of Belief," in *The Philosophy of C.I. Lewis*, ed. Paul Arthur Schilpp (London: Cambridge University Press, 1968), p. 224.

[30] See, e.g., William Alston, "Concepts of Epistemic Justification" and "The Deontological Conception of Epistemic Justification," reprinted in *Epistemic Justification: Essays in the Theory of Knowledge* (Ithaca: Cornell University Press, 1989), pp. 81–152.

[31] See, e.g., Alvin Plantinga, *Warrant: The Current Debate* (Oxford: Oxford University Press, 1993). Unlike Alston, Plantinga is cautiously sympathetic to attempts to show that will has a role in belief (see pp. 148–61), because he sees some merit in Bas van Fraassen's argument for the claim that "belief is a matter of the will" ("Belief and the Will," *Journal of Philosophy* 81 [1984]: 256). In that article, van Fraassen says little about the nature of the interaction between will and intellect, so I do not discuss his views here.

the objections against it has been the argument that the will does not have the sort of role in producing and sustaining belief that such deontological conceptions require. In fact, it has even been argued that the will *cannot* have such a role in belief.

Because Aquinas's account of wisdom depends on the claim that the will can sometimes determine intellect, it is important to look at the contemporary arguments that seem to call this claim into question.[32]

Winters's View of Believing at Will

Bernard Williams has argued that it is impossible to believe at will.[33] His arguments have been criticized effectively by Barbara Winters,[34] but she herself sides with Williams to the extent of arguing for a weaker version of his claim. According to Winters, *this* "general principle related to believing at will [is true]: [namely,] it is impossible to believe that one believes *p* and that one's belief of *p* originated and is sustained in a way that has no connection with *p*'s truth."[35]

Now the principle Winters cites is in fact false, contrary to her claim, and it is not hard to find counterexamples to it. Consider someone un-

---

[32] One caveat at the outset may be helpful. It is widely agreed that desire can influence belief: e.g., double-blind experiments in science have as their purpose minimizing the role of desire in belief. But it is not clear what the relation of desire to volition is. Harry Frankfurt defines a volition as an effective desire: that is, on his view, a desire that eventuates in action (if there are no external impediments) just is a volition. So if Frankfurt is right, then when desires for beliefs result in the mental action of belief formation, those desires are volitions; and in that case, any instance of a belief's resulting from desire will count as an instance of will's producing belief (whether directly or indirectly). Because the connection between desire and volition is a large and controversial issue, however, I set aside cases of beliefs resulting from desire and do not consider them here. For Frankfurt's view see his "Freedom of the Will and the Concept of a Person," *Journal of Philosophy* 68 (1971): 5–20; reprinted in *The Importance of What We Care About* (Cambridge: Cambridge University Press, 1988); see esp. p. 14. It is perhaps worth noting that thinkers in other periods have held similar views. Jonathan Edwards, e.g., says, "In every act of the will *for*, or *towards* something not present, the soul is in some degree *inclined* to that thing; and that inclination, if in a considerable degree, is the very same with the affection of *desire*"; and "The *will*, and the *affections* of the soul, are not two faculties; the affections are not essentially distinct from the will, nor do they differ from the mere *actings* of the will and inclination, but only in the liveliness and sensibility of exercise" (*A Treatise concerning Religious Affections*, pt. 1, sec. 1). I am grateful to Alvin Plantinga for calling my attention to this work.

[33] Bernard Williams, "Deciding to Believe," in *Problems of the Self* (New York: Cambridge University Press, 1973), pp. 136–51.

[34] Barbara Winters, "Believing at Will," *Journal of Philosophy* 76 (1979): 243–56. See also Jonathan Bennett, "Why Is Belief Involuntary?" *Analysis* 50 (1990): 87–107; Bennett also criticizes Williams's position, but for my purposes here Winters's objections are more interesting.

[35] Winters, "Believing at Will," p. 243.

dergoing a major change in worldview, someone (for example) in the process of jettisoning all the Baptist religious beliefs inculcated in him as a child. Such a person might well find himself, to his considerable annoyance, still believing that drinking is morally wrong, and he might give himself periodic stern lectures on the subject. What the lectures would consist in, presumably, is explaining to himself that his belief in the wrongness of drinking originated and is sustained in a way which has no connection with that belief's truth. But the fact that he has to give himself these lectures repeatedly shows that, even in his own view, the belief persists nonetheless. We might suppose that his lectures show he *also* does *not* believe that drinking is wrong. But unless he supposed that he perceived in himself the belief that drinking *is* wrong, his lectures to himself would be hard to explain. He might be double-minded or irrational, but it would still be true of him that he believes (and takes himself to believe) that drinking is wrong. So he is an example of someone who violates Winters's principle; he believes in full consciousness that he believes drinking is wrong *and* that his belief that drinking is wrong is not sustained by any truth considerations.

Or consider someone who finds herself believing that she must wash her hands, although she can see that they are clean and she knows that she has washed them twelve times in the last hour. She will recognize, unless she is hopelessly psychotic, that her belief that she must wash her hands is a belief which is sustained in a way that has no connection with that belief's truth, but she might find herself afflicted with the belief nonetheless. As in the preceding case, she might be double-minded or in some other way irrational; she might in some way also believe that it is not true that she must wash her hands. What makes her miserable is that in spite of everything she finds that she cannot get rid of the belief that she must wash her hands. Psychotherapy is a successful business just because Winters's principle is false. Many people make appointments with therapists as a result of believing of themselves that they hold some belief *p* but that that belief is sustained without the appropriate connection to truth; and so they enlist the help of therapists to rid themselves of their belief *p*.[36]

Suppose for the sake of argument, however, that Winters's principle is true: it nonetheless does not follow, *pace* Winters, that we have no vol-

[36] The case of enlisting the help of a therapist to rid one of a belief is, clearly, itself a case in which will has an effect on belief; but since the will's control of belief in this case is very indirect, this case will perhaps be uncontroversial. It should perhaps be added that the process of ridding oneself of a belief one thinks has no appropriate connection with truth may involve processes that have little or nothing to do with the will's control over belief.

untary control over any of our beliefs. The philosophical controversy regarding voluntary control over belief, as Winters explains, "concerns whether the model of free basic action can be applied to belief acquisition,"[37] and Winters takes her principle as relevant to this controversy, which she glosses as a controversy about believing at will.[38] But we could have voluntary control over belief, the model of free basic action could be applied to believing, even if Winters's principle were true.

Consider the three conditions Winters takes to be necessary for anything to count as believing at will.[39] According to Winters, "To constitute a genuine case of *believing at will*,"

(1) "the belief must have been acquired directly and as a result of intending to hold it";

(2) "the belief [must] be acquired independently of any consideration about its truth"; and

(3) "the action of acquiring the belief at will [must] be performed with the agent fully aware that he or she is attempting to arrive at the belief in this way."[40]

If, however, what we want to know is "whether the model of free basic action can be applied to belief acquisition," then these three conditions are much too strong. There can be cases of free basic belief acquisition that do not meet them; if these conditions do in fact capture what it is to believe at will, then not being able to believe at will is compatible with a robust degree of voluntary control over belief and also with free basic belief acquisition.

To see that this is so, it is helpful to notice that there can be cases of free basic action involving bodily movement that do not meet the appropriate analogues of (1)–(3). That is, if we think of the appropriate analogues of (1)–(3) as capturing, analogously, what it is to move at will, then there can be free basic actions of moving a body part which are not instances of moving at will.[41]

Consider, for example, the free basic action of moving your hand and

---

[37] Winters, "Believing at Will," p. 244.

[38] She gives, as a special case of her principle, "it is impossible for me to believe of a particular belief *b* that *b* is a present belief of mine and sustained at will" (ibid., p. 256).

[39] The conditions she gives also seem presupposed by others who argue against voluntary control over belief; see, e.g., Williams, "Deciding to Believe," and Alston, "The Deontological Conception."

[40] Cf. Alston, "The Deontological Conception," pp. 244–45.

[41] In fact, I don't think that (1)–(3) do capture what it is to believe at will or that their analogues capture what it is to move at will. A habitual hummer, for example, who hums without realizing that she is doing so, nonetheless seems to me to hum at will.

arm to scratch your head. This is an action which is performed directly, in normal human beings, but not necessarily always as a result of intending to perform it. The action might be absent-minded; you might not even notice that you are moving your hand and arm in this way. The action might be an example of parapraxis; you were intending to smooth your hair, but, distracted by what you were thinking about, you scratched your head instead. So, the appropriate analogue to condition (1) is not a general condition on free basic action.

The same is true of condition (3) and its appropriate analogue for free basic action of all sorts. For the same or similar reasons as before, it is not in general true that to count as free and basic an action must be performed with the agent fully aware that she is attempting to perform the action in this way. Many free basic actions are performed with less than full awareness. Besides absent-minded actions and instances of parapraxis, which involve will's commanding muscles of the limbs, there are also cases involving will's commanding muscles of the mouth and larynx; Freudian slips, instantly regretted and socially embarrassing interjections, and utterances one just finds oneself giving voice to are all cases of will's commanding muscles with less than the agent's full awareness that she is attempting to perform the action in this way.[42]

So neither the analogue of condition (1) nor the analogue of condition (3) is a condition on free basic actions which involve muscle movement. But if the analogues of (1) and (3) do not hold for all these sorts of free basic actions, why suppose that (1) and (3) should hold in cases where what the will is governing is belief? To support such a supposition, we would need to find a difference between mental acts and bodily acts that made the conditions for free basic action much more stringent in the case of mental acts than in the case of bodily acts, and it is hard to imagine what such a difference might be.

I have so far left to one side consideration of condition (2) because the way in which it is too strong is harder to see but also more important.

In general (though perhaps with some exceptions), our cognitive faculties are aimed at truth, whatever other purposes there may be for them. Their design plan is such that when they are operating according to it, they function fairly reliably to arrive at truth; or, as Aquinas puts it, each power is directed to some suitable good proper to it, and the intellect is directed to the knowledge of the truth.[43] If the will commands intellect to acquire belief "independently of any consideration about its

---

[42] Although we sometimes think of such episodes as involuntary, in fact it is clear that the muscles are not moving by themselves; they are still under the control of the will (or, as psychologists sometimes like to say, 'the executive function').

[43] *ST* Ia.82.4.

truth," then the will is commanding intellect to act against its design plan, rather than in accordance with it.[44]

It plainly is not a necessary condition on free basic action in general, however, that the will be able to act against the design plan of the system it is commanding. On the contrary, it is clear that in order to have a free basic action, the will must command in accordance with the design plan of the system it is commanding. So, for example, the will can be successful in commanding the head and neck to move only in case the volition is in accordance with the design plan of those parts. One might will that the head rotate a full circle around the neck, but (as long as the head and neck are formed in the normal way) one cannot will so successfully, and there can be no such basic action. Similarly, if the legs are not monstrously deformed, the will cannot successfully command the muscles of the lower leg to move in such a way that the leg folds over on itself with the toes touching the fronts of the thighs. The design plan of the leg will not permit that sort of motion, and there are no free basic actions of that sort.

Free basic actions, then, have to be in accordance with and not contrary to the design plan of the system or module or body part the will is commanding when the free basic action involves muscle movement. It does not seem unreasonable to suppose, as Aquinas clearly does, that this must also be the case when the free basic action involves a mental act. Aquinas thinks that when the will moves the other powers of the soul, it is to help them achieve the particular goods to which they are directed.[45] Since our cognitive faculties are in general aimed at truth, however, an attempt to command the intellect to acquire a belief independently of any consideration of the truth of that belief would be for the will to attempt to govern the intellect against, rather than in accordance with, its design plan.[46] One might attempt to will in this way, but (as long as the cognitive faculties are not malfuctioning or defective) one could not will so successfully, and there can be no such free basic actions.

[44] In order to operate in accordance with the design plan of what it commands, of course, the will does not require any recognition on the part of the intellect that it is doing so or any apprehension of the nature of the design plan on the part of the intellect. The will can command the head to turn without the intellect's apprehending the nature of the musculature of the head.

[45] *ST* IaIIae.9.1.

[46] And this point holds whether the will tries to command intellect to believe something which is evidently false or whether will tries to command intellect to believe something when the truth-value of the belief is utterly unapparent. In the latter cases, we might act as *if* we assented to the belief, but the will could not successfully command intellect to adopt it.

Condition (2) and its analogue for bodily movement are thus too strong as conditions on free basic action. Consequently, that there are no free basic actions involving belief which meet condition (2) tells us very little about whether we have voluntary control over beliefs.

Showing that there are not or cannot be such things as believings at will, then, where the conditions for believing at will are (1)–(3) above, is not sufficient to determine whether "the model of free basic action" can be applied to belief.

Alston's Counterexamples

The approach of Williams and Winters is not the only tactic for arguing that the model of free basic action cannot be applied to belief. Alston is another philosopher who takes this view, and his tactic, as he explains it, is just to get us to ask ourselves whether it is in fact in our power successfully to will to believe. His first example, designed to show us that it is not, is this: "Can you, at this moment, start to believe that the United States is still a colony of Great Britain, just by deciding to do so?"[47] Since we in fact know that the United States is not still a colony, to ask whether we can adopt the opposite belief just by deciding to do so is to ask whether the will can successfully command intellect to act contrary to its design plan. But this is the sort of thing, as we've seen, which the will cannot do in other cases—for example, when what it is commanding is body parts—and so it is not surprising to discover that the will cannot do so in the case of believing either.

Alston's other examples are like the first in this regard. It is not the case either, he says, that we have voluntary control as regards such obviously true beliefs as perceptual beliefs. If I had such control, Alston says, then I would "have effective voluntary control over whether I do or do not believe that the tree has leaves on it when I see a tree with leaves on it just before me in broad daylight with my eyesight working perfectly. And it is perfectly clear that in this situation I have no power at all to refrain from that belief."[48] But if the will were to command refraining from the belief that the tree has leaves on it in this situation, it would obviously be trying to govern the perceptual cognitive faculties (or the perceptual faculties together with other cognitive faculties of judgment) in a way contrary to their design plan. Perceptual faculties are designed to report with some reliability about whatever is presented to perceptual organs, and the will cannot successfully direct them to do

[47] Alston, "The Deontological Conception," p. 122.
[48] Ibid., p. 123.

otherwise, however much it may want to do so. When, near the end of George Orwell's *1984*, Big Brother offers to end his torture of Winston if Winston will only believe that the four fingers he sees in front of him are five, the torture continues for some time, despite Winston's passionate efforts to make it stop by trying to alter his perceptual beliefs.[49]

But once we see what the problem is with examples such as Alston's, it is not difficult to generate different examples that do, in fact, support the intuition that we sometimes have voluntary control over beliefs.

This is the case even for perceptual beliefs. Consider, for example, a man separated unwillingly from the woman he loves. Missing her desperately, he finds himself seeing her everywhere, till he gets tired of (as we say) his eyes playing tricks on him.[50] The next time he thinks he sees her, he says to himself sternly, "Stop that! You know it can't be her!" and with that command the woman he was looking at no longer looks to him like the woman he loves, and he no longer has the perceptual belief "That's Anna!" Furthermore, the will can not only successfully command the rejection of perceptual belief in this way; it can also successfully command that a certain perceptual belief occur. You are reading a psychology book on perception which contains a picture that can be seen either as a young woman or as an old lady. You see the old lady and not the young woman, but the book tells you that normal, non-brain-damaged adults see the picture both ways. Consternated, you will to see the young woman, and the result is that you do now see her. You don't work out the lines delineating that figure, crossword-puzzle fashion; you just suddenly *see* her. Because of the will's command, the image of the young woman emerges from the lines that had been the old lady; you simply see her, all at once, and you form the belief "There's the young woman!"[51] Here the perception and the perceptual belief are

---

[49] Although not entirely clear on this point, the novel suggests to some people that in the end, even if only briefly, Winston succeeds in altering his perceptual beliefs about what he in fact sees. If Orwell thought it possible for a man who sees four fingers in front of him to will successfully to believe that there are five fingers in front of him, then in my view Orwell is mistaken.

[50] This very phenomenon, of course, is an example of the way in which desire (if not volition) can influence perceptual beliefs.

[51] Nothing in this example suggests that you will *always* be successful when the will issues a command of this sort; nor is it the case that a person who can sometimes, in one free basic action, touch his toes will always be able to do so when the will commands it. On cases involving perception, see, e.g., Irvin Rock, *The Logic of Perception* (Cambridge: MIT Press, Bradford Books, 1987), esp. chap. 3. Rock sees a role for the will in the formation of perceptual beliefs also: "Consistent with my suggestion about figure-ground organization, I would like to suggest that grouping on the basis of factors such as proximity, similarity, . . . is the result of a *decision* to describe the stimulus array in one way rather than other possible ways. . . . a particular grouping is linked to a particular description

simultaneously acquired as a direct result of the will's command.[52] In these two cases, the occurrent belief (or the rejection of an occurrent belief) that the will brings about is in accordance with the agent's dispositional beliefs. That is, in these cases the will is not bringing about a belief (or the rejection of a belief) "independently of any consideration of its truth." Nonetheless, that the agent has (or rejects) the occurrent belief is a direct result of the will's commands.

There are also reasons for supposing that we have voluntary control of this sort over memory and to that extent over memory beliefs.[53] More

---

and therefore is of the nature of a *decision* rather than of a spontaneous interaction" (p. 75; my emphasis. I myself think that Rock's use of 'decision' here is infelicitous, suggesting an implausible degree of awareness or even deliberation. The claim that the will has a role in perception is a weaker claim). A neurobiology text, speaking of a different sort of figure/ground discrimination, says, "The exact shape is ambiguous. . . . With some *conscious effort* one can mentally shift the light source . . . and change the apparent curvature of the object" (my emphasis). See Eric Kandel, James Schwartz, and Thomas Jessell, eds., *Principles of Neural Science*, 3d ed. (New York: Elsevier, 1991), p. 444.

[52] Someone might suppose that this is a case in which will influences perceptual belief only indirectly and that it is analogous to a case in which the will, e.g., commands the head to turn so that the eyes can see what is behind the willer, with the result that new perceptual beliefs are formed as an *indirect* result of the act of the will. In the case I have described, of course, there is no intermediary of voluntary muscle movement between the will's command and the new perceptual belief. But someone might still object that there is nonetheless an intermediary between the command of the will and the perceptual belief, namely, the new perception. If this objection were right, any instance of perception occurring between a command of the will and the resulting perceptual belief would be enough by itself to make the will's control of the belief indirect, and it would consequently be impossible for true perceptual beliefs to be the direct result of a command of the will. In that case, the will's control over perceptual belief could be only indirect. But put this way, the objection relies on the view that perception can be cleanly dissociated from perceptual belief, and this view seems to me an implausible account of perception. I am inclined to suppose that any case of perception includes some beliefs (however tacit or unawarely held) about the object of perception. In other words, all seeing is seeing-as, in some sense. Therefore, when a perception and perceptual belief are formed at the command of the will, the perceptual belief is the direct result of the will's action if the perception is. But even those who reject the view that all seeing is seeing-as should grant this much: if the perceptual belief in question is the spontaneous and unavoidable concomitant of the perception (as it is in the case involving the ambiguous figure discussed in the text), then in virtue of being able to produce the perception directly by an act of will, the willer also has direct voluntary control over the perceptual belief, since he controls his having that perceptual belief by an act of will alone, without the intermediary of muscle movement or other intervening acts of will. I am grateful to Peter van Inwagen, whose objections helped me to think through the issues involved here.

[53] For example, you find yourself afflicted with a memory of a colleague's contumelious treatment of you, and you can feel your anger growing out of all bounds as the images of the wretched occasion recur repeatedly to your mind. "Forget it," you say to yourself sternly, "put it out of your mind." And in virtue of that act of will (perhaps repeated more than once), you succeed in moving the images of the event out of short-term memory and into dispositional memory, so that the memory beliefs become dispositional rather than occurrent. There is also considerable evidence that if the events are awful enough and the

important for our purposes here, there are cases as regards intellect as well. For example, consider Smith, who grew up in a racist part of Boston and became imbued with the racist views of the surrounding culture, but whose worldview changes in college and who becomes determined to eradicate racism in himself. When Smith catches himself with a racist belief, he says to himself, "Stop it! Don't think such a thing!" And as a result of this imperative on the part of his will, his intellect rejects the racist belief in question, at least at the moment. Or consider someone who finds himself believing, compulsively, that he must wash his hands yet again; or a person who notices that he is depressed and finds himself believing that he is worthless and would be better off dead;

---

will to erase the memory is strong enough, it is possible to move the images of the event not only out of short-term memory but out of consciously accessible long-term memory as well, so that they are repressed and entirely forgotten. Inaccessible to consciousness and not available for retrieval at the initiative of the agent, the images of such awful events remain in some sort of cognitive deep storage, where they can be jogged loose by blows to the head or equally jarring psychological shocks or probing psychotherapy. Repressed memories of traumatic childhood events, such as violent sexual abuse and mechanisms for their release have been widely discussed; there is also in some cases a little understood spontaneous release of memories. For a case in which a blow to the head releases previously repressed traumatic memories, see Oliver Sacks, *The Man Who Mistook His Wife for a Hat* (New York: Harper Perennial, 1985), pp. 161–65. It seems, then, that the will has some control over memory, too. (These cases of will's influence on memory are apparently not ones in which the will is acting in accordance with the design plan of the cognitive faculties, since the will here has a role in suppressing information that would otherwise have been available to the cognitive faculties. But some cognitive modules, or some cognitive modules in some circumstances, have something other than the cognition of truth as part of their design plan. In these cases of memory repression we might say that the primary design plan of the memory module—namely, the storage of information about past experience—is overridden in favor of a secondary design plan aimed at psychic survival. When the primary design plan would store information destructive to the psyche, the secondary design plan overrides it and represses the memory. Considered in this way, the will is acting in accordance with the design plan of memory even in bringing about the repression of memories.) In some cases, there is also voluntary control, of a limited sort, over occurrent memory beliefs. For example, the will can command memory to retain certain information in such a way as to form occurrent memory beliefs. You make an appointment to see the dean tomorrow, but you have a lamentable tendency to forget appointments, despite your best efforts, and you're worried that this one will skip your mind, too. So you issue repeated commands to memory: "Don't forget! You have an appointment with the dean at three tomorrow." And the result is that you do remember this appointment, unlike the others you characteristically forget. (That it takes effort, time, and repeated trying for will to be successful in these cases doesn't show that the acts in question aren't free basic actions. A person who was out of condition might find that it took him effort, time, and three or four tries to touch his toes, but his act of touching his toes would still be a free basic action.) Or you are being tested on digit span by an educational tester who has, unprofessionally enough, explained to you that your colleague who works in mathematical logic was able to hold in memory a span of ten digits. Eaten with envy, you will to remember at least twelve, and as a result of the determination of the will you do so.

or a person who becomes furious with a colleague and finds himself believing that nothing he could do to her would be bad enough. In each case, the will may intervene, commanding the intellect to reject the belief in question. Here, as in the cases involving perceptual beliefs, the acquisition or rejection of an occurrent belief in consequence of the directives of the will is in accordance with the dispositional beliefs of the agent, and the change in occurrent beliefs is not made "independently of considerations of truth." But it remains the case that the agent's acquisition or rejection of a belief on the occasion in question is the direct result of the will's commands.

Someone might suppose that the control of the will over belief in these cases is only indirect, that the will governs belief by having the intellect review the relevant evidence, thus strengthening a belief (or weakening its competitors). Perhaps this view is correct in some cases, but surely not in all. When the person afflicted with the belief that he must wash his hands wills to reject that belief, he does not do so by reviewing the evidence available to him about whether or not his hands need washing. He recognizes the compulsive hand-washing belief as an old enemy and, without any intervening cognitive calculations, wills straightway to reject it. Cases of this sort can be part of fierce and ongoing internal battles. Sometimes the will is not successful, and a person seeks external help from friends or religious counselors or therapists. But sometimes the will is successful, and the willer wins her battles by herself because her will has been effective in getting her intellect to abandon the compulsive or depressive or vengeful beliefs she wills not to have.

There are also the opposite sorts of cases, where one wants a belief, where one's will in fact commands one's intellect to adopt a specific belief. Smith finds himself walking the long way home at night to avoid the graveyard. As a result of his will's stern commands to his intellect, his intellect forms the belief that there is nothing to fear in the graveyard, and he takes the shortcut home. What accounts for Smith's disciplining the fear he probably still feels is not that he is being courageous about ghosts or even recklessly taking his chances with whatever stalks in the cemetery, but rather that his will's directives have resulted in intellect's holding the occurrent belief that there is nothing to fear in the graveyard. As before, the will may govern belief indirectly by bringing about a review of the evidence; it is more likely in this sort of case, however, that both the fear and the internal struggle are old and familiar and that the will governs belief directly, without any intervening review of the evidence.

These examples, and others like them, show that we do have considerable direct voluntary control over beliefs and that believing or re-fraining from believing can be a free basic action.[54] A simple way to find such examples is to look for cases where the will is working in accordance with the design plan of the cognitive faculties, or even cases such as those given above where the will is correcting the action of a cognitive faculty that is beginning to go wrong in some way.[55] Aquinas is right to hold that the will can move the intellect as an efficient cause in cases where the will is working with the powers of the soul, directing them in accordance with the aims they have by nature.

It is important, however, to add here that the will can also work with the design plan of what it commands in such a way as to damage it rather than to aid its functioning. In the most extreme case, the will can

[54] This is not to say, of course, that we have voluntary control of any sort over all our beliefs, that we are morally responsible for having the beliefs we do, that we are morally culpable for any morally wrong beliefs we have, and so on. My claim here is only the limited one stated in the text.

[55] Once we understand the way the will can govern the faculties or modules or body parts it commands, it is not difficult to find examples not only of direct voluntary control of belief, such as those above, but also of indirect voluntary control, where the will governs the intellect by directing attention. In cases, e.g., of what Alston calls immediate (although indirect) control, "the agent is able to carry out the intention 'right away,' in one uninterrupted intentional act, without having to return to the attempt a number of times after having been occupied with other matters" ("The Deontological Conception," p. 129). You have a difficult and quarrelsome colleague who is also afflicted with a brain deficit that leaves him unable to express emotion in facial expression or the pitch of speech. When he greets you in the morning, you find yourself believing spontaneously that he is angry at you. But just as your intellect is thinking up a nasty response, your will commands intellect to review the evidence available. On that basis, you bite back the unpleasant remark you were framing; you reject the belief that he is angry at you and chalk up your original reaction to a mistaken assessment of his facial expression. Or it turns out that the chief event at the party your best friend has arranged for you consists of rides in sporty little two-seater planes. You are generally unable to believe that flying is a safe and acceptable way to travel, but you want very badly not to disappoint your friend. So when your friend asks you to get in the plane, your will instructs intellect to review quickly all the evidence available to you relevant to this instance of flying. As a result, you form the belief that this one flight will be safe and acceptable, and you get in the plane. In the first of these two cases, someone might suppose that intellect is looking for "evidence to decide an unresolved issue," but in the second case it is clear that "the search for evidence was undertaken with the intention of taking up a certain attitude toward a particular proposition" (Alston, "The Deontological Conception," p. 130), which is what Alston thinks we need for a genuine case of voluntary control of belief. Here, too, for immediate indirect control of belief, a ready formula for finding examples that show the will's role in belief is to look for cases in which the cognitive faculties are beginning to go wrong, either in virtue of reacting inappropriately to something misleading in the cognitive environment (as in the case of the brain-damaged colleague) or in virtue of being swayed by the pull of a passion (as in the case of the fear of flying) or for some other reason. In such cases, the will works together with the design plan of the cognitive faculties to counteract the localized cognitive problem.

work with the design plan of the muscles in such a way as to render those muscles, and all others, permanently dysfunctional; suicide is the most obvious example. But there are plenty of smaller-scale examples. Pitchers hurt their arms pitching; ballerinas injure their legs and feet dancing; keyboard operators develop carpal tunnel syndrome on the job, and so on. In all these cases the will is working with the design plan of the relevant body parts but by that means making them less functional or bringing about damage to them.[56] Aquinas thinks that there can be such a deleterious effect of the will on cognitive capacities as well, and not just on body parts. In working with the design plan of the intellect the will can misdirect intellect, as well as aid its functioning. The misdirection works by immediate indirect control, rather than direct control, as we shall see when we look more closely at what Aquinas has to say about wisdom.[57]

Wisdom as One of the Intellectual Virtues

Aquinas's understanding of virtue is complicated, but for present purposes we can understand him as characterizing a virtue much as Aris-

[56] Or perhaps the thing to say here is that in these cases the design plan of what the will commands is being satisfied, if we take 'design plan' in a narrow sense, whereas it is being violated if we take 'design plan' in quite a broad sense. A keyboard operator's fingers are being used in accordance with their design plan when she types, and when she wills to type, the will is commanding the relevant body parts in accordance with their design plan. Carpal tunnel syndrome, however, develops in some people who regularly type many hours a day; the design plan of the fingers, taken in a larger sense, is not suited to endless repetitions of the same movements without substantial and frequent intervals of rest. So there is a sense in which operating a keyboard continuously is not in accordance with the design plan of the fingers, even if any individual movement of the fingers at the keyboard is in accordance with the design plan of the body parts used. It may be helpful here to invoke Plantinga's distinction between a snapshot design plan, which specifies how the thing works now, and a maximum design plan, which specifies how the thing will change its workings over time in different circumstances. (*Warrant and Proper Function*, pp. 22 ff.).

[57] Because I explicate wisdom by focusing on folly and because in folly the will exercises only immediate indirect control over the intellect, someone might suppose that Aquinas needs only the weaker claim that the will has such indirect control, and not also the stronger claim that the will has direct control over intellect. But this is a misimpression generated by my explication of wisdom in terms of its opposed vice, folly. The process by which the will corrupts intellect does require only indirect control over intellect on the part of the will. But the process by which the will and intellect function together to produce wisdom has as an essential ingredient direct control by the will over the intellect. Wisdom is an outgrowth of charity, which in turn depends on faith; and faith is a case in which the will exercises direct control over intellect, on Aquinas's view. If there were space here to explicate his entire account of wisdom, it would, consequently, be clear that the stronger claim is necessary.

totle does: a virtue is a habit or disposition which makes the power it is a disposition of apt to work well.[58] For intellectual virtues the power in question is primarily the intellect or reason. Aquinas divides intellect or reason into speculative reason and practical reason, and he assigns three virtues to the former and two to the latter.[59] The two virtues of practical intellect are prudence and art.[60] The three virtues of speculative intellect are wisdom, *scientia*,[61] and understanding. Understanding is a matter of grasping first principles, the starting points for the various sorts of sciences. *Scientia* involves comprehension of the causes of things and recognition of the way in which things are related to their causes. Wisdom consists in understanding the highest (or, as we would say, most fundamental) causes of everything and seeing everything else in the world in its relation to those highest (most fundamental) causes.[62]

What one thinks these highest causes are depends on the rest of one's worldview. Aquinas, who knew that Aristotle did not hold a worldview identical with his own, supposes that for Aristotle the grasp of the most fundamental causes belongs to metaphysics (or metaphysics and some natural theology), so that, Aquinas thinks, for Aristotle wisdom is a matter of mastering metaphysics.[63] For Aquinas, the highest or most fundamental cause is, of course, God, so that on Aquinas's account wisdom is a matter of knowing God's nature, God's actions, and God's decrees.[64] Just as we today suppose that all the sciences will be understood best if

[58] See, e.g., *QDV* 14.3 obj.2 and reply; also *ST* IaIIae.55.1 and 57.1. Aquinas's complete definition of virtue is more complicated than we can deal with here: virtue is a good quality of the mind, by which we live righteously, of which no one can make bad use, which God works in us without us; see *ST* IaIIae.55.4.

[59] See, e.g., *ST* IaIIae.57.2 and 4.

[60] Prudence has to do with reasoning about things that are to be done in order to obtain human good; art has to do with reasoning about things to be made in order to obtain human good: *ST* IaIIae.57.2.

[61] '*Scientia*' is often translated as 'knowledge,' but in my view this is a misleading translation; see my "Aquinas on the Foundations of Knowledge," *Canadian Journal of Philosophy*, supp. vol. 17 (1991): 125–58. (For a somewhat different approach to Aquinas's account of *scientia*, see Scott MacDonald, "Theory of Knowledge," in *The Cambridge Companion to Aquinas*, ed. Norman Kretzmann and Eleonore Stump [Cambridge: Cambridge University Press, 1993], pp. 160–95.) In order to avoid adjudicating complex issues with a translation, I leave the word untranslated. In my view, the least misleading way to translate *scientia* is as 'science,' where it is understood that science can encompass, e.g., metaphysics.

[62] See, e.g., *ST* IaIIae.66.5; also, *In PA* 2.20.15, *In NE* 6.6.1190 and 1193, and *QDP* 1.4.

[63] As Aquinas of course understood, some of what is included in Aristotelian metaphysics is what we now would think of as philosophical theology. See, e.g., *ST* IIaIIae.19.7.

[64] The discussion of Aristotle here and in the next sections should not obscure the fact that Aquinas's views of intellectual excellence in general and wisdom in particular have an Augustinian root as well. On the way Aquinas and Augustine are related here, see, e.g., Mark Jordan, *Ordering Wisdom: The Hierarchy of Philosophical Discourses in Aquinas* (Notre Dame, Ind.: University of Notre Dame Press, 1986), p. 122.

the scientist begins with a solid foundation in physics and sees the other sciences in the light of that foundation, so Aquinas supposes that physics and all the sciences, including metaphysics, will be understood most deeply and most excellently by someone who has a good grasp of God's nature and actions.[65] We and Aquinas, then, share the conviction that there is a hierarchy of knowledge about the world and that a cognitive agent's knowledge is held with more depth and richness if she knows the foundations (or, as Aquinas would say, the pinnacle) of that hierarchy. On his view, the foundation, or the pinnacle, consists in the attributes and actions of the creator of the world, and knowing these is an intellectual virtue.

Understood in this way, an intellectual virtue need not be a product of will as well as intellect. Most of what Aquinas has to say about wisdom, however, has to do not with wisdom as an acquisition of human reason but with wisdom as a gift of the Holy Spirit; and so understood, wisdom does involve the will as well as the intellect. In order to understand all Aquinas has to say about wisdom, then, we have to see it in its context among the gifts. When we see his account of wisdom in that context and in the web of the other connections in which he locates it, then it turns out that wisdom is not just one part of a rather boring taxonomy of objects of knowledge or cognitive excellences but is instead the culmination of a complex interaction between will and intellect, intimately connected to moral goodness.

Three, maybe even four, of the intellectual virtues have a twin among the gifts of the Holy Spirit.[66] The seven gifts of the Holy Spirit are courage, piety, fear, counsel (*consilium*), understanding, *scientia*, and wisdom. Besides understanding, *scientia*, and wisdom, prudence among the intellectual virtues also seems to have an analogue among the gifts, because the gifts include counsel, and counsel is regularly coupled with prudence.

There are two main differences between the intellectual virtues and their twins among the gifts.[67] The first has to do with origin. To put it roughly: if, for example, *scientia* is something we have acquired ourselves through the use of reason, then it counts as an intellectual virtue; if, on

[65] Nothing in this claim implies anything about the way in which knowledge of God's nature and actions is acquired. It might be acquired even by the simple and unlearned in consequence of being told parts of God's revelation in scripture.

[66] See *ST* IaIIae.68.1.

[67] See, e.g., *ST* IIaIIae.45.1 ad2. See also *ST* IaIIae.68.1; there Aquinas summarizes the details of the distinction between virtues in general and gifts by saying that the virtues make a person apt to follow reason, and the gifts make a person apt to follow the promptings of the Holy Spirit. See also *In Sent* III.35.2.1.1 ad1.

the other hand, God gets the credit for our having it, then it counts as a gift. The second has to do with quality. *Scientia* as a gift is more excellent, more deep, rich, and far-ranging, than *scientia* as a virtue. So if a person manifests *scientia* in an especially excellent way, then, on Aquinas's view, that *scientia* should be judged as coming from God and counted as a gift from the Holy Spirit.[68]

Given this way of distinguishing between the intellectual virtues and the gifts of the Holy Spirit, it is not surprising that Aquinas pays relatively little attention to the intellectual virtues and substantial attention to their twins among the gifts. On the other hand, in his discussions of the intellectual virtues as gifts, Aquinas devotes virtually no space to discussion of the divine origins of the gifts or to the way in which God infuses these gifts into the mind or to the way in which grace and human free will cooperate during the process of divine infusion. In short, his discussion of wisdom, *scientia*, and understanding considered as gifts of the Holy Spirit looks in all relevant respects practically indistinguishable from what we might have expected to find in a discussion of the intellectual virtues. In working on wisdom, then, I follow his lead and consider wisdom not as an intellectual virtue but as a gift of the Holy Spirit, but I leave to one side (as he himself does) any specifically theological issues raised by his claim that wisdom is infused by God.

Wisdom in Its Context

Besides the five intellectual virtues and the seven gifts of the Holy Spirit, Aquinas recognizes four other groups of ethical characteristics which are important for his discussion of wisdom.

First, there are the seven principal virtues: the three theological virtues, faith, hope, and charity, together with the four cardinal moral virtues, courage, justice, temperance, and prudence.[69] These are matched by the seven deadly sins or capital vices: from most to least serious, pride, envy, wrath, sloth, avarice, gluttony, and lust. (There are many more mortal sins than these, but these seven are picked out as the sources from which the rest flow and to which the rest can in some sense be reduced.)[70] Next, there are the twelve fruits of the Holy Spirit: faith, char-

---

[68] See *ST* IaIIae.61.2 and 62.3.

[69] These are distinguished into acquired and infused, but this distinction need not concern us here.

[70] See, e.g., *ST* IaIIae.84.4. It is easy for us to misunderstand the items on this list: e.g., we naturally tend to think of sloth as laziness, but laziness is not an interesting or important sin for the medievals; sloth is much more like garden-variety, nonclinical depression.

ity, joy, peace, patience, long-suffering, goodness, benevolence, meek-ness, moderation, continence, and chastity.[71] Both the virtues and the gifts are habits or dispositions, whereas the fruits of the Holy Spirit are to be understood either as acts—acts of self-discipline with regard to kicking the dog, for example—or else as mental states resulting from such actions. Finally, there are the seven beatitudes or blessings, a series of claims attributed to Christ in the Gospels. Seven (or eight, depending on how one counts) human actions or attributes are picked out for blessing, and each is assigned a reward: Blessed are they that hunger and thirst after justice; blessed are the peacemakers, the meek, the poor in spirit, the mourners, the merciful, and the pure in heart.[72]

In examining wisdom, as well as the other virtues, Aquinas works by interweaving all the items from all of these lists. So, for example, for each of the seven principal virtues he presents and discusses the asso-ciated gifts, fruits, and beatitudes, and the opposed vices, including both the secondary vices and the cardinal vices from which those sec-ondary vices stem. It helps us understand what he has to say about wis-dom to see it in the context of all these connections.

Wisdom and Charity

The three gifts associated with the speculative intellect are linked to the three theological virtues. None of the intellectual virtues or their

---

A person who thinks everybody hates him, nobody likes him, and he might as well eat worms has sloth, on the medieval view, and the medievals saw this attitude as a sin (per-haps at least in part on the grounds that it is not morally acceptable to treat any of God's creatures in a demeaning or degrading way, even when the creature in question is one-self). It may also be helpful to note that the medievals grouped the last three of the deadly sins—avarice, gluttony, and lust—as the carnal sins (avarice has an ambiguous charac-ter, sometimes counting as a carnal sin and sometimes as a spiritual sin; see *ST* IaIIae.72.2, esp. ad4.) The carnal sins as a group are understood by the medievals to be significantly less serious than the other sins in the list.

[71] *ST* IaIIae.70.3. Although the Latin (*'castitas'*) can be taken as narrowly as the English 'chastity,' in such contexts it often means something broader than restraint with respect to sexual desire: it refers to self-discipline with regard to desires for earthly things when those desires are morally unacceptable. Controlling yourself and not kicking your dog at the end of an exasperating day is thus an example of *castitas*, since the desire to take out your frustrations by kicking the dog is a desire which it is never acceptable to act on. The Latin for the opposite of chastity, *'luxuria,'* is typically translated 'lust,' but it can range as broadly as *'castitas,'* to pick out any lack of self-discipline with regard to morally unaccep-table desires. Continence, understood analogously, is self-discipline with regard to de-sires for earthly things when the desire considered just by itself is not morally unaccep-table. The desire to watch TV, for example, is a desire of this sort. Continence is then a matter of exercising some self-discipline over such desires.

[72] *ST* IaIIae.69.3.

twins among the gifts of the Holy Spirit is associated with hope, whereas two are associated with faith: namely, understanding and *scientia*.[73] Wisdom is the gift associated with charity.

Acts of faith are the fruit connected to faith, and two beatitudes are given for it: blessed are those who are pure of heart and who mourn sin. The theological virtue of faith, in other words, is said to eventuate in acts of faith and to be produced in those whose hearts or wills are pure— that is, not internally divided—and who mourn or mind about moral wrongdoing. The vices opposed to the gift of understanding are dullness of sense and blindness of mind, and the vice opposed to *scientia* is culpable ignorance. All these opposed vices are said to stem from the lesser or carnal capital vices. The idea here seems to be that the carnal vices result in culpable ignorance and a certain mental dullness, and these in their turn get in the way of understanding and *scientia*.[74]

The tie that Aquinas sees between wrong ethical choices and consequent misprogramming of the intellect is brought out even more strongly in his discussion of wisdom. Charity, the theological virtue with which wisdom is linked, is love of God. Since on Aquinas's account God is identical with goodness, charity is also a love of goodness,[75] and for my purposes here I understand it in this way. On Aquinas's view, charity or a love of goodness gives rise to wisdom, and wisdom and charity together eventuate in the fruits of peace and joy.[76] The beatitude associated with wisdom is "Blessed are the peacemakers. . . ."[77] The vice opposed to wisdom is, predictably enough, folly; and folly, on his view, has its source in the deadly sin of *luxuria*, taken either narrowly or broadly as the absence of self-discipline with regard to worldly desires.[78] (The nature of these connections and associations will emerge in the next sections.)

Considered as an intellectual virtue, wisdom is an excellence only of the speculative intellect. It is a sort of super*scientia*; it grasps the highest cause or causes of everything.[79] Considered as a gift of the Holy Spirit, however, and on Aquinas's view of the highest cause as God, wisdom enables a person not only to know the highest cause of everything but also to make decisive judgments about the way in which other things, such as human actions, are related to that highest cause. Since God is

[73] *ST* IIaIIae.8 and 9.

[74] *ST* IIaIIae.15.

[75] See, e.g., *QDV*, 14.8 ad10. I am grateful to Norman Kretzmann for calling this passage to my attention.

[76] *ST* IIaIIae.28.4 and 29.4.

[77] *ST* IIaIIae.45.6.

[78] *ST* IIaIIae.46.3. See also note 71 above.

[79] *ST* IIaIIae.45.1 and IaIIae.57.2.

perfect goodness, judging human acts in relation to the highest cause is a matter of distinguishing good or right actions from bad or wrong actions. For this reason, wisdom as a gift is a disposition informing both the speculative and the practical intellect.[80]

Understood in this way, wisdom is incompatible with any mortal sin, Aquinas says.[81] A person who is guilty of pride, envy, wrath, sloth, avarice, gluttony, or lust—or of the other mortal sins that flow from these—will undermine or destroy wisdom in herself. (We will see how to make sense of this view of Aquinas's as we go along.)

Perhaps the first thing to strike our notice here is how far we have come from wisdom in what Aquinas takes to be the Aristotelian sense of the mastery of metaphysics (or metaphysics and Aristotelian natural theology). The mastery of metaphysics, we naturally suppose, could be had by anyone in any moral or emotional state. It could be had by Hitler, for example, and on a day when he had neither peace nor joy, to say nothing of peacemaking and a passion for goodness. But Aquinas links an excellence of the intellect with certain actions and dispositions in the will and also with certain states of emotion. Wisdom is not alone among the intellectual virtues or gifts in being treated in this way, as the preceding remarks on faith show. Understanding and *scientia* are dealt with in the same way. The carnal vices lead to the mental states opposite to understanding and *scientia*, so that the absence of the carnal vices is presumably a prerequisite to either understanding or *scientia*. Furthermore, the first beatitude associated with faith, "Blessed are the pure in heart," indicates that a moral state is a concomitant of the intellectual condition of understanding and *scientia*. The second associated beatitude, "Blessed are they who mourn," apparently refers to a state which includes certain emotions, so that the intellectual dispositions of understanding and *scientia* on Aquinas's account are also linked to the passions.

---

[80] *ST* IIaIIae.45.3. It is therefore distinct from prudence, which is a virtue of the practical intellect alone. Aquinas holds that wisdom directs human actions, as does prudence, but wisdom directs them in light of its understanding of God and true goodness, which is God's. And so he says, "Prudence is wisdom in human affairs, but not wisdom unconditionally, because it is not about the unconditionally highest cause, for it is about human good, but human beings are not the best of the things there are" (*ST* IIaIIae.47.2 ad1).

[81] In *ST* IIaIIae.45.4 reply, Aquinas says that although wisdom which is an intellectual virtue can be in a person guilty of mortal sin, wisdom which is a gift cannot. Wisdom in this sense presupposes charity, and charity cannot occur together with mortal sin. (It is because charity can occur together with venial sin that venial sin does not preclude wisdom.) In that same question (a. 6 ad3) Aquinas says that because wisdom not only contemplates divine things but also regulates human acts, it requires distancing oneself from evil, which is incompatible with wisdom. That is why fear of God is the beginning of wisdom, because fear initiates the distancing from evils.

On Aquinas's account of wisdom, then, a person's moral wrongdoing will produce deficiencies in both her speculative and her practical intellect; it will make her less capable of understanding theology and ethics, and it will also undermine her practical intellect, leaving her prone not only to wrong moral judgments but also to self-deception. She will think her moral standards are appropriate and her moral judgments are correct when they are not. In other words, morally wrong choices on the part of the will misprogram both the speculative and the practical intellect, resulting in skewed views of God and goodness, erring conscience, self-deception, and wrong moral judgments.

If this process gets bad enough, it eventuates in the vice opposed to wisdom, namely, folly. And I think we will understand Aquinas's idea here best if we turn now to what he has to say about folly.

Wisdom and Folly

By way of a general characterization, Aquinas says that folly implies a certain apathy of heart and dullness of mind.[82] More interesting, I think, are the various descriptions he gives of the fool. He presents three, all taken from Isidore of Seville: a fool is one who through dullness remains unmoved; a fool is one who is unconcerned when he is injured; and a fool is one whom shame does not incite to sorrow.[83] What do these claims about the fool mean, and what do they have to do with the way in which wisdom is supposed to be undermined by moral wrongdoing?

I think it is most helpful here to consider a particular case. Think about the film story of Ike and Tina Turner, *What's Love Got to Do with It*? (I am not really interested in Ike and Tina's history here, so I am just going to assume that the film tells the truth in every detail. Partisans of Ike Turner may take what is said as a fictional rather than a historical example.) In the film, Tina—or Anna Mae, her real name—is a terrific person and a talented musician, a beautiful woman and a highly popular performer, whereas Ike has a limited talent and is a rotten person besides. He is a drinker and a drug addict, not only an unfaithful husband to Anna Mae but also a womanizer, and worst of all a brute who from time to time beats his wife unmercifully.

After the film came out, various media people contacted Ike, who had just been released from prison where he had served time on drug charges. Was the movie portrayal of him accurate? the reporters wanted to know. Was he really such a womanizer? Well, he said, he did sleep

---

[82] *ST* IIaIIae.46.1.
[83] Ibid.

around a lot when he was married to Anna Mae, but none of those other women really meant anything to him. Did he really beat Anna Mae in that way? Yes, he said, he did, but it was no big deal; he beat her only when she made him really mad. And so the interviews went. Ike Turner lost his one shot at glory, through no fault but his own lost a talented, beautiful, internationally acclaimed woman who was devoted to him, and his utterly shameful actions were portrayed in revolting detail for audiences throughout the country. But his reaction seemed to come only to this: "Sure, I did the things the movie portrays me as doing, but so what?" In fact, his agent said that Ike was contemplating a movie telling his side of the story. In his movie, no doubt, he would beat his wife bloody, but audiences would get to see that she was making him mad when he did it.

One's first reaction to the film is likely to be moral revulsion. Ike's behavior toward Anna Mae is outrageous; he is verbally, emotionally, and physically abusive. But more interesting from our point of view here is Ike's reaction to the release of the film, which he acknowledges to be basically accurate as regards his actions, if not his motivation. His reputation in the country fell precipitously; the movie did him incalculable damage in a host of respects, from financial and professional to personal and emotional. Now shame is a matter of a person's recognition that others around him hold a morally low opinion of him, when that low opinion is correct.[84] A shamed person, in other words, is someone who ought to have low self-esteem and who recognizes that other people see him in this way. (This is a sense of 'shame' in which a person can be *shamed* without *feeling shamed*.) So we might say of Ike Turner that the release of the movie both shamed and injured him. But what is frustrating and obnoxious about his response to it is that he doesn't seem to

---

[84] Perhaps the paradigm cases of shame are those in which a person shares with a selected set of the public around him a correct morally low opinion of himself. In that case, he both is shamed and also feels ashamed. But although it seems necessary for shame that the low opinion be correct, it is not necessary that the shamed person should understand the low opinion to be correct. Ike Turner is shamed, even if he cannot recognize that the low opinion people have of him is right. Some people might suppose that the requirement that the low opinion be correct is similarly unnecessary, but this view does not seem right. Socrates was not shamed at his trial—even though lots of people there apparently held a morally low opinion of him—just because their low opinion was incorrect. In cases where a person shares with others a low opinion of himself which he and they erroneously suppose to be correct, it seems to me better to describe such a person as humiliated rather than as shamed. It is a consequence of this way of thinking about shame that a person can be mistaken in thinking that he is shamed. Finally, if we suppose that there are cases in which a person has a correct low opinion of himself and there is no one else (not even God) who shares it with him, it seems to me better to speak of low self-esteem—or maybe humility—rather than shame.

care. Ike thus fits Aquinas's (and Isidore's) definition of a fool. Shame has not incited him to any sorrow over what he has done or become (it has not made him *feel* shamed), and he has not taken deeply to heart the injury the movie has done him.

Ike Turner's condition here is not unrepresentative of what we find when we look at people habituated to major moral evil and then brought face to face with outrage in public reaction. Consider white South Africans supporting apartheid, or Eichmann at his trial in Jerusalem. Like Ike Turner, they seem to fit Aquinas's definition of a fool: the shame their actions elicit evokes in them no sorrow for those actions, and the injury done them by their public shaming does not produce in them any deep moral concern. The camp doctor at Auschwitz, Johann Paul Kremer, personally murdered many people in dreadful scientific experiments. In his diaries, published after the war, he details both his murders and his opinion of himself as an upstanding citizen, a devoted family man, a morally good person. He thinks of himself as a person of great moral sensitivity even as he notes the pain and suffering he causes the Jews in the camp.[85] Nothing about his public disgrace at his two trials and convictions after the war seems to have changed his mind.[86] In Aquinas's sense, he is a paradigm of a fool.

How does a person get to be in such a morally frightening condition? Nazis are made; they are not born. One of the most insightful studies of the making of a Nazi is Gita Sereny's biography of Franz Stangl, the commandant of Treblinka.[87] She shows how each serious instance of moral wrongdoing on Stangl's part made it easier for him to take the next and further step into moral evil; the move into moral monstrosity is slow and gradual. When he was first assigned to head a euthanasia clinic, Stangl was morally repelled by what the Nazis were doing. But he was afraid that he would lose his job or even his position among the Nazis if he made any trouble, and so he talked himself into thinking first that the euthanasia was a necessary evil and then that it was in fact

---

[85] Johann Paul Kremer's diary is available in English translation in Jadwiga Bezwinska and Danuta Czech, *KL Auschwitz Seen by the SS. Hoess, Broad, Kremer* (New York: Howard Fertig, 1984).

[86] Kremer, previously an anatomy professor at the University of Münster, came to Auschwitz in August 1942. After the war he was tried in Poland and sentenced to death, but because of his age the sentence was commuted to ten years. On his release he returned to Münster, where he created a stir by trying to portray himself as a martyr to the German cause. The upshot was that he was tried in Münster and convicted a second time (Bezwinska and Czech, *KL Auschwitz*, p. 8).

[87] Gita Sereny, *Into That Darkness: An Examination of Conscience* (New York: Vintage Books, 1983). Also helpful in this connection is Robert Jay Lifton, *The Nazi Doctors* (New York: Basic Books, 1986), esp. pp. 193–213 on socialization.

a favor to those killed.[88] Having dulled himself in this way, he found it easier to take the next step into evil, where again he had to choose between, on the one hand, losing his promotion or his position or even his security in the system and, on the other, losing further moral ground. In each case he protected his position and security at the cost of morality. Nothing in his trial or his consequent disgrace and prison term could shake his conviction that in all his actions he was a morally good person, even a humane and morally sensitive person, who did what he did because he was following orders in a morally appropriate spirit of civic and military obedience. Nothing about the revulsion in which he was held by the whole world gave him any serious pause.

Aquinas's account of wisdom and folly give theoretical background for the example in Gita Sereny's study, and his theory of the relation between intellect and will provides an explanation of how a person can become a moral monster such as Stangl was.[89]

Like Ike Turner, though clearly in a radically more serious way, Stangl is a fool, a person whom shame doesn't incite to sorrow and who is unconcerned when he is injured. He has a severely impaired speculative intellect, unable to apprehend correctly the highest causes of things, including the nature of moral goodness; and in consequence his practical intellect is also grossly deficient in its ability to make particular moral judgments. The result is that he is self-deceived and morally monstrous. What has brought him to this condition is a disinclination, made habitual from long practice, to discipline his desires for worldly well-being when they conflict with morality.[90]

The reason these morally wrong choices can have the effect of misprogramming the intellect in both its speculative and practical parts is explained by the will's ability to exercise control over intellect—in this case, indirect but immediate control.

Stangl wants to accept his appointment at the euthanasia institute, or, at any rate, he prefers doing so to the other alternatives open to him; but he is also horrified by the nature of the assignment. In the beginning, he is double-minded, wavering between thinking he must accept the assigment and thinking that he will not be able to stick it out. "After the first two or three days," Stangl tells Sereny, ". . . I didn't think I could stand it. . . . I . . . couldn't eat—you know, one just couldn't."[91] In the

---

[88] Sereny, *Into That Darkness*, p. 48.

[89] I am not trying to argue that the only way to interpret Stangl's case is in terms of Aquinas's theory of wisdom and folly. My point is only that Stangl's story is a good illustration for Aquinas's theory and that Aquinas's theory provides a helpful elucidation of Stangl's story.

[90] That is, *luxuria*, in the broad medieval sense described in n. 71.

[91] Sereny, *Into That Darkness*, p. 55.

end, however, he does—all things considered—want to accept and remain in his assignment. As Aquinas holds, though, a wrong action can
be willed by the will only in case the intellect has succeeded in finding
some description under which it seems good.[92] And so in a case in
which the will wants what in fact is not good, as a result of the command of the will the intellect directs its attention to just the evidence
which supports the goodness of what the will wants and turns away
from any countervailing evidence.

This seems a fairly good description of what happened in Stangl's case.
Sereny asks him whether he succeeded in convincing himself that what
he was doing was right. Yes, he explains, he did so in virtue of reflect-
ing on an encounter he had with a Catholic nun who was in favor of euthanasia for disabled children. Speaking of a severely disabled sixteen-
year-old child who was not taken for euthanasia, the nun said, "Just look
at him. . . . No good to himself or anyone else. How could they refuse to
deliver him from this miserable life?" Commenting on this speech by
the nun, tacitly approved by an accompanying priest, Stangl says, "Here
was a Catholic nun, a Mother Superior, and a priest. And they thought
it was right. Who was I then, to doubt what was being done?"[93] Here
Stangl's will has directed intellect to reflect on this one encounter and
on the fact that the person who gave moral approval to euthanasia was
a person whose office generally carries moral authority, namely, a nun.
On the other hand, there was abundant evidence available to Stangl to
indicate that many Protestant and Catholic clergy were strongly opposed
to euthanasia.[94] He finds euthanasia morally acceptable on the basis of
one nun's approval of it only because his will is also directing the attention of his intellect away from the countervailing evidence.[95]

[92] See, e.g., *ST* IaIIae.19.3, where Aquinas explains that the will's object is always proposed to it by intellect, so that understood good (as distinct from what is really good) is
what the will wants. See also *ST* IaIIae.15.3, where Aquinas explains the progression toward action in this way: intellect's apprehension of the end, the desire of the end, counsel
about the means, and the desire of the means; and *ST* IaIIae.74.7 ad1, ad2, and ad3, where
Aquinas says that consent to sin is an act of the appetitive power in consequence of an act
of reason, so that reason's approving as good something which is in fact not good precedes sinful acts. Finally, in *ST* IaIIae.75.2 he explains that the cause of sin is some apparent good, and therefore both intellect and will play a role in sinning.

[93] Sereny, *Into That Darkness*, p. 58.

[94] Sereny documents the part religious authorities played in both condoning and condemning the Nazi euthanasia program, and the degree to which Germans, Stangl included, were aware of church attitudes toward euthanasia. E.g., she quotes Frau Stangl's
claim that she discussed with her husband a widely publicized sermon by the Bishop of
Münster condemning euthanasia (ibid., p. 59).

[95] It helps, of course, in this process that the Nazis were so careful with language. The
higher-up who assigned Stangl to the euthanasia institute spoke to him in abstract and
high-flown language, and Stangl records his distress at having to deal with a superior

Because he has succeeded in approving euthanasia as morally acceptable or even morally good, he has to this extent misprogrammed his intellect, and the next step is easier to take. The misprogrammed intellect allows the will to want as good what it might have rejected before the misprogramming of the intellect, and the warped will, in turn, misprograms the intellect further. So the will and the intellect are in a dynamic interaction that allows each of them to corrupt the other, one step at a time. Aquinas's theory, then, makes it easier to understand the well-documented fact that the descent into moral monstrosity tends to be gradual rather than precipitous, and it also shows, at least in part, how it is that conscience becomes dulled. Stangl went from the euthanasia institute at Hartheim to one at Bernburg, where those "eligible" for euthanasia included perfectly healthy political prisoners. From there he went to Lublin, where he was gradually inducted into the secrets of the death camps until he accepted the assignment of supervising Sobibor. When Sereny asked him how he felt when he first came in contact with the gassing of Jews at Sobibor, he answered, "At Sobibor one could avoid seeing almost all of it."[96] In Treblinka, where he couldn't help but see it, he called what he saw "Dante['s Inferno] come to life," yet he accepted his posting as commandant to that death camp.[97] In response to Sereny's question how he could have stilled his conscience into accepting, he said, "the only way I could live was by compartmentalizing my thinking"[98]—by which he meant willing *not* to think about a great deal.

With every wrong action, then, there is a misprogramming of the intellect, and the misprogrammed intellect twists the will, which in turn misprograms the intellect further. These misprogrammings can pro-

---

who did not observe such linguistic conventions: "My heart sank when I met him. . . . [He had] this awful verbal crudity; when he spoke about the necessity for this euthanasia operation, he wasn't speaking in humane or scientific terms, the way Dr. Werner had described it to me. . . . He spoke of 'doing away with useless mouths' and said that 'sentimental slobber' about such people made him 'puke'" (ibid., p. 54). Clearly, the Nazi gift for Orwellian misdescription made it easier to misprogram the intellect in the way Aquinas thinks necessary for moral evil. In this connection, see also Lifton, *The Nazi Doctors*, pp. 202–3, 445–46.

[96] Sereny, *Into That Darkness*, p. 114.

[97] Ibid., p. 157.

[98] Ibid., p. 164. Stangl sometimes suggests that cooperating with the Nazis was the only way he could live in a different sense; failure to cooperate, in his view, would have cost him not only his position but even his life. But here Stangl is unduly melodramatic; the historical record is full of people who declined Stangl's sort of cooperation and received virtually no punishment of any sort. Yet even if Stangl seriously believed that his life would have been forfeit if he hadn't agreed to participate in the torture and mass murder of Jewish men, women, and children, his decision to save his life at such cost itself shows a monumental failure of speculative and practical intellect.

gress until they reach the point where a man like Stangl, who at first could hardly bear the painless death of the severely disabled, subsequently was able to oversee with a quietened conscience tortures and killings that now sicken even those who read only pale descriptions of them.[99]

Furthermore, on Aquinas's account of the interaction of intellect and will, breaking into the cycle of the spiraling corruption will clearly be difficult. The outrage of virtually the whole civilized world was not enough to turn Stangl from his conviction that he had never been responsible for any serious evil, that he had always done what he ought to have done in the circumstances. The shame of his internationally publicized trial and the deluge of shaming publications documenting his part in mass murder inspired him to no repentance or moral sorrow. Why this should be so is easier to see on Aquinas's theory of intellect and will. A severely misprogrammed intellect with correspondingly twisted will and desires will be hard to fix, because all the previous misprogramming will have to be undone, one piece after another.[100] But this will be an undoing for which the agent has no will or desire, or which his will is even set against and which his intellect does not find good. Consequently, the corrupting interaction of will and intellect will continue. In his self-deceived state, Stangl does not see his actions or himself as the rest of the world does, and he does not want to do so either. That is why shame produces no sorrow in him. His moral evil has made him a fool.

So wisdom is undermined by moral wrongdoing because morally wrong choices corrupt not only the will but also the intellect. Because of the way in which the will and the intellect interact, it is not possible, on Aquinas's account, for a person to have the intellectual virtue of wisdom without a corresponding moral excellence in the will.

Wisdom and Peace

Although there is a great deal more to be said about Aquinas's account of wisdom, I want to conclude by considering just briefly the beatitude that he associates with wisdom. The wise person is a peacemaker, on Aquinas's view, and that in two respects. First, he is able to make peace

---

[99] I do not mean to imply that this interaction between intellect and will is all there is to say about the descent into evil. For excellent discussion of associated factors, see Lifton, *The Nazi Doctors*, pp. 418–65.

[100] In *Pilgrim's Progress* Bunyan has a vivid image for this process: the soul that strays from the right path has to walk every step of the way back; there are no shortcuts.

for others by helping them sort out the rights and wrongs of their differences. Second, he is able to make peace within himself.[101]

It is not so hard to see why Aquinas would think that wisdom, understood in this way, enables the wise person to be a peacemaker for others. But it is somewhat more difficult to see what it is about wisdom that produces peace in the person who has it. We can gain some insight into Aquinas's point here if we think of the will as a hierarchically ordered faculty. Harry Frankfurt's work on the will has made clear that persons can have not only first-order desires and volitions (desires or volitions to do something) but also second-order desires and volitions (desires or volitions to have a will of a certain sort).[102] This hierarchy in the will makes possible a variety of internal conflicts. There can be conflicting first-order desires, as when a person both desires to smoke and desires not to smoke. And there can be conflicts between first- and second-order desires, as when a person has a second-order desire for a will that wills not to smoke and a first-order desire to smoke. And, finally, there can be conflicts on the second-order level, as when a person is conflicted about whether or not to undertake a reform of his smoking habits. Frankfurt's idea is that for a person to be free, there needs to be harmony within the will. A free person's second-order desires and volitions cannot be in disagreement with his first-order volitions.

It is clear that Frankfurtian harmony in the will is needed for peace as well as freedom. An agent whose will is divided against itself is an agent who is at war with himself. Whatever such an agent does or gets for himself, he will not have what he wants.

Now Frankfurt thinks that there can be harmony in the will, whatever the will wills, as long as the will is unified in that wanting. That is, if Stangl wanted to have the will of a mass murderer and if his first-order volitions were in harmony with that second-order volition and he had no discordant willings, then to that extent—on Frankfurt's theory—Stangl would be free and (we might add) at peace with himself. But Aquinas would not agree with Frankfurt on this score. On Aquinas's view, moral evil will always result in internal divisions in the self, in disharmony in the will and corresponding double-mindedness in the intellect, and so moral evil is incompatible with inner peace.[103] For single-mindedness and harmony in the will, on Aquinas's account, we need moral goodness and the wisdom that moral goodness accompanies.

---

[101] *ST* IIaIIae.45.6.

[102] Harry Frankfurt has written much that is pertinent; his classic work on this subject is "Freedom of the Will and the Concept of a Person," *Journal of Philosophy* 68 (1971): 5–20.

[103] It is not hard to understand why this claim is true with respect to subjective moral evil, but Aquinas also means it to hold for objective moral evil, for the reasons given below.

For Aquinas, no one ever gets so evil that there is nothing in his intellect or will which holds back from the evil he is immersed in, which disapproves of that evil or desires something better. Aquinas's account is thus a much more optimistic view of human beings than Frankfurt's is. Frankfurt's view allows a person to be utterly unified in evil. For Aquinas, a morally evil person will always be divided within himself; somewhere, however deeply buried in the psychic structure, there will be some part of the evildoer's intellect and will which dissents from the evil approved of by the rest of the intellect and desired by the rest of the will. And so, Aquinas thinks, in distinction from Frankfurt, that to the extent to which the will wills moral wrongdoing, to that extent the agent's peace is undermined. That is why Aquinas connects peace and wisdom. A moral monster such as Franz Stangl, on Aquinas's view, is not only a fool but also a restless person.

Conclusion

To comprehend Aquinas's theory of wisdom, we must understand it not only in the web of his moral categories—the deadly sins and principal virtues, the beatitudes and the fruits of the Holy Spirit—but also in the context of his views of intellect and will. We have to be clear about Aquinas's rich account of the nature of the will and of the way in which the will interacts with the intellect. I have tried to show that, contrary to much contemporary opinion, Aquinas is right in supposing that the will can influence belief, both directly and also indirectly. Furthermore, on Aquinas's theory of the intellect and will, the relations between them are not simple but dynamic and full of interactive feedback; each can progressively shape and influence the other. As a result, it is possible for there to be a series of morally wrong acts which culminates in a bland and self-satisfied moral monstrosity, corrupting the intellect as well as the will.

Wisdom is the virtue opposed to this sort of vice, on Aquinas's account. Understood in this way, wisdom turns out to be a mixed moral and intellectual excellence; and it is noteworthy that on Aquinas's view all true excellence of intellect—wisdom, understanding, and *scientia*—is possible only in connection with moral excellence as well. Wisdom, in particular, is undermined by moral evil, and a person utterly devoid of wisdom is a fool. The conscience of a fool is dulled, his standards are wrong, and he is hugely self-deceived about his own actions and character. No one is born a fool; a person becomes a fool gradually, as a result of a series of wrongdoings in which his will and intellect progressively misprogram each other, as Aquinas's account of intellect and will explains. Aquinas's conception of wisdom thus gives us some understanding of the perplexing phenomenon Hannah Arendt called "the banality of evil," signaled, for example, by the lack of anguish or remorse or even insight on the part of an Eichmann or a Stangl.[104] For Aquinas, the evil a person does can have the fearful consequence of making him morally stupid.

Wisdom, on the other hand, carries powerful benefits with it, among the chief of which is inner peace. Because Aquinas has an essentially optimistic attitude toward human beings and human nature, he supposes that moral evil will always fragment a person: that no person, however morally monstrous, can ever be wholly unified in willing and approving of what is objectively wrong. That is why there is no peace for the wicked; peace is the natural reward for the wise.

In explaining just this much of Aquinas's account of wisdom, I have left a great deal to one side. I have hardly discussed the connection between wisdom and charity, and I have said only a little about the fruits and beatitude that Aquinas associates with wisdom. Space does not permit a full consideration of the whole of Aquinas's conception of wisdom, but this is, I think, enough to show that it constitutes an impressive and useful theory.[105]

---

[104] For an excellent study of Arendt's views, see Richard Bernstein, *Hannah Arendt and the Jewish Question* (Cambridge: MIT Press, 1996).

[105] I am grateful to William Alston, Scott MacDonald, Peter van Inwagen, and Linda Zagzebski as well as audiences at Syracuse University, Bar-Ilan University in Tel-Aviv, and the University of LaVerne Conference of the Society of Christian Philosophers for helpful comments on earlier versions of this paper. I am indebted to Norman Kretzmann for many useful questions and suggestions.

GARETH B. MATTHEWS

ð▲

Saint Thomas and the Principle of Double Effect

Although the Natural Law tradition in ethics is not strongly represented in very many philosophy departments in the United States, it remains influential in this country in the practice of medical ethics. No doubt one reason for its influence is institutional. Natural Law ethics has been embraced by the Roman Catholic Church, and many hospitals in this country are Catholic hospitals.

Yet it would be a mistake to attribute the influence of Natural Law theory in medical ethics solely to the institutional role of the Catholic Church. Consider the Principle of Double Effect. This principle is clearly identified with the Natural Law tradition in ethics. Yet many medical practitioners who have no commitment to Roman Catholicism and have had no formal training in Natural Law ethics nevertheless find at least one form of the principle immediately attractive.

Still, not everyone finds the Principle of Double Effect plausible. Although it does strike some medical decision-makers with the force of revelation, it seems to others little more than sophistry. Precisely this disparity makes it an especially important principle to subject to careful examination and reflection.

The Principle of Double Effect is also intriguing in another way. To some people it seems clearly Thomistic, even if they are unable to say why this is so, let alone where in Saint Thomas it is to be found. The provenance of the principle, including its Thomistic credentials, is a matter of both scholarly and philosophical debate.

In section 1 of this essay I present and discuss one recent formulation of the Principle of Double Effect and say something about how it is applied to two questions in medical ethics. In section 2, I discuss the

self-defense passage in Saint Thomas which is often taken to be the
Thomistic source of the principle. Next, in section 3, I consider a second
formulation of the principle, one taken directly from the self-defense
passage in Aquinas. Section 4 shows how one scholar has tried to derive something very close to the first formulation from the self-defense
passage, and section 5 offers my own interpretation of the self-defense
passage in Aquinas. Finally, in section 6 I take up yet another principle
that has been discussed recently as "the Principle of Double Effect" and
say a little about how it differs both from the first formulation considered here and from the best interpretation I can offer of the self-defense
passage in Saint Thomas.

1

Here is a formulation of the Principle of Double Effect from a current
textbook in medical ethics:

> [Formulation A]
> A particular kind of moral conflict arises when the performance of an ac-
> tion will produce both good and bad effects. . . . The [Principle of Double
> Effect] holds that such an action should be performed only if the intention
> is to bring about the good effect and the bad effect will be an unintended or
> indirect consequence. More specifically, four conditions must be satisfied:
> 1. The action itself must be morally indifferent or morally good.
> 2. The bad effect must not be the means by which the good effect is
>   achieved.
> 3. The motive must be the achievement of the good effect only.
> 4. The good effect must be equivalent in importance to the bad effect.[1]

The editor of the text from which this formulation is taken applies the
Principle of Double Effect to the standard example: a pregnant woman
found to have a cancerous uterus. According to the Principle of Double
Effect, the woman may be operated on to remove her uterus if each of
the four conditions is satisfied.

Since the action of removing the uterine cancer is good, condition 1 is
satisfied. The bad effect, killing the fetus, is not, it seems, the means by
which the good effect, ridding the woman of cancer, is achieved; so condition 2 is satisfied. If the motive is simply to rid the woman of cancer
and not to rid her of her fetus, condition 3 is satisfied as well. And, finally,

---

[1] Ronald Munson, ed., *Intervention and Reflection: Basic Issues in Medical Ethics*, 4th ed.
(Belmont, Calif.: Wadsworth, 1992), p. 27.

the good effect, ridding the woman of cancer and so saving her life, is equal in importance to the bad effect, killing the fetus; so condition 4 is satisfied.

A standard case in which condition 2 is *not* satisfied would be one in which a pregnant woman has a weak heart and, although she might be able to carry the fetus to term, she could not do so without seriously damaging her heart. In that case, performing an abortion would perhaps have the good effect of prolonging the woman's life; but the means to that good effect would be killing the fetus, which according to the Natural Law position would certainly be a bad effect, since according to Natural Law it would be homicide.[2]

The relevance of the Principle of Double Effect to abortion has been much discussed. But perhaps the principle is even more important to recent controversy over euthanasia. Consider this passage from a Presidential Commission's report, *Decisions to Forgo Life-Sustaining Treatment* (1983):

> No death is more agonizing for the aware patient . . . than one from respiratory insufficiency. Untreated, the patient will struggle for air until exhausted, when carbon dioxide narcosis and progressive hypoxia finally bring death fairly quickly. With the consent of the family morphine may be given. . . . If the patient is already quite exhausted, the slowed respirations will induce hypercapnia [that is, abnormally high levels of carbon dioxide in the blood], which will perpetuate the sedation and the patient will die in the ensuing sleep.[3]

In an article in the *Journal of the American Medical Association*, Kenneth L. Vaux, who seems not to have any general commitment to Natural Law ethics, supports, at least in certain circumstances, the use of what he calls *"double-effect"* euthanasia."[4] In particular, Vaux mentions cases like that described by the Presidential Commission. He does not spell out exactly how, on his view, such a case would meet the necessary and sufficient conditions for double effect. But he seems to think of the bad effect of the morphine injection as hastening death and the good effect as relieving suffering. His idea may be that hastening death is not the

[2] According to the theory of human generation called "mediate animation" (see *ST* Ia.118.1–3 for Aquinas's statement of this view, and Joseph F. Donceel, S.J., "A Liberal Catholic's View," in *The Problem of Abortion*, 2d ed., ed. Joel Feinberg [Belmont, Calif.: Wadsworth, 1984], pp. 15–20, for a modern account), there is first a human being at about 90 days of gestation. Only after that point would there be homicide.

[3] Quoted in Munson, *Intervention and Reflection*, pp. 170–71.

[4] Reprinted in ibid., 170–72, from *Journal of the American Medical Association* 259 (April 8, 1988): 2140–41.

means by which suffering is relieved, though it is an expected consequence of the action of giving the patient the morphine injection. And this seems plausible. Of course, one might undertake to shorten a patient's life as a means of relieving suffering by simply shortening the *total time* of suffering. But in the kind of case under consideration, morphine could be administered for its normal analgesic effect; it would relieve suffering for whatever time the patient lived. The additional consequence that the patient's life is thereby shortened would not have to be thought of as a way of relieving suffering.

Would this case also satisfy condition 4? That is, would the good effect of relieving suffering be at least equivalent in importance to the shortening of the patient's life? Perhaps that would depend on how severe the suffering was and how much the life was shortened. But it is plausible to think that there are indeed cases in which this condition would also be satisfied.

2

Is the Principle of Double Effect to be found in Saint Thomas? Commentators seem to be agreed that no such principle is ever formulated explicitly by Aquinas. But some sort of double-effect principle is found in his discussion of self-defense (*ST* IIaIIae.64.7). Here is the *responsio* of that article:

> It must be said that nothing prevents there being two effects of a single act, of which only one is in accordance with the [agent's] intention [*in intentione*], whereas the other is really beyond [that] intention [*praeter intentionem*]. However, moral acts get their character [*speciem*] according to what is intended, but not from what is beyond that intention [*praeter intentionem*], since [what is beyond the intention] is *per accidens*, as is clear from what was said above [IIaIIae.43.3; IaIIae.1.3; 18.6; 72.1]. Therefore from the act of self-defense there can follow a double effect: one, [the effect of] saving one's own life; the other, however, the killing of the attacker. Since saving one's own life is what is intended, such an act is not, therefore, impermissible; for it is natural for anything to keep itself in existence as far as possible. However, it is possible for an act that proceeds from a good intention to become impermissible, if it is not proportioned to its [intended] end. Thus if one uses greater force than is necessary to defend one's own life, [the act] will be impermissible. If, however, one repels the force with true moderation, it will be a permissible defense; for according to law, it is permissible to repel force with a force under properly defensive control. Nor is it necessary for salvation that a person forgo a moderate defense to avoid killing someone

else, since one is under a greater obligation to protect one's own life than the life of another.

But because it is not permissible to kill a human being except by public authority in accordance with the common good, as is clear from what was said above [64.3], it is not permissible for a human being to intend to kill a human being in self-defense, except for one who has public authority and who, intending to kill a human being in self-defense, puts this down to the public good. So it is clearly, for example, in the case of a soldier fighting against the enemy, and in the case of a minister of justice fighting against robbers, although even these would sin if they were moved by a private passion.[5]

Does a case such as Saint Thomas has in mind here fit the four conditions of Formulation A?

Suppose I am attacked by a man with a knife. Seeing a large stone nearby, I pick it up, throw it at my attacker, and hit him in the head. Suppose my action has the unintended effect of killing my attacker, as well as, of course, the intended effect of saving me from his knife attack. According to Saint Thomas, my action would be licit, provided these conditions were met:

  a. It was my intention to defend myself against the attacker.
  b. It was not my intention to kill the attacker.
  c. Throwing this rock at my attacker was, in fact, proportionate to the end of defending myself against the attacker.

Would my action also satisfy the four conditions of Formulation A of the Principle of Double Effect?

A first problem is to identify what is to be considered in this case "the action itself." Here are some descriptions that might be thought to pick out the action itself (where Adam is my attacker):

  (i) throwing a large rock at Adam.
  (ii) throwing a large rock at my attacker.
  (iii) defending my life against a threat to it.

If the good effect of this action is supposed to be defending my life against a threat to it, we had better not describe the action as (iii), lest the good effect be identical with the action whose effect it is. So the action had better be (i) or (ii). As for (i), that action seems to be, in and of itself, bad, rather than "morally indifferent or morally good," as the first

---

[5] My translation.

condition of Formulation A requires. Either we need to understand something about the context in which the action is performed, or else, perhaps more straightforwardly, we should describe the action in such a way as to make clear that it is a response to an attack. Suppose, then, that we choose (ii) as the description of the action.

So identified, or described, the action does seem to be one that could be plausibly described as "morally good," certainly if one supposes, as Aquinas asserts in the passage quoted above, that "one is under a greater obligation to protect one's own life than the life of another." The third and fourth conditions also seem to be satisfied. Thus my motive, as I am imagining the case, was "the achievement of the good effect only." That is, I wanted to defend myself against this attack, but I was not trying to defend myself by actually killing my attacker. So condition 3 is satisfied. Moreover, the good effect, defending my life from an attack against it, is, we can suppose, "equivalent in importance to the bad effect," namely, killing the assailant. So condition 4 is satisfied.

What about the second condition? Was the bad effect (killing the attacker) the means by which the good effect (defending myself) was achieved? It seems the answer would have to be yes. We must conclude that the kind of case Saint Thomas wants to justify in this article cannot be justified by appeal to the Principle of Double Effect in Formulation A. Thus the Principle of Double Effect, understood according to Formulation A, is not what Saint Thomas is presenting in this article.

Someone may protest that we should not answer so quickly. We have been supposing that I actually killed my attacker, so as to make the case fit Saint Thomas's discussion. (After all, he does speak of "killing the attacker.") But, of course, I could have killed him unintentionally. Not having a great deal of practice at stopping attackers by hitting them with rocks, I might not have been able to judge accurately how much force would be needed to stun but not kill my assailant.

What this consideration shows is that there could have been a somewhat different incident, one in which I threw my rock at the attacker all right, but with somewhat less force. In that alternative incident I would have achieved my goal without killing the assailant. No doubt I would have damaged him, but I would not have killed him.

Yet the possibility of an alternative scenario of this sort does not show that, in the case as initially conceived, the bad effect is "not the means by which the good effect is achieved." What it shows is rather that my purpose could have been achieved without actually killing the assailant. But it does not show that the actual bad effect was not, in the event, the means by which the good effect was achieved, where, as in Saint Thomas's case, I do actually kill the attacker.

Moreover, even in a case in which the assailant was hit and knocked unconscious, but not killed, there would again be a bad effect—hitting him and knocking him unconscious—as well as the good effect of defending my life against an attack. And in this case, too, the bad effect would be the means by which the good effect was achieved.

It seems, therefore, that the kind of case Saint Thomas had in mind does not lend itself to moral justification along the lines of Formulation A of the Principle of Double Effect. In this respect, killing—or even just hurting—someone in self-defense is very different from giving morphine to a dying patient who is in great agony, or removing the cancerous uterus of a pregnant woman. To be sure, the good effect, relieving pain (or removing the woman's cancer and thus saving her life), may be bound up with the bad effect, shortening life (or killing the fetus), in such a way that we can be sure the first comes at the cost of the second. But it does not seem right to say that shortening the patient's life (or killing the fetus) is the means by which the good effect is achieved. Or, to concentrate on the euthanasia case, we can say that these are distinguishable aims in the sort of situation described by the Presidential Commission:

(I) shortening the life of the patient so as to limit the patient's suffering;

(II) relieving suffering through the use of morphine, with the understanding that one effect of this treatment will likely be to shorten the patient's life.

It is (II) that the commission condones, not (I). And it is (II), not (I), that seems likely to satisfy condition 2 of Formulation A of the Principle of Double Effect. Saint Thomas (in *ST* IIaIIae.64.7) shows no interest in drawing a distinction of this sort.

3

So far it looks as though the Principle of Double Effect is not to be found in Saint Thomas. More circumspectly, if the Principle of Double Effect is properly stated in Formulation A and the quoted passage on self-defense (*ST* IIaIIae.64.7) is the best candidate for a statement of that principle in Saint Thomas, then the principle is not to be found in him.

Some commentators begin at the other end and, taking the self-defense discussion in Saint Thomas to presuppose the Principle of Double Effect, conclude that Formulation A is an incorrect formulation of the principle. Perhaps the most prominent of these commentators is Germain Grisez, whose formulation is neatly summarized by Alan Donagan as follows: "It is lawful to perform a unitary intentional action which has two effects, one good and one bad, provided that the intention with which it is done is to bring about the good effect, and provided that the good effect is a proportionally serious reason for permitting the bad effect."[6] As Donagan goes on to explain, "Whether or not the good effect is a proportionately serious reason is determined according to the principle that evil is to be avoided or prevented wherever possible, except at the cost of an equal or worse evil."[7]

From Grisez, as interpreted by Donagan, we may formulate the Principle of Double Effect his way:

[Formulation B]
An action with both a bad effect and a good effect may be performed if
1. the intention with which the action is performed is to bring about the good effect and it is not to bring about the bad effect; and
2. producing the good effect is a proportionally serious reason for permitting the bad effect [since failure to perform the action would result in there being more net evil in the world].

Formulation B is, of course, radically different from Formulation A. B1 is a little like A3. And B2 is a little like A4. But nothing in B corresponds to A1 or A2.

That the two formulations yield radically different principles can be seen in the case of the pregnant woman for whom the continuation of the pregnancy is a threat to her life. Here is Donagan again:

> Grisez holds that his principle [i.e., Formulation B] justifies craniotomy. Provided that only so can the mother's life be saved, and that his intention is solely to save it, and not to kill the child, a surgeon may perform a craniotomy, because saving the mother's life is a proportionately serious reason for causing the child's death. However, there is a catch. "On the same principle," Grisez points out, "one would be equally justified in cutting away the mother to rescue the baby."[8]

Both operations—the craniotomy, as well as "cutting away the mother to rescue the baby"—would, of course, be ruled out by the Principle of Double Effect in Formulation A, since either killing the child (to save the

---

[6] Alan Donagan, *The Theory of Morality* (Chicago: University of Chicago Press, 1977), p. 161.
[7] Ibid.
[8] Ibid., p. 162.

mother) or killing the mother (to save the child) would be the means by which the good effect is achieved.

What motivates A2 is something that Donagan calls "the Pauline Principle," after Saint Paul's famous rhetorical question at Romans 3:8—"And why not do evil that good may come?" In Donagan's statement of it, the Pauline Principle says this: "It is impermissible to do evil that good may come of it."[9]

Clearly, Formulation B makes no appeal to the Pauline Principle. Moreover, there is no obvious reliance on the Pauline Principle in the Aquinas passage (*ST* IIaIIae.64.7). In that respect, Grisez is right. If Saint Thomas does appeal to the Principle of Double Effect in his justification of self-defense, then the Pauline Principle is no obvious part of his understanding of that principle.

I must add, though, that if Formulation B is to be accepted, then the Principle of Double Effect will not be very helpful in medical ethics—or elsewhere, for that matter. It tells us that (a) where a contemplated action can be expected to have both good and bad consequences, we must not intend the bad consequences but only the good; and furthermore, (b) we must not, by the actions we choose, increase the net evil in the world. No one with a serious ethical problem is likely to be much helped by those boring bits of advice.

4

It is not immediately obvious exactly what cases St. Thomas has in mind when he discusses self-defense. Is he thinking of cases in which

(a) one believes, or has good reason to think, that the means of self-defense one employs is very likely to kill the attacker?

Or is he thinking only of cases in which

(b) one believes, or has good reason to think, that the means of self-defense one employs is not likely to kill the attacker?

We could answer those questions if we knew whether *intendo* and *praeter intentionem* in this article are to be given technical meanings, or whether they are assumed to have ordinary senses in such a way that

---

[9] Ibid., p. 149.

the ordinary English meanings of 'intend' and 'beyond the agent's intention' would translate them quite satisfactorily.

The scholar who seems to have given this question the most careful examination is Joseph M. Boyle Jr.[10] In this section I am guided by his discussion.

Let us ask, first, whether Saint Thomas counts the *means* an agent chooses to achieve a certain end as something within the agent's intention (*in intentione*) or something beyond the agent's intention (*praeter intentionem*). Boyle discusses this question at some length. He concludes that according to Saint Thomas the agent "does not intend the means as such."[11] However, Boyle adds, "the means are intimately connected with the intended ends in such a way that one's chosen means cannot be *praeter intentionem*."[12] So, though not intended as such, the means, according to Boyle's reading, are still not beyond the intention.

What about the merely foreseen effect of one's action? Can a foreseen effect be outside one's intention (*praeter intentionem*)? Here Boyle notes that, following Aristotle, Saint Thomas distinguishes between an effect that is "always or for the most part" joined with an action of a certain kind and one that is only "in a few cases and rarely" joined with the action. Something always or for the most part conjoined with a certain sort of action presumably counts as a foreseen or expected consequence.

Boyle adduces one passage (*In Ph* 2.5, from the commentary on Aristotle's *Physics*) in which Saint Thomas seems to be counting foreseeable consequences as something within the agent's intention in such a way that they could not be *praeter intentionem*. "For what always or frequently is joined to an effect falls under the same intention," Saint Thomas writes in that passage. He goes on: "It is foolish to say that someone intends something and does not will that which is frequently or always joined to it."[13]

Yet in the end Boyle decides that, according to Saint Thomas, even what is always or frequently joined to an intended effect may be beyond the intention of the agent. One important text upon which Boyle bases his interpretation is this one from Saint Thomas's *De malo*:

> It should be said that sometimes an accidental effect is joined to it in few cases and rarely [*ut in paucioribus et raro*]; and then the agent need not intend in any way the accidental effect while he intends the effect *per se*. But sometimes an accident of this type is attached either always or for the most

---

[10] Joseph M. Boyle Jr., "*Praeter Intentionem* in Aquinas," *Thomist* 42 (1978): 649–65.
[11] Ibid., p. 657.
[12] Ibid.
[13] *In Ph* 2.8.8, using Boyle's translation in "*Praeter Intentionem*," p. 658.

part to the effect which is principally intended; and then the accident cannot be separated from the intention of the agent. If therefore, something evil is joined only infrequently to the good which is intended, it is possible to be excused from sin; for example if someone cutting down a tree in a forest where people rarely pass, kills a person by cutting down the tree. But if the evil is joined either always or for the most part to the good which is intended *per se*, one is not excused from sin although he does not *per se* intend this evil.[14]

Here Saint Thomas makes a threefold distinction. Boyle fits it to the twofold distinction of the self-defense passage (*ST* IIaIIae.64.7) in the following way:

In sum, we can distinguish what is *per se* intended and what is *per accidens* intended. And we can distinguish two kinds of accidental effects: Those which follow rarely and those which follow always or for the most part. The former are not intended in any way.[!] The latter, although they are not *per se* intended and thus [!] can be called *praeter intentionem*, cannot be separated from the agent's intention; he must . . . will them. . . . The death of the attacker is *praeter intentionem* even though it can be foreseen with certainty to follow; it is not *per se* intended. This is not to deny that in some sense it cannot be separated from the agent's intention, or that it is *per accidens* intended, or that it is in some sense willed by him.[15]

If all this is right, then Saint Thomas's view is that one may, in self-defense, repel an attacker in a way that one expects and foresees will kill the attacker, as long as (i) one does not intend *per se* to kill the attacker, and (ii) the means one uses in self-defense are proportional to the threat.

On this reading we may offer the following formulation of the principle that lies behind St. Thomas's comments:

[Formulation C]
An action with both a good effect and a bad effect may be performed if
1. the agent intends per se the good effect;
2. the agent does not intend per se the bad effect; and
3. the action is proportioned to its end.

Following a tradition that goes back to Cajetan, Boyle uses Saint Thomas's reply to Augustine (*ST* IIaIIae64.7 ad 1) to supply a fourth condition. Augustine had written, "I cannot bring myself to advise any

---

[14] *QDM* 1.3 ad15, Boyle's translation in ibid., p. 659.
[15] Ibid., p. 660.

people to kill others to prevent those others killing somebody except in the case of a soldier or public servant who is doing this not for himself but for others, within the terms of the authority duly given to him."[16] For reasons that elude me altogether, Boyle, following Cajetan, takes Aquinas's response to Augustine to rule out killing *as a means* to self-defense, but not killing "as a consequence of the act of self-defense—as "what follows from the necessity of the end" in Cajetan's language."[17]

If, indeed, Augustine does mean to say that the bad effect (killing the attacker) cannot be a means to the good effect (defending oneself), then we may add this condition to the three above:

4. the bad effect is not the means by which the good effect is achieved.

Now we have something reasonably close to the formulation with which we began, namely, Formulation A. C1 and C2 correspond roughly to A3 ("The motive must be for the good effect only"). C3 corresponds, again roughly, to A4 ("The good effect must be equivalent in importance to the bad effect"). And C4 corresponds to A1 and A2.

Is this a satisfactory reading of Saint Thomas (*ST* IIaIIae.64.7)? Well, it is certainly a useful one in that it connects Aquinas with an important modern formulation of the Principle of Double Effect. And it is defensible insofar as it relies on sophisticated interpretations of *intendo* and *praeter intentionem* from other writings of Saint Thomas. But as a reading of this passage it seems to me too clever by half.

For one thing, there is no distinction in this article between intending *per se* and intending *per accidens*. Saint Thomas does tell us here that what is *praeter intentionem* is *per accidens*, but he does not tell us that it is, or can be, intended *per accidens*. Moreover, Cajetan's distinction between the means chosen to bring about an end and "what follows from the necessity of the end" is not found in the article either. If Aquinas's response to Augustine can be interpreted in a plausible way that does not appeal to such a distinction, simplicity should favor such an interpretation.

Can the Aquinas passage be given a simpler and, at least for that reason, more plausible interpretation? I think so.

---

[16] Augustine *De libero arbitrio* 1.5.

[17] "St. Augustine, [Aquinas] says, regarded as sinful that case in which 'someone intends to kill a man in order to free himself from death' [*ST* IIaIIae.64.7 ad1]. So Aquinas admits that the killing of another may be within the intention (presumably as a means) but contrasts it with the kind of deadly self-defense which can be morally justified" (Boyle, "*Praeter Intentionem*," pp. 660–61).

5

Here is my précis of Saint Thomas's discussion of self-defense (*ST* IIaIIae.64.7):

T1. Some acts have both a good and a bad effect, only one of which is "aimed at."

T2. It is what is aimed at that gives a human act its moral or immoral character.[18]

T3. An act of self-defense can have two effects, namely, (a) saving the agent's own life and (b) killing the attacker.

T4. An act of self-defense may have a morally legitimate purpose, since it is natural to preserve one's life as far as possible.

T5. Even an act that aims at some good may be morally wrong, however, if it is not proportioned to its end; for example, using more force than is necessary to defend one's life is wrong.

T6. It is (prima facie) wrong to kill a human being except when one is acting in a public capacity for the common good (for example, as a soldier, or executioner); therefore, it is wrong to aim at killing a human being except when one is acting in a public capacity for the common good.

In my judgment the passage makes perfectly good sense if it is read to assert T1 through T6 and nothing more. I am myself inclined to read it that way. So read, it yields these two principles concerning homicide:

P1. It is impermissible to aim at killing another human being unless one is acting in a public capacity for the common good.

P2. It is permissible to kill another human being even though one is acting only in a private capacity if
(a) one's own life is threatened;
(b) one aims at one's own defense and not at killing the attacker; and
(c) one's response is proportional to the attack.

Do these two principles suggest the Principle of Double Effect in any of the formulations we have considered so far? They certainly do not suggest Formulation A, since they do not include anything like A1 ("The action itself must be morally indifferent or morally good") or anything like A2 ("The action itself must not be the means by which the good effect is achieved").

What about Formulation B? Does either P1 or P2 or the combination of the two suggest Formulation B? It seems not, since it is quite

---

[18] This claim is, presumably, to be understood as subject to qualification.

unclear how the exception for public persons—soldiers, police, and the like—is supposed to accord with the Principle of Double Effect in Formulation B.

My conclusion is that Saint Thomas does not present anything strongly suggestive of either Formulation A or Formulation B. Still, it can be viewed as a sort of seed bed for the Principle of Double Effect, even for Formulation A. That is, reflection on this passage, in the light of distinctions Saint Thomas makes elsewhere, could and apparently did lead Thomistic philosophers to Formulation C, which is very much like A.

6

I conclude by considering yet another conception of the Principle of Double Effect, something different from anything I have discussed so far. Warren Quinn offers these characterizations of the principle I have in mind:

> According to one of the common readings of this principle, the pursuit of a good tends to be less acceptable where a resulting harm is intended as a means than where it is merely foreseen.[19]

> The principle is sometimes put in terms of the difference between a harmful *result* that is "directly" intended and one that is "indirectly" (or "obliquely") intended. But it also might be put in terms of the difference beween a directly and an indirectly intended *act* of harming.[20]

Even more generally, Quinn tells us that the principle he is discussing "discriminates in favor of agency that involves only foreseeing, but not that kind of intending, of an objectionable outcome."[21]

As Quinn understands the Principle of Double Effect, either the principle itself, or else an important assumption that forms a central part of that principle, may be formulated this way:

[Formulation D]
If what the agent does in situation S1 and what an agent does in situation S2 have the same [as Quinn puts it] "consequential profile," that is, the

---

[19] Warren S. Quinn, "Actions, Intentions, and Consequences: The Doctrine of Double Effect," *Philosophy and Public Affairs* 18 (1989): 334–35.
[20] Ibid., p. 335.
[21] Ibid.

same distribution of good and bad consequences, but in S1 the agent actually intends to bring about one or more of the bad consequences whereas in S2 the agent merely foresees those bad consequences and does not intend to bring them about, what the agent does in S1 is morally worse than what the agent does in S2.

Quinn's own project is, first, to say how it can be that S1 and S2 are really different and, second, to explain why this difference might be thought to be morally significant.

How is Formulation D related to Formulation A? One's first reaction might be to think that although Formulation A is much richer than D, A does indeed presuppose D. But that reaction, I think, is wrong. In fact, D is in an important way much richer than A.

To see that this is so, suppose that, like Euthyphro's father in Plato's dialogue *Euthyphro*, I bind my murderous worker, throw him into a ditch, and go off to Boston to find out what should be done with him. Suppose further that he dies of neglect in the ditch. Make S1 the case in which I intend his death and S2 the case in which I merely foresee it. D tells me that S1 is worse than S2. But the Principle of Double Effect in Formulation A is silent on this issue.

What else, you may ask, could justify A3 ("The motive must be the achievement of the good effect only"), if it is not D? One plausible answer is that it is the already mentioned Pauline Principle ("It is impermissible to do evil that good may come of it") that motivates A3, just as it is the Pauline Principle that gives plausibility to A2 ("The bad effect must not be the means by which the good effect is achieved"). In fact, the Pauline Principle can plausibly be thought to lie behind all four conditions of Formulation A.

Thus, requiring that "the action itself must be morally indifferent or morally good" (A1) assures us that performing the action itself will not be, in itself, doing something evil. Insisting that "the bad effect must not be the means by which the good effect is achieved" (A2) assures us that the good effect is not contaminated by the bad effect. Adding that "the motive must be the achievement of the good effect only" (A3), guarantees that the agent will not be aiming to bring about evil. And the fourth condition, "The good effect must be equivalent in importance to the bad effect," certifies that fixing on the good, irrespective of foreseen evil, does not undermine the proportionality of one's motivational structure.

Formulation D is a dubious principle anyway—dubious first in its meaning, and then also dubious as to its acceptability. The Pauline Principle is, at least, clearer in its meaning. To a pure consequentialist it is also clearly unacceptable. But to the rest of us it may have some appeal.

As I mentioned at the outset, the Principle of Double Effect in Formulation A is certainly attractive to many health care professionals, including some who have little understanding of or appreciation for Thomistic ethics as such. Thinking of it as an expression of the Pauline Principle may help us to appreciate why this should be so.

Is Formulation D presupposed in Saint Thomas's discussion of self-defense, if not in Formulation A of the Principle of Double Effect? I think the answer must be no. Perhaps the easiest way to see that this is so is to recall that Saint Thomas, when he says that we should not aim at the death of another person, makes an exception for public officials acting for the common good. The police officer who is attacked may, in certain circumstances, aim at killing the assailant, and not just in self-defense. It need not even be the case, as D requires, that what the police officer does who intends a bad consequence (for example, the death of the assailant) is morally worse than what the officer does who merely foresees the bad consequence. In fact, the contrast between what is intended and what is merely foreseen is not raised in this context. Thus Formulation D does not underlie the Thomist discussion of self-defense.

I conclude that modern discussions of the Principle of Double Effect, whether in Formulation A, or in Formulation D, do not have a direct basis in Aquinas (assuming, as I have throughout, that the best candidate for such a direct basis would be the discussion of self-defense in *ST* IIaIIae.64.7). There is, however, an indirect way to get from what Saint Thomas says about self-defense to Formulation A, as I tried to bring out in section 4. Perhaps Formulation A evolved historically in just this way. If so, modern medical ethicists are right to consider the principle at least broadly Thomistic, even if it is not a principle Saint Thomas himself ever formulated, or even clearly presupposed. Finally, the principle can be thought to derive its force from the Pauline Principle that we should not do evil that good may come of it.[22]

---

[22] Pope John Paul II testifies to the continued appeal of the Pauline Principle when, in his encyclical *Veritatis Splendor* (1993), he insists forcefully that "it is never lawful, even for the gravest reasons, to do evil that good may come of it" (*Boston Globe*, October 5, 1993, p. 6).

M A R K   D.   J O R D A N

ﾞ▲

Ideals of Scientia moralis *and the*
Invention of the Summa theologiae

Is there a moral philosophy in Thomas Aquinas? The question is not merely verbal, though it requires attention to phrases in Thomas that might be candidates for translation as "moral philosophy." The question is rather about the character and limits of moral knowing as Thomas conceived them. A plausible answer to the question would govern local readings of Thomas's remarks on individual moral matters. It would also be a prerequisite for responsible dialogue between Thomas's moral teaching and contemporary conversation in what we call "ethics" and "moral theology."

The answer I hope to make plausible is that there is no moral philosophy in Thomas if by "moral philosophy" we mean a complete *scientia moralis* possessed by unaided reason. Thomas's construction of the *secunda pars* of the *Summa*, his most sustained labor of moral teaching, is a deliberate criticism of the philosophical ideals of *scientia moralis* known to him. He criticizes them on a number of grounds, not least because they are both more incomplete and more powerless than they profess. But it is equally true, and no less significant, that Thomas in the *secunda pars* criticizes inherited ideals of theological *scientia moralis*. The theological ideals suffer from a confusion of too many principles, distinctions, judgments, and cases—a confusion at once conceptual and pedagogical. A better form of moral science, one that lies between the unavowed incompleteness of moral philosophy and the confusion of inherited moral theology, is just the form of the *Summa theologiae*. Of course, the *Summa* remains incomplete and powerless in important respects. It is incomplete so far as a theologian's knowledge about human acts must be too general. It is powerless so far as the theologian's knowl-

79

edge begins and ends with the necessity for grace. But the achievement of the moral part of the *Summa* is to acknowledge clearly, by statement and by structure, its incompleteness and its powerlessness.

I undertake to make this answer plausible in four steps. The first considers both what is meant by an ideal of *scientia moralis* and how such ideals can best be discovered in texts. The second and third treat, respectively, of structural innovations in the *prima* and *secunda secundae* of Thomas's *Summa* itself as the depiction of an avowedly self-limiting ideal of theological *scientia moralis*. The fourth section, the conclusion, considers the whole *Summa* as an act of theological teaching.

Ideals of *Scientia moralis*

At several points in the *Summa* Thomas invokes an ideal of *scientia moralis* to settle some problem of textual order. He invokes it first in regard to the location of the discussion of divine providence.[1] The sequence of topics in *scientia moralis* serves as paradigm or analogue—the relation is not stated—for the sequence of questions about God. Later, more crucially, Thomas cites *scientia moralis* to postpone the discussion of appetitive powers into the second part.[2] Finally, and most obviously, Thomas recalls the order of *consideratio moralis* and the structure of *sermo moralis* to justify the largest structural features of the *prima* and *secunda secundae*.[3]

The ideal invoked in these passages is a pattern for the differentiation and disposition of teaching on moral matters. At its fullest, the pattern would presumably settle a number of issues: What individuates a moral science among other sciences? What ought a distinctively philosophical or theological moral science to treat and in what order? Medieval Latin

---

[1] *ST* Ia.22.prologue: "Nam et post morales virtutes, in scientia morali consideratur de prudentia, ad quam providentia pertinere videtur." Given the number of roughly equivalent editions of the *Summa*, and the standardization of internal textual divisions across them, I do not supply page citations to any particular one. For this essay I have used the edition by the Ottawa Institute of Medieval Studies (Ottawa: Studium Generalis O. Pr., 1941–1944), because it gives a wider sample of textual traditions than the "critical edition" of the Leonine *Opera omnia*.

[2] *ST* Ia.84.prologue: "Actus autem appetitivae partis ad considerationem moralis scientiae pertinent, et ideo in secunda parte huius operis de eis tractabitur, in qua considerandum erit de morali materia."

[3] *ST* IaIIae.6.prologue: "Moralis igitur consideratio quia humanorum actuum, primo quidem tradenda est in universali; second vero, in particulari." *ST* IIaIIae.prologue: "Necesse est considerare singula in speciali. Sermones enim morales universales sunt minus utiles, eo quod actiones in particularibus sunt."

writers were familiar with set lists of questions to be asked about *scientia moralis* or any other science.[4] Thomas uses one of these lists by way of introducing his literal exposition of the *Nicomachean Ethics*.[5] Unfortunately, many of the lists are mechanical, and even Thomas's list glosses over many issues about moral science. We cannot use them to determine what an ideal of moral science would contain. But Thomas's invocations of an ideal do show that it has decided the science's autonomy and disposition or order.[6] Both autonomy and disposition are pedagogical concerns. They arise within that tension between knowledge and its learners that Thomas confesses at the end of the *Summa*'s first prologue: "to pursue what pertains to holy teaching briefly and clearly, so far as the material permits" (Ia. prologue).

If the invocations of the ideal are too brief, and the prologues devoted to it elliptical or mechanical, where might one look to find depictions of it? The usual thing is to look in Thomas for explicit remarks about sciences or moral science. Explicit remarks can be useful, but they are not nearly so telling as the actual organization of the texts in which moral science is offered. Thomas remarks on *scientia moralis* rarely and then usually to repeat a commonplace. Outside his literal expositions of Aristotle, he has only a handful of things to say about moral knowledge. He takes *scientiae morales* generally as a name for the whole of practical knowledge. These sciences constitute one of the principal parts of philosophy.[7] Thomas does not seem to assign any singular, technical mean-

---

[4] For samples of schematic analyses of ethics contemporary with Thomas, see Robert Kilwardby, *De ortu scientiarum* 36 (*de quo est, finis, definitio*), ed. Albert G. Judy, Auctores Britannici medii aevi 4 (London: British Academy; Toronto: Pontifical Institute of Mediaeval Studies, 1976), p. 126, no. 357; Albert the Great, *Super Ethica: Commentum et quaestiones*, prologue (*materia, finis, utilitas*), ed. Wilhelm Kühle, *Opera omnia* 14/1 (Münster: Aschendorff, 1968–1972), p. 1, lines 1–55. (References to the latter and to similar editions are reduced to page and line numbers: "1.1–55.") Dominic Gundissalinus provides one of the most elaborate schemes for analyzing sciences but does not apply it to ethics, which he passes over in a few lines. See his *De divisione philosophiae*, "De partibus practice philosophie," ed. Ludwig Baur, Beiträge zur Geschichte der Philosophie des Mittelalters 4 (Münster: Aschendorff, 1903), p. 140.

[5] *In NE* 1.1 (*de quo est, modum tractandi, qualis debeat esse auditor*), Leonine 47/1, 5:110–15.

[6] Under "autonomy" I include various issues in the individuation of the science: the source and character of its starting points, its relations with other sciences, its position in the order of study, and so on. Under "disposition" I include such issues as what is taught, in what order, and by what means of rational persuasion.

[7] *In Sent* I.prologue.1.2 obj.1 (Mandonnet-Moos 1:9) and 3.23.2.4.2 obj.2 (3:735–36); *In BDT* 5.1 (Decker 169.14–18); *In Matt* 2.3 (Busa 6:139a). I have tried to clarify the relation of moral knowing to science and art in "The *Pars moralis* of the *Summa theologiae* as *Scientia* and as *Ars*," in *Scientia und ars im Hoch- und Spätmittelalter*, ed. Ingrid Craemer-Ruegenberg and Andreas Speer, Miscellanea Mediaevalia 22 (Berlin: Walter de Gruyter, 1994), 468–81.

ing to the phrase *scientia moralis* and so regularly alternates it with *philosophia moralis, doctrina moralis, consideratio moralis,* or simply *moralia.* *Scientia moralis* and its alternates name the study of voluntary human acts, of their sources and ends.[8] Any doctrine that denies voluntariness in human acting immediately abolishes moral science.[9] Because moral science deals with voluntary actions, with contingent particulars, it cannot have the certainty of mathematics or metaphysics.[10] Its lessons hold only for the most part.[11] Moral instruction aims at the practical end of judging what ought to be done in particular circumstances.[12] Hence its language is the language of the *exemplum,* the concrete and clarifying instance.[13] It is also the language of exhortation.[14] Still, the possession of moral science is not identical with the possession of virtue. Someone instructed in moral science can say what a particular virtue requires without having to possess that virtue.[15]

These are, as I said, commonplaces of the moral traditions that Thomas inherits. They are not therefore vacuous. They make clear, for example, that *scientia* is an analogous term for Thomas. Moral science cannot be science in the same way that metaphysics is. It cannot have the same demonstrative necessity, universality, certitude, or kind of end. To say this positively, Thomas's ideal of moral science requires that the science be self-limiting in ways that metaphysics is not. I mean by "self-limiting" to refer to ways in which a teaching or a text resists temptations to overstate its certainty or comprehensiveness. The ways of resisting range from explicit admonition through self-mockery or irony to implicit self-contradiction. Thomas prefers the quieter, structural means of self-limitation. So he multiplies terminologies, juxtaposes rival accounts, and places every utterance—his own included—within an ongoing dia-

---

[8] *In Sent* III.34.1.1 (Mandonnet-Moos 3:1114); *ST* Ia.1.4 sed contra; *QDVC* 2 ad15 (Marietti, no. 745b). See also the early division of moral matter into *delectabilia, difficilia,* and *communicabilia* at *In Sent* III.34.3.2 solutio 1 (Mandonnet-Moos 3:1165).

[9] *SCG* II.60 no. 5 (Marietti, no. 1374) and II.76 no. 20 (no. 1579); *DUI* 3 and 4 (Marietti, nos. 232 and 239); *QDM* 6 (Leonine, 23: 148.253–56).

[10] *In Sent* II.24.2.2 (Mandonnet-Moos, 2:606); *In BDT* 6.1.1. ad4, and 6.1.2 (Decker 207.25–29, 209.2–5); *ST* Ia.86.3 sed contra, IaIIae.30.1.

[11] "In pluribus," *In Sent* IV.14.1.2.1 (Mandonnet-Moos 4:596); *QDM* 8.1 ad4 (Leonine 23:195.389).

[12] *In Sent* I.prologue.1.1 obj. 2, III.34.1.2, III.35.1.3 solutio 2 (Mandonnet-Moos 1:7, 3:1118, 3:1184).

[13] *Principium biblicum* 2 (Busa 3:648a); *In Sent* I.prologue.1.3.2 (Mandonnet-Moos 1:13); *ST* I.1.2 ad2.

[14] Here the best evidence is from the scriptural commentaries. See, e.g., *In Rom* 6.3 (Busa 5:463a), *moralis exhortatio*; *In Phil* 1.2 (Busa 6:466a), *moralis monitio*; *In Heb* 13.1 (Busa 6:554a), *moralis instructio,* which requires *commendatio* and *exhortatio*.

[15] *ST* I.1.6 ad3 and IaIIae.45.2, to which cf. *In BDT* 5.1 ad3 (Decker 168.20–169.1).

lectic. If his textual devices for self-correction are less obvious than So-
cratic irony or Maimonidean self-contradiction, they must still be appreciated fully if Thomas is not to be badly misunderstood.

Lessons about the self-correcting character of moral science can be
drawn from the commonplaces I mentioned. They can also be seen in
the works of moral instruction that Thomas receives. The clearest case
is the *Nicomachean Ethics*, because Thomas documents his reading of
that work most carefully. If Thomas is at pains in his reading of the
Ethics to exhibit the work's coherence, he also insists on the limits
around Aristotle's inquiries.[16] Thomas emphasizes that ethics depends
on a number of prior studies and that it issues immediately in politics.
Even if one judged Thomas's views on moral science identical with
those of Aristotle, his science would still be neither autonomous nor
apodictic. Similar cases could be made for the ideals known to Thomas
from Cicero, Seneca, or Augustine's doxographies of ancient philosophy. The philosophical ideals of moral science received by Thomas are
already professedly incomplete because self-limiting.

Thomas never passively accepts an ideal of moral science from ancient philosophy. He writes not as a philosopher but as a Christian theologian. Whatever the internal delimitations of moral philosophy, the
limits on it discovered by moral theology are more severe. If we want to
see Thomas's judgment on the ideals of moral science known to him, we
had best look beyond his borrowing of philosophical commonplaces to
his deliberate composition of the second part of the *Summa*. Reading the
structure of that second part against the received ideals of moral philosophy will show us Thomas's detailed judgments on them.

The second part of the *Summa* is itself divided, as everyone knows,
into a *prima* and a *secunda*. Everyone knows this, but few reflect on its
implications. Indeed, it is astonishing how many studies of moral topics in the *Summa* still run on for hundreds of pages without ever attending to that work's basic structure. When they do look to structure,
they rarely look beyond the first part. The character of moral teaching
in the *Summa* is expressed in the structure of the second part, which is
by far the longer and more detailed. According to Thomas, the *prima
secundae* speaks more universally of the kinds and starting points of
human acts. The *secunda secundae* speaks more particularly of virtues

---

[16] E.g., *In NE* 1.3 (Leonine 47:11.170–78), lacking *perfecta certitudo*; and 2.2 (81.72), *incer-
tus* and *variabilis*. Add to these the difficulties over the appropriate audience for ethics, 1.3
(12.94–160), 1.4 (15.30–16.161), 2.4 (88.116–129). I have discussed these passages and
Thomas's activity as commentator in "Aquinas Reading Aristotle's Ethics," in *Ad litteram:
Authoritative Texts and Their Medieval Readers*, ed. Mark D. Jordan and Kent Emery Jr.
(Notre Dame, Ind.: University of Notre Dame Press, 1992), pp. 229–49.

and the states of human life.[17] The division is hardly simple. Its distinction between universal and particular, for instance, is relative, because moral science always remains universal in its terms and arguments. Again, the distinction between universal and particular is here curiously paired with a distinction between elements and compounds. The more universal consideration treats as if analytically the end, elements, and causes of human acting. The more particular consideration treats as if synthetically concrete actualizations in durable dispositions and choices about ways of life. Whatever the outcome of these reflections, the division between the *prima secundae* and the *secunda secundae* is the first and presumably the most fundamental difference that Thomas wishes to mark in moral science.[18] Any study of the structures in the *Summa* had best begin by treating the two separately.

Structural Innovations in the *Prima Secundae*

For a reader accustomed to the textual arrangement of its predecessors, the *prima secundae* of the *Summa* is surprising in at least four ways: in its divided presentation of the soul's powers; in its placement of beatitude; in its digression on the passions; and in its postponing the appearance of law and grace. Each of the four innovations marks a stubborn question about the order of moral philosophy. Something must be said about each, and then about the effect of all.

1. Many moral works known to Thomas contain unified treatments of powers of the soul. Their patterns cannot be called Aristotelian, since Aristotle leaves unstated the relations between *On the Soul* and *Nicomachean Ethics*. Nor does *On the Soul* comprise what are obviously pro-

---

[17] *ST* IaIIae.6.prologue; IIaIIae.prologue.

[18] Despite that, the distinction has not been well explained by modern commentators on the *Summa*. Sometimes it is collapsed into other distinctions, as that between *exitus* and *reditus*. See Th.-André Audet, "Approaches historiques de la *Summa theologiae*," in *Etudes d'histoire littéraire et doctrinale* (Montreal: Institut d'études médiévales; Paris: J. Vrin, 1962), pp. 7–29, at 15. Sometimes the two sections of the *secunda pars* are likened to the premises of a syllogism, their connection being somehow a deduction. See, e.g., Martin Grabmann, *Einführung in die Summa theologiae des heiligen Thomas von Aquin*, 2d ed. (Freiburg: Herder, 1928), pp. 84–88; Francis Ruello, "Les intentions pédagogiques et la méthode de saint Thomas d'Aquin dans la *Somme théologique*," *Revue du moyen âge latin* 1 (1945): 188–90; Marie-Dominique Philippe, "La lecture de la *Somme théologique*," *Seminarium* 29 (1977): 898–915, at p. 904. Even book-length studies of the *Summa*'s organization refuse to enter into the plan or position of the *secunda secundae*; see, e.g., Ghislain Lafont, *Structures et méthode dans la Somme théologique de S. Thomas d'Aquin* (Paris: Desclée de Brouwer, 1961), p. 262.

legomena to ethics. Aristotle did not intend that it should. Early on he faults his contemporaries for confining themselves to human souls.[19] Afterward he conceives himself as moving within natural philosophy.

Thomas could not easily read *On the Soul*, however, without fixing its relation to moral science. This is due in part to the circumstances of the work's reception in antiquity and the medieval West. The circumstances include both general impulses to make the Aristotelian corpus coherent and particular modifications to *On the Soul*. So one finds the Aristotelian order under the five parts of Avicenna's *Book of the Soul*, where it is stretched to include a sustained dispute on optics and rewritten to accommodate treatments of visions and prophecy as highest acts of mind.[20] Less grandly, the Aristotelian pattern is adapted for such works as John Blund's *Tractatus de anima* by replacing the original remarks on desire and motion with chapters on the soul's immortality, separate ontology, creation, and free choice.[21] The Aristotelian pattern can even be made to fit with the very different and more easily moralized schemata of Galenic medicine, as in book 3 of *De proprietatibus rerum* of Bartholomæus Anglicus.[22]

Alongside traditions built around Aristotle's *On the Soul*, Thomas received authoritative patterns for assimilating anthropology or psychology to the purposes of moral science. There is one pattern in Nemesius of Emesa's *On the Nature of Man*, known to Thomas as a work of Gregory of Nyssa.[23] Nemesius's purpose is not to summarize received opinions on soul so much as to use philosophical and medical doctrines in constructing an account of man that would justify human freedom under divine providence. His anthropological accounts are given on the way to conclusions about fortune, freedom, and providence. Although Nemesius includes Aristotelian material in his compilation, the purpose and order are certainly not Aristotelian.

---

[19] Aristotle *On the Soul* 1.1 (402b3–5).

[20] Avicenna *Liber de anima* 3 and 5.6, ed. S. van Riet, Avicenna Latinus 4–5 (Louvain: Peeters and Éds. Orientalistes; Leiden: E. J Brill, 1968–72).

[21] Johannes Blund (Blondus) *Tractatus de anima*, ed. D. A. Callus and R. W. Hunt, Auctores Britannici medii aevi 2 (London: British Academy, 1970).

[22] Bartholomew first goes through the Aristotelian order (3.7–13), then switches to the order of Constantine the African (3.14–24). See the partial edition of his *De proprietatibus rerum* 3 and 4, published as *Bartholomæus Anglicus: On the Properties of the Soul*, ed. R. James Long (Toronto: Centre for Medieval Studies/Pontifical Institute of Mediaeval Studies, 1979).

[23] The work was translated by Alfanus of Salerno in the eleventh century and again by Burgundio of Pisa in the twelfth. It suffered several confusions over authorship, including the transformation of "Nemesius" into "Remigius." There is a trace of the ascription to "Remigius" in Thomas's earliest treatment of the passions, *In Sent* III.15.2.1 solutio 2 (Mandonnet-Moos 3:485).

A variation on Nemesius appears in another of Thomas's authorities: John of Damascus *On the Orthodox Faith* 25–44. John's discussion of soul is evidently part of a grander scheme. It is preceded by a study of the whole visible world and followed by a much longer study of Christ. This order, taken just as stated, sounds much like the order of Thomas's whole *Summa*. Indeed John of Damascus is the only nonscriptural authority to be quoted by Thomas in the prologues to the parts of the *Summa*.[24] But I want to notice now that John's chapters on the human creature rehearse—indeed, confirm—the Nemesian pattern for teaching about the soul, even if they reduce the amount of physical lore.

How surprising, then, that the consideration of the human soul in the *Summa* follows none of these patterns. No part of it is a treatise on the soul. Consider both its exclusions and its divisions, exclusions first. The *Summa* treats neither basic physiology nor sensation and the other 'inner senses' subserving the mind. That Thomas knew much more of these things than appears in the *Summa* can be seen from such contemporary works as his literal expositions of *On the Soul* and *On Sense and What Is Sensed*. Thomas explains the exclusions as dictated by limitations on a theologian's interest. The theologian studies the human body only so far as it has bearing on the soul (Ia.75.prologue). Further, among the powers of the soul, the theologian attends to intellect and appetite; other powers are mentioned only on the way to intellect (*praeambula*, Ia.78.prologue, Ia.84.prologue).

Consider, next, Thomas's divisions of what is discussed. The most notable is the division of psychological topics between the first and second parts. After a cursory treatment of the ground of the passions (*sensualitas*, Ia.81), will, and free choice (Ia.83), Thomas excuses himself from discussing their acts in the first part by invoking an ideal of *scientia moralis*. "The acts of the appetitive part, however, belong to the consideration of moral science: so they will be treated in the second part of this work, in which moral matter will be considered" (Ia.84.prologue). I set aside the question of how the tripartite construction of the *Summa* expresses Thomas's final conception of theology. What I can say now is that the *Summa*'s division prevents any unified treatment of psychological and moral matters. The topics postponed from the *prima* are not just treated elsewhere; they are treated differently. The speed of the *prima* requires Thomas to reduce his accounts to what is simplest. We learn nothing from the question on the human soul in the *prima* that we could not learn in more detail from Thomas's earlier works. This is not true for

---

[24] *ST* IaIIae.prologue: "Quia, sicut Damascenus dicit . . ." The other authorities are 1 Corinthians 3:1 (Ia.prologue) and Matthew 1:21 (IIIa.prologue).

the *prima secundae*. Its slow examinations of the acts of human will or of the passions greatly exceed what Thomas had written earlier. The division between the *prima* and the *prima secundae* is not just a division within a sequence; it is a division of two teachings that differ sharply in pace and scope. The division cuts through every unified pattern of moral psychology.

Thomas's exclusions and divisions in the *Summa* are by no means a triumph of Aristotle. If Thomas is cutting moral science off even more cleanly from natural philosophy, he is not doing so as an Aristotelian. He reads the Aristotelian corpus as a strong unity. Thomas's exclusions and divisions in the *Summa* are dictated not by Aristotle but by a self-limiting ideal of theological moral science. This science is less ambitious of a unity treatment, less interested in detailing how moral matters arise from the psychological, than its philosophical predecessors.

2. The second innovation in the *prima secundae* is the placement of the treatise on beatitude. It is not unusual for medieval moral treatments to begin with discussions about the good as such. Philip the Chancellor's *Summa de bono* and Albert's work of the same name proceed in just this way. But it is odd to combine an inquiry into the highest good with remarks on happiness. Philip's "showing" (*ostensio*) of the highest good is accomplished on hierarchical grounds, not by exhausting other candidates for human happiness.[25] Albert's initial treatment of the good includes a wider range of authorities but is concerned chiefly to define the good and to consider some of its conceptual relations.[26]

Thomas himself offers a reason for his starting place. We can understand things ordered to an end only in view of that end.[27] This is an Aristotelian maxim, and the placement of the discussion must recall the opening of *Nicomachean Ethics*. But the discussion is in fact quite different from that in the *Ethics*. Aristotle's diffident search for some archer's mark at which to aim human action is replaced in Thomas by a chain of arguments purporting to show that the highest human end lies only in the contemplation of God after this life. To Aristotle's outline sketch of the good, to his dialectical investigation of happiness, Thomas opposes a refutation of every false beatitude. The immediate structural precedent is not Aristotle but Thomas's own *Contra gentiles* III. *Contra gentiles* III

[25] Philip the Chancellor *Summa de bono* prologue.4, ed. Nicolaus Wicki, Corpus philosophorum medii aevi 2 (Bern: Francke, 1985), 1:20–22.

[26] Albert the Great *Summa de bono* 1.1.1–10, ed. Wilhelm Kühle in *Opera omnia* 28 (1951), pp. 1–21.

[27] *ST* IaIIae.1.prologue: "ex fine enim oportet accipere rationes eorum quae ordinantur ad finem."

owes its structure to patristic sources, especially to Augustine and Hilary of Poitiers.[28] Indeed, Thomas elsewhere quotes to great effect Augustine's report of Porphyry's despair over philosophical disagreements about the good.[29] The confident discernment of the highest good, of human happiness, at the beginning of the *secunda pars* is, just by itself, a decisive criticism of ancient philosophy. It announces that we stand at the doorway to a theologian's treatment of *materia moralis*.

The revision of Aristotle accomplished by the beginning of the *secunda pars* introduces us, if we will reflect, to a string of revisions. Any survey will show how different Thomas's order in the *secunda pars* is from the order he reads in Aristotle's *Ethics*. Leaving aside entirely the insertion of Christian matter, it is plain that Thomas rearranges what philosophical elements he shares with Aristotle. First, he strictly segregates the definitions of virtue and the other principles or elements from the treatment of particular virtues. Thomas insists, second, that the four cardinal virtues suffice for a comprehensive organization of all moral virtue. The virtues are the organizing principles, and such matters as friendship or continence must be subordinated to them.[30] Third, Thomas suppresses Aristotle's separate treatment of the intellectual virtues.[31] Fourth, he inserts into the investigation of principles the long treatment of the passions.[32] Fifth, Aristotle's discussion of law is transposed from the end of book 10, where it forms a bridge to the *Politics*, to a point in book 3 just before the consideration of particular virtues. Under Thomas's reorganization, then, the *Nicomachean Ethics* would proceed as follows: investigation of happiness; definitions of virtue, choice, passions, and law; the four cardinal virtues; and the personal attainment of happiness in a state of life, especially the contemplative. The theologian's ideal of

[28] Cf. Augustine *De civitate Dei* 6.12, 8.8–10, 9.14, and so on, Corpus Christianorum Series Latina 14 (Turnhout: Brepols, 1960); Hilary of Poitiers *De Trinitate* 1.1–14, ed. P. Smulders, Corpus Christianorum Series Latina 62 (Turnhout: Brepols, 1979). Joseph Wawrykow has shown the importance of Hilary's *De Trinitate* for Thomas's conception of the *Contra gentiles* in "The *Summa contra gentiles* Reconsidered: On the Contribution of the *De Trinitate* of Hilary of Poitiers," *The Thomist* 58 (1994): 617–634.

[29] *In BDT* 3.3 (Decker 121.26–127.7). The whole passage depends explicitly on Augustine's *De civitate Dei*.

[30] In the *Summa*, friendship becomes a quasi-potential part of justice, continence a potential part of temperance (*ST* IIaIIae.114; IIaIIae.155).

[31] Prudence is combined with the similarly named cardinal virtue. Art is excluded as not pertaining to moral matters. Wisdom, understanding, and knowledge are treated with their related gifts of the Spirit under the appropriate theological virtue. Thomas explains this in *ST* IIaIIae.prologue, but he does not admit how remarkable the consequences are: e.g., the condensation of the last three intellectual virtues with the gifts of the Spirit qualifies the very possibilities for an ungraced philosophy.

[32] Thomas thinks that Aristotle has relegated the passions from the *Ethics* to the *Rhetoric*. See *In NE* 4.17 (Leonine 47:261.137–39), to which cf. 2.9 (109.166–67).

scientia moralis does not merely add new topics to philosophy; it reorders the whole study.

3. The third structural innovation in the *prima secundae* is the large space given over to the passions. Many of the patristic and medieval works already mentioned lay out classifications for the passions and point to them as a problem for the conduct of rational life. Indeed, Thomas counts among his sources the pertinent sections in Nemesius, John of Damascus, and Albert's *De bono*. But because Thomas has learned from Augustine, sometime after commenting on Peter Lombard,[33] about the importance of the passions in ancient moral theory, he expands the four chapters in Nemesius and John of Damascus and the single question in Albert into the twenty-seven questions that constitute one of the largest single blocks in the second part.

At first glance, this expansion might seem to contradict the theological selectivity Thomas had promised. Aristotle had used anger as an example on the border between physics and moral philosophy, and many of the ancient discussions of the passions were to be found in medical works. Does not Thomas's unprecedented concern with the passions digress from theology into natural philosophy? On the contrary, Thomas spends attention on the passions because he wants to win them over from physics. He means to show, with Augustine, that the passions must be discussed as elements of rational action. *De civitate Dei* had given Thomas the history of the conflict over the goodness of the passions between Stoics and Peripatetics. It records Augustine's insistence that what matters in the passions is human will, not physiology.[34]

Thomas elaborates Augustine's suggestions in detail. To assert that the passions fall under moral discourse is to assert that they are, in significant ways, subject to rational control. "Rational control" is neither mechanical nor mathematical. For Thomas, the chief thing for the moralist to know about the passions is that they are open to rational persuasion. Indeed, Thomas begins by explaining that they are morally good or morally bad only so far as they "lie under the rule (*imperium*) of reason and the will" (IaIIae.24.1). The political connotations of "rule" are important. In the *prima*, Thomas has argued that the irascible and concupiscible powers do obey reason and the will (Ia.81.3). The relation of appetite to reason is not despotic, he has written, but political and

---

[33] I argue the case more fully in "Aquinas's Construction of a Moral Account for the Passions," *Freiburger Zeitschrift für Philosophie und Theologie* 33 (1986): 71–97.

[34] See esp. *De civitate Dei* 14.6. Augustine goes so far as to criticize both Cicero and Virgil for naming grief in terms that carry overly strong physical connotations (14.7, just at the end).

regal (Ia.81.3 ad2). In the *prima secundae's* teaching on the passions, images of rule, obedience, and measure (*imperium, obedientia, regula*) can be found on every side. Now political and regal governance is exercised in the city by means of education, habituation, and rational persuasion. So too within the soul. The enormous space given to the passions captures them for moral inquiry, but it also reminds the reader that the uncertainties of moral education are to be found inside the soul as well. The limitations that Aristotle recognized in the teaching of ethics must now be repeated for an internal pedagogy. Since reason has to persuade the passions, reason's rule over them is subject to the limits on every moral persuasion.

4. The fourth and last structural innovation in the *prima secundae* is the delayed entry of grace and its pairing with law. In Peter Lombard, grace appears immediately after the discussion of free choice. It is treated both generally and as characteristic of man's state before the Fall.[35] The Old Law is not discussed until the next book, where the Lombard uses it to preface the discussion of particular sins.[36] The pattern is picked up in William of Auxerre's *Summa aurea*, except that a treatise of natural law is inserted between the theological and cardinal virtues.[37] The Old Law and its sins still come near the end of the third book.[38] In Philip the Chancellor, the entire discussion of human life takes place under the heading of grace.[39] Albert's *Summa de bono* is concerned with the political virtues and so includes neither grace nor divine law.

Thomas justifies the joint and delayed appearance of law and grace when he describes them as exterior principles of human acts leading toward the good and given by God. God "instructs by law" and "helps by grace" (IaIIae.90.prologue). The reader is brought to law and grace from inside the human soul, from the prior study of the internal starting points (*principia*) of human action. This approach does not denigrate God's assistance. It helps the "beginners" to whom the *Summa* is addressed by starting with what is nearer to hand, with what they can control. The entire *prima secundae* is put under the teleology of the highest human end. The part begins with the end of human life because only the end renders the rest intelligible. The sequence of articles is

---

[35] Peter Lombard *Sententiae* 2.26 and 2.28–29, ed. Ignatius Brady (Grottaferrata: Collegio S. Bonaventura, 1972).

[36] Ibid., 3.37–40.

[37] William of Auxerre *Summa aurea* 3.18, ed. Jean Ribaillier, Spicilegium Bonaventurianum 16–20 (Paris: CNRS: 1980–   ).

[38] Ibid., 3.44–49.

[39] Philip the Chancellor *Summa de bono* "De bono gratiae in homine" (Wicki 2:489).

then dictated by approach to the end, starting with the primary possibility of choice and ending with the uniquely efficacious gift of grace (IaIIae.6.prologue).

So far Thomas's explicit reasons. Delaying the discussion of grace and joining it to divine law also gives Thomas more room to describe the elements of moral science before he must confront the paradoxes of direct divine intervention. The moral philosophy of the ancients has been declared disordered, more incomplete and insufficient than it knew. The declaration is made by a theologian, who himself must begin teaching from a theological view of the human end. The theologian concludes that this end, however much it is naturally desired, can be attained only with the aid of divine grace. The theologian's moral science is even less able to deliver this grace, to compel this gift, than ancient philosophy was able to produce uninterrupted contemplation.

The tensions produced by the questions on grace were hardly absent earlier in the *prima secundae*. From the beginning, Thomas insisted that happiness is not attainable without divine assistance. He made the same point later and in other ways—saliently in the teaching on the necessity and preeminence of divinely infused virtues. But the questions on divine law and grace emphasize that moral life depends on a free gift from God. Thomas must now show how any moral science whatever can be constructed in the face of such dependence. He shows it by writing a *secunda secundae*.

Structural Innovations in the *Secunda Secundae*

If it was important to notice several structural innovations in the *prima secundae*, it is important to concentrate in the *secunda secundae* on the one that is most obvious: namely, the disposition according to the three theological and four cardinal virtues. The innovation is bold for being so simple.

Organizations of the virtues and vices reach back through the desert monastic traditions and the Church Fathers to pagan mythographers and philosophers.[40] The *Summa* presupposes no exact knowledge of the stages of transmission and elaboration. It is enough to know that by the twelfth century catalogues of virtues and vices were well established, but without a fixed order for their elements. Theological variations on

---

[40] Morton W. Bloomfield, *The Seven Deadly Sins* ([Lansing]: Michigan State College Press, 1952), pp. 43–87; Siegfried Wenzel, "The Seven Deadly Sins: Some Problems of Research," *Speculum* 43 (1968): 1–22, esp. 3–14.

the catalogues lengthen them by adding other elements in sequence—
virtues, vices, gifts, and beatitudes one after another. The sequences
grow longer still as later writers distinguish more carefully between
theological and cardinal virtues, and as they continue to add new elements such as the commandments. So William of Auxerre considers in
turn the virtues as such, the theological virtues, the cardinal virtues (with
their annexes), the gifts, the beatitudes, the properties and comparisons
of the virtues, and finally the commandments, with respective sins and
cases.[41]

The appearance of cases is significant. Alongside the sequential treatments, there had developed before Thomas the *summa de casibus*, or con-
fessor's casebook. An early example can be had in the sprawling *Summa
de sacramentis et animae consiliis* that goes under the name of Peter the
Chanter.[42] The third part of this *Summa* is a *Liber casuum conscientiae*
of sixty-four 'chapters.' Some of the chapters do report particular cases
calling for delicate moral judgments.[43] Others deal with fundamentals—
the virtues, merit, and sin as such.[44] The variety of material is exceeded
by its disorder, which worsens near the anthology's end.

By contrast, and with the benefit of intervening works, Raymond of
Peñafort codifies the casuistic material by applying to it a schema of
crimes. Crimes are committed either against God or one's neighbor, and
they are fully direct, less direct, or indirect.[45] Raymond then establishes
order within each crime, usually by adopting some of a standard list of
questions: What is it? Why is it called that? How many senses does the
name have? How is it distinguished? What are its kinds? What are its
punishments? What doubtful cases are there? Raymond's order is an
achievement, I think, and is directly connected with his efforts at codi-
fying canon law. The achievement has its price. The crimes here catego-

[41] William of Auxerre *Summa aurea* 3.11, 3.12–16, 3.19–29, 3.30–34, 3.38–43, and 3.44–
45, respectively.

[42] According to the best arguments, it was finished by his colleagues and students
shortly after his death in 1197. See the chronological hypotheses in Peter the Chanter
Summa de sacramentis et animae consiliis, ed. Jean-Albert Dugauquier, Analecta mediaevalia Namurcensia 4, 7, 11, 16, 21 (Louvain: Eds. Nauwelaerts; Lille: Libr. Giard, 1954–67),
11:187–98.

[43] See the medieval headings for 3.5, 3.29, 3.37, 3.44, 3.59, and 3.61 (ibid., 21:892–909).

[44] See the medieval headings for 3.20, 3.58, 3.49, 3.60, and 3.63 respectively (ibid).

[45] In Raymond's *Summa de casibus*, direct crimes against God are simony (1.1–3), simple
unbelief (1.4), heresy (1.5), schism (1.6), or the combination of these last two in apostasy
(1.7). Less direct crimes against God are breaking vows (1.8), breaking oaths and other
perjuries (1.9), mendacity or adulation (1.10), divination (1.11), and disrespect for solemn
feasts (1.12). Indirect crimes against God are sacrilege (1.13), crimes against church sanc-
tuary (1.14), refusal of tithes, first fruits, or oblations (1.15), and violations of the laws of
burial (1.16).

rized do not even constitute a complete list of sins, much less a frame for a full account of the moral life. So the discussion of sinful cases still proceeds apart from the teaching on virtues and vices.

Something nearer a full account is given by William Peraldus in his *Summae de vitiis et virtutibus*. The combined work is large, at least 10 percent longer than Thomas's *secunda secundae*. Peraldus returns to the serial or sequential treatment but with an extraordinary thoroughness that permits him to include cases. His *Summa de vitiis* is organized around the seven capital sins, treated at very unequal lengths.[46] A host of lesser sins is attached to the seven. There is also a long appendix on sins of the tongue. In the *Summa de virtutibus*, William adopts a familiar serial order: the virtues in common, theological virtues, cardinal virtues, gifts, and beatitudes. There is a regular sequence of subtopics. Each cardinal virtue, for example, is given its several senses, then described, next commended, and finally divided into parts. Before or after the division, mention is made of helps and hindrances to the particular virtue.

William's *Summae* were certainly on Thomas's mind, though not as models to be copied. Thomas begins the *secunda secundae* by announcing that he wants to avoid the needless repetition required by sequential treatment. It is more helpful—more teacherly, more persuasive—to gather in one place a virtue, its corresponding gifts, its opposed vices, and the entailed positive and negative commands. But Thomas also insists that the table of the vices should itself be constructed by real differences rather than by accidental ones: "Vices and sins are distinguished by species according to their matter and object, not according to other differences of the sins, such as 'of the heart,' 'of the mouth,' and 'of the deed,' or according to weakness, ignorance, and malice, and other such differences" (IaIIae.prologue).

The immediate references are to two distinctions passed down by Peter Lombard.[47] Both distinctions are used by Thomas himself in other texts, even within the *Summa*, though he is always careful to point out that they are not classifications by genera or essential species.[48] What is more important, both triplets are akin to the sorts of classifications in

---

[46] The sections are allotted as follows: gluttony, 8; self-indulgence (*luxuria*), 36; avarice, 96; sloth (*acedia*), 49; pride, 138; envy, 4; and anger, 25.

[47] The division according to "heart, mouth, and deed" is from Jerome *Super Ezechielem* 43.23–35, ed. Franciscus Glorie, Corpus Christianorum Series Latina 75 (Turnhout: Brepols, 1964), p. 642, through Peter Lombard *Sententiae* 2.42.4 (Brady 1:569). The division according to "weakness, ignorance, and malice" goes back to Isidore *Sententiae* 2.17:3–4, Migne PL 83:620A–B, through Peter Lombard *Sententiae* 2.22.4 (Brady 1:445).

[48] For the use of the first triplet see, e.g., *In Sent* III.37.1.2 solutio 3 (Mandonnet-Moos 3:1242); *QDM* 9.2 sed contra 3 (Leonine 23:212.84–85). For its qualification, see *In Sent* II.42.2 solutio 1 (2:1072–2074), IV.16.1.1 solutio 3 ad1 (4:775), *ST* IaIIae.72.7. For the use of

Peraldus's *Summae* and other works like them. Thomas's criticism would surely apply to Peraldus's addition of a special supplement on sins of the tongue. It must also count against Peraldus's practice of distinguishing sins by their external occasions.[49] But the force of Thomas's criticism is felt most by the main principle of Peraldus's *Summa*, namely, the order of the seven chief vices.

One of the best-calculated effects of Thomas's organization of the *secunda secundae* is to push the seven capital vices to the margin.[50] They appear, each in turn, but without obvious connection or special importance.[51] Now this may seem odd, because Thomas himself uses the list of seven to arrange his disputed questions *De malo*. Indeed, the two articles in the *Summa* that introduce the seven vices are extremely close to the parallel article in *De malo*. But a study of either text will show that Thomas makes very limited claims for a division of moral teaching by capital vices. Thomas insists that the seven are not the "roots" or "starting points" of all sin. They are, in *De malo*, the ends that desire seeks "principally" or "for the most part."[52] They are, in the *Summa*, the vices out of which others arise "most frequently," but not exclusively.[53] For Thomas, then, a treatment of sins and vices organized around the Gregorian list of seven is fundamentally misleading.

The *secunda secundae* innovates when it replaces the serial order with a more compendious, 'simultaneous' order according to a list of virtues. The list itself is traced back from accidental or causal classifications to an

---

the second triplet, see *QDM* 3.6–12 and *ST* IaIIae.76, IaIIae.77.3, IaIIae.78, where the triplet is classed among the causes of sin.

[49] See, e.g., the multiplication of types of pride by types of ornament or, indeed, by subtypes—horse-trappings, buildings, books, singing, and so on—in Peraldus *Summa*, fols. 293ra–299rb and 304ra–306vb, respectively.

[50] Thomas's recasting of moral theology did not stick, even within the Dominican Order. For instances of return to old classifications according to the seven capital sins, see Martin Grabmann, "De Summae divi Thomae Aquinatis theologicae studio in Ordine fratrum Praedicatorum jam saec. XIII et XIV vigente," in *Miscellanea Dominicana in memoriam VII anni saecularis ab obitu sancti patris Dominici (1221–1921)* (Rome: F. Ferrari, 1923), pp. 151–61.

[51] In the *secunda secundae*, see questions 35–36 for sloth and envy, 118 for avarice, 132 for vainglory, 148 for gluttony, 153 for self-indulgence, and 158 for anger. Thomas is well aware of the authority of Gregory the Great's list of seven capital sins. Indeed, he relies on it in arguing that each of the seven sins is a capital vice (35.4, 36.4, 118.7, 132.4, 148.5, 153.4, and 158.6). Moreover, Thomas explicitly defends Gregory's list as an appropriate classification of seven final causes for other sins (IaIIae.84.3–4). But he also explicitly denies that the classification of sin by final causes—or any causes—ought to count as an essential classification (IaIIae.72.3 corpus and ad3).

[52] *QDM* 8.1 ad1, *principaliter* (Leonine 23:195.370); 8.1 ad6, *in pluribus* (195.402); and 8.1 ad8, *in pluribus* (196.432).

[53] *ST* IaIIae.84.4 ad5.

essential one. The result is not only greater clarity and compression but also a theoretically justified form within which to arrange the sprawling matter of both the moral catalogues and the casebooks. The *secunda secundae* thus hybridizes the theological genres it receives by a telling application of certain philosophical lessons about what is essential in virtues.

If the innovations of the *prima secundae* seem to apply a theologian's interests and inspirations to the forms of ancient philosophy, the central innovation of the *secunda secundae* seems to do the reverse. It applies the conclusions of a philosophically astute moral analysis to what had been taught in the unruly theological forms of *sententiae*, exhortations, *exempla*, cases, and other *pastoralia*. What are the consequences for moral science of the mutual applications of theological and philosophical principles to the received forms of the other? What ideal of *scientia moralis* is enacted by the *Summa* itself?

The *Summa* as an Ideal of *Scientia moralis*

In the hybrid structure of the *Summa*, Thomas gives most obviously the ideal of a clarified and unified theological ordering for *materia moralis*. There is no mention of "moral philosophy" in the *Summa*, much less the labeling of any part of it as philosophy, moral or otherwise. It is all formally theology. Indeed, Thomas sometimes draws explicit contrasts between the theologian's procedure, which is his own, and the procedure of the philosopher. Thus the theologian considers fault (*peccatum*) principally as an offense against God, while the moral philosopher considers it as contrary to reason (IaIIae.71.6 ad 5).[54] Indeed, Thomas elsewhere counts the word *ethica*, which does not appear in the *Summa*, a foreign term—not only Greek, but philosophical.[55] The *Summa* is not a philosophical ethics; it is moral theology. The difference between the theologian and the philosopher makes for exclusions and shifts of attention in the *Summa* that we have already seen. Others are required so far as the second part is a component of an integral theology. The ideal theological order, unified and clarified, is strongly selective. That is the first of its self-limitations.

The second self-limitation can be seen not in order but in content. Thomas presents through the *Summa* the ideal of a set of patterns for the

[54] Cf. *In Sent* II.40.1.5 (Mandonnet-Moos 2:1024): "non tantum secundum theologum, sed etiam secundum moralem philosophum."

[55] *In Sent* III.23.1.4 solutio 2 (Mandonnet-Moos 3:713), where the *nos* is not so much "we speakers of Latin" as "we Christians."

analysis of moral life. One staple of Dominican moral preaching was the sermon *ad status*, the sermon concerned with the perils and opportunities of a particular profession or social class. The closest Thomas comes to that kind of direct address is in the final questions of the *secunda secundae*, which concern the choice of religious life. Even here, however, the *Summa* keeps considerable distance from the particular. It seems to offer no more than schemata for moral applications or analyses yet to be done. A few particular issues are treated, of course. Thomas considers whether it is licit to baptize non-Christian children against the will of their parents (IaIIae.10.12), how one is to proceed in fraternal correction (IIaIIae.33.7–8), and when one is to fast (IIaIIae.147.5–7). But the overwhelming majority of questions in this "more particular" part of the *Summa* concern the classification, causality, order, and opposition of virtues or vices. It is more taxonomy than exhortation, more causal classification than spiritual direction. So Thomas's ideal of moral science would seem to be self-limiting in a second way: it recognizes the intrinsic universality of moral teaching and does not pretend to misleading particularity.

Then, third, Thomas reminds his readers of the limitation of any theological teaching about morals. What is required for a complete life of virtue is the personal gift of divine grace. The gift brings more vivid awareness of one's place under God's very personal providence. It thus threatens the whole enterprise of *scientia moralis*. What is the point of teaching a Christian moral doctrine if the enactment of that doctrine depends utterly on God?[56] The *Summa* addresses the question with two explicit correctives to any overestimation of the value of human teaching. One comes, prominently, at the end of the *prima pars* (Ia.117.1). It is the opening article in a set of three questions "on human action" (Ia.117.prologue). Thomas argues that a human teacher can do no more than minister externally to the learner. The human teacher can provide "helps and instruments" such as examples, analogies, disanalogies, or more proximate propositions. The human teacher can propose, again, an order of learning—can trace out a path for the learner's work of understanding. That is all. The *Summa*'s other reminder about teaching comes at the end of the *secunda secundae*. In the final question on special graces and conditions of life, human teaching itself is analyzed as a divine gift. There is, for example, the freely given grace of the "word of wisdom" or "of knowledge" (*sermo sapientiae, scientiae*) by which the human teacher becomes an instrument for the Holy Spirit.[57]

---

[56] Thomas knows one formulation of this puzzle in Augustine's anti-Manichean writings: *De correptione et gratia* 1.2.3–6.9 (Migne PL 44:917–21).

[57] *ST* IIaIIae.177.1. Cf. the remarks on teaching for the sake of saving souls in IIaIIae.181.3, 187.1, and 188.4–5.

These remarks on teaching are not casual asides. They are deliberate reminders of a third self-limitation in the ideal of *scientia moralis* which Thomas embodies in the *Summa*. The *Summa* is neither scriptural exegesis nor preaching. It is intermediate between them—dependent on scripture, intended for the formation of preachers. The *Summa* is intermediate between divinely inspired books that embrace every important genre of teaching and the specialized genres of direct spiritual formation. It is at once a clarifying simplification of scripture for the sake of preaching or confessing, and a clarifying generalization of pastoral experience brought back under the science of scripture, which is to say, under the whole of theology. Nothing more ought to be asked of a theologian's moral teaching. The ideal of *scientia moralis* ought to insist first and last that it is ancillary to the workings of divine grace in individual human souls.

In drawing this conclusion, I have spoken of the whole *Summa*—and quite deliberately. I believe that Thomas wrote the *Summa* for the sake of second part—that is, in order to situate the moral component of theology within a properly ordered account of the whole. Thomas undertook the writing at the end of a series of experiments in comprehensive theological composition: a first commentary on the Lombard, a projected series of Boethius commentaries, the so-called *Contra gentiles*, an abandoned *Compendium*, and the bare beginnings of a second commentary on the Lombard.[58] Reading through these experiments, we can argue over Thomas's motives for moving from one project to another. But the largest contrast between the *Summa* and the earlier works seems to me beyond argument: it is the contrast created by the *secunda pars*, by the large and ingeniously arranged teaching of *scientia moralis* at the center of theology. Any account of the *Summa*'s purposes that fails to explain the unprecedented size and scope of the moral teaching in the work will be an inadequate account.

I argued above that we discover Thomas's self-limiting ideal of *scientia moralis* from the shape of the *Summa*. I want to end by suggesting that *scientia moralis* ought to be our guide to seeing the shape of the whole *Summa*, which centuries of Thomism have hidden behind a preoccupation with "treatises," if not just with the first questions of the first part. We are still preoccupied. What causes our preoccupation? Why do our notions of moral philosophy or moral theology make it so difficult for us even to begin seeing Thomas's ideal of *scientia moralis*?

[58] If I must still disagree with Norman Kretzmann about Thomas's purposes in the *Contra gentiles*, I am happy to agree with him that the shape of the *Summa theologiae* is a critique or correction of that earlier work. See Kretzmann, *The Metaphysics of Theism: Aquinas's Natural Theology in* Summa contra gentiles *I* (Oxford: Clarendon Press, 1997), esp. p. 40.

II

~

MORAL PSYCHOLOGY
AND PRACTICAL REASON

PETER KING

ॐ

Aquinas on the Passions

Following Aristotle's lead, medieval philosophers generally accepted, first, a distinction between the cluster of principles and capacities that account for movement and sensation, known as the *sensitive* part of the soul, and the cluster of principles and capacities that account for thought and volition, known as the *intellective* part of the soul;[1] and second, a distinction between the apparatus of powers whereby information about the world is acquired and assimilated, known as the *cognitive* or *apprehensive potencies*, and the apparatus of powers whereby one engages the world, known as the *appetitive potencies*.

These distinctions cut across each other. The intellective and sensitive parts of the soul each have cognitive and appetitive faculties; cognition and appetition take place in both the intellective and sensitive parts. There are thus four fundamental departments into which psychological experience may be divided. The principle of cognition in the intellective part of the soul is the intellect itself, where thinking and reasoning take place. The principle of appetition in the intellective part of the soul is the will, responsible for volition and choice; the will is literally 'intellective appetite.' The principle of cognition in the sensitive part of the soul is called 'sensing,' where sensation and perception occur.

---

[1] The sensitive and intellective parts of the soul sit astride another fundamental cluster of principles accounting for nourishment, growth, and reproduction, known as the vegetative part of the soul. There are psychological experiences founded solely on the vegetative part: for instance, hunger, thirst, and sexuality (as mere physical reactivity). But medieval philosophers, along with modern psychologists, do not classify these together with the passions of the soul or emotions; they are more primitive motivational forces, now called 'drives' or 'urges,' which I discuss only incidentally in what follows.

My focus is on Aquinas's treatment of the fourth department of psychological experience: the principles of appetition in the sensitive part of the soul, namely the eleven kinds of *passions of the soul*: the six concupiscible passions of love and hate, desire and aversion, and joy and sorrow; the five irascible passions of hope and despair, confidence and fear, and anger.[2] Aquinas's account of the nature and structure of the passions as psychological phenomena, developed in his *Summa theologiae* (especially in IaIIae.22–48), is a model of the virtues of medieval scholasticism. This essay concentrates on making sense of Aquinas's theory. The first section explores his analysis of the nature of the passions, and the second takes up the structure of the passions by considering the complex ways in which they are related to one another. At this point we turn to exploring the ways in which passions can be controlled by us (if at all). The third section deals with the extent to which Aquinas's theory renders us passive with regard to our passions, and the fourth examines his account of how reason controls the passions. I hope to show that Aquinas deserves a distinguished place in debates over the passions or emotions.

1. The Nature of the Passions

Aquinas gives the theoretical background to his analysis of the passions in *Summa theologiae* Ia.77.3. Passions are *potencies*; a passion is something the soul is *able* to experience, where the modality is interpreted as roughly akin to the modern notions of an 'ability' or 'capacity.' Now these modern notions correspond to a fundamental distinction among kinds of potencies: abilities correspond to *active* potencies, capacities to *passive* potencies. I have the ability, or the active potency, to climb trees. Water has the capacity, or passive potency, to be heated— say, to make tea. Active potencies enable their possessor to 'do' something, whereas passive potencies enable their possessor to 'suffer' or 'undergo' something. This intuitive sense is captured in the idea that the reduction of a potency to act[3] requires a cause or explanation: those potencies whose actualization is due to an internal principle are active

---

[2] All translations are my own; I use the Marietti edition of *ST*. The term 'passion' is cognate to the Latin *passio*, and as such is a term of art with no relation to the ordinary English word: there need be nothing vehement, forceful, or heartfelt about Aquinas's passions. For a critique of the traditional terminology, see Eric D'Arcy's introduction in *ST* (Blackfriars, 19:xxiii).

[3] *Acts* are not to be confused with *actions*. The latter are a special case of the former, namely, realizations of potencies where the principle is within the agent.

potencies; those potencies whose actualization is due to an external principle are passive potencies. The grammatical voice of the verb used to express the act in question is often a linguistic test of the kind of potency involved. Thus we can offer as paradigms:

The act of an active potency is φ-ing.

The act of a passive potency is being Ψ-ed.

Acts have *objects*, and therefore so do the potencies that are individuated by the acts.[4] An acorn has an active potency for growth, for absorbing nutrients from the surrounding soil and converting them to upward growth (stem, seedling, sapling . . .). Yet the acorn's potency is not for unlimited growth. Oak trees stop growing when they reach their adult form, which limits their potency. To reach the full adult height is the 'goal' of the acorn, the culmination and terminus of its growth. Biochemical processes are the efficient cause of the acorn's growth, whereas its formal and final cause are its end. This end is the object of the act, and hence the object of the acorn's potency for growth. The point may be summarized as follows:

[OAP] The object of an active potency is the act's end.

Now consider the case of vision, which is a passive potency. (Here the linguistic test offered above is misleading: 'seeing' is in the active voice but is a passive potency.) The act of seeing, which is the exercise of the passive potency of vision, comes about from an external principle or cause and exists so long as the external principle is reducing the potency to act, just as water's capacity to be heated is actualized by a fire so long as it actively heats up the water. The external principle acts as the formal and final cause of the actualization of the passive potency—

[4] Potencies are individuated by their corresponding acts because potencies and acts are not capable of definition: the division potency/act is a transcendental division of being, on a par with the division of being into the ten categories and hence unable to be captured in a genus-species hierarchy (which is what makes Aristotelian definition possible). Yet because act is *prior* to potency, potencies can be distinguished by their corresponding acts. This doctrine is at the root of the pair of distinctions mentioned at the beginning of this essay: cognitive and appetitive potencies are distinguished by their objects, and the object of appetite is the good, whereas the object of cognition is the real (or the true), as Aquinas argues in *ST* Ia.80.1 ad1; the sensitive and intellective parts of the soul are themselves distinguished by their objects, which, for Aquinas, differ as particular and universal, respectively.

its end.[5] As above, the end is the object of the act. Hence the object of seeing is the thing seen; the object of being heated is heat (more exactly being hot), which is imparted by the fire. The point may be summarized as follows:

[OPP] The object of a passive potency is the act's external principle.

Acts are themselves distinguished by their objects, which determine the kind of act in question.

Since the actuality (or realization) of an active potency is an act that is defined by reference to its end, there are as many kinds of potencies as there are distinct ends. These are roughly of two kinds: *activities*, where the goal of the act is the act itself, such as dancing or walking; *performances* or *achievements*, where the end or completion of the act is the state that obtains at or after the temporal limit of the act, such as winning the race or being married.[6] Both activities and achievements are kinds of actions.

Since the actuality (or realization) of a passive potency is an act that is defined by reference to an external principle, according to [OPP], such acts must therefore be occurrent *states* of the subject: the external principle exercises its influence on the subject, causing a change within it in some way, one that persists so long as the external principle continues to exercise its influence. The subject of a passive potency may be put into a state by the exercise of a passive potency that persists after the potency is no longer being exercised, but the state is not properly the exercise of the passive potency; it is instead the result of its exercise. Jones has a passive potency to be beaten with a stick; his passive potency is actualized just as long as Smith is beating him with a stick. Once Smith is done, Jones has been beaten with a stick and is no longer actualizing his potency to be (actively) beaten; his bruised condition is the actualization not of his potency to be beaten but rather of his potency to have been beaten, a different matter altogether. Since the passive potency is actualized only by an external principle, the acts of passive potencies

---

[5] In the case of vision, the external principle is also the efficient cause of the passive potency's reduction from potency to act. The efficient cause actualizing a passive potency may differ from its formal and final cause, however; see the discussion at the end of section 1.

[6] This distinction, taken from Aristotle's *Nicomachean Ethics* 2.5 and 10.4, is reflected in the different kinds of tensed statements that can be made about the acts in question. For a discussion and application of the point to the case of the passions, see Anthony Kenny, *Action, Emotion, and Will* (London: Routledge & Kegan Paul, 1963), chap. 7; Ronald de Sousa, *The Rationality of Emotion* (Cambridge: MIT Press, 1987), chap. 8.

are examples of what the subject *suffers* or *undergoes*; they are not actions, but passions.

So it is with the passions of the soul. They are passive potencies, the actualization of which is a matter of the soul's being put into a certain state: being angered by a remark about one's ancestry, for example. Anger, joy, sorrow, fear, desire—these are all states of the sensitive appetite, conceptually on a par with the pangs of hunger originating in the vegetative part of the soul.[7] (This fits well with the common view that the sensitive part of the soul is essentially passive, whereas the intellective part is essentially active.) Three consequences follow from this point. First, for Aquinas, the surface grammar of passion-statements is misleading, just as it is for perception-statements: hating, like seeing, is grammatically active but describes a state of the subject induced by some external agency. Second, the grammatical formulation of a passion-statement may conceal an ambiguity. A remark such as

I want a sloop

may be interpreted either as a *description* of a state experienced by the subject (referring to the presence of the passion of desire in the sensitive appetite) or as a *report* of a choice or decision (referring to an act elicited by the intellective appetite, that is, the will). Aquinas regiments the distinction between these two interpretations, introducing specialized terminology (in *ST* IaIIae qq. 8–17) for reporting acts of the will so as to avoid such ambiguities (the vocabulary of 'intention,' 'choice' or 'election,' 'consent,' and the like). Third, passions are individuated by their objects in line with [OPP] above, as any passive potency is, so that the formal difference between, say, fear and love is a matter of the distinct objects each has.[8]

In general, then, we can say that the passions of the soul are *objectual*

---

[7] Aquinas holds that there are analogues to the passions pertaining to the purely intellective part of the soul—call them pseudopassions. These pseudopassions, unlike the passions, do not involve any somatic reactions or indeed any material basis at all. They are located in the intellective appetite as rational acts of will. Angels and disembodied human souls experience only these pseudopassions; animals experience only passions; living human beings alone are capable of both. The *amor intellectualis Dei* is a pseudopassion, one that may be deeply held. Likewise, the dispassionate drive to destroy something evil, the reflective judgment that something—for example, smallpox—should be eradicated, is a pseudopassion. On a more prosaic level, the desire to stop smoking is typically a pale pseudopassion, quite unlike the passion (the craving) for nicotine. The account given here applies strictly to the passions, not the pseudopassions, which play a major role in Aquinas's theology and merit investigation in their own right.

[8] I explore this point in detail in the next section.

intentional states of the sensitive appetite. The sense of this claim can be unpacked by considering a structural parallel between the cognitive and appetitive potencies of the sensitive part of the soul, at the core of which is an analogy between *experiencing a passion* and *having a perception*: the passions are a kind of 'appetitive perception.'[9]

What happens when Jones sees a sheep? The act of seeing the sheep is the actualization of Jones's passive potency of vision. Technically , the sense organ (Jones's eye) receives the form of the sheep without the sheep's matter, and the inherence of the form of the sheep in Jones's sense organ simply *is* the actualization of Jones's faculty of vision. That is what it is to see a sheep. The inherence of the dematerialized form of the sheep in Jones's sense organ actualizes his faculty of vision in a particular way, distinct from the way in which a dematerialized form of an elephant would actualize it. The different ways in which the faculty of vision may be actualized are classified and understood by reference to the external principles that produce them, whereas the form of the sheep, when it inheres in ordinary matter (flesh and bone and wool) and makes it a sheep rather than an elephant, is classified and understood directly through itself. Jones's act of seeing is therefore *intentional*: it is directed 'toward' something, which, as defined above, is the object of the passive potency—in this case, the sheep. It always makes sense to ask *what* someone is seeing, hearing, touching, and so on.[10] Furthermore, given the underlying Aristotelian mechanism, the act of seeing is *objectual*: Jones receives, and can only receive, forms from particular things.[11] What kinds of things can be seen? What is the most general characterization of the object of vision as such, that is, *qua* object of vi-

[9] The parallel between emotions and perceptions has been exploited, with some degree of success, by several contemporary philosophers; see, e.g., de Sousa, *The Rationality of Emotion*, chap. 5.

[10] There is a sense in which someone can 'see' without seeing anything, namely, while looking *for* something. (This is perhaps more plausible for hearing than for seeing, as in the case of a person listening for something: "Quiet—I thought I heard a burglar upstairs! Listen!") In such cases one is still looking or listening *for* something, and so the directedness of the act is preserved. Furthermore, they are cases in which a person sees or hears many things and rejects each in turn as not the object in question: "This noise is just the furnace (not the burglar), that one is the cat meowing (not the burglar)," and so on. The sensing is clearly intentional, with an intellectual 'filter' on the input.

[11] This is not to be confused with the claim that the received form is itself particular or individual. The point here is that there are no 'forms' of states of affairs, propositional objects, abstract entities, and the like. Forms are received from individuals rather than complexes—independent of whether the content of the perception is singular or universal, and also of whether the received form by means of which perception takes place is singular or universal.

sion? The answer to this question specifies the *formal object* of vision.[12] The answer can appear trivial—as in the reply "the formal object of vision is the visible"—but often a nontrivial specification of the formal object is available: the formal object of vision, for example, is *color* (more precisely it is *the colored*).

Now consider the parallel for sensitive appetite. What happens when Jones loathes a sheep? There are two questions at stake: about the intentionality of the passion (what it is that is loathed), and about the character of the passion (what makes the passion loathing rather than loving). I start with the first. The act of loathing the sheep is the actualization of Jones's passive potency of loathing (*odium*). Technically, the actualization of Jones's potency for loathing requires some form's inhering in the sensitive appetite once it has been apprehended and assimilated: the preceding cognition 'supplies' the sensitive appetite with the form toward which the passion is directed.[13] A physiological account of passion is available, just as it is for perception. The inherence of the form of the sheep in Jones's sensitive appetite has as its material element some somatic condition (*ST* IaIIae.22.2 ad3).[14] Jones loathes sheep, and seeing one chills the blood around his heart. Thus passions, like perceptions, are intentional in character: they are directed toward something, which, as defined above, is the object of the passive potency, in this case the sheep. It always makes sense to ask *what* someone loathes, loves, or hopes for, and so on. Furthermore, since the sensitive appetite

---

[12] The terminology was not fixed. Aquinas usually says 'object' rather than 'formal object.' The formal object of a cognitive potency is usually called its 'per se object' or 'primary object.'

[13] See *ST* Ia.81.2: "The sensitive appetite is an inclination that follows upon the sensitive apprehension (just as natural appetite is an inclination that follows upon the natural form)." See also *ST* Ia.80.2 and elsewhere for this claim. The sensitive appetite receives not only the form from perception but also the associated *intentiones* (*ST* IaIIae.22.2), as discussed in section 4.

[14] In *ST* IaIIae.44.1 Aquinas begins his reply by remarking: "In the case of the passions, the formal element is the motion of the appetitive potency and the material element is a bodily change, where one is proportionate to the other; accordingly, the bodily change appropriates the nature of and a resemblance to the appetitive motion." Aquinas examines the somatic reactions associated with each of the passions in considerable detail: e.g., the several articles of *ST* IaIIae.44 are devoted to the effects of fear. Vital spirits are concentrated in the higher region, deflected from the heart, which is contracted; this chills the rest of the body and may produce trembling, the chattering of teeth, and fluttering in the stomach. Depending on the kind of fear, blood may rush into the head to produce blushing (if the object is shameful) or away from the head to produce paleness (if the object is terrifying). If the onset of fear is sudden and sharp, control over bodily limbs and functions will be lost. Knocking knees, shuddering, heaving chest, difficult breathing, voiding of the bowels or bladder—all these accompany a general paralysis.

depends upon sensitive cognition, the act of loathing is thereby *objec-tual*: Jones receives, and can only receive, forms from particular things. He can, in a derivative way, loath all of sheepdom, but this is a matter of loathing any particular sheep that comes along, not a matter of loathing sheephood or sheepness.[15]

The formal object of a potency is the most general characterization which anything that counts as the object of the potency can fall under; it is the condition any object must satisfy in order to be intelligible as an object of the potency, whether the potency be active or passive.[16] Something must be colored in order to be visible at all; the response to the question "What do you see?" cannot be "A colorless object." The formal object of the appetitive faculties is *the good*, as the formal object of the cognitive faculties is *the true*; the formal object of the sensitive appetite is *the sensible good*, and that of the intellective appetite, the will, is *the immaterial good* (*ST* Ia.80.2).[17] In keeping with [OPP], the nature of any passion is given as a formal object falling under *the sensible good*. The differentiae of formal objects define distinct kinds of potencies defined through those formal objects. Thus the concupiscible passions (love and hate, desire and aversion, joy and sorrow) have the common formal object *sensible good or evil taken absolutely*, and the irascible passions (hope and despair, confidence and fear, anger) have the common formal object *sensible good or evil taken as difficult or arduous* (*ST* Ia.81.2).

The analogy with perception breaks down at this point. Aquinas argues in several cases that the formal object of a given passion, such as loathing, must also be the cause of loathing (*ST* IaIIae.26.1). The parallel claim in the case of perception is plausible: the formal object of vision, namely, the visible, is also what causes the act of vision to take place. Likewise it may be the case that Jones loathes the very sheep in

---

[15] *ST* IaIIae.29.6 clarifies this point: "Hatred in the sensitive part [of the soul] can therefore be directed at something universally, namely, because something is hostile to an animal because of its common nature and not only in virtue of the fact that it is a particular thing—for instance, the wolf [is hostile] to the sheep. Accordingly, sheep hate the wolf generally." Sheep do not hate wolfhood but all wolves *qua* having a wolf-nature inimical to sheep, which is to say that the sheep's hatred is directed at any given wolf. This is akin to hatred *de dicto* rather than *de re*, in contemporary terminology, although sheep do not hate (or do anything else) under descriptions. Only particular things are the objects of passions; see *QDV* 25.1 resp. This much said, Aquinas is liberal about what may count as a 'particular thing': in *ST* IaIIae.42.4 he describes the ways in which someone might, e.g., fear fear itself.

[16] The medieval notion of 'formal object' has passed directly into the contemporary debates over the emotions, apparently by way of Kenny, *Action, Emotion, and Will* 189: see, e.g., de Sousa, *The Rationality of Emotion*, pp. 121–23.

[17] When Aquinas says that the formal object of the appetite is *the good*, for example, he means that any item that counts as an object of appetite must be characterized as good, not that goodness itself (whatever that may be) is the object of appetite. See note 15 above.

front of him as a palpable evil. But, strictly speaking, Aquinas admits that the efficient cause of Jones's loathing is his perception or cognition of the sheep as an evil.[18] This marks a sharp difference between the objects of perception and passion: perception is always of what is present, whereas passions need not be. Smith's insulting letter to Jones causes Jones's anger at Smith, though Smith may be nowhere in the vicinity when his letter is read by Jones. Perception, on the other hand, requires the presence of its object for its actualization. The passions have *targets* at which they are aimed, and these targets may not be present (or indeed exist at all).[19]

To summarize the results of Aquinas's analogy between perception and passion: the passions are physiologically based potencies of the sensitive appetite, the proximate efficient cause of which is a perception, whose actualities are objectual intentional states; they are targeted at some individual that must fall under a given formal object, which defines their nature.

Aquinas therefore explains the passions of the soul as complex psychophysiological states that, like beliefs, are intentional and objectual.[20] The passions involve feelings, which are mental states known primarily through their phenomenological and qualitative properties, but they are not explicable solely in terms of feelings. (If they were, the passions would be analogous to sensations rather than perceptions.) Furthermore, Aquinas's account of the nature of the passions rules out classifying 'objectless' psychological experiences as passions: nonspecific emotions such as angst or dread on the one hand, and moods on the other hand.[21] By the same token, each of the eleven kinds of passions of the

---

[18] It is not clear whether Aquinas holds that (a) Jones perceives the sheep as an evil, or (b) Jones perceives the sheep and thereafter judges or esteems it as an evil; the neutral word 'cognition' covers both alternatives. See the discussion of *intentiones* in section 4. Furthermore, according to Aquinas, Jones's loathing of the sheep is ultimately due to some form of love; the efficient cause of *love* is the cognition of something as good (*ST* IaIIae.27.2), and love, surprisingly, is the ultimate cause of hatred (*ST* IaIIae.29.2), on the grounds that you can only hate what in some fashion you care about.

[19] The terminology is derived from Wittgenstein, *Philosophical Investigations* I §476; see de Sousa, *The Rationality of Emotion*, pp. 115–16. The targets of passions need not exist: e.g., I can fear the (nonexistent) burglar or love the dear departed.

[20] Aquinas's theory of the passions is therefore *cognitivist* in much the sense described in Robert Kraut, "Feelings in Context," *Journal of Philosophy* 83 (1986): 642–52: "Cognitive processes are somehow essential to emotion," where such processes include "complexity, intentional focus, susceptibility to appraisal" and issue in theories that explain emotions in terms of belief and desire (p. 643). Kraut, among others, defends a 'feeling theory' of the emotions, which is strictly incompatible with the account Aquinas provides. The debate is well known in the modern literature (see de Sousa, *The Rationality of Emotion*, chaps. 3–5).

[21] This means not that Aquinas denies the existence of such psychological phenomena but that his account of them does not depend on treating them as passions. Anxiety, e.g.,

soul Aquinas identifies must have a target. For example, joy (*gaudium*) is a matter of rejoicing *over* something; sorrow (*tristitia*) is also directed *at* something and in this regard is more similar to grief than to sadness; and so on for the rest of the passions.[22] Yet so far all we have is a disorderly heap of passions. What kind of logical structure do the various passions of the soul exemplify?

2. The Structure of the Passions

Aquinas offers a taxonomic account of the passions. That is to say, he separates the passions into kinds that are distinguished by various forms of contrariety. But the taxonomy of the passions is not the strict taxonomic division ideally given in biology; the passions are not divided into pairs of coordinate species that are exclusive and exhaustive, defined by opposite differentiae. Instead, the different passions are specified by a multiplicity of criteria that allow several coordinate kinds at the same level and different modes of opposition between different pairs of passions, which are traditionally arranged in pairs (each of which is called a 'conjugation') at the same level—except for anger, which has no contrary. All in all, things are fairly messy, and a good deal the more interesting for it.[23]

From section 1 above we know that the differentiae of formal objects define the distinct kinds of potencies that are defined through those formal objects. The formal object of the appetitive faculties is *the good* and the formal object of the sensitive appetite, as a subordinate appetitive faculty, is *the sensible good* (*ST* Ia.80.2). Not too much emphasis should be put on 'sensible' here, I think. Aquinas only means that, as the sensitive appetite depends on sensitive apprehension (perception), its object must be capable of being perceived. He certainly does not mean to exclude non-present targets of the passions, and he carefully allows some passions to be directed at things in virtue of the kind of thing they are.[24]

---

is a matter of the proper physiological conditions for fear being present (or at least some of them) without the corresponding form in the sensitive appetite. He also uses the theory of the four humors to provide a purely physiological account of moods.

[22] This is not to deny that there may be corresponding 'objectless' forms of these passions, as some have argued that anxiety is nonspecific fear, but—as suggested in the preceding note—whatever these phenomena may be, they are not passions.

[23] Most of the following discussion is drawn from *ST* IaIIae.23.1-4.

[24] See note 15 above on this last point. Aquinas's restriction of the passions to the sensible good, understood as the demand that the target of the passion be perceptible even if not perceived, is connected with his distinction between sensory and intellective goods (and perhaps the distinction between passions and pseudopassions as well: see note 7).

In *Summa theologiae* Ia.81.2 and again in IaIIae.23.1, Aquinas begins his discussion of the passions by dividing them into two broad kinds. The concupiscible passions have the formal object *sensible good or evil taken absolutely*, whereas the irascible passions have the formal object *sensible good or evil taken as difficult or arduous*. In explaining the distinction in his earlier discussion, Aquinas appeals to the claim that natural substances on the one hand pursue what appears good and avoid what appears evil, and on the other hand resist and overcome contrary forces and obstacles that prevent the attainment of good or the avoidance of evil. Aquinas offers two arguments in support of his distinction (*ST* Ia.81.2):

> These two impulses are not reduced to one principle [for the following reasons]:
>
> [First], because sometimes the soul occupies itself with unpleasant things, against concupiscible impulse, so that it may fight against contrary [forces] in line with the irascible impulse. Accordingly, the irascible passions even seem to be incompatible with the concupiscible passions—the arousal of concupiscence diminishes anger, and the arousal of anger diminishes concupiscence, as in many instances.
>
> [Second], this point is also clear in virtue of the fact that the irascible is the champion and defender of the concupiscible, so to speak, when it rises up against whatever gets in the way of suitable things that the concupiscible desires, or it attacks harmful things from which the concupiscible flies. (And for this reason all the irascible passions arise from concupiscible passions and terminate in them: e.g., anger is born from sorrow and, taking revenge, terminates in joy.)

I shall return to the details of these two arguments shortly. But perhaps the most remarkable thing about these arguments is that Aquinas gives them at all. Imagine the analogous case for metaphysics: after dividing the genus *animal* by the differentia *rational*, further arguments are given to establish that rational animals really are not the same as irrational ones! The explanation, presumably, is that the distinction between the formal objects of the concupiscible and irascible appetites is not a strict differentia, as would be, say, *sensible good or evil taken absolutely* and *sensible good or evil taken relatively (non-absolutely)*. But then why didn't Aquinas distinguish them in this manner?[25] (The problem is not isolated to this case; it holds for the definitions of all the passions by their

---

[25] For that matter, why didn't Aquinas distinguish them as *sensible good taken absolutely* and *sensible evil taken absolutely*? He uses the opposition between good and evil as one of the contrarieties that give structure to the interrelations among the passions; why not use it from the beginning?

formal objects, which are opposed only within a conjugation.) Aquinas does not say, but I think the only plausible answer is that this is how he found the passions—not organized into mutually exclusive and exhaustive classes of phenomena, but clustering around types of formal objects that are not strictly contradictory. The ideal of a strict taxonomy is a Procrustean bed for a scientist who is sensitive to the nuances of the phenomena. For example, the irascible passions have an internal complexity absent from concupiscible passions. Jones's anger at Smith is more than his aversion to Smith (he doesn't simply avoid him); it involves a shift of focus to seeing Smith as an obstacle that none of the concupiscible passions can account for. Likewise, hope is more than future-oriented desire, since it includes the consciousness of its (possible) realization. In addition to such complexity, the passions will also have richly nuanced interrelations—sorrow giving rise to anger, as Aquinas notes.

This reconstruction has the consequence that Aquinas's account of the passions and their structure is not, appearances to the contrary, a matter of definition. Instead, he is engaged in a scientific (or proto-scientific) enterprise: that of arranging his data in the most general classes possible consistent with illuminating analysis. The justification for the definitions Aquinas does offer is not his arbitrary fiat but the fruitfulness with which they help us understand the passions as psychological phenomena. In other words, the taxonomic structure he articulates has no independent explanatory value; its worth is cashed out in its fidelity to the phenomena it seeks to explain and in the utility of its classification scheme. Aquinas is thus proposing a 'scientific taxonomy' to account for the structure of the passions.

We can appreciate the distinctive character of Aquinas's explanation by contrasting it with two other accounts, one modern and one contemporary, which take fundamentally different approaches. Consider first the compositional theory of the passions proposed by Descartes, who identifies six 'primitive' passions—wonder, love, hate, desire, joy, and sadness—the combination of which generates all the passions we experience.[26] These primitive passions are like chemical elements; they are mixed and blended in different proportions and modes to produce the rich variety of emotional textures we encounter in psychological experience. Aquinas's model is biological rather than chemical. He takes

---

[26] René Descartes, *Les passions de l'âme* §69. In §68 he rejects Aquinas's taxonomy of the passions on the grounds that (1) the soul has no parts; (2) he does not see why concupiscence and anger should have any explanatory primacy; (3) Aquinas's account does not give equal recognition to all six primitive passions.

the passions to be essentially different from one another, so that they are related causally rather than by mixture.

Yet Aquinas does not define the passions solely in terms of their causal role in psychological experience, as a functionalist theory does. Instead, he allows for a sharp distinction between the passions and their effects, so that causal connections among the passions are a matter for investigation rather than analytic truth. In his parenthetical remark at the end of the second argument in the passage given above, for example, he says that "anger is born from sorrow and, taking revenge, terminates in joy." One of the merits of Aquinas's account is that such claims can be made and perhaps falsified. Functionalist theories can also allow for contingent connections between causally defined items, but were two passions to have the same causal inputs and outputs, a functionalist account could not distinguish them, whereas Aquinas's scientific taxonomy could. He examines the causes and effects of each of the passions carefully, showing how each is embedded in a causal nexus, but he does not reduce them to mere roles in this nexus. Rather, each passion has a definition in terms of its intrinsic features, which partially explains the causal relations in which it can stand.[27]

How satisfactory is Aquinas's taxonomy? There is, I think, no obvious way to answer this question, other than to consider whether it can in fact account for all our psychological experiences in an illuminating way. Rage, wrath, annoyance, and irritation all seem to be classified under the heading of 'anger' (*ira*); they are presumably distinguished, though not essentially distinguished, by their degree of intensity. Likewise, fright, fear, timidity, and reticence are all forms of 'fear' (*timor*). The adequacy of Aquinas's taxonomic classification depends on how useful such classifications are. They are at least plausible.[28] For our purposes

---

[27] Aquinas's discussion of the causes, the effects, and often the remedies for each passion are wide-ranging, penetrating, and occasionally humorous, as when he considers in *ST* IaIIae.40.6 whether youth and inebriation are causes of hope (they are), or in *ST* IaIIae.48.3 whether anger notably interferes with the ability to reason (it can). Aquinas investigates serious questions of all sorts, such as whether transport and jealousy (*extasis* and *zelus*) are effects of love (*ST* IaIIae.28.3–4), whether someone can hate himself (*ST* IaIIae.29.4), whether sympathy from friends can help alleviate sorrow (*ST* IaIIae.38.3), whether love is the cause of fear (*ST* IaIIae.43.1).

[28] I don't know how to prove that they are any *more* than plausible, however. Consider the following remark in John Haugeland, *Artificial Intelligence: The Very Idea* (Cambridge: MIT Press, 1985), p. 234, about fear and anger: "What I call EMOTIONS, on the other hand, are more measured, more discriminating. The point is not that they are less powerful— *fear and anger are not fright and rage watered down*—but rather they are more intelligent, more responsive to argument and evidence" (my emphasis). Haugeland rejects Aquinas's classification of rage and anger, or fright and fear, under the same heading. Which theory is right? How do we tell?

here it is enough to have shown that despite the disrepute into which taxonomic theories have fallen outside of biology, there is no prima facie reason to rule them completely out of court. Further evaluation will depend on a closer look at the details of his theory. With this in mind, consider Aquinas's arguments for distinguishing the concupiscible passions from the irascible passions.

Aquinas's distinction between the concupiscible and the irascible passions runs contrary to the trend of affective psychology, stemming from Locke, which holds that only concupiscible passions, and indeed perhaps only desires, are needed for adequate psychological explanations.[29] These 'push-pull' theories, typically based on the claim that pleasure and pain alone are the sole motivating psychological factors, are incompatible with Aquinas's analysis. But his two arguments for the distinctness of the irascible passions from the concupiscible passions are based on the claims that (a) the two kinds of passion act independently[30] and can interfere with each other, and (b) they are both required to explain psychological experience, since they are directed at different objects. These claims can be made plausible by an example. Suppose that Jones shows Rover a bone and then teases him by almost, but not quite, letting him have it. After a while Rover will no longer pursue the bone, even when it is available, but direct his energies to attacking Jones and chewing his ear off. According to Aquinas, Rover becomes gripped by the passion of anger *as well as* by the desire for the bone, and after sufficient provocation Jones becomes the sole and unfortunate focus of Rover's attention. According to Lockean psychology, either Rover should immediately pursue the bone as soon as it becomes available—which, after teasing, does not happen—or the original desire to pursue the bone is *replaced* by the desire to chew Jones's ear off, and then replaced again by the desire for the bone. Slightly more sophisticated versions of Lockean psychology allow for a new desire to arise in Rover—the desire to chew off Jones's ear—*concurrent* with and outweighing Rover's (standing) desire for the bone. But no matter which explanation the Lockean theory adopts, a basic question is unanswered and indeed unaddressed. What prompts Rover to adopt the desire to attack Jones

---

[29] See John Locke, *Essay concerning Human Understanding* 2.20, for his claim that the passions are simply ideas of pleasure and pain. Jones's hope, e.g., is simply mental pleasure generated by the occurrent idea of "a probable future enjoyment of a thing, which is apt to delight him" (2.20.9).

[30] This claim is too strong: irascible passions depend on concupiscible passions, since they presuppose some kind of conative attitude toward whatever is regarded as difficult or arduous. That is why Aquinas holds that the irascible passions arise from and terminate in the concupiscible passions. He treats these relations among kinds of passions at length in *ST* IaIIae.25.

at all? Jones is not edible, as the bone is. Jones is not a natural target of canine aggression. Why does Rover attack Jones rather than merely circumventing him as quickly as possible? The answer is familiar from experience. Rover attacks Jones because Jones is a present evil, a threat to Rover's pursuit of pleasure, an obstacle to be overcome. But that is precisely to allow Aquinas's point that obstacles or difficulties *themselves* can be objects of passions. Furthermore, they are certainly not desires on a par with the simple push-pull model. The burden, therefore, is on the Lockean to explain how desires alone can account for (a) and (b) in ordinary cases.

The rest of Aquinas's discussion (*ST* IaIIae.23.2–4) is concerned with differentiating the six kinds of concupiscible passions and the five kinds of irascible passions: that is, with describing the kinds of opposition relating the formal objects that define each of these eleven passions. Aquinas lays out the two kinds of opposition (*ST* IaIIae.23.2):

> Passion is a kind of motion, as stated in *Physics* 3.3 [202a25]. Therefore, one must take the contrariety of passions according to the contrariety of motions or changes. Now there are two kinds of contrariety in motions or changes, as stated in *Physics* 5.5 [229a20]:
>
> (a) according to the [subject's] approach to or withdrawal from the same terminus
>
> This contrariety belongs properly to changes—that is, generation (which is a change *to* being) and corruption (which is a change *from* being). The other kind is:
>
> (b) according to the contrariety of the termini
>
> This contrariety belongs properly to motions. For example, whitening (which is the motion from black to white) is opposed to blackening (which is the motion from white to black).

A subject can be changed by its relation to a single terminus, as in (a); in such cases the subject acquires or loses something, where such acquisition and loss are opposed processes. If we have not a single terminus but two 'poles' of the change, as in (b), we can describe the subject as moving from one terminus to the other, or the other way around; the direction of movement yields different motions.[31] Aquinas immediately applies these cases to the passions:

---

[31] Aquinas's distinction between (a) and (b) reflects a real difference in physics. In the case of substantial change, generation and corruption do not involve, in addition to being,

Therefore, two kinds of contrariety are found in the passions of the soul: [32]

(a*) according to the [subject's] approach to or withdrawal from the same terminus
(b*) according to the contrariety of objects, i.e. of good and evil

Only (b*) is found in the concupiscible passions, namely [contrariety] according to the objects, whereas (a*) and (b*) are both found in the irascible passions.

Why shouldn't there be the motion of 'worsening' (from good to evil) and the contrary motion of 'bettering' (from evil to good)—parallel to whitening and blackening—for both kinds of passions? Aquinas offers the following explanation:

> The reason for [the claim that only (b*) is found in the concupiscible passions] is that the object of the concupiscible, as stated above [in *ST* Ia-IIae.23.1], is sensible good or evil taken absolutely. Yet good *qua* good cannot be a terminus that change is directed away from but only one that it is directed towards, since nothing evades good *qua* good; rather, all things strive for it. Likewise, nothing strives for evil as such; rather, all things evade it, and for this reason evil does not have the nature of a terminus that change is directed towards but only [the nature] of a terminus that change is directed away from. Therefore, every concupiscible passion in respect of good is [directed] towards it (as in love, desire, and joy); every [concupiscible] passion in respect of evil is [directed] away from it (as in hate, aversion or abhorrence, and sorrow). Therefore, contrariety according to the approach to or withdrawal from the same terminus, [namely (a*)], cannot exist in the concupiscible passions.

It is one of Aquinas's fundamental principles that all of creation tends toward the good. In the case of creatures that have at least sensitive abilities, he takes this principle to have the consequence that all action is directed to the (apparent) good. Since the passions are part of the affective structure of living creatures, they tend toward something only to the extent that it is seen as a good. Hence there cannot be any passion that tends toward (apparent) evil. In terms of motion, no creature can, in any

---

a 'real' terminus of non-being. That is to say, there is no readily identifiable substrate persisting through the entire change. In accidental change, however, there are two opposed forms that successively inhere in the persisting substrate. Aquinas argues, as we shall see, that concupiscible passions can only involve something like substantial change, whereas irascible passions have features similar to both substantial and accidental change.

[32] Aquinas inverts the order of presentation here, giving (b*) before (a*).

of its passions, withdraw from the good. Pursuit of the (apparent) good is automatic and innate. Hence (a*) is impossible.[33] The concupiscible passions are grouped into conjugations as pairs of contrary opposites with regard to good and evil (as Aquinas lists them above), that is, with respect to (b*): love/hate, desire/aversion, joy/sorrow.

The argument given in the preceding paragraph does not turn on any special feature of the concupiscible passions. Thus it seems as though (a*) cannot hold for any of the passions, including the irascible passions. Yet Aquinas says that it does hold for the irascible passions. How is this possible? He continues his explanation (*ST* IaIIae.23.2):

> The object of the irascible is sensible good or evil—not taken absolutely but under the aspect of difficulty or arduousness, as stated above [in *ST* Ia-IIae.23.1]. Now the arduous or difficult good has a nature such that (i) something tends to it insofar as it is good (which pertains to the passion *hope*), and (ii) something recedes from it insofar as it is arduous or difficult (which pertains to the passion *despair*). Likewise, the arduous evil has a nature such that (i) it is shunned insofar as it is evil (and this pertains to the passion *fear*); and (ii) it has a nature such that something tends to it as something arduous through which it avoids being subjected to something evil (and *confidence* tends to it in this fashion). Therefore, in the irascible passions we find both (a*) [contrariety] according to the approach to or withdrawal from the same terminus, as between confidence and fear, and again (b*) contrariety according to the contrariety of good and evil, as between hope and fear.[34]

These four irascible passions are grouped into the conjugations hope/despair and confidence/fear according to (a*) rather than (b*) like the concupiscible passions; Aquinas describes (a*) for each irascible conjugation of (i)–(ii). The answer to the question raised above, then, is that irascible passions characterize approach and withdrawal not in terms of good or evil but in terms of the surmountability or insurmountability of the difficulties associated with the (good or evil) object. Hope is the passion that sees its object as a surmountable (attainable) difficult good, so that the difficult good 'approaches' the agent's possession; despair is the passion that sees its object as an insurmountable (unattainable) difficult

---

[33] This argument also rules out the motion of 'worsening' (contrary to the motion of 'bettering'). Aquinas is playing fast and loose with (b*) when it comes to the concupiscible passions: he characterizes them in terms of their motions with regard to each member of a single pair of contradictorily opposed termini—namely, good (motion toward) and evil (motion away from)—not in terms of motions *between* contradictorily opposed termini. Love, for example, is not a motion *from* evil *to* good but only a motion to good.

[34] Aquinas again inverts the order of presentation here, giving (b*) and then (a*).

good, so that the difficult good 'withdraws' from the agent's possession. Likewise, confidence is the passion that sees its object as a surmountable (avoidable) difficult evil, and fear the passion that sees its object as an insurmountable (unavoidable) difficult evil.

Irascible passions also include contrariety of type (b*). Aquinas only mentions and does not explain one of the two pairs, hope/fear, but his reasoning is not hard to uncover. Hope and fear regard their (difficult) objects as likely to be possessed by the agent—hope directed at the good and fear at the evil. We can invert the reasoning for the other pair, confidence/despair: each regards its (difficult) object as likely not to be possessed, confidence doing without the evil and despair doing without the good.

There is an exceptional irascible passion: anger. Aquinas argues (*ST* IaIIae.23.3) that it has no contrary of any sort. Anger has for its object a difficult evil already present which it strives to attack and overcome (revenge). Since the evil is present, there is no movement of withdrawal, so (a*) is impossible. Likewise, the opposite of present evil is an obtained good—but, as Aquinas remarks, "this can no longer have the aspect of arduousness or difficulty"; nor does any motion remain after the acquisition of a good (except for the repose of the appetite in the acquired good, which pertains to *joy*, a concupiscible passion). The other four irascible passions are defined by the variety of contrary oppositions they bear to one another, but anger is defined solely in terms of its formal object, without any other kind of passion opposed to it.

The various kinds of contrariety among the irascible passions (including the lack of contrariety for anger) defines each formal object and specifies the essence of each kind of irascible passion. The situation is not so clear-cut in the case of the concupiscible passions, each conjugation of which is characterized by contrariety of the sort described in (b*). Why are there three *distinct* conjugations of concupiscible passions rather than just one? In taking up this question (*ST* IaIIae.23.4) Aquinas exploits the technical resources available in the theory of motion:

> Every mover in some fashion either draws the patient[35] to itself or repels it from itself. In drawing [the patient] to itself [the mover] does three things in it. First, [the mover] imparts to it an inclination or aptitude to tend to [the mover]. For example, an airborne light body imparts lightness to a body generated [by it], through which [the generated body] has an inclination or aptitude to be airborne also. Second, if the generated body is outside its

---

[35] The 'patient' is the item that suffers or undergoes the action of the mover (formed on analogy with 'agent').

proper place, [the mover] imparts *movement towards its place*. Third, [the mover] imparts *repose in its place* to it once it arrives there, since something reposes in its [proper] place by the same cause whereby it is moved to that place. A similar account holds for repulsion.

Now in the motions of the appetitive part, the good has a 'power of attraction' (so to speak) and evil a 'power of repulsion.' Therefore, first of all the good causes in the appetitive potency a certain inclination or aptitude or affinity towards the good. This pertains to the passion *love*. The corresponding contrary is *hatred* in the case of evil. Second, if the good is not yet possessed, it imparts [to the patient] a motion towards attaining this beloved good. This pertains to the passion of *desire* or *cupidity*. The opposite in the case of evil is *aversion* or *abhorrence*. Third, once the good has been acquired, it imparts to the appetite a certain repose in the acquired good. This pertains to *pleasure* or *joy*; the opposite in the case of evil is *pain* or *sorrow*.

Each thing has its proper place, to which it moves when possible; even when not moving toward its proper place (for example, when prevented from doing so), it has a natural aptitude toward its proper place. The proper place for a stone is the center of the earth. When a stone is released in the air, unless a contrary (violent) motion is imparted to it, the stone will tend downward toward the center of the earth. Nor does it lose this tendency when not exercising it. The theory of motion he relies on may be quaint, but the point of Aquinas's comparison should be evident: the three conjugations of concupiscible passions differ in representing the simple tendency to move toward the good (love) or away from evil (hate); actual motion toward the good (desire) or away from evil (aversion); and the 'repose' found in the possession of the good (joy) or evil (sorrow). The first conjugation represents the purely evaluative aspect of the passions; the second, their motivating features; the last, the enjoyment taken in attaining the desired and loved object or the sorrow in not avoiding the hated object. Aquinas concludes, on the basis of his analogy with movement, that love/hate is the start of all passions and joy/sorrow the end of all, with desire/aversion and all the irascible passions denoting kinds of affective movement (*ST* IaIIae.25.1–2).

Aquinas's overall taxonomic structure of the sensitive appetite may therefore be represented, in first approximation, in tabular form.

Passions

Concupiscible Passions		Irascible Passions
Love—Hate	[simple tendency]	Hope—Despair
Desire—Aversion	[movement]	Confidence—Fear
Joy—Sorrow	[repose]	Anger

These are the most general classifications Aquinas identifies within the sensitive appetite, where each class is singled out by the kinds of contrariety it bears to the other passions and its role in the stages of motion. These, of course, are consequences of the formal object of each passion.

Much more could be said about the elements of this structure; the account given here is not simplified, but certain complexities have been put to one side, and it is certainly incomplete.[36] But rather than pursue these issues, I want to focus the discussion by considering the sense in which the passions are *controllable* by us. (This will mean a focus on humans to the exclusion of other animals). There are two sides to this question. First, since the passions are by definition passive potencies, their passivity might be thought to prevent our exercise of control over them. We are no more than the passive subjects of our passions; their actualization is involuntary—a spasm of desire is on all fours with a sneeze, and loathing is like digestion. Second, modern discussions of the emotions recognize that they are, to at least some extent, 'cognitively penetrable': they are affected by shifts in belief and related desires.[37] But how can the passions be affected by anything taking place in the higher faculties, posterior to the act of the sensitive appetite? I take up each question in the next two sections.

3. Passions and Passivity

The passions are passive potencies: objectual intentional states of the sensitive appetite elicited by an external principle, defined by their formal objects and structured as described in the preceding section. Nonhuman animals, having no higher faculties, are clearly at the mercy of their passions, which determine their actions completely. But since the analysis of the sensitive part of the human soul is continuous with that of the sensitive soul belonging to nonhuman animals, why should the case be any different for us? The passivity of the passions seems to militate against the possibility of human control.

---

[36] This account does no more than scratch the surface of Aquinas's account of the passions. Among the complexities it ignores are these. (1) There are kinds of passion subordinate to those listed here. For instance, *amor* (love) is divided into *amor amicitiae* and *amor concupiscentiae*; anger comprises wrath, ill-will, and rancor. (2) Joy is a kind of pleasure and sorrow a kind of pain; more exactly, pleasure and pain are generic terms applying equally to body and soul, whereas joy and sorrow apply strictly to the soul. These passions are nevertheless named after joy and sorrow as the most 'exalted' form of the passion. Similar remarks apply to love and 'dilection,' desire and cupidity, and others. (3) The formal object of each passion needs to be spelled out in precise detail.

[37] The notion of 'cognitive penetrability' used here is taken from Zenon Pylyshyn, *Computation and Cognition* (Cambridge: MIT Press, 1984).

Aquinas holds that the passivity of the passions goes only so far. He is careful to avoid what Robert Gordon has termed "the two fallacies" that attend discussions of "the passivity of the emotions."[38] These fallacies are, first, passivity of this sort entails that we are ultimately at the mercy of our passions; second, passivity entails that the passions are not voluntary.[39] These seem to be the core intuitions underlying the worry that passivity prevents control. We'll look at each in detail in this section.

First, given that fear, for instance, is a way (or the product of a way) of being acted upon, it does not follow that we are completely passive with regard to fear—that fear overwhelms us or that we are subject to the vagaries of our affective experience. Now distinguish two questions: (*i*) whether we are entirely passive with respect to experiencing fear; (*ii*) whether we are entirely passive in the face of the fear we happen to be experiencing. Even if we were to grant (*i*) to be the case (discussed more fully below), there are serious complications for (*ii*). It is true that the sensitive appetite is passive with respect to the external principle that puts it into the state it is in—namely, fear. Because the sensitive appetite is a part or faculty of the soul as a whole, we can even say that the entire soul is *per accidens* passive with regard to fear. But the qualification *per accidens* is important. From the fact that the sensitive appetite is passive with regard to its external principle it does not follow that the soul as a whole is passive with regard to the state of its sensitive appetite—that fear, the state of the sensitive appetite, is an active cause putting the entire soul into some given state. If a soldier is wounded in his hand, the damage inflicted to his hand licenses our asserting that he (as a whole) has been wounded; we pass from a strict assertion about a part to a general claim about the whole, which is very different from saying that the wound in his hand causes damage to the rest of his body. His wounded hand is not a cause of the wound with regard to the rest of the soldier's body, or to his whole body, which is the fallacy in question. In like manner, the passivity of the passions does not make us passive with respect to our passions.

This argument depends on two assumptions. First, it supposes that the sensitive part of the soul is a proper part of the whole soul, an assumption that holds for humans but fails for animals. (Animals are therefore passive with respect to their passions: they cannot but act on them.)[40]

---

[38] Robert M. Gordon, *The Structure of Emotions* (Cambridge: Cambridge University Press, 1987), chap. 6, esp. pp. 117–21.

[39] See ibid., chap. 6, on the extent of these fallacies in contemporary philosophical work on the emotions.

[40] Aquinas's story here is more complex than I have made it out to be, for reasons he expounds in *ST* Ia.80.1. As a part of his metaphysics he holds

Second, it supposes that the intellective part of the soul contributes to the condition of the soul as a whole—that is, that motivation is not exhausted by the sensitive appetite; since the will is intellective appetite and operates in close conjunction with the intellect, this assumption is well founded.[41] For Aquinas, the will can be and typically is at least a partial co-cause of the state of the soul as a whole. We have to *choose* something as well as *want* it to be motivated by it in the relevant way.

Yet even if it is in general fallacious to move from the passivity of the passions to our passivity vis-à-vis the passions, Aquinas recognizes that we often explain actions by referring to the motives of the agent, where a passion is cited as the sole motive for action. For example, when we say that Jones struck Smith out of anger, we explain Jones's action (striking Smith) by referring to the passion he is experiencing (anger). It seems as though passions do completely explain actions, Aquinas's insistence notwithstanding.

Aquinas takes such 'explanations' of action to conflate two very different cases: the rare circumstances in which people are literally overcome by their passions, and the ordinary case in which some degree of cognitive and volitional control is retained. He describes the difference between these cases as follows (*ST* IaIIae.10.3):

(F) Form is the principle of action

But for animals and humans (F) does *not* automatically reduce to

(F*) The determinate form of a thing is the principle of its action

Now (F) is not equivalent to (F*) because, in the case of creatures that have sensitive or intellective abilities, in addition to the determinate form that, say, an elephant has (the form that makes it to be the kind of thing it is, namely, an elephant), additional forms are acquired through the cognitive or apprehensive powers. When the elephant sees a mouse, its sense organs transmit the mouse-phantasm to its sensitive soul; the behavior of the elephant is fixed by its determinate form and how the acquired form interacts with the determinate form: mouse-phantasm combined with elephant-form produces trumpeting and rearing, a response that likely involves a mixture of physiological structure and conditioned responses ('habits').

[41] To say this does not explain *how* the higher powers (intellect and will) interact with the passions. The case of intellect is discussed in section 4 below. Aquinas has this to say about the will in *ST* IaIIae.17.7: "The sensitive appetite is also subject to the will with respect to execution, which takes place through a motive power. In the case of other animals, motion immediately follows upon the concupiscible and the irascible appetite: e.g., a sheep that fears a wolf immediately flees [from it], since there isn't any higher appetite in them to act against it. But man is not immediately moved in accordance with the irascible and concupiscible appetite; instead, he awaits the command of the will, which is a higher appetite. For in all ordered motive potencies, the second mover moves only by the power of the first mover. Accordingly, the lower appetite is not sufficient to move unless the higher appetite consents. And this is what the Philosopher [Aristotle] says in *De anima* 3.11 [434a12–15]: "The higher appetite moves the lower appetite, as the higher sphere the lower one." The will is the source of the activity of the causal power possessed by the sensitive appetite, since it is a higher power to which the lower power is ordered.

The influence of a passion on a man occurs in two ways. First, such that a man does not have the use of his reason, as happens in the case of those who become crazed or maddened through vehement anger or desire—as with any other bodily disorder, for passions of this sort don't happen without a bodily change. And the explanation of such cases is the same as for brute animals, which follow the impulse of their passions of necessity: there is no movement of reason within them and consequently none of will. [Second], at times reason is not totally devoured by passion, but preserves the free judgment of reason with regard to something, and in line with this preserves some movement of the will.[42] Therefore, to the extent that reason remains free and not subject to passion, so too the movement of the will that remains does not of necessity tend towards that to which the passion inclines it.

Thus either (i) there is no movement of the will in the man, but rather he is dominated by the passion alone; or (ii) if the movement of the will is [in the man], then he doesn't follow the passion of necessity.

Passions that literally overwhelm reason and will can reduce humans to the level of brute animals, so that they are not 'acting' at all, strictly speaking, but merely reacting blindly to circumstances.[43] This is one interpretation of what is going on when Jones strikes Smith. Jones is so overcome with rage that he lashes out blindly and only later, when he 'returns to his senses,' learns what he has done.

More common, however, are cases in which the agent is not overwhelmed by a passion but rather 'goes along' with it. Aquinas says that the will gives its *consent* to a passion (ad1). In this instance, "reason is not totally devoured by passion," and at least in principle the faculties of the intellective part of the soul could dictate action contrary to the passion. If not blinded by an overwhelming rage, Jones could refrain from striking Smith. When we explain his striking Smith by citing his (non-overwhelming) anger, we simultaneously describe the state of Jones's soul and report on a choice Jones has made. The description may pick out something passive, but the report does not. The sense in which Jones's anger is a passion doesn't make him passive with respect to it. The explanation of a human action by passion, then, does not run contrary to Aquinas's analysis—not, at least, once it is understood in this way.

The second fallacy identified by Gordon is to conclude that passions, in virtue of their passivity, are not voluntary.[44] There is a clear sense in

[42] See also *ST* IaIIae.17.7 ad2 for this point.

[43] In terms of the famous distinction Aquinas draws in *ST* IaIIae.1.1, such blind reactions are not *actiones humanae* but merely *actiones hominis*.

[44] Gordon's explanation of the fallacious character of this inference turns on the sense in which we may have control over purely passive responses, so that experiencing

which the passions are subject to our control. The will's consent to a passion is required, in normal circumstances, for the passion to serve as a basis for action. But a related issue here is less clear. Aquinas recognizes that we seem to *excuse* actions by referring to the motives of the agent, where a passion is cited as the motive for action. Jones struck Smith, his lawyer might protest, only because Smith made him angry with his insults. Even if a choice is somehow involved, his anger (deliberately incited by Smith) makes his action less culpable. Jones did not simply walk up to Smith and strike him, after all; he was provoked. Thus Jones's anger is at least one of the background circumstances in which Jones made his choice to strike Smith. Jones's action is therefore not as purely voluntary as his deciding in cold blood to strike Smith would be. Aquinas seems to endorse this line of thought (*ST* IaIIae.9.2): "Accordingly, something seems fitting to a man when he is in a passion that doesn't seem so apart from the passion—for instance, something seems good to an angry man that doesn't seem so when he is calm."[45] The passions influence our behavior (even if they do not determine it), and so our actions under the influence of the passions are not entirely voluntary. Or so it might be argued.

Aquinas attacks this question with his analysis of the *voluntary*, the *nonvoluntary*, and the *involuntary*. He sets forth two requirements for voluntary action (*ST* IaIIae.6.1 and 2):

(1) The principle of action is *within* the agent
(2) The end of the action is known *as* the end

Aquinas points out (6.1 ad1) that the internal principle of an action need not be the first principle of the action; there may be an external prin-

---

the passive response can reasonably be described as voluntary (*The Structure of Emotions*, pp. 119–20). He is certainly correct that passivity does not rule out control. My eyes must see whatever is in front of them, but I can open or close them at will, change the direction of my gaze, and so on. I can likewise put myself in frightening situations so as to feel fear—freely walking into a haunted house, say. For that matter, we can exercise similar control over the functions of the vegetative part of the soul: my stomach digests whatever is in it, but I control whether something is in it, as well as what and when. Yet the mere possibility of exercising control over passive responses does not mean that we can always exercise such control, and hence that such actions are always voluntary. Whether we can dominate our passions so completely depends on the extent to which they are subject to the higher faculties of the intellective part of the soul (see section 4). Yet this is a less interesting way of taking the question. Surely what matters is not whether we have voluntary control over experiencing the passions but whether the action that is (at least partially) caused by the passions is voluntary—and that is the question under discussion here.

45 See also *ST* IaIIae.17.7 ad2.

ciple that occasions the action of the internal principle (as passions are prompted by circumstances), or the operation of the internal principle in itself requires the prior action of other principles (as the passions ordinarily need the will to operate). Now the action generated by the internal principle must have an end, as noted in section 1 above, which must be known as the end for the action to be voluntary; it must be seen as some kind of good, be it in fact real or merely apparent.[46] Failure to meet either (1) or (2) prevents an action from being voluntary; it renders it *nonvoluntary*. Yet these two requirements are ordinarily satisfied when someone acts on the basis of a passion. The influence of the passion does not prevent an action from being voluntary.

Aquinas recognizes that an action considered in itself, apart from the circumstances in which it is performed, might be opposed to the will; he calls such an action *involuntary* (see *ST* IaIIae.6.6). He discusses Aristotle's case of an action done out of fear, when the ship's captain jettisons the cargo during a storm (*Nicomachean Ethics* 3.1 [1110a9–11]). Technically, such an action is voluntary, for it satisfies (1) and (2). Throwing the cargo overboard, an action performed to avoid the greater evil of the ship's foundering (that is, done out of fear), is voluntary. Whether the cargo is thrown overboard depends solely on the captain; it is his command that determines the fate of the cargo. Yet the captain's action is involuntary. In other circumstances, or independent of these particular circumstances, the captain would not throw the cargo overboard— far from it; he is entrusted with its protection. Therefore, although his action is voluntary, it is involuntary in a respect (*secundum quid*). In such cases, the agent wills what he does not want to will. The correct moral, it seems, is that we are responsible for what is done out of fear, since the actions are voluntary, but the circumstances may be extenuating. So too with Jones's anger. Striking Smith does not seem like a good idea in other circumstances; were it not for Smith's provocation, Jones would not strike Smith at all. Jones is responsible for striking Smith but, perhaps, should be excused for doing so.[47]

[46] To be known as the end of an action—to fall under the *ratio finis*—is to be seen as some sort of good. Animals may know their ends, but humans know their ends as ends. It's one matter to be hungry and so tear apart the wrapping and eat the food within, and quite another to recognize one's tearing apart the wrapping as an action that has the food within as an end, as Aquinas notes in *ST* IaIIae.6.2 (he adopts Aristotle's practice of referring to the thing that is the end as itself 'the end'). The ability to recognize an end as an end is in turn dependent on something more fundamental, namely, the capacity for self-reflection: one has to conceptualize oneself as an agent engaged in an action to recognize an end as an end and that, in its turn, depends on having a conception of oneself.

[47] Whether Jones should in fact be excused for striking Smith is another question, one that pertains to moral theory rather than an account of the passions. (Aquinas will say that

The cases of anger and fear contrast sharply with concupiscence (*ST* IaIIae.6.7). Aquinas argues that concupiscence (*concupiscentia*) is simply voluntary. There is nothing of the involuntary in it, for the agent wills to have what he would will to have in other circumstances. The desired object would be chosen in other circumstances as well; hence there cannot be any extenuating circumstances for concupiscence.[48] Therefore, action on the basis of a passion is voluntary but may include an involuntary component. But even if it does, whether the involuntary component should free the agent from blame is a separate issue.

4. Reason and the Passions

Aquinas holds, *contra* Hume, that reason is and ought to be the ruler of the passions: since the passions *can* be controlled by reason they *should* be controlled by reason (*ST* IaIIae.24.3). But this bit of moralizing depends on reason's being able to control the passions in a more robust way than that described in section 3, where the cases under discussion do no more than somehow affect what seems good to the agent. Aquinas recognizes several external factors that can affect the content of the apparent good: bodily dispositions (*ST* IaIIae.17.7 ad2); the physiological states of the organs involved in the somatic reaction associated with the passion (*ST* IaIIae.10.3); the condition of the recipient in the attendant circumstances as well as the condition of the object itself (*ST* IaIIae.9.2), and so on. Yet none of these ways in which the content of the apparent good can be affected is under the control of reason, except indirectly. Digestion is just as 'controllable' by reason, since it too is a process that proceeds largely autonomously but can be influenced by bodily disposition, the state of the stomach, what is eaten and the circumstances in which it is eaten, and so on. Aquinas needs to explain the way in which

---

there is no general principle that defines exculpating circumstances.) For our purposes it is enough to note that Aquinas preserves the force of both intuitions: that Jones was in control of his actions when he struck Smith (he acted voluntarily) and that Jones was provoked (his action was involuntary in a respect). Gordon's second fallacy is thereby avoided, and the reason why people are tempted by the fallacious inference is explained.

[48] Why the asymmetry? Aquinas thinks there is a moral distinction to be drawn between Jones's being provoked by Smith and Brown's being enticed by Green. I suspect he has not distinguished three cases: (i) Brown would choose Green apart from the enticing circumstances; (ii) Brown would desire Green but not choose Green apart from the enticing circumstances; (iii) Brown would neither choose nor desire Green apart from the enticing circumstances. Aquinas's argument depends on understanding the baseline as in (i), but the parallel to the case of Jones and Smith is (ii) or (iii). Surely circumstances can make something seem desirable just as much as they can make something seem provocative.

passions can be controlled in a robust sense: how beliefs and reasons can influence the passions themselves (if they can), as opposed to merely influencing action based on the passions. In short, Aquinas needs to explain how the passions are cognitively penetrable.

The mere presence of the higher faculties in humans is not enough to explain the cognitive penetrability of the passions. For the passions might be caused by their external principles regardless of our beliefs, as the sense of taste responds to hot peppers no matter what our cognitive state may be. Instead, there must be some means by which the cognitive and the appetitive faculties can interact.[49] The intellect must be connected to the sensitive appetite, in some fashion yet to be determined, so that belief can directly affect desire.

Aquinas describes the connection between perception and passion in the case of nonhuman animals (*ST* Ia.78.4):

> If an animal were moved only according to what is pleasant and unpleasant to sense, it would only be necessary to postulate in the animal the apprehension of forms that sensing perceives, in which [the animal] takes pleasure or shudders at. But an animal must search out or avoid some things not only because they are suitable or unsuitable to the senses, but also according to some other uses and advantages or disadvantages. For example, a sheep seeing an approaching wolf runs away—not because of its unsightly color or shape, but as if it were a natural enemy. Likewise, a bird collects straw not because it pleases sense but because it is useful for building a nest. Thus it is necessary for an animal to perceive intentions [*intentiones*] of this sort, which the exterior senses do not perceive. There must be some distinct principle for the perception of this, since the perception of sensible forms takes place in virtue of a sensible transmutation, but not the perception of the aforementioned intentions. Therefore, the *proper sense* and the *common sense* are appointed for the reception of sensible forms . . . but the *estimative power* is appointed for apprehending intentions, which are not received through sensing.

Animals do not respond solely to the perceptible properties of the objects they encounter. They also respond to such objects as useful or useless, as harmful or harmless, which are not perceptible properties of these objects. Sheep run when they see wolves; birds gather straw for nests. The nonperceptible properties of an object are the *intentiones* associated

[49] The particular case of the interaction between cognition and appetite in the intellective part of the soul—that is, between intellect and will—has been exhaustively studied in Aquinas. The connection between perception (sensitive cognition) and passion (sensitive appetite) has been granted to be largely one way, the latter depending on the former. It is the link between intellective cognition and sensitive appetite that remains obscure.

with it.[50] The behavior of sheep and birds, Aquinas maintains, cannot be explained solely in terms of the perceptible properties of wolves or straw. The intentions associated with wolves and straw, however, provide the beginnings of an explanation. We need to postulate a faculty for the reception of these nonperceptible properties—the estimative power.[51] While Aquinas does not here spell out the connection to the passions, the link should be obvious: when a sheep receives the intention of enmity from the wolf in the estimative power, it has the passion *avoidance* (or perhaps *fear*), which is the proximate cause of and explanation for the sheep's flight. Animals subsume perceived objects under the formal objects of the passions by the estimative power.

Aquinas does not explain the mechanics of the connection between the estimative power and the sensitive appetite, but the details are of no interest for our purposes; sheep necessarily respond to certain intentions with certain passions, whether this is in the end due to their physiology, conditioning, or a mixture. Matters are more complicated in the case of humans (who are themselves more complicated), as Aquinas immediately points out (*ST* Ia.78.4):

> It should be noted that there is no difference as regards sensible forms between man and the other animals, for they are similarly transmuted by the exterior senses. But there is a difference as regards the aforementioned intentions, for other animals perceive intentions of this sort only by a kind of natural instinct, whereas man does so through a kind of combination. And so [the power] that is called the natural *estimative* in other animals is called the *cogitative* in man, which discloses intentions of this sort through a kind of combination. Accordingly, it is also called *particular reason*. Physicians assign a determinate organ for this [faculty], namely the middle part of the head, for it combines individual intentions just as intellective reason [combines] universal intentions.

The natural estimative power, common to all animals, is replaced in humans by the cogitative power: particular reason. Aquinas is unhelpful as to its nature. Localized in the middle part of the head, particular reason is said to 'combine' intentions: more exactly, it combines individual intentions, as reason (in the intellective faculty) combines universal

---

[50] These *intentiones* are problematic. Does a wolf 'give off' an intention of harmfulness? Does an elephant therefore find the wolf dangerous? Are such intentions located in the object, the subject, or relationally between the two? See Katherine Tachau, *Vision and Certitude in the Age of Ockham* (Leiden: E. J. Brill, 1988), for an account of medieval philosophical attempts to grapple with *intentiones*.

[51] The name for this faculty, the *vis aestimativa*, is linked to 'evaluating' (*aestimatio*) and to 'esteem' (*aestimare*). This nicely captures the non-judgmental assessment of objects as useful or useless, harmful or harmless, and so on.

intentions. This faculty is the mediating link between cognition and the passions. We can make some headway on understanding particular reason by looking at what Aquinas says later (*ST* Ia.81.3):

> [The irascible and the concupiscible appetite] obey reason with respect to their own acts. For in other animals the sensitive appetite is apt to be moved by the estimative power; for example, a sheep that esteems a wolf as inimical is afraid. But the cogitative power takes the place of the estimative power in man, as stated above [in *ST* Ia.78.4]. Some call it 'particular reason' because it combines individual intentions. Accordingly, the sensitive appetite in man is apt to be moved by it. Yet particular reason itself is apt to be moved and guided in accordance with universal reason. Singular conclusions are thus drawn from universal propositions in logic. And so it is clear that universal reason commands the sensitive appetite (which is divided into the concupiscible and the irascible) and that the [sensitive] appetite obeys [reason]. Now because deducing singular conclusions from universal principles is not the work of the simple intellect but of reason, the irascible and the concupiscible are said to obey reason rather than to obey the intellect. Also, anyone can experience this in himself: by applying some universal considerations, anger or fear or the like can be mitigated—or even stirred up.

Particular reason is a faculty that stands apart from all the other cognitive faculties and receives their input. It deals with singular propositions. Now it is a fundamental thesis of Aquinas's philosophy of mind that sense deals with particulars and intellect with universals; reason joins universal concepts together in propositional judgment.[52] But singular propositions can follow from universal ones, and particular reason is the faculty that draws such inferences. Furthermore, particular reason may supply singular propositions that are combined with other propositions, singular or universal, to draw conclusions. As he says, "particular reason is moved and guided by universal reason."[53]

Aquinas's remark at the end of the passage confirms this interpre-

---

[52] See Peter King, "Scholasticism and the Philosophy of Mind: The Failure of Aristotelian Psychology," in *Scientific Failure*, ed. Tamara Horowitz and Allen I. Janis (London: Rowman & Littlefield, 1994), pp. 109–38, for a discussion of Aquinas's philosophy of mind. My identification of 'particular reason' in this passage with the faculty of drawing singular conclusions is based on Aquinas's connection between particular and universal reason in the latter part of the passage; his initial description of particular reason as the faculty that "combines individual intentions" certainly seems unlike any inferential ability. Scott MacDonald has proposed that universal reason may draw singular conclusions which then affect the intention-combining faculty, in part on the grounds that the combination of intentions is a much lower-level function than syllogistic inference.

[53] Nothing in the passage cited above forces us to identify the particular reason Aquinas is discussing here with the faculty of drawing singular conclusions.

tation. From the singular proposition "This is a lion" (provided by sensible apprehension) and the universal proposition "All lions eat human beings" (known to the intellect), the particular reason draws the conclusion "This lion eats human beings"—a singular proposition that should trigger a response of fear. Other universal considerations, such as "All lions prefer eating humans to anything else," should in the appropriate way increase my fear. Alternatively, the intellect can be left out of account, and I can lessen my fear by combining "This is a lion" with the singular proposition "This is Chicago, the well-known vegetarian lion."[54] In either case, particular reason is the place where the logical 'combinations' take place.

In replying to an objection, Aquinas lists the psychological faculties that are directly linked to the sensitive appetite the way particular reason is (ad2):

> Now intellect or reason is said to rule the concupiscible and irascible "with a politic rule" [*Politics* 1.2 (1254b2)], because the sensitive appetite has something belonging to it that can resist reason's command. For the sensitive appetite is apt to be moved not only by the estimative power in other animals and by the cogitative power in man, but also by the imaginative power and by sensing.[55] Accordingly, we experience that the irascible and the concupiscible struggle against reason, in that we sense or imagine something pleasurable that reason forbids, or [something] unpleasant that reason enjoins. Yet the fact that the irascible and the concupiscible struggle against reason in some instance does not stop them from obeying it.

Reasons and beliefs, then, can directly affect the sensitive appetite through imagination and particular reason. These cognitive faculties are naturally linked to sensitive appetite, and, just as sensitive apprehen-

---

[54] More exactly, the individual intention "This lion is dangerous" is combined with "This lion, namely Chicago, is not dangerous." Here 'combination' seems to mean 'is replaced by.' Aquinas owes us an account of the forms of combination.

[55] A parallel listing is given in *ST* IaIIae.17.7: "Whatever is due to the power of the soul follows upon an apprehension. Now the apprehension of the imagination, although it is particular, is governed by the apprehension of reason, which is universal, just as a particular active power [is governed] by a universal active power. On this score the act of the sensitive appetite is subject to the command of reason. . . . Sometimes it also happens that a movement of the sensitive appetite is suddenly aroused upon the apprehension of the imagination or of sensing. In this case, the movement is outside the command of reason, although it could have been prevented if reason had foreseen it. Accordingly, the Philosopher says that reason controls the irascible and the concupiscible not 'with a tyrannical rule,' which is that of a master over his slave, but 'with a politic or regal rule' [*Politics* 1.2 (1254b2–5)], which is over free men who are not completely subject to command." Sensitive apprehension, imagination, and particular reason directly affect the sensitive appetite; presumably the first two also provide input to the particular reason.

sion does, they provide content for the passions. The cognitive penetrability of the passions depends on the mediating activity of the imagination and of particular reason.

The truth of this general claim is compatible with the passions being more or less open to reasoning and persuasion on any given occasion. People may persist in the fear of flying even while mumbling the air-safety statistics to themselves; weakness of the will is possible; other factors (such as organic dysfunction) may intervene. The passions are recalcitrant; they are not slaves to reason's commands but free citizens (mostly) following the ruler's advice. Yet the difficulties that stand in the way of making the passions completely rational are minor compared to the importance of Aquinas's basic claim that reasons and beliefs *can* affect the passions. The passions are not, after all, similar to our reaction to hot peppers. They can be affected by reasons and beliefs. Their cognitive penetrability will turn out to be fundamental to Aquinas's moral and theological psychology, since this allows people to perfect themselves through the virtues.

How sensitive apprehension, imagination, and particular reason actually interact with sensitive appetite, though, is left obscure. All Aquinas says is that "the sensitive appetite in man is apt to be moved by [particular reason]," and "the sensitive appetite is apt to be moved not only by . . . the cogitative power in man, but also by the imaginative power and by sensing." All well and good, but how do they do it?

Aquinas has no real answer to this question, and that, I think, is one of the virtues of his account. He describes psychological activity at a high level of abstraction, where the relation among psychological faculties is characterized functionally: sensitive apprehension, imagination, and particular reason are treated as so many *inputs* to sensitive appetite. This is the level of abstraction common in contemporary cognitive science. Aquinas does suggest where the answer may be found: in the realization of the functional system he mentions the physiological basis, the middle part of the head, where, he vaguely suggests, the interface among the faculties might be. But he does not pursue the matter, leaving it to future neurophysiologists if any should be interested, preferring to concentrate instead on the substantive claims made in his functional psychology. In this regard, Aquinas (and scholastic philosophy of mind generally) is far superior to its successors. Descartes's account of the passions and their somatic bases, for instance, is shot through with his attempts to identify the underlying neurophysiological mechanism in terms of brain-pores and animal spirits. Neurophysiology is not psychology, though, and all the latter demands are functional mechanisms, which may be physiologically instantiated in one way or another.

Aquinas should not be blamed for not giving an account of how the interaction among the various psychological departments takes place; he was, rightly, more concerned with the logic of such interaction than with the nuts and bolts of how it worked.

Conclusion

Aquinas's account of the nature and structure of the passions as psychological phenomena is as fine a piece of philosophical analysis as the Middle Ages had to offer. And, apart from its historical merits, I have tried to argue that his theory is attractive in its own right. His emphasis on a faculty psychology and scientific taxonomy is a more sophisticated philosophical approach to psychological inquiry than that found in the early modern period, bearing remarkable similarities to contemporary questions and accounts being developed in cognitive science. The subtlety and penetration of Aquinas's analysis of the passions is unparalleled, and the questions he addresses are still philosophically pressing and acute. His discussion deserves to be taken seriously by anyone concerned with the issues he examines, not just by those with primarily historical or systematic interests. That is his genuine philosophical legacy to us, and it is a rich legacy indeed.

Scott MacDonald

ह०

Practical Reasoning and Reasons-Explanations: Aquinas's Account of Reason's Role in Action

1. A Puzzle about Reasons-Explanations

We often suppose that by citing a relevant piece of an agent's practical reasoning we can explain why she chose to act as she did. Following an ancient tradition—one first given systematic exposition by Aristotle and later developed in great detail by Aquinas—I'm going to suppose that the pieces of practical reasoning we appeal to in offering explanations of this sort must have two basic components, one of which is orectic or appetitive (an intention, want, or wish directed toward some end), the other non-orectic or cognitive (a deliberative judgment or belief about how to attain that end). We can explain Socrates' refusal to escape into exile, for example, by citing his desire to avoid harming Athens and his belief that his accepting Crito's invitation to escape would be harmful to the city. We can bring out the structure in our explanatory account of Socrates' action in the following way:

(A) (1) Socrates wanted to avoid harming Athens
    (2) He believed that escaping into exile would harm the city
So (3) He chose to refuse to escape[1]

[1] I assume without argument that the 'conclusions' of relevant pieces of practical reasoning are the agent's choices or determinate intentions to act in certain ways, which (barring impediments) give rise straightaway to the specified actions. There is dispute about whether Aristotle's claim that the conclusion of practical reasoning is an action implies his rejection of this assumption; see, e.g., *De motu animalium* 7 (701a12–14). Aquinas clearly supposes that an elicited act of will, choice, precedes overt human actions (which are acts commanded by the will)—see, e.g., *ST* IaIIae.6.prologue and 8–14—and so I take myself to be following his position on this matter. Aquinas, however, also thinks of deliberation or the practical syllogism as concluding with a judgment: that is, a cognitive element to

We can think of the propositional attitudes referred to in parts (1) and (2) of this schema—Socrates' desire and belief—as together constituting his *reason for acting* in the way specified as the object of choice in part (3). We can think of the explanation of his choosing to act in that way that appeals to this reason for acting as a *reasons-explanation* of that action.[2]

The remaining part of our explanatory account—the connective 'so' preceding the schema's third part, which here expresses the relation of explanation—is the locus for a good deal of what philosophers have found puzzling about reasons-explanations and the practical reasoning that underlies them. The connective 'so' in this sort of schema seems to

---

which the act of choice is an immediate response (*ST* IaIIae.13.1 ad2, 13.3). On this conception, the agent's want (reported in [A1]) and choice (reported in [A3]) would, respectively, precede and follow deliberation proper and would not be part of it. As I am using the term, then, 'practical reasoning' refers to a process that includes what Aquinas calls the practical syllogism but extends beyond it to include the relevant acts of will both anterior and posterior to it.

[2] By substituting the first-person pronoun for the subject terms in (A) and putting the main verbs of propositional attitude in the present tense, we can present from the point of view of the deliberating agent the bit of practical reasoning referred to in that account:

(A*) (1) I want to avoid harming Athens
     (2) (I believe that) escaping into exile would harm the city
  So (3) I choose to refuse to escape (or: I'll refuse to escape; or: I must refuse to escape)

When we use this first-person version of the schema, however, we must keep in mind that it is intended as a way of representing the actual content of the agent's own practical reasoning and not as the agent's report or explanatory account of his reasoning. Hence, we must take its first part, represented at (A*1), as an expression of his actual want or desire rather than as a proposition expressing that he has a certain want or desire. (It is Socrates' want, not some proposition ascribing a want to him, that plays the relevant role in his practical reasoning.) Similarly, the conclusion of (A*) must be taken as an expression of the agent's choice or intention to act in a certain way. It follows, then, that practical reasoning (as I am understanding it) is not reasoning of the ordinary sort, the components of which are propositions, not propositional attitudes. In order to avoid confusions of this sort, we might try to isolate the propositional content of a piece of practical reasoning by removing references to propositional attitudes. Thus, we might represent the case at hand as follows:

(A**) (1) Actions that would harm Athens are to be avoided (or: One must avoid actions that would harm Athens; or: An action that would harm Athens is a bad thing to do)
      (2) Escaping into exile is an action that would harm Athens
   So (3) Escaping into exile is to be avoided (or: One must avoid escaping into exile; or: Escaping into exile is a bad thing to do)

For the sake of clarity I use the term 'practical reasoning' broadly to cover all these variations and the term 'practical inference' to refer only to *propositional* practical reasoning of the sort presented at (A**); hence, (A), (A*), and (A**) all present instances of practical reasoning, whereas only (A**) presents a practical inference (the practical inference that corresponds to the practical reasoning reported or expressed in [A] and [A*]). See G. E. M. Anscombe, *Intention* (1957; Ithaca: Cornell University Press, 1963), sec. 33; and G. H. von Wright, "Practical Inference," *Philosophical Review* 72 (1963): secs. 3–8 (reprinted in G. H. von Wright, *Practical Reason* [Ithaca: Cornell University Press, 1983]).

raise questions of two different sorts. First, there are the well-known questions about whether the relation between reasons and the choices and actions they explain is *causal* and, if it is, just what sort of causal relation it might be. Although part of my argument in this essay presupposes that the reasons we cite in reasons-explanations of action cause the choices and actions they explain, I do not defend that claim here or give very much attention to questions of this first sort. Second, it seems natural to think that the connective 'so' in our account must do something besides, or in addition to, expressing a causal relation. It seems to express or point to what we might call the rational or inferential force in our practical reasoning: our choices and actions seem to follow from and be constrained by our practical reasoning in much the way certain of our beliefs follow from and are constrained by the sorts of ordinary theoretical inference and argument we engage in. Whatever else they do, reasons-explanations display in the choices and actions they explain a kind of inherent intelligibility or rationality. The issues I discuss here have to do with understanding the way in which reasons-explanations accomplish this latter part of their explanatory task.

It has seemed to many people that a piece of practical reasoning of the sort reported in (A) can provide a reasons-explanation of an agent's choice or action only when that reasoning rationally *requires* the agent to have chosen or acted in that way—that is, only when the connective 'so' in our schema expresses a requirement of rationality or what I call a kind of *rational necessity*. It has seemed that if it is possible for the agent to have had precisely the wants and beliefs cited in a putative reasons-explanation of her acting in a given way and nevertheless reasonably to have chosen to act differently, then in appealing to this reason we have not adequately explained her choosing to act in that way. If the agent's reasoning is to explain, it must be conclusive; her rationality must dictate her choice. On this way of looking at it, an adequate reasons-explanation must be such that the agent could not consistently have taken the propositional attitudes constitutive of the reason proposed as the explanation without also choosing to act in the way that is to be explained. I call this the requirement that explanatory practical reasoning manifest a rational necessity—or simply the *necessity requirement*. Aristotle might well be read as endorsing something like this requirement. According to Martha Nussbaum, for example, "To illustrate the completeness of the explanation [for which the practical syllogism is a schema], . . . Aristotle tells us that it is like the case of theoretical reasoning: the conclusion follows 'of necessity.'"[3]

---

[3] Martha Nussbaum, *Aristotle's De motu animalium* (Princeton: Princeton University Press, 1978), p. 175. See also G. E. M. Anscombe: "[Aristotle] is marked by an anxiety to

The necessity requirement, then, places a restriction on the way in which reasons-explanations display the intelligibility or rationality of the choices and actions they explain: reasons-explanations must show how the relevant choice is rationally required by the agent's reasons. The requirement might be thought of as a kind of analogue for reasons-explanations of a requirement many philosophers have found it attractive to impose on straightforwardly causal explanations, namely, that adequate causal explanations cite or presuppose factors that causally necessitate or determine the events they explain. I want to emphasize, however, that as I am understanding it, the claim that explanatory practical reasoning must manifest a rational necessity leaves open whether any other restrictions on reasons-explanations might be necessary and, in particular, whether adequate reasons-explanations must cite or presuppose factors that causally necessitate the choice or action they explain. I do not discuss the validity of any causal requirements on reasons-explanations.[4]

Now, accepting what I call the necessity requirement leaves us with a difficulty. A good deal of our day-to-day practical reasoning and a good many garden-variety reasons-explanations seem not to satisfy it. Some of Aristotle's so-called practical syllogisms are notorious in this respect.[5] Consider the following example from *De motu animalium*:

---

make practical reasoning out to be as like as possible to speculative reasoning. 'They work just the same,' he says in the *Movement of Animals*, and he seems to be referring to a necessitation of the conclusion" ("Thought and Action in Aristotle," in *Articles on Aristotle*, Vol. 2, *Ethics and Politics*, ed. Jonathan Barnes, Malcolm Schofield, and Richard Sorabji [London: Duckworth, 1977], pp. 67–68).

[4] If we think of a choice or an action as being made rationally necessary by an agent's practical reasoning just in case she cannot consistently or reasonably fail to choose or act in that way while endorsing that practical reasoning, then we can see that a choice's or an action's being rationally necessary is distinct from its being causally necessitated or determined. For it is surely causally possible to fail to choose or act in ways that practical consistency or rationality require (just as it is causally possible to fail to believe things that one's theoretical reasoning makes it irrational to fail to believe).

[5] Aristotle's examples of pieces of practical reasoning are found primarily in two places, *De motu animalium* and the *Nicomachean Ethics*. Here are the relevant texts, with the examples individuated: "For example, [1] whenever someone thinks that every man should take walks, and that he is a man, at once he takes a walk. Or [2] if he thinks that no man should take a walk now, and that he is a man, at once he remains at rest. And he does both of these things, if nothing prevents him or compels him. [3] I should make something good; a house is something good. At once he makes a house. [4a] I need a covering; a cloak is a covering. I need a cloak. [4b] What I need, I have to make; I need a cloak. I have to make a cloak" (*De motu animalium* 7 [701a13–19], trans. Nussbaum, *Aristotle's De motu animalium*); "Perhaps [5] someone knows that dry things benefit every human being, and that he himself is a human being, or that this sort of thing is dry. . . . [6] If, e.g., everything sweet must be tasted, and this, some one particular thing, is sweet, it is necessary for someone who is able and unhindered also to act on this at the same time" (*Nicomachean Ethics* 7.3 [1147a5–7, 28–31], trans. Terence Irwin [Indianapolis: Hackett, 1985]).

I need a covering
A cloak is a covering
Therefore I need a cloak

Or consider Alan Donagan's example of an apocryphal Dr. Watson who, on entering the kitchen on a particular morning hungry for a good breakfast, undertakes a bit of practical reasoning which Donagan presents as follows:[6]

(B) (1) Can I make myself a good breakfast?
     (2) Well, fried bacon and eggs would be a good one;
     (3) and, how jolly! bacon and eggs are in the larder.
     (4) So, I'll fry myself some.

These bits of practical reasoning look familiar enough, but if practical reasoning that adequately explains an agent's choice must be such that the agent is rationally required by it to choose in that way, then these bits of reasoning cannot provide adequate reasons-explanations. Watson's desire for a good breakfast together with his belief that the bacon and eggs that are ready to hand would be a good one cannot explain his choice to fry himself some bacon and eggs, for it is consistent with Watson's reasoning in the way described by (B1)–(B3) that he choose to have porridge or Pop-Tarts rather than bacon and eggs. Thus, as Donagan points out, (B1)–(B4) is logically defective and, because of its defect, fails to satisfy the necessity requirement; Watson's reasoning does not rationally require him to choose as he does. The same sorts of remarks apply to Aristotle's cloak syllogism.

Assuming for present purposes that we don't want simply to rule out of court practical reasoning of the sort represented by these cases and the straightforward reasons-explanations they seem to license, there are two ways we can go. On the one hand, we can try to find a model for practical reasoning that satisfies the necessity requirement, to which pieces of practical reasoning of this sort can be accommodated. Perhaps reasoning of the sort found in (B1)–(B4) and Aristotle's cloak syllogism can be supplemented or modified in ways that will fix its logical defect and bring it in line with the necessity requirement. On the other hand, we can reject the necessity requirement, taking pieces of practical reasoning of this sort more or less at face value and finding some other explanation of their suitability for grounding adequate reasons-explanations. On my view, this latter direction is the right way to go, and I am con-

[6] Alan Donagan, *Choice: The Essential Element in Human Action* (London: Routledge & Kegan Paul, 1987), p. 45.

vinced of this by Aquinas's account of practical reasoning. I think his understanding of the nature and structure of practical reasoning both shows why non-necessitating practical reasoning of the sort found in these examples should be a common occurrence in our practical lives and suggests how an agent's reasons can sometimes adequately explain her choices and actions even when they impose on her no rational requirement of any sort to choose or act in the relevant way. I argue for the rejection of the necessity requirement on reasons-explanations primarily by developing and defending Aquinas's views on these matters.

Donagan and a host of other philosophers, however, have gone in the other direction, accepting the necessity requirement and taking up the challenge of accommodating logically defective reasons-explanations to it. Before turning to Aquinas, we need to see what some of these philosophers have to say about the indisputably large part of our ordinary practical reasoning characterized by the sort of logical flaw that infects Aristotle's cloak syllogism and Watson's breakfast ruminations.

2. Rationally Necessitating Practical Reasoning

I am going to look at four attempts to show how logically defective instances of practical reasoning that we ordinarily suppose to be explanatory can be brought into line with the necessity requirement.

2a. Formal Necessity

The first attempt is, in one respect, the most straightforward but also the least plausible. Following out the analogy between practical and theoretical reasoning, it proposes that the rational necessity required of reasons-explanations be grounded in the logical form of the inferences underlying those explanations. If a practical inference supporting a conclusion that a particular action must be done were deductively valid, then as a matter of straightforward logical consistency an agent could not accept the premises of that inference without also accepting its conclusion.

Since a common pattern of practical inference—what we might call the rule-case pattern—fits this description, we might suppose that explanatory practical reasoning must conform to rule-case reasoning. In practical inferences of this sort, the application of a universal practical rule or principle ("All passengers on departing flights must pass through the security checkpoint") to a particular case ("I am a passenger on a departing flight") validly yields a conclusion about what to do ("So I must pass through the security checkpoint"). Now, although the account I introduced at (A) above as a kind of schema for explanatory units of practical reasoning does not provide us with an inference of this sort, we can often distill a rule-case practical inference from an instance of practical reasoning that conforms to that schema.[7] We might imagine, for example, that Socrates' reasoning is of the following sort:

(C) (1) Any action of mine that would harm Athens is to be avoided
    (2) My escaping into exile is an action of mine that would harm Athens
So (3) My escaping into exile is to be avoided

If Socrates accepted (C1) and (C2), it might seem that he could have failed to accept (C3) only on pain of logical inconsistency. And (we may suppose) his accepting (C3) either logically guarantees or rationally requires his choosing to act in the appropriate way.[8] On this proposal, then, adequate reasons-explanations of an agent's action satisfy the necessity requirement precisely because they attribute to the agent practical inferences of this sort.

Now, we clearly do engage in rule-case practical inference. But it is also clear that not all our practical reasoning can be made to fit this model. In particular, requiring reasons-explanations to conform to the rule-case model leaves us in a hopeless position for dealing with cases such as (B1)–(B4). This is because it is not at all clear what universal rule might be at work in cases of this sort. Perhaps the most plausible way of attributing to Watson reasoning that appeals to a universal rule is to imagine that his ruminations about breakfast take the following form:

(D) (1) I want a good breakfast
    (2) (I believe that) fried bacon and eggs would be a good one and are ready to hand
    (3) (I believe that) whenever anyone wants a good breakfast and believes that bacon and eggs would make a good one and are ready to hand, that person must fry himself some bacon and eggs
So (4) I must fry myself some bacon and eggs

[7] See note 2 above.

[8] Of course, it does not follow from Socrates' wanting to avoid harming Athens (see [A1] above) that he endorses a universal proposition of the sort expressed in (C1); he may not think that literally *any* action that would harm Athens is to be avoided. Moreover, in order to get a conclusion strong enough strictly to require the appropriate action, we would need to read the phrase "to be avoided" in (C1) and (C3) as meaning "to be avoided no matter what"; if (C3) could be understood as meaning "my escaping into exile is to be avoided (except in extreme circumstances)" or as being implicitly qualified in some other way, then Socrates's commitment to (C1)–(C3) would not rationally require him to act in the appropriate way, since he might also judge himself to be in extreme circumstances.

We might make explicit the rule-case structure of the inference under-lying this piece of first-person practical reasoning in the following way:

(E) (1) Whenever anyone (a) wants a good breakfast and (b) believes that fried bacon and eggs would be a good breakfast and are ready to hand, that person must fry himself some bacon and eggs
(2) I am a person who satisfies conditions (1a) and (1b)
So (3) I must fry myself some bacon and eggs

If Watson were committed to an inference of this sort, then the practical inference leading to his choice to fry himself some bacon and eggs would indeed be logically tight. But inferences of this sort illustrate Anscombe's point that transforming pieces of practical reasoning into rule-case inferences often purchases validity in the reasoning only at the cost of requiring insanity in the agent who endorses it.[9] It seems clear that Watson's reasoning does not and need not contain a universal proposi-tion of the sort required by this proposal.[10]

2b. Hypothetical and Optimific Necessity

The other three proposals to be considered abandon the attempt to understand the rational necessity in explanatory practical reasoning in terms of formal validity. The two I take up in this section can be thought of as describing patterns of practical reasoning that instantiate or express some substantive principle of practical rationality. These proposals argue that explanatory practical reasoning restricts a rational agent to some single course of action not because of the reasoning's logical form but because of what it is to be practically rational.

The first proposal builds a model of practical reasoning around the

---

[9] Anscombe, *Intention*, sec. 33.

[10] It would be more natural, I think, to represent the practical inference underlying Watson's reasoning at (B1)–(B4) in the following way:

(E*) (1) A good breakfast would be a good thing to have
(2) Fried bacon and eggs (which are ready to hand) would be a good breakfast
(3) Fried bacon and eggs (which are ready to hand) would be a good thing to have

If Watson's reasoning rests on this inference, he reasons validly, but his reasoning fails to satisfy the necessity requirement. (E*3) might be thought to show that Watson has *a* rea-son for choosing to fry himself some bacon and eggs, but it is consistent with his having a reason for choosing in that way that he fail to do so (since he may, for example, have other, better reasons against choosing in that way). This suggests a particular way of stat-ing the problem of reasons-explanations that we are trying to resolve: ordinary reasons-explanations often purport to explain an action by identifying *a* reason the agent had for performing that action, but an agent's having *a* reason to perform a given action does not seem sufficient to account for the agent's choosing to perform that action.

principle that a rational agent will, other things being equal, choose to do what she believes to be necessary for achieving her goals.[11] Nussbaum, for example, drawing on Aristotle's discussions of cases of this sort, develops a model that displays a kind of *hypothetical necessity* in practical reasoning.

> This pattern of practical reasoning, which, after von Wright, I shall call the "anankastic" (because of its inclusion of a premise descriptive of a hypothetical necessity), translates readily into a third-person teleological explanation of the agent's action: "He did A because he wanted G and believed that it was necessary to do A in order to bring it about." This is a complete account of why he did it; and the conditions alleged are sufficient conditions for the action.[12]

We might represent that pattern schematically as follows:

Hypothetical necessity:
  (1) S wanted G
  (2) S believed that doing A was *necessary* for bringing G about
So (3) S chose to do A

We might suppose that, other things being equal, an agent who has a want and belief of this sort is bound by practical rationality to choose or act in the relevant way; she cannot, consistent with her want and belief, fail to choose or act in that way.[13]

Now clearly, practical reasoning manifesting hypothetical necessity

---

[11] As G. H. von Wright has pointed out, Kant endorses a principle of this sort: "Who wills the end, wills (so far as reason has decisive influence on his actions) also the means which are indispensably necessary and in his power" (*Groundwork of the Metaphysic of Morals*, trans. H. J. Paton [New York: Harper & Row, 1964], pp. 84–85).

[12] Nussbaum, *Aristotle's De motu animalium*, p. 176. A claim of the sort Nussbaum has in mind occurs at *Metaphysics* 7.7 (1032b6–9).

[13] In actual fact Nussbaum, following von Wright, holds the stronger view that an agent's having the relevant want and belief is *logically sufficient* for his acting. See Nussbaum, *Aristotle's De motu animalium*, pp. 178–80, 205–6; and von Wright, "Practical Inference," sec. 5. But this stronger view is clearly too strong: I may want G and believe that doing A is necessary for attaining G but nevertheless not do A for the simple reason that there are things incompatible with G that I want more. Interestingly, in his later paper "On So-Called Practical Inference" (*Acta Sociologica* 15 [1972], reprinted in *Practical Reason*), secs. 2–5, von Wright hedges his original claim, arguing that what is logically sufficient for an agent's acting in the relevant way is not his *wanting* to attain some end and believing that performing some action is necessary for attaining it but his *intending to make it true* that he attains his end and his believing that performing some action is necessary for his making it true. He expresses a similar qualification in note 4, added to the 1983 reprinting of "Practical Inference." In this discussion I have taken the Nussbaum–von Wright view as suggesting the weaker and more plausible view that it is a requirement of practical ratio-

cannot be the whole story of practical reasoning for the simple reason that we often do not view our actions as necessary for attaining our goals: Donagan's Dr. Watson, presumably, does not think that he cannot have a good breakfast without frying himself bacon and eggs. In order to meet this kind of objection, Nussbaum—again appealing to precedent in Aristotle—suggests that we can preserve the hypothetical necessity in such cases by appropriately augmenting the orectic component of the practical reasoning. As she explains it, we sometimes introduce into our deliberation supplemental goals (perhaps having to do with efficiency or some other sort of optimality) which have the effect of narrowing the range of alternatives ultimately to one (the easiest or best way of achieving our original goal).[14] We can imagine, for example, that Watson wants not just to obtain a good breakfast but to obtain one *as quickly as possible.* If we supplement the account of Watson's wishes in this way and add to our account of his reasoning his belief that he can fry himself some bacon and eggs more quickly than he can prepare any other available breakfast, then we can see how Watson's reasoning will manifest hypothetical necessity and rationally require him to choose as he does.

Instead of following Nussbaum's suggestion that we accommodate cases involving considerations of optimality by augmenting the model of hypothetical necessity, I propose that we distinguish practical reasoning that appeals to *optimality* from practical reasoning that appeals to hypothetical *necessity.*[15] One might suppose it to be a distinct principle of practical rationality that a rational agent will, other things being equal, choose the course of action she judges to be best among the alternatives she takes to be open to her.[16] We might call the sort of necessity intro-

---

nality (though not of logic) that an agent with the appropriate wants and beliefs choose or act in relevant ways.

[14] "Now we need only recast the desire statement in the form, e.g.: 'I want to realize G as quickly as possible,' and the compound belief statement, 'If G is to be realized, I must do either A or A_1, but A_1 will bring G about more rapidly than A,' will yield a conclusion as binding as those of our previous examples" (Nussbaum, *Aristotle's De motu animalium,* p. 177). For the Aristotelian precedent, see *Nicomachean Ethics* 3.3 (1112b15 ff.).

[15] I am inclined to think that if either of these two models of practical reasoning is more basic than the other, it's optimific reasoning. We might think of practical reasoning that manifests hypothetical necessity as optimific reasoning applied to the special case in which there is only one alternative. When an action is necessary for attaining some goal, it is *eo ipso* the best way of attaining it.

[16] Leibniz's view that God is bound to create the best of all possible worlds seems to be based on a principle of this sort: "Now, this supreme wisdom, united to a goodness that is no less infinite, cannot but have chosen the best. For as a lesser evil is a kind of good, even so a lesser good is a kind of evil if it stands in the way of a greater good; and there would be something to correct in the actions of God if it were possible to do better" (*Essays on the Justice of God and the Freedom of Man in the Origin of Evil,* trans. E. M. Huggard [La Salle, Ill.: Open Court, 1985], pt. 1, para. 8, p. 128).

duced into practical reasoning by considerations having to do what's best *optimific* and present it schematically as follows:

Optimific necessity:
    (1) S wanted G
    (2) S believed that doing A was the *best* way of bringing G about
So (3) S chose to do A

Thus, if Watson judges not just that frying himself bacon and eggs is one way of getting a good breakfast but that it is the best alternative open to him, then we can see how, in virtue of an optimific necessity, he will be bound by rationality to choose to fry himself some bacon and eggs.[17]

We should recognize, of course, that considerations of optimality can be brought to bear on reasoning about the desirability of deliberation itself, and optimific necessity can enter into practical reasoning at what we might call the meta-level. We sometimes choose a particular course of action not because we take it to be, in itself, the best way of attaining our goal but because we judge that there is no overall utility in searching for or evaluating alternatives to the course of action that has presented itself; we might, for example, lack the time necessary for an exhaustive search for the unqualifiedly best way of satisfying our goal. Despite not having ascertained that bacon and eggs are, strictly speaking, the uniquely best breakfast available to him, Watson might nevertheless choose to fry himself some bacon and eggs on the grounds that, given his particular circumstances and other goals and needs, it is best for him on this particular occasion to cease deliberating about how to fulfill his desire for a good breakfast (or to forgo deliberation altogether) and simply to fry himself some bacon and eggs. Cases of this sort conform to the model of optimific necessity in an indirect way. As I have described them, Watson's grounds for choosing to fry himself some bacon and eggs do not have to do solely with the intrinsic preferability of bacon and eggs as a breakfast food or with the relative contribution

---

[17] As I describe it here, optimific necessity in practical reasoning constrains the rational agent to choose what she judges to be uniquely best, but we might extend the notion to cover cases in which there is no unique best course of action but only a set of equally good alternatives. In cases of this sort, which we might think of as Buridan's-ass cases, optimific practical reasoning might be thought of as constraining the agent to choose some, but not any particular, member of the relevant set. Having noted that Buridan's-ass cases can be thought of as conforming in this extended way to the model of optimific necessity, I henceforth ignore such cases and, for simplicity's sake, talk of optimific necessity as if it always constrains an agent to some uniquely best course of action. In doing so, I am assuming that cases like that of Watson's ruminations about breakfast are not to be understood as Buridan's-ass cases. On Buridan's-ass cases in their historical context, see Jack Zupko, "Freedom of Choice in Buridan's Moral Psychology," *Mediaeval Studies* 57 (1995): 75–99.

of this course of action to other supplemental or subsidiary goals. They do, however, give him reason to think that frying himself some bacon and eggs is the best course of action (even if, for all he knows, bacon and eggs may not be the best breakfast) available to him.

2c. Nihil obstat *necessity*

Both hypothetical and optimific necessity are important and common in practical reasoning, but Donagan thinks that we must acknowledge the importance of yet another model. He supposes that it is essential to the kinds of cases he has in mind—cases like that of Watson's reasoning about a good breakfast—that the agent does not judge the course of action he chooses to be the one and only thing it is reasonable of him to do. The models of hypothetical and optimific necessity, however, are designed precisely to show how the rational agent is restricted by her practical reasoning to some one course of action. On Donagan's view, those who try to make reasoning of the sort found in (B) satisfy the necessity requirement by stretching it to fit forms of practical reasoning that are formally valid or that manifest hypothetical or optimific necessity fail to see that "processes of deliberation like our apocryphal Watson's are attempts to answer not questions of the form 'What *must* you do that will bring about such and such, which you wish?' but rather those of the form 'What *can* you do that will bring it about?'"[18] Insofar as deliberation is practical reflection on how to gratify a given wish, it will quite often come to a stop when it has found a way—any suitable way—to do so.

> You will hesitate only if some reason for not choosing it occurs to you; and in most cases none will. That is why formulations of bits of deliberation usually omit both the question whether there are such reasons and the answer that there are not. But strictly they should not. Hence formulations like [B] above are logically defective. Insert the missing question and answer, and the objection will vanish that Watson's wish and deliberation, as stated, do not logically require him to choose as he did.[19]

So when it's all cleaned up and filled out in the ways Donagan suggests, the story of Watson's ruminations takes the following form:[20]

---

[18] Donagan, *Choice*, p. 45 (my emphasis).

[19] Ibid., p. 47.

[20] Ibid., p. 49. Following Donagan's subsequent suggestions (pp. 49–50) for emending (F1), I have substituted 'intended' here for the original 'wished.'

(F) (1) Watson intended: *that he get himself a good breakfast.*

(2) He began with the belief: *that fried bacon and eggs make a good breakfast;*

(3) and, upon investigating, arrived at the further belief: *that what he needed to make such a breakfast was in the larder.*

(4) He then asked: *whether there was any reason to deliberate further, for example, to inquire whether some other breakfast he could get himself would be better;*

(5) and answered: *No.*

(6) So he chose: *that he fry himself some bacon and eggs.*

Steps (F4) and (F5) supply what was left out of (B) above and, as Donagan sees it, fix its logical (and explanatory) defect. He concludes that "Watson could not have had the propositional attitudes described by (F1)–(F5) and consistently have believed it to be reasonable to refuse to take that described by (F6)."[21]

Now, it might seem that Donagan's suggestions for making Watson's practical reasoning logically tight amount to converting it into an instance of optimific reasoning, since the function of the part of the reasoning made explicit by (F4) and (F5)—at least as Donagan describes these steps—is to verify that there is no option open to Watson that is better than the one he is considering. But Donagan's point is really broader. His idea is that a piece of practical reasoning such as Watson's can be logically tight so long as it includes the agent's considered belief that there are no reasons standing in the way of choosing the option under consideration. So long as Watson considers and judges that there are *no* reasons for *not* choosing to fry himself some bacon and eggs, he will have a principled way of bringing his practical reasoning to a conclusion. So Donagan is requiring only that Watson's reasoning satisfy what we might think of as a negative condition: it must ascertain that there are *no reasons against* his choosing the option that has occurred to him. By contrast, straightforward optimific reasoning imposes a positive condition on Watson's reasoning: it must ascertain that there is a reason of a particular sort *for* choosing that option, namely, that the option under consideration is the best alternative open to him. Now we might argue that one can be in a position to judge that there are *no* reasons for *not* choosing to fry oneself some bacon and eggs only if one is in a position to judge that frying oneself some bacon and eggs is the *best* option open: that is, that Donagan's negative condition will be satisfied only when the positive condition required by optimific reasoning is satisfied. But it is not obvious that this is so, and since Donagan's position allows us

[21] Ibid., p. 49.

to leave that question open, we can treat it as offering an account of the necessity characteristic of practical reasoning that is distinct from the account provided by the model of optimific reasoning.[22]

Donagan, then, can be taken as suggesting what we might call the *nihil obstat* model of practical reasoning: practical reasoning that identifies a way in which the agent can attain the end she wants (whether or not that way is judged to be the optimal or a necessary way of attaining that end) makes rationally necessary—and hence can explain—the agent's choosing that way of attaining her end, provided that the agent believes nothing stands in the way of her choosing it. Reasoning of the sort Donagan describes in (F) may be presented schematically as follows:

Nihil obstat necessity
    (1) S wanted G
    (2) S believed that doing A was a suitable way of bringing G about
    (3) S judged that there was *no* reason for *not* doing A
So (4) S chose to do A

Donagan's model, I think, constitutes a genuine advance over the other models we have looked at and brings to light an important characteristic of practical reasoning, namely, that its primary function is to uncover some *suitable* way of attaining our end rather than to narrow the range of our alternatives to some single course of action that is, from a rational point of view, *unavoidable*. But Donagan's account of Watson's ruminations, like the other accounts, still requires too much of practical reasoners, as I now argue.

3. Practical Reasoning without Necessity

My own view is that practical reasoning fully explanatory of human actions need not manifest *nihil obstat* necessity or any other form of rational necessity. I defend this view in two stages. First (in this section), I explain what I take to be important about cases like that of the apocryphal Dr. Watson. Then (in sections 4 through 6) I develop and defend a part of Aquinas's general account of practical reasoning that explains both why cases of this sort should be central to our understanding of practical reasoning and how the practical reasoning they involve can be

---

[22] Perhaps Donagan's account should be thought of as describing a genus of which straightforward optimific reasoning is a species.

logically defective, strictly speaking, and nevertheless adequately explain the choices and actions to which it gives rise.

Let me be clear: I do not want to deny that practical reasoning sometimes conforms to one or another of the models we have looked at or that practical reasoning conforming to these models can adequately explain the choices and actions to which it gives rise. I want to insist, however, that there are important sorts of cases in which the agent has some goal, decides on some way of achieving it which she judges to be suitable, and acts in that way for that reason *without* ever having decided (or believed) what the models we have looked at require her to have decided or believed. We can imagine that the story lying behind Donagan's example is just as simple as it at first seems: Watson wanders sleepily into the kitchen one morning wanting breakfast; it occurs to him that fried bacon and eggs would make a nice breakfast and that bacon and eggs are in the larder; and, straightaway, without giving it another thought, he sets about frying himself bacon and eggs.

Two features are essential to the example as just described—and, it seems to me, to a great deal of ordinary practical reasoning: (a) the agent's practical reasoning turns up a course of action that seems to the agent a *suitable* way of attaining her goal, and (b) the agent chooses that course of action straightaway, without any significant further reflection, *solely* on the basis of the judgment that it is a suitable way of attaining her goal. In virtue of these characteristics, the reasoning manifested in cases of this sort will fail to be conclusive or exhaustive, and so will fail both to narrow the range of reasonable options to some one course of action— as is required by the models of hypothetical and optimific necessity— and to bring deliberation to a principled close in the way Donagan's *nihil obstat* model requires. We might think of the cases that manifest these features as being cases of choice or action that are to some extent spontaneous insofar as they spring from practical reasoning that is not exhaustive or conclusive in either of these ways.

I am supposing, then, that the story of Watson's ruminations about breakfast is complete as I have told it, that there are no suppressed or implicit deliberations, judgments, or beliefs which, if made explicit, would show his reasoning to be an instance of one of the sorts of necessity we have looked at. I am supposing, in other words, that Watson's reasoning can be presented without lacunae in just the way Donagan first presents it at (B) above. My thesis, then, is that (B) can be a correct and complete description of Watson's practical reasoning and that (B1)–(B3) can both identify the reason on the basis of which Watson chooses to fry himself some bacon and eggs and constitute an adequate reasons-explanation of that choice. Put more generally, in cases of the sort I have in mind, given the agent's desire or intention, the mere belief on the agent's part that a given way of satisfying that desire is suitable is sufficient to account for her choosing to satisfy it in that way.

4. Aquinas on Non-Necessitating Practical Reasoning

I want now to turn to Aquinas's account of practical reasoning. Aquinas explains practical reasoning on analogy with theoretical reasoning. But he parts company with many philosophers—including some of those whose views we have been looking at—in supposing that practical reasoning is not to be understood, on analogy with the paradigms of theoretical reasoning, as characterized by any sort of necessity. His view seems to be that far from rationally requiring an agent to choose or act in certain ways, practical reasoning is the source or root of a kind of rational *indeterminacy* in the will: "Therefore, since the will moves itself by means of deliberation and deliberation is a non-demonstrative kind of inquiry that can go in different directions [*ad opposita viam habens*], the will moves itself not necessarily" (QDM 6.1).[23] He expresses this view in a number of texts in which his primary objective is to establish that human beings are significantly free, and he clearly thinks that establishing the possibility of non-necessitating practical reasoning is crucial for establishing that human beings have freedom of choice.[24]

Moreover, Aquinas views the analogy between practical and theoretical reasoning as supporting and explaining the claim that deliberation is a source of a kind of indeterminacy, not as undermining that claim. His elaborate development of the analogy provides the framework for

---

[23] See also *ST* IaIIae.6.2 ad2: "A human being is master of his own acts by virtue of the fact that he engages in deliberation about them, for by virtue of the fact that deliberating reason can go in different directions, the will can go in any of them"; and *ST* IaIIae.17.1 ad2: "As far as its subject is concerned, the root of freedom is the will, but as far as its cause is concerned, it is reason. For it is because reason can have different conceptions of what is good that the will can incline freely toward different things. Hence philosophers define free will as '*liberum arbitrium* arising from reason,' implying that reason is the cause of freedom." Aquinas understands the phrase *ad opposita* (which I render 'toward different things' and 'in different directions') broadly, as allowing for the possibility of both contrary and contradictory deliberative results—see section 5 below.

[24] "Does the will will anything of necessity?" (*ST* Ia.82.1); "Does the will will everything it wills of necessity?" (*ST* Ia.82.2); "Do human beings have *liberum arbitrium*?" (*ST* Ia.83.1); "Is the will moved necessarily by its object?" (*ST* IaIIae.10.2); "Do human beings choose with necessity or freely?" (*ST* IaIIae.13.6; cf. QDM 6.1). Other contexts containing important expressions of this view include his discussion of natural and human law (*ST* Ia-IIae.92–94) and of the intellectual virtue associated with practical reasoning, namely, prudence (*ST* IaIIae.57–58 and IIaIIae.47.6).

sorting out the respects in which acts of will are and are not subject to rational necessity.

It is not of necessity that the will wills whatever it wills. In order to make this evident we must notice that just as the intellect adheres to the first principles naturally and of necessity, so the will adheres to the ultimate end. . . . Now there are some intelligible objects that are not necessarily connected with the first principles: for example, contingent propositions, the denial of which does not lead to a denial of [any] first principles. The intellect does not assent of necessity to these. But there are some necessary propositions that have a necessary connection with first principles: for example, demonstrable conclusions, a denial of which leads to a denial of first principles. The intellect assents to these of necessity, once it has recognized the necessary connection these conclusions have to the principles through the demonstrative inference; but it does not assent of necessity until it recognizes the necessity of a connection of this sort through the demonstration. The case is the same with regard to the will. For there are certain particular goods that are not necessarily connected with happiness, because one can be happy without them. The will does not adhere of necessity to things of this sort. But there are some things that have a necessary connection with happiness, namely, the things by virtue of which a human being adheres to God, in whom alone true happiness consists. Nevertheless, until the necessity of this sort of connection is demonstrated through the certitude of the divine vision, the will does not adhere to God of necessity, nor does it adhere of necessity to the things that are associated with God. . . . Hence, it is clear that it is not of necessity that the will wills whatever it wills. [*ST* Ia.82.2][25]

That which is always and necessarily true moves intellect to its act (intellectual assent to that truth) out of natural necessity; that which is perfectly and unqualifiedly good moves the will to its act (the willing of that good) out of natural necessity.[26] But because acts of intellect and will require the cognition of their objects, their being necessitated by certain objects depends not only on the nature of those objects but also

[25] See the appendix to this essay for my schematization of the distinctions Aquinas draws in this passage. See *ST* Ia.82.2 ad2 and *ST* IaIIae.10.2 ad3: "The ultimate end moves the will of necessity because it is the complete good; so, too, whatever is ordered to this end, without which the end cannot be attained: for example, existing and living and things of this sort. But one who wills the end does not of necessity will other things without which the end can be attained, just as one who believes the principles does not of necessity believe conclusions without which the principles can be true." Passages such as these and those cited in note 23 above place it beyond doubt that Aquinas does not view practical reasoning as proceeding deductively from a priori first principles, contrary to what Nussbaum claims about his position (*Aristotle's De motu animalium*, pp. 167–70).

[26] *ST* IaIIae.10.2c and the replies to the objections; see also Ia.82.2 ad2.

on the agent's being cognizant of them. Hence, only truths that are *recognized* as being necessary—those that are evident to the cognizer and those that are seen to be demonstrable—necessitate intellectual assent, and only that which is *conceived* as the perfect good (and any good seen to be necessarily connected with it) necessitates the will.

If we focus for a moment on the case of intellect and its act of assent, we can see how this sort of account of the rational soul's powers and their activities leaves room for indeterminacy of two sorts.[27] On the one hand, certain things can be objects of intellect which nevertheless are not of the right sort to necessitate assent. Aquinas tells us that these are contingent truths.[28] We might think of the sort of indeterminacy the intellect has when confronted with such things as being due to a kind of *ontological* gap between the power and its object, since it depends on the nature or character of the particular objects. On the other hand, certain objects, which in themselves are of the right sort to necessitate intellect, can nevertheless fail to do so because they are not recognized as the sort of things they are: Aquinas's example is demonstrable truths whose demonstrations we don't know. We might think of this sort of indeterminacy as being due to an *epistemic* gap between the power and its object, since it obtains because of the possibility of our failure to recognize certain objects for what they are.[29]

Aquinas uses the analogy between practical and theoretical reasoning to motivate his claim that both these kinds of indeterminacy can characterize acts of the will. The will is necessitated by its nature with respect to willing its ultimate end, the perfect and complete good—happiness—and anything that is seen to be necessary for attaining it. But epistemically grounded indeterminacy enters here because in this life we lack certainty about what things satisfy these descriptions: we needn't will God as our ultimate end because we may (mistakenly, on Aquinas's view) suppose that our ultimate end is to be found in some-

---

[27] Both of these sorts of indeterminacy have to do with what Aquinas calls the *specification* of the act (of intellect or of will). He locates a third kind of indeterminacy in our *exercise* of these acts, allowing that in many cases in which the power is necessitated with respect to its act by a particular object, the act remains unnecessitated in another respect: namely, by virtue of its being open to us not to exercise the act. See, e.g., *ST* IaIIae.10.2 and *QDM* 6.1.

[28] Aquinas does not explicitly provide for exceptions for special sorts of contingent truths: namely, those to which we are epistemically related in such a way that our awareness of them guarantees their truth and compels our assent. Contingent propositions such as "I exist," "I am in pain now," and "I seem to see white" may be of this sort.

[29] For more on Aquinas's epistemology, see my "Theory of Knowledge" in the *Cambridge Companion to Aquinas*, ed. Norman Kretzmann and Eleonore Stump (Cambridge: Cambridge University Press, 1993), pp. 160–95.

thing else.[30] With respect to our willing of things we take to be necessarily connected with our ultimate end, there will typically be epistemically grounded indeterminacy twice over. For in most cases we will lack certainty about whether these things are truly necessary for our ultimate end and whether that particular ultimate end is in fact the perfect, complete good. With respect to its willing of other things—the particular goods that are the analogues of contingent intelligible objects—there will be ontologically grounded indeterminacy.

Aquinas's notion of epistemically grounded indeterminacy in the will is interesting and important to his general account of practical reasoning, but I am leaving it aside in order to focus on the other sort of indeterminacy brought to light by his analogy. The logical gap that prevents a piece of practical reasoning from manifesting any sort of rational necessity can be due to an underlying ontological shortcoming in the will's object, and this locus of indeterminacy in the will is crucial for making sense of practical reasoning that has the features essential to cases such as that of Dr. Watson.

5. Ontologically Grounded Indeterminacy in the Will

As we have seen, Aquinas's idea is to exploit not the analogy between practical reasoning and theoretical *demonstrative* reasoning (where there is both logical necessity in the inference and ontological necessity in the subject matter) but rather the analogy between practical reasoning and the non-demonstrative reasoning characteristic of a certain kind of theoretical thought about contingent matters (where there is no necessity). "Reason having to do with contingent matters can go in different directions [*habet viam ad opposita*], as is clear in the case of dialectical syllogisms. . . . Now particular cases of things that might be done [*operabilia*] have a kind of contingency, and so in such matters reason's judgment is open to different things and is not determined to one" (*ST* Ia.83.1).

Aquinas claims that what he here calls dialectical reasoning "can go in different directions," and he explains this by saying that the truth of its premises is consistent with the falsity of its conclusion.[31] Given the truth of its premises, dialectical reasoning gives reason to believe that its conclusion is true, but the conclusion need not be true. Typically, human infants are born with five fingers on each hand, and so in the case

---

[30] See *QDM* 6.1 ad9.
[31] For Aquinas's account of the general scope and structure of theoretical reasoning, see his prologue to *In PA* and my discussion of it in "Theory of Knowledge."

of a given birth one has reason to believe that the infant will have five fingers on each hand. The infant's being born with a deformed hand, however, is consistent with the evidence one has for believing that it will be physically normal. Aquinas holds that in many cases practical reasoning is analogous to this, and we can see the point in thinking of Watson's ruminations about breakfast in this way. Given what Watson wants and believes, he has reason to fry himself bacon and eggs, but it is also consistent with what he wants and believes that he choose otherwise: his practical reasoning can go in another direction even while he retains his desire for a good breakfast and his belief that frying himself some bacon and eggs would satisfy that desire.

The essential feature in cases of practical reasoning that can go in different directions is that the end the agent has set herself can be realized in more than one way. In keeping with Aquinas's metaphor, we might think of the various alternatives as being, from the deliberating agent's perspective, distinct but convergent paths each of which leads to the agent's end and all of which are open to her. The metaphor of directions or paths (*viae*) makes it natural to think of the relevant alternatives as external means to the end: preliminary courses of action or purely instrumental means that in some way lead to or are causally productive of the end—for example, the various routes a person might take to get to the grocery store are relevant alternatives open to him in respect of his end of doing his shopping. But clearly Aquinas does not intend the alternatives open to the deliberating agent to be restricted to external means only. Many of his examples are what we might think of as specifications of an abstract or generic end: God (or the vision of God) is a way of specifying our ultimate end, not an external means to it; it is a way of identifying what our ultimate end consists in. But it is only one alternative specification among many. Traveling by horse or by foot are two alternative specifications of the end of *traveling to* Rome (though they are external means to *attending a meeting in* Rome). Swimming and playing tennis are two alternative specifications of the end of taking some exercise. Settling on particular specifications of more general ends is an important function of practical reasoning and one that Aquinas often has in mind in these contexts.[32]

In any case, he typically lumps these different kinds of alternatives together, calling them "things that are for the sake of the end" (*ad finem*) or, as here, "particular goods." The latter designation is appropriate not only because goods of this sort are often concrete, individual things or actions we can attain or perform here and now but also because Aquinas

[32] See my "Ultimate Ends in Practical Reasoning: Aquinas's Aristotelian Moral Psychology and Anscombe's Fallacy," *Philosophical Review* 100 (1991): 31–66.

thinks of practical reasoning—which starts from our ends or goals and moves toward fully specified individual actions we think we can actually perform—as a process from what is general or universal to what is particular and fully specified. The starting points of our practical reasoning are often general in the sense that they lack the specificity, the particularity required to elicit immediate action. That is why we must deliberate about how to attain them and continue our deliberation until we reach something we can actually do. I cannot act on my desire to take some exercise until and unless I have specified it sufficiently ("I'll swim rather than play tennis") and settled on means I can undertake without further deliberation ("I'll walk to the pool rather than take the bus"). My end of taking some exercise is a universal of which relevant particular instances for me are swimming and playing tennis. Practical deliberation, then, is essentially a process by which we particularize our ends in order to be able to act on them. In many cases, the relation between our ends or universal goods and the particular goods by virtue of which they are realizable will be indeterminate. That is to say, in many cases the realizability of our ends will not depend on any one particular way of realizing them.

Aquinas bases his view that there is a kind of ontological indeterminacy with respect to certain acts of will on this idea of the indeterminacy in the relation between a universal good and its particular realizations. Practical reasoning is the process whereby we instantiate our universal ends in certain particular, realizable goods, and that sort of process is often logically indeterminate: "It need not always be the case that a human being, by virtue of its end, is subject to necessity with respect to choosing things that are for the sake of the end. This is because it is not the case that everything that is for the sake of the end is such that the end cannot be attained without it, or, if there is something of this sort, it is not always thought of under that description" (*ST* IaIIae.13.6 ad1). In certain cases, then, there can be a gap between a piece of practical reasoning and the choice to which it gives rise because the reasoning's non-orectic component identifies as a particular good what is only one particular way of realizing the general end identified by its orectic component. The ontological gap between the will and its particular object is mirrored by the logical gap between the reasoning and the choice.

6. Rational Indeterminacy and Adequate Reasons-Explanations

This much of Aquinas's account suggests, I think, why choice and action that are more or less spontaneous should be relatively common features of our reason-governed practical lives. A significant portion of practical reasoning is by its nature bound to be inconclusive and non-exhaustive. But we have not yet seen how practical reasoning of that sort can be explanatory. If Watson's choosing to fry himself bacon and eggs and his choosing to make himself some other good breakfast are both consistent with his endorsing (B1)–(B3), how can his endorsing that piece of practical reasoning explain his doing the former? In order to answer this question we need to look at another part of Aquinas's account of practical reasoning: his account of the nature of *the will* and its role in practical reasoning. A reasons-explanation is sufficient to explain an agent's choice or action not by virtue of some feature of the reasoning it cites but by virtue of the reasoning's being backed and driven by an act of will. It is the volitional component of practical reasoning that makes it genuinely practical and suitable for giving rise to action.

On Aquinas's view the will is, by nature, an appetitive power and as such is naturally inclined toward its object, namely, the good as it is conceived by intellect.[33] To say that the will is inclined toward its object is almost to put it too weakly, for in this Aristotelian psychological theory the appetitive powers are the motive powers in human beings, the powers without which human beings would be utterly inert. The will, then, is the causal power behind our actions. Of course, it depends in certain ways on intellect: for its ends, which intellect must apprehend for it, and for the sort of deliberation that finds ways of attaining those ends.[34] But it is the presence of will that ultimately makes our reasoning practical, that makes us agents.

To say that we are beings with rational appetite or will, then, is to say that we are characterized by a motive power that is incessantly pulsing toward action but can find no outlet unless and until it is given a specific object, a good as conceived and made sufficiently particular by intellect. As Aquinas sees it, it is a mistake to think of the will as being at rest or in equilibrium until it is activated or energized by something else. The will *is* the motive force, the activator in human beings; it is not in equilibrium but rather positively inclined toward the good, actively pressing for its realization. Given its natural inclination, then, all that's required for the will to act is apprehension by intellect of a way of attaining the good. When presented with a particular way of attaining the good, the will will act—unless it is impeded.[35]

---

[33] *ST* Ia.80.1; IaIIae.8.1–2; IaIIae.19.3.

[34] *ST* IaIIae.9.1, 4; IaIIae.13–14.

[35] "Not every cause produces its effect of necessity, even if it is a sufficient cause, because a cause can be impeded in such a way that sometimes its effect does not follow: for example, causes in nature, which produce their effects not of necessity but for the most part. . . . In this way, therefore, the cause that brings about the will's willing a given thing need not bring this about of necessity. This is because an impediment can be set up by the will itself

This general point about the will is illustrated in a particular piece of practical reasoning. As we have seen, it is essential to practical reasoning that it start from or be backed by appetite: practical reasoning is directed toward action in the full-blooded sense that it is prompted by a real desire for some end—what Aquinas calls an intention—which moves reason to deliberate about how to attain the end.[36] Given that the force of appetite is pressing through the reasoning toward action—that the will is already intending or aiming at attaining the end—all that is required for this instance of practical reasoning to give rise to action is that deliberation uncover some suitable way of attaining the end. Having been presented with what the deliberating agent recognizes as a suitable way of proceeding, the agent will act. All that is needed to provide an outlet for Watson's intention to have a good breakfast is his judgment that the bacon and eggs that are ready to hand would make a good one.

We might say, then, that because will's positive inclination stands behind it, practical reasoning's function is primarily to satisfy appetite, to find a way of attaining what appetite seeks. Higher aspirations—for example, finding the *best* way of attaining the end—may be laudable and, in special circumstances, important, but they are not central to practical reasoning. Donagan seems to me to have put this point nicely in the passage we have already looked at: "Processes of deliberation like our apocryphal Watson's are attempts to answer not questions of the form 'What *must* you do that will bring about such and such, which you wish?' but rather those of the form 'What *can* you do that will bring it about?'"[37] The conceptually central case, then, is the one in which the agent finds her way through to a *suitable* choice or action, not the case in which she finds her way through to the best or only one. It is evidence of this that in situations of special importance where we feel we must do better than what is merely suitable, we make a conscious effort to engage in optimific practical reasoning, being careful to search thoroughly and creatively for alternatives and for evidence relevant to their relative preferability. That situations of this sort call for special effort shows that optimific reasoning of this sort is not the standard case.

So genuinely practical reasoning—reasoning that is prompted and driven by appetite or intention—has a sort of presumption in favor of action, which is rooted in the will's natural inclination toward the good. Acting when presented with a good—that is, when in possession of a

---

either by removing the sort of thought that leads it to willing or by thinking the opposite, namely, that the object proposed as good is not good in some respect" (QDM 6.1 ad15).

[36] *ST* IaIIae.9.4; IaIIae.12.

[37] Donagan, *Choice*, p. 45.

reason composed of an intention to attain some end and a corresponding belief that a certain action is a suitable way of attaining that end—
constitutes a kind of default setting. A simple reason of that sort, therefore, can by itself be rationally sufficient for action.

Having located the root of explanatory practical reasoning's sufficiency in the will's motive power, we can see where the accounts that require reasons-explanations to manifest some sort of necessity or con-
clusiveness go wrong. Supposing that the impetus for action must come
from the *reasoning*, they understandably require that the reasoning be
compelling. In terms of the metaphor I have been using, they suppose
that practical reasoning must provide sufficient force to move us from
an initial state of rest or inaction. If our initial state as we undertake deliberation is rest, if practical reasoning has a presumption in favor of inaction, then in order to account for our acting our reasoning must necessitate, that is, must identify something we cannot reasonably avoid
doing. We will have to think of deliberation as trying to answer not the
question "What *can* I do to bring about such and such, which I wish?"
but the question "What *must* I do to bring it about?"

Moreover, we are now in a position to see why we need not follow
Donagan in reintroducing a kind of reason-based sufficiency at a different point in the process. Donagan recognizes that an agent's desire
for some end together with her judgment that a certain course of action
is a suitable way of attaining that end can be sufficient to account for her
choosing to act in that way, *provided it is not the case that she believes there
to be some reason against* her choosing to act in that way. That's right. But
what Donagan mistakenly goes on to assert—and schematizes in steps
(F4) and (F5) of his account of Watson's ruminations—is that the agent's
desire and judgment of suitability can fully account for her choice
provided she believes that there is no reason against her choosing in that
way. Of course, it does not follow from the fact that it is not the case
that someone believes that P, that that person believes that it is not the
case that P: it is not the case that Alice believes that Socrates died in
399 B.C., but it does not follow that she believes that Socrates did *not* die
in 399 B.C.—being only seven years old, Alice as yet has no beliefs at all
about Socrates' death.

It is not clear whether Donagan's proposal for filling out Watson's reasoning rests essentially on a fallacious inference of this sort, but we can
see how the allure of a certain way of thinking about practical reasoning—the idea that, because practical reasoning is *reasoning*, its capacity
for accounting for an agent's choices and actions must depend on its
logical tightness—might tempt one toward his solution. The same idea
has led others to suppose that all our genuinely explanatory practical

reasoning must manifest hypothetical or optimific necessity. Those who take up this idea are forced by it to require practical reasoners to be far more sophisticated and thorough than they in fact generally are or need to be. Contrary to what these philosophers suppose, we are not, most of the time, terribly concerned about whether the alternative courses of action that occur to us are somehow rationally compelling; like Dr. Watson we very often simply seize on the first thing that comes along that will satisfy our want. In doing so we are no doubt sometimes irresponsible, imprudent, or stupid, but practical reasoning that is irresponsible, imprudent, or stupid can nevertheless be perfectly intelligible and can adequately explain our choices and actions.

So Donagan was right to point out that simple practical reasoning of the sort described by (B1)–(B3) can explain choices like that described in (B4), provided the agent sees no reason against choosing in that way. But he was wrong to think that, in order to take account of this proviso, practical reasoning of the sort described by (B1)–(B3) needs to be supplemented with more practical reasoning on the agent's part. The correct view is that if practical reasoning such as that described by (B1)–(B3) is to be an adequate reasons-explanation of the choice described by (B4), it needs to be *true* that no such countervailing reasons occurred to the agent. It need not be the case, however, that the agent *judged or believed* that there were no such reasons.

Because it need not be grounded in any sort of rational necessity, this will-based sufficiency in practical reasoning leaves open the possibility of practical reasoning's taking different courses. Given that the intention to attain some end is in place, deliberation's having identified a suitable way of attaining that end can be sufficient, from a rational point of view, to move us to act in that way. But the fact that we judge it to be only a suitable course of action leaves room for our entertaining considerations that can lead us in different directions. That is to say, the rational force that characterizes these simple pieces of practical reasoning is defeasible. We might think of what Aquinas calls impediments as being considerations or reasons that can defeat the standing presumption in favor of a given suitable good. As he points out, for any particular good there will always be respects in which the object is not good, and in many cases there will be other ways of attaining the same end. If Watson, for example, calls to mind the fact that bacon and eggs are high in fat and cholesterol, that may well impede his desire for a good breakfast from giving rise to action via his belief that bacon and eggs, which are ready to hand, would be a good one. Similarly, Watson's fondness for kippers or his loathing of the prospect of having to wash the frying pan might defeat his reason for frying himself some bacon and eggs or, even if not defeating it, might nevertheless require practical reasoning on his part that is more complex than our simple account describes. Of course, the presence of potential defeaters of this sort is a common feature of practical reasoning, and so in many cases a simple reasons-explanation of the sort I have insisted on for Watson's case will not capture practical reasoning's complexity and, hence, will not constitute an adequate explanation. But if I am right, the simple account will sometimes capture it both correctly and completely.

I have set aside questions about reasons as the causes of human action in order to focus on issues associated with the rational force of pieces of practical reasoning and the role that sort of force plays in our reasons-explanations of action. But I would like to conclude by at least pointing in the direction of that other part of Aquinas's account. Aquinas holds that the desires and beliefs that explain our actions also cause them. But he also wants to argue that in many cases the practical reasoning that causes a given action does not causally necessitate it, and so he denies not only that explanatory practical reasoning must be rationally necessitating but also that it must be causally necessitating.[38] His argument for the causal indeterminacy of our free choices gives a central place to the notion of the defeasibility of practical reasoning which has emerged in my discussion of the rational force of practical reasoning. The presence or possibility of potential defeaters of a given reason for acting represent the possibility for alternative deliberative results, that is, for an agent's obtaining or giving herself effective countervailing reasons. If it is sometimes up to the agent herself whether or not she undertakes or extends her practical reasoning so as to look for and take account of potential defeaters—that is, if on some occasions she is not causally necessitated with respect to the reasons she includes in her practical reasoning—then the reasons on which she acts can sometimes be causally sufficient and non-necessitating. Insofar as she can cast about for relevant reasons for acting otherwise—either reasons she possesses but has been hitherto inattentive to or reasons she does not possess but that are accessible to her—she is not causally constrained by reasons that are nevertheless sufficient for acting. On Aquinas's view, therefore, free choice is grounded not so much in an irreducible ability to *choose* between alternatives (as many proponents of an incompatibilist account of free will have maintained) as in an irreducible ability to give oneself alternative reasons for acting. This, I think, is what he means when he says that "as far as its subject is concerned, the root of freedom

[38] I argue for an incompatibilist reading of Aquinas in "Aquinas's Libertarian Account of Free Choice," *Revue Internationale de Philosophie* 2 (1998): 309–28.

is the will, but as far as its cause is concerned, it is reason; . . . that is why philosophers define free will as 'free judgment [*liberum arbitrium*] arising from reason,' implying that reason is the cause of freedom" (*ST* IaIIae.17.1 ad2).[39] But as I say, this is another part of Aquinas's rich account of human practical activity.[40]

[39] I find a view similar to the one I attribute here to Aquinas in Augustine. See my "Primal Sin," in *The Augustinian Tradition*, ed. Gareth B. Matthews (Berkeley: University of California Press, 1999), pp. 110–39.

[40] I am grateful to John Boler, Richard Fumerton, Norman Kretzmann, David Schmidtz, Christopher Shields, Eleonore Stump, and Terry Irwin for comments on drafts of this paper, and to audiences at the ninth International Congress of Medieval Philosophy in Ottawa, the University of North Carolina at Chapel Hill, the University of Iowa, and Cornell University to whom I read previous versions of it. I also acknowledge support for work on this project from the National Humanities Center in 1992–93 and from a University of Iowa Faculty Scholarship.

Appendix

	Intellect	Assent	Will	Willing
Proper object	What is true (intellect assents to propositions insofar as they are true)		What is good (will wills things insofar as they are good)	
Perfect object[a]	necessary truths		perfect good	
primary	first principles known unknown	NECESSITATED E-INDETERMINATE[b]	happiness known unknown	NECESSITATED E-INDETERMINATE[b]
secondary	demonstrable conclusions known unknown	NECESSITATED E-INDETERMINATE[b]	things necessary for happiness known unknown	NECESSITATED E-INDETERMINATE[b]
Imperfect object (not necessarily connected with the perfect object)	contingent truths	O-INDETERMINATE[c]	particular goods	O-INDETERMINATE[c]

ST Ia.82.2: It is not of necessity that the will wills whatever it wills. In order to make this evident we must notice that just as the intellect adheres to the first principles naturally and of necessity, so the will adheres to the ultimate end. . . . Now there are some intelligible objects that are not necessarily connected with the first principles: for example, contingent propositions, the denial of which does not lead to a denial of [any] first principles. The intellect does not assent of necessity to these. But there are some necessary propositions that have a necessary connection with first principles: for example, demonstrable conclusions, a denial of which leads to a denial of first principles. The intellect assents to these of necessity, once it has recognized the necessary connection these conclusions have to the principles through the demonstrative inference; but it does not assent of necessity until it recognizes the necessity of a connection of this sort through the demonstration. The case is the same with regard to the will. For there are certain particular goods that are not necessarily connected with happiness, because one can be happy without them. The will does not adhere of necessity to things of this sort. But there are some things that have a necessary connection with happiness, namely, the things by virtue of which a human being adheres to God, in whom alone true happiness consists. Nevertheless, until the necessity of this sort of connection is demonstrated through the certitude of the divine vision, the will does not adhere to God of necessity, nor does it adhere of necessity to the things that are associated with God. . . . Hence, it is clear that it is not of necessity that the will wills whatever it wills.

[a] That which is in every respect of the kind to move that power (*ST* IaIIae.10.2 ad1).
[b] = epistemically indeterminate.
[c] = ontologically indeterminate.

JOHN BOLER

∂⋅

Aquinas on Exceptions in Natural Law

In the Treatise on Law—that is, *Summa theologiae* IaIIae.90–97[1]—
Aquinas develops in somewhat more detail an analogy he alludes to in
a number of places between practical reasoning and speculative reasoning (that is, the reasoning of demonstrative science).[2] In setting out his
case, however, he calls attention to an important difference between the
two because of a certain mutability in practical reason.

> It is clear, therefore, that as regards the common principles of speculative
> or practical reason, there is same truth and rectitude for all, and it is
> equally known [by all]. Indeed, with regard to the proper conclusions of
> speculative reason, truth is the same for all but not equally known to all. . . .
> But as to the proper conclusions of practical reason, truth or rectitude is not
> the same for all, and even among those for whom it is the same, it is not
> equally known. Thus it is right and true for all that action be carried out ac-
> cording to reason. From this principle it follows, however, as if a proper

---

[1] The Latin text I have used is the Leonine edition as presented in *ST* (Marietti). I have
followed the translation, with some adjustments, in *ST* vols. 28–29 (Blackfriars). The secondary literature on Aquinas's discussion of natural law is extensive and that on his moral
theory even more so. M. B. Crowe, *The Changing Profile of the Natural Law* (The Hague:
Martinus Nijhoff, 1977), has a good bibliography, but of course some very significant
work has been done since then. Robert Henle, S.J., *The Treatise on Law* (Notre Dame, Ind.:
Notre Dame University Press, 1993), provides a detailed commentary. In part because of
my special focus, the works I cite form an idiosyncratic group.

[2] There is no one text in which Aquinas sets out the comparison and contrast in full detail. In the Treatise on Law it is introduced briefly in *ST* IaIIae.90.1 and 91.3, developed at
greater length in 94.2 and 4, and alluded to in passing at a number of other places. The full
text (in English and Latin) of the body of articles 2 and 4 of question 94 appears in an appendix to this essay.

conclusion, that deposits [i.e., goods held in trust] be returned; and this is true for the most part. But it can happen in some case that it would be ruinous [*damnosum*], and as a result irrational, if the deposit were returned: for example, if someone sought it to fight against [one's] country.[3]

The immediate setting of Aquinas's remark, of course, is a discussion of law. But traditionally, and I think correctly, commentators have seen this treatment of practical reason as an essential element in his moral theory. While the relation of practical reason to morality and that of morality to law are themselves complex and controversial matters, I think the issue of mutability in practical reason can and deserves to be treated in relative isolation.[4]

What concerns me, then, is not that one might be led to expect Aquinas to say, for example, "Killing the innocent is wrong for the most part," or "Adultery is wrong *ceteris paribus*." It is, rather, a more basic and in a way more abstract issue: that is, the original analogy between speculative and practical reason requires that morality and law be matters of principled reasoning, but it would make a shambles of that if there were no objective way—a way in some sense "the same for all"—to assess claims of exception in any area open to whatever sort(s) of mutability Aquinas means to allow.[5] By analyzing cases where Aquinas, in the Treatise on Law and elsewhere, describes exceptions to practical

[3] *ST* IaIIae.94.4; see appendix.

[4] It is impossible to ignore the relevance of Aquinas's moral and legal theory, of course, but I hope to focus on the peculiar issue of mutability as much as possible. E.g., I stay with the somewhat awkward "common conceptions and proper conclusions" and purposely avoid the more familiar "primary and secondary precepts." The latter usage plays an important role in the secondary literature on Aquinas's moral theory, but that involves more than the contrast of mutable and immutable precepts. (Crowe, *The Changing Profile*, pp. 179–80, offers the useful caution that primary and secondary precepts here should not be confused with Aquinas's talk—later abandoned—in *In Sent* about primary and secondary goals.) For traditional (if controversial) accounts of the Treatise in relation to Aquinas's moral theory, see R. A. Armstrong, *Primary and Secondary Precepts in Thomasitic Natural Law Teaching* (The Hague: Martinus Nijhoff, 1966); D. J. O'Connor, *Aquinas and Natural Law* (London: Macmillan, 1968); Henle, *The Treatise on Law*; and Ralph McInerny, *Aquinas on Human Action* (Washington, D.C.: Catholic University of America Press, 1992), chaps. 5 and 6.

[5] The obvious general precedent is Aristotle's remark in *Nicomachean Ethics* 1.3 (1094b13) about not introducing a precision beyond what the subject matter will bear. But to take the Aristotelian maxim as an open-ended license to allow exceptions is simply to sanction mischief. We are all familiar, after all, with the unhealthy tendency in moral crises to view our own case as unique, or to rely on fashion or social pressure in allowing the "obvious" exception. The problem has been recognized by both Armstrong (*Primary and Secondary Precepts*) and Crowe (*The Changing Profile*); my concern is to introduce some structure into the complaint.

precepts,[6] I hope to cast some light on the problem and go at least part of the way toward its resolution.

I begin with a brief summary account of the analogy and the disanalogy between speculative and practical reason—since that is the context in which Aquinas introduces the idea of mutability of precepts—augmented with reference to some texts from his discussion of the Old Law. In section 2, I try to focus the problem of mutability by showing why it is not easily resolved. In section 3, I discuss examples that Aquinas gives of precepts that are seen to "fail" (*deficit*); in section 4, I provide a classification of the different kinds of mutability at stake, emphasizing a specific notion of "exception" that I think is essential to the distinction of "common conceptions and proper conclusions." Sections 3 and 4 represent the primary concern of the paper: to show that an understanding of different kinds of mutability and how each works will both deflect the charge of irrationality and give a more developed picture of the relation of mutable and immutable precepts. In section 5, I want at least to broach the topic of the status of mutable precepts as more than mere rules of thumb and to indicate further lines of investigation into the unique character of that sort of mutability whose instances I identify as exceptions.

1

Aquinas introduces his most detailed single account of the analogy of practical to speculative reasoning (*ST* IaIIae.94.2) with the claim he means to explain: natural law stands to practical reason as the first principles of demonstration (*principia prima demonstrationum*) stand to speculative reason, "because they are both *per se nota*."[7] Since I focus on the issue of mutability, let me emphasize at the beginning Aquinas's basic,

---

[6] What Aquinas calls principles (or premises or propositions; see note 10 below) in speculative reason, he sometimes calls precepts in practical reason. Perhaps today we automatically think of moral and legal precepts, but for Aquinas they represent only a special kind of precept within the broad range of practical reason, which is properly concerned with what is "suitable" in achieving certain ends. Aristotle's often-cited example "Dry food is good for humans to eat" or, say, "Attending concerts is a good thing for humans to do" would need a very elaborate background to make it carry moral or legal force; see also note 49 below. At least, one should resist the legalistic implications of describing Aquinas as holding a "natural law morality": see Gregory Stevens, "Moral Obligation in St. Thomas," *Modern Schoolman* 40 (1962): 1–21; and Russell Hittinger, "Natural Law and Virtue: Theories at Cross Purposes," in *Natural Law Theory: Contemporary Essays*, ed. Robert George (Oxford: Clarendon Press, 1992).

[7] See appendix. Sometimes Aquinas allows a broader sense of natural law which extends to derived precepts as well: cf. 94.6.

positive motivation for drawing the analogy.[8] In its simplest form, it is this: in practical as well as speculative matters, we have to and we can think things out. What we come to know as conclusions (that is, things known *per aliud*) is ultimately grounded in premises or principles known *per se*.[9] The latter, for Aquinas, are not innate; but he thinks that we can determine the truth of such propositions (either in obvious cases or where some special background is needed) by an understanding of their terms. One might put the point in this way: in our ratiocinations (speculative or practical) we are self-movers—that is, we undergo change in acquiring knowledge we did not have—but we are able to bring this about because of our natural intellectual capacities for making use of principles[10] that can be known to be true without themselves being conclusions.[11]

The analogy aside, however, Aquinas is clear from the beginning that there is a structural difference between practical and speculative reasoning. When he introduces the issue of mutability (IaIIae.94.4), he concentrates on the idea that practical reason deals with what is particular and contingent.[12] The Aristotelian scheme in which the object of

[8] Although Aquinas discusses mutability in *ST* IaIIae.94.4 and 5, the context of each article (indicated in the title and sed contra) is clearly oriented to the stability of natural law.

[9] Michael Tkacz, in a paper read at the 1993 American Philosophical Association Pacific meetings, argued for an interpretation of Aquinas's account of such *per se nota* propositions along the lines of Miles Burnyeat's reading of Aristotle ("Aristotle on Understanding Knowledge," in *Aristotle on Science: The Posterior Analytics*, ed. Enrico Berti [Padua: Editrice Antenore, 1981], pp. 97–139). In practical reasoning as well I think the common notions, though technically indemonstrable, are not meant by Aquinas to be a set of a priori intuitions that can be arrived at before being engaged in practice (moral or legal). They are not derived as conclusions from other propositions but discovered only as presuppositions to practice (see also note 21 below). Notice that the makeup of even the common notions can change depending on the kind of inquiry: see *ST* IaIIae.100.3 ad1, 4 ad1, and 104.1 ad3, where Aquinas includes matters of faith in the common notions (presumably of moral theology).

[10] "Principle" is one of the broadest cover terms in the scholastic vocabulary; it is anything from which anything in any way proceeds. A cause, of course, is a principle: e.g., one animal is the principle of generation of another. Moreover, for Aquinas, a concept can be a principle: as we shall see, he says that the *ratio boni* is a first principle of practical reasoning. A proposition can be a principle: e.g., the principle of noncontradiction. Conclusions as such, of course, are not principles; but if something further follows from a conclusion, or if one were to act on the basis of believing some conclusion, the conclusion (or the believing of it) could in turn be said to function as a principle. Among propositional principles we might distinguish premises (from which a conclusion follows) and principles of inference (according to which a conclusion follows). The difference is important, I think, in understanding the controversy about the status of "the" first precept of practical reason; see note 19 below.

[11] See note 21 below.

[12] "Sed ratio practica negotiatur circa contingentia, in quibus sunt operationes humanae; et ideo, etsi in communibus sit aliqua necessitas, quanto magis propria descenditur tanto magis invenitur defectus" (see appendix). Mutability, of course, can cover a variety of

science is universal and necessary, reflected even today in some contrasts between pure and applied science, takes the work of scientific inquiry (strictly speaking) to be complete with the discovery of physical laws and properties. In that setting it is a different (almost "blue-collar") activity to apply the results of "pure" science to actual, individual cases. In any event, in application to particulars, speculative reasoning is no better off than practical reasoning for Aquinas, for the conclusions of speculative reason apply to actual individuals only "for the most part."[13] The important point, however, is that the possible application to particulars does not at all affect the status of principles or conclusions in speculative reason, which Aquinas says are "the same for all."

Practical reasoning, then, is not just speculative reason applied to particular action; it must be somehow basically different in structure. The primary reason for that, I think, is brought out by Aquinas early in the Treatise. Where in speculative reason conclusions are justified or supported as following from premises (and ultimately first principles), in practical reason a conclusion that some action is to be done is supported or justified in terms of precepts oriented to some goal.[14] One might say that justification in speculative reason is a matter of "looking back" to more basic truths that support a conclusion, whereas in practical reason it is a matter of "looking ahead": that is, of orienting an action or type of action to some goal or goals that make the proposed action worth doing. The ultimate conclusions one draws in any particular case, of course, will involve an application of a precept to a particular. But the conclusions that Aquinas says hold only for the most part are not applications to particulars (as "This action is to be done") but the precepts themselves that are to be applied (as "Goods held in trust are to be returned to their rightful owner").

In sum, practical reason has to do with intelligent, goal-directed activity and is essentially concerned with the propriety (or lack of it) of par-

---

things, as I show in sections 3 and 4. In *QDM* q. 2, a. 5 ad13 Aquinas speaks of the mutability of human nature, but he clearly means variable response to varied surroundings: "et hoc continget propter mutabilitatem naturae humanae et diversas conditiones hominum et rerum, secundum diversitatem locorum et temporum." See also *ST* IaIIae.95.2 ad3, where he attributes mutability to the variety in human affairs: "propter multam varietatem rerum humanarum."

[13] "Ut in pluribus," *ST* IaIIae.94.4. The similarity to speculative reason is instructive. "Donkeys are quadrupeds" is a property that biology discovers; however, sometimes a donkey will be born with only three legs. "Some quadrupeds are three-legged" will be false if taken to mean that there is a species of quadruped that normally has three legs, but it will be true if it means that some of those individual things that are essentially quadrupeds do have only three legs. See note 74 below.

[14] See *ST* IaIIae.90.1 ad2, and 94.2 (on the place of *ratio boni*).

ticular actions. Ultimately, it is these two features that underlie the special character of practical reason, of which the mutability of its derived precepts is a symptom. An important difference in types of derivation is therefore relevant. There are some cases, Aquinas says, where one precept is deduced from another; his example is that "Killing is not to be done" is deduced from "Harm is not to be done to anyone."[15] More often, however, the conclusions of practical reason are not deductions but "determinations."[16] To cite a modern example, the U.S. traffic code requiring that one drive on the right is a determination of the idea that traffic should be orderly. The traffic law is binding because *this* determination has been established somehow (whether by edict or general agreement or convention).[17] What makes it reasonable, however, is that it is a determination of—that is, one way of achieving—the more general or higher end that traffic be orderly. In any event, defeasible precepts will be determinations and not deductions.

To return to the analogy of speculative and practical reason, then, its general lines (very roughly) go as follows.[18] There is for each a base - concept (my term): *being* for speculative reason and *good* for practical reason. Following on that, there is a "first principle": as the principle of non-contradiction stands to the *ratio entis*, so for the *ratio boni* the first principle is "Good is to be done and pursued, and evil is to be avoided."[19] Along with this first principle there are some other *per se*

---

[15] *ST* IaIIae.95.2. O'Connor, *Aquinas and Natural Law*, p. 75, says this is not a deduction because qualifications have to be put on wrongful killing (e.g., to exclude judicial execution, actions in war, and self-defense). He does not seem to notice that the very same qualifications would apply to harm. In general, O'Connor adopts a somewhat uncritical fact-value distinction that colors his assessment of Aquinas's position (cf. pp. 67–69). In fact, Aquinas, following Augustine, resorts here to what I call "interpretation" to exclude killing in war and judicial execution. This is, he thinks, a matter not of adding qualifications but rather of understanding what "killing" amounts to in the context; see *ST* IaIIae.100.8 ad3 (and note 68 below).

[16] *ST* IaIIae.95.2. One might claim that determinations (and therefore exceptions, as we shall see) arise only in connection with positive legislation (see note 33 below). But many of the examples Aquinas gives seem to me to have moral implications as well. And whether he recognized it or not, the present-day challenge to moral objectivism (much less absolutism) requires, I think, a broader relevance of the phenomenon of determination in moral issues.

[17] Aquinas points out that the force of a law derives in part from its being just (and as such being based in natural law) and in part from the authority that has established the determination; see *ST* IaIIae.95.2. This is important when assessing dispensations or exceptions.

[18] Because of the scattered character of Aquinas's presentation (see note 2 above) and variations in his terminology (see note 23 below), some reconstruction is unavoidable in setting out the full scheme. Because of my own narrow interests (see note 4 above), I omit many details.

[19] See note 10 above on the broad use of "principle." On the status and content of the first principle, see Germain Grisez, "The First Principle of Practical Reason," *Natural Law*

nota principles that are, in both speculative and practical reason, "the same for all and known to all."[20] They make up what Aquinas, following Boethius, calls "common conceptions." And then there are other propositions, either more "proper" *per se nota* propositions or conclusions,[21] which are in speculative reason "the same for all but not known to all" but which in practical reason may not be the same for all and, where they are, may not be known to all.[22]

The full scheme for the comparison and contrast of speculative and practical reason is not set out in any one text, and perhaps because of that there are anomalies in Aquinas's different descriptions.[23] He is also not lavish with examples.[24] All of that leads to some controversy in the reconstruction of the scheme as part of his moral theory. In the latter setting it is significant that after setting out "the" first principle of practical reason (*ST* IaIIae.94.2), Aquinas simply goes on to propose that the order of precepts follows the order of natural inclinations: "inclinations to good according to the nature of human beings." That order he describes as follows: first, those shared by any substance in tending to preserve itself in being; second, those shared with the other animals, involving the conjunction of male and female and the nurturing of offspring; and finally, those proper to humans, which involve tendencies to know the truth concerning God and to live in society. Inclinations, of

---

Forum 10 (1965): 168–96. I have tried to be cautious in my formulations throughout so as not to commit the text to one side of a controversy about the character of the "first precept" of natural law and the nature of moral reasoning in Aquinas. As it happens, I side with Grisez—because, in brief, the "first principle" is supposed to be an analogue to the principle of non-contradiction, and I think it must function more as a principle of inference than as a premise (see note 10). But nothing (I think) in my thesis or its support depends on this.

[20] The "same for all" and what is "known to all" are best regarded as technical expressions; Aquinas apparently takes them from Boethius: see note 21.

[21] When discussing speculative reason, Aquinas draws a distinction within *per se nota* propositions between those "known to all" and those "known only to the wise." One can perhaps gloss them to eliminate the psychological (and so inexact) aspect in their description. The category of those known only to the wise is of some interest, however, since it allows that a priori truths can be discovered empirically: e.g., that water is H_2O—a claim better known to the modern reader through the work of Saul Kripke and Hilary Putnam. One could, I think, find something similar among the precepts of practical reason, but Aquinas does not follow out the parallel there, speaking only of common conceptions and proper conclusions.

[22] This paragraph is a résumé of *ST* IaIIae.94.2 and 4. See the appendix for the full texts.

[23] This is no doubt due in part to the many different textual sources (scriptural, legal, and so on) from which he draws.

[24] It is tempting but risky to try to make up for this. Armstrong, *Primary and Secondary Precepts*, attempts (unsuccessfully, I think) to reconstruct a set of "primary precepts." The nature and difficulty of the task can be seen in the effort to establish basic goals ("human flourishing") and to identify precepts associated with them; see Alan Donagan, *The Theory of Morality* (Chicago: University of Chicago Press, 1977).

course, are not precepts, but the precepts arise from using reason in pursuing them[25]—something that reinforces the idea that "Actions are to be in accord with reason" is one of the common conceptions. But again, Aquinas himself gives only a few examples, all in connection with the third inclination: "that one shun error and not offend those among whom one has to live, and others of this sort." It is an issue I return to in the next section, but it should be clear that the order of natural inclinations is not of itself going to provide a criterion for distinguishing immutable from mutable precepts (that is, those that are and are not "the same for all").[26]

In any event, from what Aquinas says (in *ST* IaIIae.92.4, the text I cited in the beginning), it seems clear enough that "Actions are to be carried out according to reason" is a common conception. And at the beginning of the Treatise (*ST* IaIIae.90.1 ad2) he said "The first principle in practical matters, which are the object of practical reason, is the last end [i.e., happiness or beatitude]."[27] Again, a goal or end is not a precept, but "Happiness is to be sought and its opposite avoided" is a plausible candidate. These two precepts, along with "the" first principle ("Good is to be done" etc.) would seem to be presupposed not only in the application of all other precepts but in any rational assessment of any exceptions or modifications of practical precepts.[28]

Just what others should be numbered among those common conceptions that are "the same for all" is not immediately clear. "Harm is to be done to no one" seems a favorite of Aquinas; for example, he says that "Killing is not to be done" is deduced from it.[29] In his questions on the

[25] Cf. *ST* IaIIae.90.1. This is brought out clearly by McInerny, *Aquinas on Human Action*, pp. 121–22.

[26] How one gets from practical reason to morality is a complex and controversial issue which I am setting aside in order to concentrate on the mutability issue. In the final analysis (see note 4 above), mutability may not be a satisfactory criterion for distinguishing what have traditionally been called "primary and secondary precepts" of natural law. The latter distinction is probably of interest mainly for moral theory. But that is another story from the mutability distinction itself, which is my concern here. See also note 49 below.

[27] "Primum autem principium in operativis, quorum est ratio practica, est finis ultimus Est autem ultimus finis humanae vitae felicitas vel beatitudino" (*ST* IaIIae.90.2). See note 10 above as a caution for the wide use of "principle." That happiness or beatitude should be (in some sense) the first principle in human affairs fits with Aquinas's position that the desire for happiness is voluntary but not free (*ST* Ia.83.1).

[28] The three precepts—Good is to be done and evil avoided; Happiness is to be pursued and its opposite avoided; Action is to be undertaken according to reason—are clearly not subject to the mutability Aquinas attributes to "proper conclusions." And one can argue that they are "known to all" in a relevant sense. But it is unlikely that Aquinas means three precepts only when he claims that there are as many principles of practical reason as there are of speculative reason (*ST* IaIIae.94.2).

[29] *ST* IaIIae.95.2.

Old Law he cites instances from the Decalogue, but the context should make one cautious about coming down too hard on the exact formulations. Still, this is worth quoting at length (and should be compared with the texts of *ST* IaIIae.94.2 and 4 in the Appendix).

> The moral precepts [of the Old Law], as distinct from the ceremonial and judicial, are those which pertain to right conduct [*bonos mores*]. Since human conduct is so-called in relation to reason, which is the proper principle of human acts, conduct is said to be good which conforms to reason and bad which is discordant with reason. However, just as every judgment of speculative reason proceeds from a natural cognition of first principles, so every judgment of practical reason proceeds from certain naturally known principles, as was said above. From these, [practical reason] is able to proceed to assess differently diverse sorts of case. For there are certain kinds of human action that can be approved or disapproved of immediately, with only little reflection [*cum modica consideratione*], using the common and primary [*prima*] principles. Others require a greater consideration of diverse circumstances, which is not for everybody but only for the wise—just as the consideration of particular conclusions of the sciences are pertinent to philosophers alone and not to everyone. Other kinds of action require the help of divine instruction for their assessment, as pertaining to [the province of] faith.
>
> It is clear, therefore, that since the moral precepts [of the Old Law] pertain to right conduct (which are precepts which accord with reason), [and] all judgments of human reason are derived in some way by natural reason, it is necessary that all the moral precepts [of the Old Law] pertain to the law of nature though they do so in different ways. There are some which the natural reason of anyone immediately of itself judges to be done or not to be done: e.g., "Honor thy father and thy mother," and "Thou shalt not kill," "Thou shalt not steal." Precepts of this sort belong absolutely to the law of nature. That other precepts are to be observed is judged by the wise through more subtle considerations of reason. Thus these also belong to the law of nature, but as requiring some teaching [*disciplina*], by which ordinary people are instructed by wiser ones: "Rise up before the hoary head and honor the person of the aged," and the like. Finally, there are [kinds of action] to judge of which human reason needs divine instruction: e.g., "Thou shalt not make to thyself a graven image, nor any likeness," "Thou shalt not take the name of the Lord in vain."[30]

[30] "Dicendum quod praecepta moralia, a caeremonialibus et judicialibus distincta, sunt de illis quae secundum se ad bonos mores pertinent. Cum autem humani mores dicantur in ordine ad rationem, quae est proprium principium humanorum actuum, illi mores dicuntur boni qui rationi congruunt, mali autem qui a ratione discordant. Sicut autem omne judicium rationis speculativae procedit a naturali cognitione primorum principiorum, ita etiam omne judicium rationis practicae procedit ex quibusdam principiis naturaliter cognitis, ut supra dictum est. Ex quibus diversimode procedi potest ad judicandum de di-

And again:

> The precepts contained in the Decalogue are those the knowledge of which man has in himself from God. They are such as can be known immediately from first principles with little reflection (*modica consideratione*). . . . Therefore, two general sorts of precept are not numbered among those of the Decalogue: i.e., [1] those which are primary and common—which need no promulgation other than being inscribed in natural reason, as if *per se nota*, e.g., that one should do harm to no one, and others of this sort—and [2] those which, through the diligent inquiry of the wise, are found to be in accord with reason. The latter God provides to the people through instruction by the wise. Nevertheless, both kinds of precept [can be said to be] contained in the precepts of the Decalogue, though in different ways. Those which are primary and common are contained [in the precepts of the Decalogue] as principles are contained in conclusions; those which are known to the wise are contained in them conversely, as conclusions in principles.[31]

---

versis. Quaedam enim sunt in humanis actibus adeo explicita quod statim, cum modica consideratione, possunt approbari vel reprobari per illa communia et prima principia. Quaedam vero sunt ad quorum judicium requiritur multa consideratio diversarum circumstantiarum, quas considerare dilgentur non est cuiuslibet, sed sapientum: sicut considerare particulares conclusiones scientiarum non pertinet ad omnes, sed solos philosophos. Quaedam vero sunt ad quae diiudicanda indiget homo adiuvari per instructionem divinam: sicut est circa credenda. Sic igitur patet quod, cum moralia praecepta sint de his quae pertinet ad bonos mores, haec autem sunt quae rationi congruunt, omne autem rationis humanae iudicium aliqualiter a naturali ratione derivatur: necesse est quod omnia praecepta moralia pertineant ad legem naturae, sed diversimode. Quaedam enim sunt quae statim per se ratio naturalis cuiuslibet hominis diiudicat esse facienda vel non facienda: sicut Honora patrem tuum et matrem tuam, et *Non occides. Non furtam facies.* Et huiusmodi sunt absolute de lege naturae. Quaedam vero sunt quae subtiliori consideratione rationis a sapientibus iudicantur esse observanda. Et ista sic sunt de lege naturae, ut tamen indigeant disciplina, qua minores a sapientioribus instruantur: sicut illud, *Coram cano capite consurge, et honora personam senis,* et alia huiusmodi. Quaedam vero sunt ad quae iudicanda ratio humana indiget instructione divina, per quam erudimur de divinis: sicut est illud, *Non facies tibi sculptile neque omnem similitudinem: Non assumes nomen Dei tui in vanum"* (*ST* IaIIae.100.1).

[31] "Praecepta decalogi ab aliis praeceptis legis differunt in hoc, quod praecepta decalogi per seipsum Deus dicitur populo proposuisse; alia vero praecepta proposuit populo per Moysen. Illa ergo praecepta ad decalogum pertinent, quorum notitiam homo habet per seipsum a Deo. Huiusmodi vero sunt illa quae statim ex principiis communibus primis cognosci possunt modica consideratione; et iterum illa quae statim ex fide divinitus infusa innotescunt. Inter praecepta ergo decalogi non computantur duo genera praeceptorum: illa scilicet quae sunt prima et communia, quorum non oportet aliam editionem esse nisi quod scripta in ratione naturali quasi per se nota, sicut quod nulli debet homo malefacere, et alia hujusmodi; et iterum illa quae per diligentem inquisitionem sapientum inveniuntur rationi convenire, haec enim proveniunt a Deo ad populum mediante disciplina sapientum. Utraque tamen horum praeceptorum continentur in praeceptis decalogi, sed diversmode. Nam illa quae sunt prima et communia, continentur in eis sicut principia in conclusionibus proximis: illa vero quae per sapeintes cognoscuntur, continentur in eis, e converso, sicut conclusiones in principiis" (*ibid.*, art. 3). Note the shift to assessing (called for by the context) rather than legislating or formulating precepts. Even

This completes my brief sketch of Aquinas's comparison and contrast of speculative and practical reason in the Treatise on Law. For anyone primarily interested in the place of this discussion of natural law within Aquinas's moral theory, of course, it cannot but seem distortingly selective.[32] But my concern, as I say, is exclusively with the mutability issue, which I think is an important problem in its own right. Perhaps that can be made clearer by considering some ways in which it might be thought easily resolvable.

2

The simplest way to isolate the issue of mutability that Aquinas has raised is to suppose that it can be restricted to the context of formulating positive laws. And there is some textual support for this hypothesis.[33] The idea would be that while vagueness can be a crucial defect in laws, Aquinas is pointing out the problems in trying to make laws absolutely precise and explicit. There is not only the practical problem of foreseeing all the possible eventualities but a theoretical problem in supplying clauses that will not themselves be open to the same mutability as the original precept.[34] It is an important point, moreover, that a system of laws cannot be made automatic, as if one could dispense with the need for judges (and juries).

At the same time, however, unless practical reason operates differently in moral and legal contexts, it is hard to see why one should think Aquinas's intentions here are so limited. In the example of returning goods held in trust, I suppose one could insist that the case is a matter

---

if the need for a little thought in assessing them makes it sound as if the moral precepts in the Decalogue are conclusions, Aquinas says they admit of no dispensations (ibid., art. 8) which would suggest that they are like common conceptions. The "little bit of thinking," of course, could be deductive reasoning. The claim in reply to 100.8 ad3 (see Part II of the appendix, under Interpretation) that the precepts of the Decalogue "as applied to particular acts . . . admit of change" has to do with "whether they constitute homicide, theft or adultery." It is a special type of mutability to which all precepts are susceptible; I discuss it in the following section.

[32] For a readable overview of the traditional position, see McInerny, *Aquinas on Human Action*, chaps. 5 and 6; and Henle, *The Treatise on Law*.

[33] In *ST* IaIIae.91.3 (see appendix) Aquinas identifies the common and indemonstrable principles of practical reason as natural law and says that the particular dispositions worked out from them are "called human laws." This is, after all, a treatise on law, and one might want to claim that the contrast between immutable and mutable precepts is simply that between moral principles and certain legislative actions based on them. I think the issue is more complex; see note 35 below.

[34] "Quanto enim plures conditiones particulares apponuntur tanto pluribus modis poterit deficere" (*ST* IaIIae.94.4).

of contract, and so a matter of law or social convention. But the same considerations would seem to apply to moral cases such as promising or perhaps lying. In addition, the way Aquinas talks of our recognizing the rightness of elements of the Decalogue presupposes a strongly moral context.[35]

One might agree that in the Treatise Aquinas is dealing with a broader context than positive law but still think that whatever flexibility he means to allow in the moral assessment of action is something that he has already accounted for in his earlier discussion of the goodness and malice of human actions.[36] In that context, he holds (in effect) that the application of precepts speaking to actions of a certain kind (species) will be affected when one fills in the circumstances, intention of the agent, and consequences of the action.[37] Where an act is morally indifferent in its species (as the vast majority of kinds of act will be), these other factors will serve to determine whether the act is morally good or evil. Even for actions that Aquinas considers good or evil just by being the kinds of action they are, he allows that such factors mitigate or compound the good or evil of the act.[38]

Specifying the conditions of a particular action, however, would not seem to produce the mutability that Aquinas talks of in connection with practical reason. No doubt it is "particular conditions" that we look to in assessing whether, in this case (or any other), it is right or wrong to return the deposit. But if we were then to set out a precept that includes all those conditions, it will still not have escaped the possibility of yet another exception; in fact, Aquinas suggests, each of the itemized con-

[35] See ST IaIIae.100 passim; Aquinas seems to consider some of them as conclusions. But it is always relevant to ask, and not always easy to decide, whether some claim that Aquinas makes about a case of positive law (human or divine) is meant to be limited to or is somehow specific to a legal setting: cf., e.g., the passage from *De malo* cited in note 12 above with 94.6 ad3, where he says some legislators have enacted ordinances that violate secondary precepts; the latter would imply that (at least some of) the derived precepts are not themselves positive legislations. Of course, the Treatise itself can be viewed as a "set piece" expected of any master of theology; and one should keep that in mind when dealing with its variable terminology, paucity of examples, and other symptoms of an apparent casualness about underlying problems. Still, if one thinks Aquinas's moral theory involves the Aristotelian project of practical reason-*cum*-theory of human flourishing, the Treatise on Law assumes a substantive role as the evident locus for Aquinas's account of practical reason. In any event, my interest in the mutability of the conclusions of practical reason takes them to have moral and not merely legal implications.

[36] ST IaIIae.18 and 19, but for the general context see 6–21.

[37] I say "in effect" because Aquinas does not put the case in the referenced text in terms of precepts.

[38] See ST IaIIae.18.11. Since, for Aquinas, an act to be good unqualifiedly must be good in all respects, it is relatively easy for circumstances to render evil an action that is good in species. An action that is evil in its kind can be made good only in some respect.

ditions will itself be open to exception.[39] In sum, while particularizing circumstances are essential in the moral assessment of actions, what Aquinas is after in bringing up the mutability of derived precepts seems to be something different and in a way more radical.

In the case of deductions, we can see how any "necessity" in a more basic precept would carry through to its derivation (as it does in speculative reason). What needs to be explained is how determinations can be mutable when the precepts from which they are derived are not—or, equally important, how the common conceptions can be indefeasible if their derivations are not. The closer one gets to the particular, Aquinas says, the more occasion there will be for a precept to fail [*deficere*].[40] But the idea of a gradation of mutability may be a distraction. In the same text Aquinas has already said that none of the common conceptions is susceptible to mutability, and all of the proper conclusions are. The problem, or part of it, is that the gap between general principle and particular case would, on the face of it, seem to be formally no different for basic and derived principles: that is, the common conceptions of practical reason must apply to particulars as much as their proper precepts do.[41]

A more promising hypothesis emphasizes the peculiar role that goals or ends play as principles in practical reason.[42] And it thus has at least an initial advantage in locating the source of mutability in the derivation of the precepts themselves rather than leaving it for their ultimate application to individual cases. One way to appreciate what is at stake is to compare "means-ends" reasoning with inductive or probabilistic reasoning.[43] The rules of demonstrative reasoning preserve truth: if the premises are true, the conclusion will be true. And this holds most importantly even if new "premises" are added (so long as they are not

[39] See note 34 above.

[40] *ST* IaIIae.94.4; and see my discussion of the Siege in section 3.

[41] Aquinas does say that "the common principles of natural law cannot be applied in the same way to all because of the great variety of human affairs [Principia communia legis naturae non eodem modo applicari possunt omnibus propter multam varietatem rerum humanarum]": *ST* IaIIae.95.2 ad3. This does not mean that those principles change, but rather that they apply differently through the more specific precepts, as I try to explain in section 5.

[42] See note 14 above. In what follows I draw on Anthony Kenny, *Will, Freedom, and Power* (New York: Barnes & Noble, 1992), pp. 43–45; for a more extended treatment, see Kenny, *The Metaphysics of Mind* (Oxford: Oxford University Press, 1975), pp. 94–110, where he makes frequent reference to Aquinas in developing the point about the defeasibility of practical reasoning in the context of goals. He approaches the problem there, however, from a different issue: a disanalogy between "good" and "true." Kenny is not in either place offering an interpretation of the Treatise on Law.

[43] I want to include under the heading of "means-ends" not only cases where an action is purely instrumental in attaining a goal but also those where an action "realizes" a goal: e.g., in the way the natural inclinations realize human flourishing.

contradictions themselves or do not produce a contradiction). In non-demonstrative reasoning, however, the likelihood that the premises confer upon the conclusion is subject to change with the addition of further information—hence the familiar addition of a *ceteris paribus* clause. Something rather like the defeasibility of likelihood affects the justification of a means as desirable in terms of the desirability of a goal. Unless a means is the only way of achieving the goal, additional information may make a means that was desirable independently of that into something less desirable. In fact, even if it is the only means, further information about the means may undercut the desirability of the goal; the end, as we say, does not justify the means.[44]

One can, in fact, give a plausible interpretation of what is "the same for all" in terms of what is desirable or valuable in itself. What is valuable only as one among many means to or ways of achieving something else may indeed not be the same for all. It seems fairly clear, for example, that at least one thing Aquinas has in mind when he describes three "natural inclinations" in the Treatise on Law is that they are directed at goals or ends which, for human beings, are valuable in themselves. As "natural," those goals will be "the same for all" in the sense that any rational person must find them desirable or valuable and in no need of further justification to establish that pursuing or satisfying them is a good thing to do.

But unlike the pursuit of happiness or human flourishing itself, the goals of these natural inclinations are good things to do only *ceteris paribus*.[45] That is to say, being associated with a basic goal—that is, the object of one of the natural inclinations—does not guarantee that a precept will be indefeasible, which is the central contrast I am trying to understand. Consider the (presumably basic) goals associated with the three natural inclinations Aquinas identifies.[46] Self-preservation, for example, is a natural goal and therefore needs no further justification to be desirable. But "one's own life is to be preserved" holds only *ceteris paribus*; additional information may make it reasonable to sacrifice one's life in the service of a just cause. Moreover, Aquinas is a celibate and so has eschewed the "conjunction of male and female." And he presum-

---

[44] When discussing derivations in practical reasoning as opposed to deducing one precept from another, Aquinas sometimes speaks of "quasi-conclusions," and at one point he even seems to hesitate about the necessity of its first principles (see note 3 above). But I think this only reflects his belief that reasoning in practical reason is importantly different from the paradigm demonstrations of speculative reason.

[45] See notes 25, 26, and 43 above. One may be able to generate unexceptionable precepts in connection with the reasonable pursuit of natural inclinations. But the inclinations and their goals, though desirable in themselves, are not dominant. See note 48 below.

[46] *ST* IaIIae.94.2.

ably approves of the Desert Fathers, say, who chose to live apart from the society of their times.[47]

These natural inclinations play a very important role in the articulation of human flourishing, and so there will be an order, as Aquinas says, in the precepts associated with them. But it is hard to see how they can provide the order that distinguishes mutable proper conclusions from immutable common conceptions. What we expect of the latter precepts, I think, is that they will be "dominant" in a sense often associated with moral precepts.[48] That is, the moral option is commonly thought to be overriding when opposed to any alternatives that would constitute a violation of the relevant moral precept. But the only goal that is dominant in this way, for Aquinas, is human happiness itself. Clearly, if the common conceptions of practical reason contain precepts that take precedence over any alternatives—or if the common conceptions are supposed to constitute a "proto-morality" of some sort—that fact must come from something in addition to their being associated with "natural" inclinations (or goals desirable in themselves).[49]

To summarize this section then, the mutability Aquinas alludes to (*ST* IaIIae.94.4) is not just an issue in the context of positive law but something that applies to practical reasoning more broadly construed. The hypothesis that the mutability of derived precepts is due to their application to individual cases does not explain why basic precepts

[47] These natural inclinations, and the precepts associated with them, are not altogether malleable: e.g., Aquinas would not sanction someone's committing suicide in the service of a just cause. And from a legislative viewpoint the basic goals described give a plausible base for determining certain "rights" that society should protect. My point is not that the basic inclinations are irrelevant to the development of moral precepts but only that some further account is needed about how moral precepts might be derived from them. See note 49 below.

[48] I take the idea of "dominance" from discussions of choice theory: A is not dominant if we prefer A to B and B to C but not A to C. The standard example is that of a shopper who might prefer the brand-name product to another if it is no more than 10 percent more expensive. The Prisoner's Dilemma also involves nondominant alternatives. As I use it here, a choice is dominant if it takes precedence over all alternatives. Moral precepts characteristically carry a demand (or obligation) that claims dominance. See note 49.

[49] Two of the ways people have proposed for getting to dominance from basicness in an Aristotelian scheme are (a) to make it a demand of rationality that one do the *best* of the possible alternative courses, and (b) to require that human flourishing (happiness) involve having a life plan in which it is required that any "package" of basic goods meet certain specifications. And, of course, those who think that practical reason simply manipulates moral premises derived independently can avoid the problem, but only at what seems to me the price of distorting Aquinas's moral theory. In *The Theory of Morality*, chap. 7, no. 3, Donagan points out that a moral theory cannot be generated from a theory of practical reason alone, without a theory of human nature. See also the helpful account of the controversy surrounding the efforts of Finnis, Grisez, et al., in Robert George, "Natural Law and Human Nature," in his *Natural Law Theory*. See also note 26 above.

(which are also applicable to individual cases) should be indefeasible. And although Aquinas allows a kind of flexibility where circumstances or intentions can place an otherwise indifferent act in the moral species of good or evil, that does not account for the more radical issue of mutability in precepts that seem to proscribe moral evil. Finally, the hypothesis that defeasibility comes from the character of means-ends reasoning—where added information changes the likelihood that premises would confer on conclusions—seems on the right track. But the possibility of glossing what is or is not "the same for all" in terms of goals that are or are not desirable in themselves, though it may provide some order among precepts, does not supply a criterion for distinguishing the mutability of "proper conclusions" from the immutability of "common conceptions."

That the Treatise on Law does not itself provide a simple and explicit explanation of the difference it introduces between mutable and immutable precepts does not at all affect the overall contribution of the Treatise or the significant place it has come to occupy in accounts of Aquinas's moral theory. In fact, I have gone into this much detail about it only in order to articulate the problem about mutability in practical reasoning and to show why it is not easily resolved. I want now to examine more closely some of the cases Aquinas treats, in the Treatise and elsewhere, in which precepts are seen to "fail." It is from them, I think, that one must develop the resources for a resolution to the problem.

3

There is no one place where Aquinas discusses as a group the different cases of putative mutation in legal or moral precepts which I describe below. The order, therefore, is mine, but I think it serves to bring out some of the important principles at stake.[50]

The Siege

Of all the examples Aquinas gives, the most straightforward sort of exception seems to me to be that where, as Aquinas says, observing the letter of the law would violate the spirit of the law. The Siege is a simple case that can serve as a model for the interpretation of some of the

---

[50] I have gathered some relevant texts in the appendix, following this order. Aquinas also takes up mutability in a general way under the heading of *epikeia* in *ST* IIaIIae.120.

things Aquinas has to say about exceptions in other contexts. Imagine then that in a city under siege the authorities have decreed that the gates are to remain closed. This, Aquinas says, "serves the common welfare in most cases; but it may happen that the enemy is pursuing some citizens through whom the city is maintained: it would be most ruinous [*damnosissimum*] for the city if the gates were not opened [to admit the citizens being pursued]. And so in such cases, the gates are to be opened, against the letter of the law, in order to serve the common advantage that the legislator intended."[51]

Note first of all that this is clearly an exception. As Aquinas points out in answer to an objection, the judgment that the gates should be opened in this case does not reflect on the propriety of the original order or its continuing to hold.[52] Moreover, one can easily see why adding specifications to the original order would not have resolved the need for considering exceptions. For example, to "The gates are to be kept closed *unless people important to the city need immediate entry*," one is going to have to add "unless the pursuing enemy is so close that they would also gain entry . . . well, unless the pursuers are few and could easily be overcome by the defenders . . . unless, of course, the soldiers that happened to be available were not experienced," and so on. One could, of course, use language that masks the problem by its vagueness: "Do not open the gates if the enemy is *too* close," or "unless it is safe to." Or perhaps one might simply add, "Use a little common sense!" But the problem is not that a lack of specification puts the onus on the judgment of the gatekeeper; the issue is what principles he (or anyone else) can make use of to resolve the inevitable problematic cases.

Aquinas, here and in his other examples, has no doubt about the right course of action: the gates are to be opened. In fact, a number of things make this particular case clear. First of all, it has to do with positive law.[53] Second, the order that the gates are not to be opened is clearly desirable only as a means: that is, the justification for the order is instrumental or conditional, not something that of itself directly and independently serves the common good but only something that does so in time of siege. More important, "The gates are not to be opened" is clearly a determination: that is, the order or precept has not been *deduced* from a more basic or general precept but is one arrangement or disposition for meeting the more basic need or goal: providing for the welfare of the city. Since the whole rationale for the order derives from its serving the

---

[51] *ST* IaIIae.96.6; see the appendix, under the Siege. See also IIaIIae.120.1 ad1 and 2.

[52] *ST* IaIIae.96.6 ad1.

[53] See notes 33 and 35 above.

higher purpose, one can see why it is reasonable not to thwart that purpose. In fact, Aquinas explicitly builds in the feature upon which the conflict turns.[54] The guard is not presented as, say, opening the gate for a friend (as if *any* good purpose were relevant) or because he made a promise (as if there were a conflict of obligations). Rather, these are citizens important for maintaining the city, and not saving them therefore directly conflicts with the purpose of the order to keep the gates closed: that is, conserving the city.

In sum, the Siege is a case where almost anyone can see just what the point of the order is, just how it is supposed to fulfill the higher purpose, and just why not allowing the exception would conflict with doing so. And because of that, the case meets the requirement for justifying the exception that I called attention to in the introduction: that is, one can see in the appeal to a higher-order goal the reason why the exception should be granted and why the original order or precept is not thereby being challenged. All this may seem so obvious as to make my repetitive account altogether tedious. My point, as I hope will become clear, is that an appeal beyond the immediate precept to a higher goal or purpose that gives the lower precept its authority is essential to the justification of what I am calling exceptions (and other cases Aquinas raises as like exceptions); and exceptions, as I hope to show, provide the main clue to the distinction between the immutability of the common conceptions and mutability of proper conclusions that Aquinas identifies (*ST* IaIIae. 94.4).

The Starving Family

A more complex and subtle case, one that in addition seems explicitly to have moral as well as legal bearing, is the example Aquinas gives of the Starving Family.[55] No doubt it was a familiar example, but he states the case somewhat casually, only gesturing at the many qualifications that would be necessary in a fuller account.[56] One can easily enough get the general drift, however. The question is whether anyone might be allowed to steal because of the press of necessity. The simple answer is

---

[54] I take it Aquinas has put in the phrase about "citizens through whom the city is maintained" to make explicit that this is a case of "spirit and letter of the law." It may be politically incorrect of one or both of us, but I assume that the important citizens Aquinas is thinking of are military or political leaders. One might gloss it differently and come up with the same result.

[55] *ST* IaIIae.66.7; see the appendix under this heading. Putting "family" in the label is my gloss; as Aquinas presents it, the case deals simply with a person in dire straits.

[56] Cf. "immediate danger," "cannot be met otherwise," in ibid.

given in the sed contra: "On the other hand, in a condition of necessity, all things are common; and thus it is not a sin if someone takes something of another's which necessity has made common."[57] The crucial idea, of course, is that necessity can somehow "make things common." My explanation draws on other contexts to fill in the details but is not, I think, controversial.[58]

The institution of private property, for Aquinas, is a "determination" and not a basic right. He is familiar with communities that do not allow private ownership: for example, religious communities such as his own Dominican Order, and the early Christian community described in the Book of Acts. But that is equally a determination: neither common property nor private property is the right arrangement *tout court*, for one or the other is better suited to certain conditions. Aquinas seems to favor the idea of private ownership as the more practicable scheme for the broader political community in achieving the higher goal or purpose: that is, providing for a just and effective distribution of goods (which in turn is supposed to support the general health and welfare of the community).

When Aquinas speaks of things as held in common "in the condition of necessity," therefore, he is not suggesting that there is a shift from the one sort of determination to the other. He has, in effect, moved back to the perspective of the higher (or more basic) purpose or goal, the just and effective distribution of goods, but that is not being offered here as an alternative economic arrangement.[59] What Aquinas imagines in the Starving Family is a case where the (otherwise appropriate) system has temporarily or for a particular family broken down. That is to say, he proposes an exceptional situation that calls for immediate redress but does not require a reconsideration of the community's having adopted

---

[57] "In necessitate sunt omnia communia, et ita non videtur esse peccatum, si aliquis rem alterius accipiat propter necessitatem sibi factem communem" (ibid.). Cf. ad3; a. 2, ad1; q. 57, a. 2; IaIIae. 94.5 ad3.

[58] See Marcus Lefebure, "Private Property according to St. Thomas and Recent Papal Encyclicals," which is app. 2 in *ST* (Blackfriars, vol. 38). See also *ST* IaIIae.99.5 ad3; and IIaIIae.66.2 and the replies.

[59] Let me anticipate a point that will be important later on. So long as one thinks of attending to the higher goal (viz., the just distribution of goods), the case may seem straightforward enough. But there is something odd about the idea that in such cases of necessity as this the situation reverts, as it were, to a condition in which goods are to be held in common. That cannot be the specific commonness of a competing, communitarian determination (or institution) but must be a kind of generic commonness of the supposed condition "prior" to any determination—though we cannot be talking here of any actual condition, as if things once (long ago) were like this and we are now returning to that. See *ST* IaIIae.94.5 ad3. The "common" condition is like that of something in a genus but not of any species, as I try to explain in section 5.

the institution of private property itself. Under the institution of private property, as he understands it, the poor are to be taken care of by others who have things in abundance. But something has gone wrong for a particular family whose need is "immediate," and the proper course of action is not in doubt: "Should there be an urgent and evident need, where it is clear the immediate need must be met from whatever is available—for example, when a person is in imminent danger—and cannot be met otherwise, then one can legitimately supply the need out of someone else's things, either secretly or openly. And this does not have the character properly of theft or plunder."[60]

The principles we saw in the more straightforward case of the Siege are implicit in the case of the Starving Family as well. Private property is a determination of a higher (more basic or general) goal; in a case where sticking to the rules of the more specific arrangement or disposition works against the purpose of the general goal, an exception is called for lest the general goal be thwarted. I return to the issue of appeal to "general" goals later. What I want to emphasize here is an important difference between this case and the Siege.

What is special about the Starving Family case is the idea that the action that would constitute the exception is now said not to be itself an act of theft or stealing. That is to say, the family is not, under the circumstances, taking property that *belongs to another*, where the latter is an essential feature of the definition of stealing.[61] To a modern reader, perhaps, the difference between allowing that stealing—or lying, or whatever—may sometimes be justified and insisting that in some cases it is not "really" stealing after all may seem a tenuous one.[62] Aquinas, however, holds that some acts are morally evil in their object: that is, just for being the kind of act they are.[63] It is important in his moral scheme, therefore, to distinguish the more straightforward cases of exception from cases where the issue is whether the formal criteria for a kind of action are present or not. The investigation of the latter procedure is not central to my thesis in this essay, but some recognition of it is in keeping with the emphasis I think should be placed on the centrality in

[60] *ST* IIaIIae.66.7 (text in the appendix).

[61] One might want to claim that the guard in the Siege is not really violating the order, but one could not say he is "not really opening the gates"—whereas in the Starving Family it is not really a case of "taking property belonging to another."

[62] It is not enough, of course, just to claim that an act is not really stealing (or whatever); one must give reasons to show why the formal conditions of an action of that kind have not been met. And the whole enterprise depends on a system of agreed-upon definitions or specifications of actions; in Aquinas, see *ST* IaIIae.6–21.

[63] *ST* IaIIae.18, esp. art. 5.

Aquinas's moral theory, as I understand it, of "knowing what one is do-ing": that is, of knowing what kind of action one is undertaking rather than focusing primarily on what the results of one's actions might be. In any event, the appeal to a higher-level principle behind a determination in the Starving Family is what makes it like an exception. But for Aquinas it will not be a case of "spirit versus letter of the law," since the claim is that the letter of the law has not been formally violated.

Special Divine Commands

It is not a surprise, I think, that Aquinas adopts a device similar to that of the Starving Family in handling many of the Old Testament examples of prima facie dubious actions undertaken at the command of God. A fairly simple example (from Exodus 12:35) is sometimes called "the plun-der of the Egyptians": the Israelites, as they leave Egypt, take with them gold and precious jewels given them by the fearful Egyptians. Aquinas makes rather short work of the case: "What makes something theft is that a thing is taken [that belongs to] another. But whoever takes some-thing at the command of God, who is the Lord of the Universe, does not take it against the will of the lord [owner], which [would be] theft."[64]

I do not want to pursue the question of how successful Aquinas was in handling such cases, for I think they are significantly different from the Starving Family. In both sorts of case Aquinas will claim that it is not actually stealing. But in this and other Old Testament cases he seems to be proposing a more straightforward defense of the questionable action. That is to say, the appeal is not to some breakdown in a determination. It is more as if, for example, I were charged with theft for taking a book from my colleague's office and pointed out, in my defense, that the true owner of the book had directed me to take it; I would not then be asking that an *exception* be made in my case.[65]

---

[64] "Et eadem ratio est de furto, quod est acceptio rei alienae: quidquid enim accipit aliq-uid ex mandato Dei, qui est dominus universorum, non accipit absque voluntate domini; quod est furari" (*ST* IaIIae.94.5 ad2). Other cases there involve commands to kill the in-nocent or commit fornication or adultery. See also 100.8 ad3, where he treats some of the same cases under what I call "interpretation."

[65] I have the feeling that Aquinas's handling of these Old Testament cases is rather spe-cial, and so I tend to distinguish them somewhat from straightforward exceptions. Given a perhaps more "theological" reading of his position on property, however, where all things belong to God and the more familiar property arrangements depend for whatever legitimacy they have on God's permission, cases like the plunder of the Egyptians could be considered dispensations; and they would then fall more directly under the standard type of exception, as in the Siege. In *ST* IaIIae.100.8 Aquinas seems to run together inter-preting a precept and determining that a particular action is not really such and such. I separate the relevant paragraphs in the appendix.

Interpretation

Aquinas's discussion of Old Testament examples provides another rather special case of mutability. Although Aquinas says the precepts of the Decalogue are in no way dispensable, he allows at one point that they are subject to "interpretation." For example, the Maccabees' decision to defend themselves on the Sabbath was undertaken, he says, not as an exception to the command that the Sabbath be kept holy but as an interpretation of what observing the Sabbath amounts to.[66] And I assume it is also a matter of interpretation, in this sense, that Aquinas takes the biblical prohibition against killing to be unqualified. Claiming the authority of Augustine in *De libero arbitrio* 1.4, he says that judicial execution, for example, is just not "the homicide that is forbidden."[67]

Here again Aquinas supplies no rules for assessing putative interpretations, but it is clear enough that they constitute a new category, different both from straightforward exceptions and the "not really stealing" sort of case. It should also be clear that the process of devising and assessing interpretations is not only very important, because of its wide application (for any precept will be susceptible to interpretation), but also very difficult to provide criteria for. Since interpretation is relevant even to indispensable precepts, however, it cannot ground the distinction between mutable and immutable precepts, which is my main concern here. For my present purposes, then, it is enough to mention this form of mutability and pass on.[68]

The Deposit

We can now return to the case Aquinas uses (*ST* IaIIae.94.4) to exemplify the general claim that the conclusions of practical reason are "not the same for all." It is the (old and familiar) example of keeping, say, a sword for someone; the issue is the propriety of not giving it back when

[66] *ST* IaIIae.100.8 ad4 (see appendix).

[67] Ibid., ad3.

[68] Interpretation, for Aquinas, is not likely intended to be an occasion for showing one's originality. A genuine interpretation, I assume, must at least satisfy a reasonable observer that it covers no more and no less than the original precept. I cannot emphasize too much the need for rational canons of assessment for claims about exceptions or mutability generally. One can legitimately claim that it is not to Aquinas's purpose in (this part of) the Treatise on Law to enter into that difficult project, but any theory about mutability is still seriously incomplete until one can deliver on the promise to do so. This does not mean that one can set out now what will apply to all future cases, but one has to be able to give the principles one operates on now. And one has to consider not only successful cases but those where some form of interpretation or claim of defeasibility has gone wrong. See also note 85 below.

one knows that he means to use it to fight against one's country.[69] Since it is the only example he uses when describing the disanalogy between speculative and practical reason, Aquinas evidently thinks it is a good one in which to see the general problem. Before trying to explain why that might be so, I want first to call attention to what makes it somewhat radical. Consider the way the case is raised in the following text:

> It is clear that those things which are beyond the order of lower principles or causes are sometimes traced back to principles of a higher order: for example as monstrous births of animals are beyond the order of the active power of the seed but still fall under principles of a higher order, such as that of celestial bodies or, ultimately, divine providence. Hence a firm judgment cannot be made about this sort of monstrosity by considering the active power of the seed; although a judgment can be made from a consideration of divine providence.
>
> Now it sometimes happens that something is to be done outside the common rules for action: for example, that a deposit is not to be returned to an enemy of the country, or something else of this sort. And so one has to assess this sort of case in accordance with some higher principles than the common rules with which *synesis* deals. And the higher principles require a higher power of judgment which is called *gnome*, and which implies a certain perspicacity of judgment.[70]

It is important for my thesis that Aquinas speaks here of higher principles of some sort. The appeal, so to speak, "over the head" of one precept to the authority of some higher precept from which it derives its force is the characteristic I take as the mark of exceptions. Unfortunately, however, the flexibility that the analogy with monstrous births brings with it also raises the stakes for the problem of understanding how the actual practice of justifying exceptions might work. In the example of the Deposit, the judgment not to return the sword to its rightful owner is doubtless the "perspicacious" one. But just why is that true?[71]

In the account of the Deposit (*ST* IaIIae.94.4), the only higher principle Aquinas cites—pretty clearly offered as an example of a common conception—is that one is to act according to reason (*secundum rationem agatur*). It is said to follow as a proper conclusion that goods held in

---

[69] Actually, Aquinas does not mention the sword—an example one finds as early as Plato—but he does allude to the deposit being used against the country. Nothing turns on that detail.

[70] *ST* IIaIIae.51.4. See appendix under the Deposit.

[71] One has to be careful not to fall back on some general principle such as the greatest happiness, for that would essentially alter Aquinas's moral theory. If, as seems plausible, he holds to a virtue ethics, no such rule will do the work.

trust are to be returned. And I assume that it is the very same higher principle about acting reasonably that one appeals to in justifying the exception; after all, does not Aquinas say that returning the deposit in the case described would be ruinous and therefore irrational? But saying that something is reasonable or unreasonable only promises a reason; it does not itself amount to a reason.[72]

Aquinas, of course, is not likely to think it does. That he leaves a gap here between the very basic common conception (about being reasonable) and a very proper conclusion (about goods held in trust) might be explained in a number of ways. Perhaps the simplest is that he wants to avoid any distraction from the basic point about the disanalogy between speculative and practical reason which might arise in connection with examples of particular, intermediate precepts. One might also say that he wants to allow for cases where thwarting a higher goal or principle is not so direct as in the contrast of spirit and letter (in the Siege) or the breakdown of an institution (in the Starving Family). The passage just quoted, however, suggests that the Deposit—or at least his use of it there—introduces a gap that is very wide indeed: the higher principle one has to appeal to may be as remote as the influence of celestial bodies or providence would be in accounting for monstrous births.[73]

For all its difficulties, the analogy with monstrous births seems to me to provide an essential clue to the (at least prima facie) unsettling aspect of Aquinas's contrast of mutable and immutable precepts (*ST* IaIIae 94.4). In the summary classification of mutability in the following section, my isolation of a special category of exception turns largely on the contrast of other, relatively clear and straightforward cases (of defeasibility, for example) with the peculiar status that results from allowing something "monstrous" within practical reason.[74] In section 5 I try to

[72] It is the vice of virtue theory to break out of the apparent circle of identifying good action through good persons and vice versa by assuming that the better persons are the "establishment" in which, of course, "everyone" just sees the proper thing to be done, thus reasons do not have to be examined explicitly.

[73] Considering in isolation whether or not to return the sword, one might come up with a number of possibilities. Aquinas's account of the kinds and conditions of human actions, and his basic analysis of being and goodness, provide him with considerable resources in assessing actions. But what I said earlier in connection with the Siege example seems to me implicit from the context here: the issue is not moral or rational assessment generally but something peculiar to the derived precepts of practical reason. Even there, various readings are possible. It would not be implausible to suppose that the precept about returning goods held in trust is (or is associated with) a determination—e.g., the institution of private property again—and thus on a par with the Siege. Or one might deal with it on the model of not really (or formally) stealing. The reference to monstrous births, however, makes me think that this case is meant to be different.

[74] Some exceptions may be analogous to less serious "deformities": a three-legged donkey is still a donkey, though it may lack some property that is definitive of the species (e.g., being a quadruped; see note 13 above). What is usually meant by "monstrous births,"

say something about the status of monstrous births in the Aristotelian scientific scheme.

4

The analysis of cases in the preceding section contains, I think, the resources for constructing (at least in outline) a general defense of Aquinas against the charge that his allowing mutability in the results of practical reason undercuts the rationality of the process of moral and legal reasoning. What is needed to counter the appearance of an unmanageable variability is a classification of the different kinds of mutability, along with the development of reasonable canons for assessing individual cases. The following classification is, I believe, implicit in Aquinas's practice, but the terminology involved is my regimentation.

Kinds of Mutability

(1) There are two ways that even dominant precepts are susceptible to a kind of mutability: (a) they are open to "interpretation," and (b) it is always possible to claim that an action is not "really" such-and-such (stealing, for example).[75] Both these procedures, of course, are brought to bear on difficult cases. If successful, however, they do not justify our saying of the precept under consideration that it holds *ceteris paribus* or for the most part. That is, if successful, they show that the relevant precept simply does not apply to the case. I have mentioned before the importance of the "not formally such-and-such" move for Aquinas, and I am not suggesting that the brief account I have given is adequate to the full complexities of the procedure.

(2) The kind of mutability with the next broadest application is what I have called defeasibility, for it is applicable not only to derived but also to basic precepts if they are not dominant or are indeterminate (or general). It is useful, therefore, to distinguish two forms of defeasibility: (a) a goal (such as the preservation of one's own life) will be basic for

---

however, is not just any sort of deformity but such a radical sort that one cannot even call the offspring an instance of the species of its parents. They are also usually only briefly viable. I assume that Aquinas means to allow for a similarly wide variety of exceptions.

[75] Cf. *ST* IaIIae.100.8 ad3. Although Aquinas's example involves a precept of the Decalogue (cf. the Maccabees and the Sabbath), the implication is that any precept (basic or derived) could (at least theoretically) be open to interpretation (cf. ibid., ad4). E.g., in "Harm is to be done to no one," the understanding of *harm* and the notion of *person* can undergo some development over time (see note 15 above). The "not really such-and-such" move is actually more exact: there is no dispute about just what the criteria for an action are, and the claim is that they are not formally present in a certain case.

being desirable in itself and not just instrumentally, but there may also be circumstances (such as the defense of a just cause) in which the desirability of that basic goal is overridden; (b) the weight one gives to certain precepts formulated in terms of kinds of action may vary when we specify for a particular case the circumstances, intention of the agent, and consequences. An action that is morally evil in kind will not be made good by the specification of added conditions, but an action that is indifferent may become not just more desirable but the morally right or wrong thing to do.[76] Defeasible precepts of both kinds are typically identified by the presence (or applicability) of a *ceteris paribus* clause, just because it is added information in their case that makes for mutability.

(3) A somewhat different kind of "failing" occurs with what I am calling exceptions. And here, the appropriate tag for susceptible precepts is "for the most part." The source of mutability is not added information but the possibility of an appeal, in particular cases, to some higher precept that gives the exceptionable precept its force. Such an appeal requires, as I see it, (a) that the higher-level precept have significant content—legal, if the context is legal; moral, if it is moral—and (b) that the exceptionable precept be a (proximate or remote) determination of it. Exceptionability is therefore a somewhat narrower phenomenon than defeasibility. Precepts associated with basic goals—if there is more than one basic goal—will be unexceptionable just because there are, by definition, no higher goals of which they are determinations.[77] Dominant precepts will also be unexceptionable, not because they are dominant but because they are not determinations (although they may be deductions from basic precepts, in the way "Do not kill" is deduced from "Do not harm").

Exceptionability, I want to claim, when specified as I have suggested, is the mark of precepts that are "not the same for all," as opposed to common conceptions in practical reason as that distinction is drawn in the Treatise on Law.[78] That is to say, though all forms of mutability are important for an understanding of Aquinas's moral and legal theory, it is only defeasibility

[76] To reverse the case, one can try to defeat a charge of immorality by retreating to some description of an action that is indeterminate: e.g., "All I did was pull the trigger." To show why this is cheating is not always easy—but not impossible.

[77] It is common enough nowadays to consider the possibility of a conflict between basic goals and moral precepts themselves, but Aquinas apparently thinks that an adequate specification of moral precepts (along with careful analysis of putative conflicts) precludes any real conflict.

[78] Should this claim seem too strong, I would be satisfied with a weaker version. That is, although mutability of all the kinds I have mentioned may be relevant to the mutability Aquinas allows for practical in contrast to speculative reason, it is exceptionability that make for the unsettling form of variability which is introduced on the analogy to monstrous births.

and exceptionability that address specifically the relation of basic and derived (or what I have sometimes called higher and lower) precepts. But compared to exceptionability, defeasibility is a relatively straightforward and mannerly phenomenon: one simply has to supply the relevant circumstances or indicate the alternative options to provide the data on which a claim for defeasibility is to be assessed. In choosing the Deposit for his paradigm and comparing its problematic to that of monstrous births, Aquinas seems to me to locate the ground for what it is for a precept not to be "the same for all" in the rather messier phenomenon of exceptionability. In the following section, I look somewhat more closely at the problem of monstrous births as an analogue for exceptions. Before closing this section, however, I want to return briefly to the general issue of mutability.

Canons of Assessment

In discussing "Whether Natural Law Is the Same for All" (*Utrum lex naturae sit una apud omnes, ST* IaIIae.94.4), Aquinas clearly opts for the affirmative. But there is no confusion or mistake in his going on to allow for, even emphasize, mutability in the process of defending the stability of natural law. The point of developing canons of assessment and making use of distinctions such as common and proper precepts, determination and deduction, dominance and basicness has more to do with rationality than flexibility. The idea is a perfectly valid one: the better one understands the great variety in human affairs, the clearer it becomes that certain basic principles do not change when they are differently applied to different situations. One can admit that the Treatise on Law is not always of great help on the details without denigrating the importance of the general point.

Here I wish to make only two remarks. First, the fact that Aquinas only gestures at the reasoning process behind various precepts can be taken in two ways. One is to suppose that he thinks the procedures so obvious and the basic principles both a priori and so accessible that they need no explanation. The other, with which I am more comfortable, is to suppose that the procedures are so complex and so open to adjustment because of context that he does not want the general principle to be lost in the possible qualifications one might have to make explicit in discussing any particular example. For although we can and should be clear and explicit about techniques and fallacies of assessment which we have developed and refined from past experience, it is still possible that new experience and new techniques—especially in connection with interpretation—may require us to adapt.

Second, however one cashes in "common conceptions," it is important not to lose sight of what I take to be the central point of Aquinas's appeal to them in both speculative and practical reasoning: that we have to learn most of what we can know about things, but that we are able to do so because of our intellectual capacity to relate those things to common conceptions which are knowable through themselves. And here again, the common conceptions are not armchair deductions from the contemplation of the notions of being and good; they are rather the presuppositions we discover and reconstruct from our best understanding of science and practical affairs.[79] In the final analysis, of course, an adequate defense of Aquinas's position on mutability turns on the assumption that one can supply or develop reasonable canons for assessing claims of mutability (or immutability). The problems in developing such canons, however, are of a piece with the problems of developing an adequate moral or legal outlook or apparatus, for they require reflection on our moral and legal practices themselves.

5

Beyond the more practical question of working out the principles of assessment for mutability, there remains a significant theoretical problem about Aquinas's approach. We are almost comfortable nowadays with the idea that our best results are open to revision, that what we now find obvious may turn out to be false, and that our concepts often prove inadequate to the full dimensions of concrete particulars. And Aristotle's now familiar remark that it is foolish to impose a precision on a field that will not bear it is easily (though I think lazily) glossed along those lines. But Aristotle was not talking about fallibilism or about being "flexible" in our moral attitudes; he was pointing to something about the *field* of practical affairs which involves both our concepts and the sorts of things they are meant to capture. At a minimum, to put the case in modern terms, he meant to contrast the "exact" concepts of mathematics with the nonexact concepts used in practical affairs—not just moist and dry, but stealing and happiness. The implications of that contrast, along with the claim that nonexact concepts are unavoidable in the areas of ethics, politics, and the like, carry us into theoretical questions of considerable complexity and active concern. In this section I want to indicate (if only in a preliminary and sketchy way) how exceptionability, as I have described it, introduces this theoretical dimension.

[79] One's interpretation of the role and character of the common conceptions is relevant here; see note 9 above.

In the Treatise on Law at least, the cases of exception Aquinas introduces are not as difficult cases that lead to refinements of the relevant precept. He treats the exceptions as (pretty) obviously the right thing to do in a case where the precept itself requires no revision.[80] But if one can objectively determine the rightness of particular cases (that is, whether an exception is justified or not) by appeal to higher principles that ultimately are "the same for all," what is the point of having intermediate precepts at all?

One way to approach the issue is to ask whether intermediate precepts might be merely rules of thumb that serve only a heuristic purpose.[81] It is unlikely, of course, that this is what Aquinas had in mind. Rules of thumb are essentially eliminable. In bridge, for example, "Third hand high!" is a helpful rule for the beginner—who must then be warned not to assume that it is always the best play—whereas the expert who is familiar with the principles of bridge strategy does not really need the rule but can decide the individual case directly from them. With rules of thumb, one might say, it is the rule that gives way when there are accepted variations in practice. With Aquinas's account of the mutability of practical precepts, however, the "blame" seems to fall at least equally on something about particulars.[82]

To repeat, then, if the common conceptions are the same for all, and individual claims of exception can be definitely decided by appeal (ultimately) to them, why does not the "middle" hold? The answer, I think, is that it does; but to see why, we must return, ironically enough, to the

[80] In both moral and legal reasoning, the examination (and experience) of borderline or "difficult" cases can be crucial to the process of clarifying and refining our intuitions. Although this is clearly not what Aquinas had in mind in his account of the mutability of derived principles in practical reasoning, there is no reason to think he would deny its relevance in legal or even moral matters.

[81] Armstrong emphasizes this point (using "counsels" where I speak of "rules of thumb" in *Primary and Secondary Precepts*, e.g., p. 172), and I think it is generally agreed to. Of course, there is room for considerable variety between significant precepts and mere rules of thumb; rule utilitarians would have something to say here. Moreover, precepts that speak to kinds of action are not simply counsels or rules of thumb, yet they are defeasible by the addition of circumstances and the like. I am concerned here, however, with the particular case of exceptions (as I described that category above).

[82] The place of the individual in the Aristotelian system is an important topic for inquiry, I think, but also a very difficult one. It is, at least on the face of it, different from our modern view—and that of most thirteenth- and fourteenth-century Franciscans. For the latter, the idea is that the (human) individual somehow "transcends" our attempts at conceptualization; for the Aristotelian, the (material) individual somehow fails to measure up. I am not arguing here for one or the other. My point is that to understand what Aquinas is up to in talking about exceptions, one must recognize the Aristotelian context. That is to say, it is not something about our concepts or conceptual scheme that creates the need to recognize exceptions but rather something about the subject matter of practical (and hence moral) reasoning.

analogy with monsters. In the context of Aristotelian scientific explanation, monsters are a significant phenomenon—something more than the merely unusual—precisely because of the central role that classification by genus and species plays within that scheme. Monsters are an anomaly for being, we might say, in a genus but not a species, so that they are not fully intelligible in their own right (in the way a new species of animal would be).[83] They can be recognized for what they are, therefore, only as lacking or somehow failing to measure up to complete specificity.

In the context of practical reasoning, determinations are products of our thinking out what is suitable for rational natures (as individuals or in community), and they function after the fashion of species in scientific classification. The context of practical reason is action, so the analogy will not be exact. But the idea I want to suggest is, roughly put, that if an individual case does not fall directly under or follow deductively from a common conception, we can fully understand that particular case only if we can place it either as an instance of or exception to some derived precept which is a (proximate or remote) determination of a common conception.

It is true, of course, that we sometimes appeal to difficult cases to show that something is wrong about a certain determination (a statute or precept or principle upon which we have been operating). But where, in practical reason, exceptions stand to determinations as monstrous births to species, they are neither adjustments to a determination nor competitors claiming, as it were, to be a new species.[84] When we consider exceptions in this radical way, therefore, we do not simply ignore the derived precept and apply the higher-level precept directly to the facts of the case. For the higher-level precept does not apply to the exception as species to individual, or even as a genus would to a normal individual; it applies rather in the anomalous way that a genus applies to something that does not fully (or perhaps not at all) fulfill the properties of

[83] "Being in a genus but not in a species" is the anomaly I have emphasized as characteristic of exceptions. One might think that being in a species simply adds certain properties to those covered by being in a genus. But Peter Geach has pointed out that there may not always be an identifiable "genus property." For example, a thing is not at one time (or at any time) "just colored" and then made specifically red or blue by the addition of something to that "property." Red and blue are rather *ways* of being colored. See G. E. M. Anscombe and Peter Geach, *Three Philosophers* (Oxford: Blackwells, 1961), p. 81. And Aristotle at one point describes the developing fetus as "just animal": *The Generation of Animals*, 3.2 (736b2–5), cited in Gareth B. Matthews, "Aristotelian Essentialism," *Philosophy and Phenomenological Research* 50, supp. (1990): 257.

[84] The individual does not stand to a determination as a further determination of it. In the analogy, the individual does not stand to the species as the species does to genus; it is an instance of the species. See also note 75 above.

any species.[85] Practical reason, therefore, cannot do without intermediate or derived principles any more than speculative reason can. There is still a unity to the process, Aquinas insists, because "the" first principle of practical reason—that good is to be sought and evil avoided—governs the derivation and the application of all other precepts.[86]

One might claim, however, that Aquinas's *moral* theory is significantly independent of the plurality of precepts within the process of reasoning in practical affairs. One might hold, for example, that practical reason is only a (relatively) formal scheme for getting from general principles to particular cases of action, where the normative major premises are supplied by an independent process for establishing moral claims: in effect, "Morality in, morality out." Or one might hold that for Aquinas the morally right thing to do is established by some "maximizing" procedure. As it happens, I favor the idea that, in his moral theory, substantive moral (legal or political) principles and precepts are generated by practical reason in a process of "thinking things out" with an eye to basic (or "natural") human goals.[87] Establishing that claim, however, goes beyond anything I have developed in this essay.

What I do want to emphasize is that the deduction of a more specific from a less specific precept (as in the case of "killing" from "harm") is relatively trivial compared with the derivation (broadly speaking) of moral precepts and the determination of what is basic among them—and, even more specific to my present purposes, that to assess claims about mutability of any of the sorts I have set out is to engage in the very reasoning that recognized or derived the precept under consideration. It follows that if determination is relevant within morality as such, the possibility of exceptions is an important symptom for understanding the structure of Aquinas's moral theory. And if that is right, the somewhat "messy" quality of exceptionability, as separate from defeasibility, will be found in morality as well.

[85] In developing the analogy of exceptions to monsters, I do not mean to imply that one must subscribe to a genus-species system of explanation in science in order to make use of Aquinas's ideas about practical reasoning. Our current intuitions about the method and results of the sciences are importantly different from those of Aristotelian science. If one defines the object of science in terms of prediction and control, e.g., it will already be more "practical" than Aristotle would allow for speculative reason. And this is only one feature that would affect our immediate sense of any contrast or comparison between science and ethics. In the analogy I have been developing, it is the relation of ultimate to intermediate goals—including the relation of ends to means, or of goals to ways of realizing goals—that takes the place of a structure of genus and species.

[86] Aquinas argues explicitly for a plurality of precepts within the unity of practical reason in *ST* IaIIae.94.2, and the first reply.

[87] In this respect, at least, I am on the side of such people as Grisez and Donagan; see notes 19 and 49 above.

6

In sections 3 and 4 I tried to develop a classification of kinds of mutability that allows one to see in some detail how Aquinas can be defended against the charge that adjustments to the precepts of natural law—and especially, the possibility of exceptions to derived precepts—is not after all a loose cannon in his system of practical reasoning. That is the main purpose of my essay. The missing canons of assessment, as I have pointed out, constitute a difficulty for any full-scale reconstruction of Aquinas's system, but I do not think they need to be a threat to the theory.[88]

What I wanted to bring out in section 5 is that Aquinas's allowing for exceptions should be seen not as a mere adjustment within his account of practical reasoning but in fact as pointing to deep structural elements in the theory. Despite its familiarity, I think, Aristotle's comment about the exactness to be expected of different fields of inquiry needs to be pressed critically—much more fully than I have done here—in order to reveal the basic picture of reasoning about affairs both scientific and practical which it presupposes. I have tried to show how understanding different kinds of mutability need not unsettle a theory that emphasizes principled reasoning. At the same time, I have tried to use the radical character of exceptionability to emphasize what I have done no more than point to: the need for a more careful analysis of how the structure of practical reasoning, of which mutability is a symptom, affects any moral theory in which practical reasoning plays an essential role.[89]

[88] In a virtue theory of ethics, e.g., the judgment of "the virtuous person" (however that is to be established) will always take some precedence in the application of rules. But see note 72 above.

[89] I have benefited greatly from the suggestions of the editors of this volume as well as from two anonymous referees. Norman Kretzmann had already provided me with extensive comments on a much earlier version of this paper which was read at the annual joint conference of the Society for the Study of Islamic Philosophy and Science and the Society for Ancient Greek Philosophy, held at Baruch College, New York, in October 1986.

Appendix

Many of the passages I cite and quote from deserve to be read whole. I have gathered them here under two headings: those (primarily) relevant to the comparison and contrast of speculative and practical reason, and those (primarily) relevant as cases of mutability in practical precepts.

Part I. On Speculative and Practical Reason

A. ST IaIIae.91.3

WHETHER THERE IS ANY HUMAN LAW: ... *I answer that,* as stated above [90.1 ad2], a law is a dictate of practical reason. The procedure found in practical and speculative reason is similar; for both proceed from selected principles to their conclusions, as was said above [ibid.]. Accordingly, it should be said that, just as in speculative reason from naturally known indemonstrable principles there are produced the conclusions of the diverse sciences, the knowledge of which is not naturally found in us but is acquired by the work of reason, so from the precepts of natural law, as it were from certain common, indemonstrable principles, it is necessary for human reason to proceed to some more particular dispositions. And these particular dispositions arrived at by human reason, are called human laws, provided the other essential conditions of law are observed. ...

Utrum sit aliqua lex humana: ... Responsio: Dicendum quod, sicut supra [90.1 ad2] dictum est, lex quoddam dictamen practicae rationis. Similis autem processus esse invenitur rationis practicae et speculativae; utraque enim ex quibusdam principiis ad quasdam conclusiones procedit, ut superius [ibid.] habitum est. Secundum hoc ergo dicendum est quod, sicut in ratione speculativa ex principiis indemonstrabilibus naturaliter cognitis producuntur conclusiones diversarum scientiarum, quarum cognitio non est nobis naturaliter indita, sed per industriam rationis inventa; ita etiam ex praeceptis legis naturalis, quasi ex quibusdam principiis communibus indemonstrabilibus, necesse est quod ratio humana procedat ad aliqua magis particulariter disponenda. Et ista particulares dispositiones adinventae secundum rationem humanam, dicuntur leges humanae, servatis aliis conditionibus quae pertinet ad rationem legis. ...

B. *ST IaIIae.94.2*

WHETHER THE NATURAL LAW CONTAINS MANY PRECEPTS OR ONE ONLY: ... *On the contrary*, the precepts of the natural law in humans stand in relation to actions as first principles do to demonstration. But there are several first indemonstrable principles. Therefore, there are several precepts of natural law.

I answer that, as was said above [91.3], the precepts of natural law are in this way related to practical reason, just as the first principles of demonstration are related to speculative reason: for both are certain principles known *per se*. However, something is said to be *per se nota* in two ways: in one way, in itself; in the other, with respect to us. A proposition is said to be *per se nota* in itself if its predicate pertains to the very idea [*ratio*] of the subject. But it can happen that to someone ignorant of the definition of the subject, such a proposition will not be *per se nota*. For example, this proposition, "Man is rational" is *per se nota* of itself, since who says *man* says *rational being*. And yet to someone ignorant of what man is, this proposition is not *per se nota*. And hence it is that, as Boethius says, certain axioms or propositions are commonly *per se nota* for all; and of this sort are those propositions of which the terms are known to all: e.g., "The whole is greater than its part" and "Equals added to equals give you equals." But certain propositions are *per se nota* only for the wise, for only the intelligent know what the terms of those propositions signify: e.g., to those who know that an angel is not a body, it is *per se nota* that "Angels are not circumscribed in place"; but that is not clear to the unlearned for they cannot grasp it.

With those things which fall within the apprehension of all, there is found a certain order. For that which first falls under apprehension is being, the understanding of which is included in anything whatever anyone apprehends. And therefore the first indemonstrable principle is that the same thing cannot be affirmed and denied, upon which the idea of being and non-being is grounded. And upon this principle all the others are grounded, as is said in *Metaphysics IV*. However, just as being is the first that falls under apprehension unqualifiedly, so good is the first that falls under the apprehension of practical reason (which is ordered to action): for any agent acts because of an end, which has the *ratio* of good. And therefore the first principle of practical reason is what is grounded on the *ratio* of good: i.e., "Good is what all things seek." This is, therefore, the first precept of law: that good is to be done and pursued, and evil is to be avoided. And upon this are founded all other precepts of natural law; so that whatever practical reason naturally apprehends as a human good (or evil) belongs to the precepts of natural law as something to be done or avoided.

Because good has the *ratio* of an end, and evil that of the contrary, it follows that anything to which humans have a natural inclination, reason naturally apprehends as good and consequently as something to be pursued and its contrary as evil and to be avoided. Therefore, the order of the precepts of natural law follows the order of natural inclination. In humans, there is first of all an inclination to good in accordance with a nature shared with all substances: inasmuch as every substance seeks to conserve its own existence according to its nature; and by reason of this inclination there pertains to natural law that through which human life is conserved and its contrary impeded. Secondly, there is in the human an inclination to something more specific, inasmuch as its nature is common with the other animals. And according to this, those things are said to be of natural law which nature teaches all animals: e.g., the conjunction of male and female, the education of the young, and like things. Thirdly, there is in the human an inclination to good according to the rational nature which is proper to it: thus humans have a natural inclination to know the truth about God and to live in society; and in this respect, whatever pertains to this inclination belongs to natural law: for example, to shun ignorance, to avoid offending those among whom one has to live, and other such things regarding the above inclination.

Utrum lex naturalis contineat plura praecepta, vel unum tantum: . . . Sed contra est quia sic se habent praecepta legis naturalis in homine quantum ad operabilia sicut se habent prima principia in demonstrativis. Sed prima principia indemonstrabilia sunt plura. Ergo etiam praecepta legis naturalis.

Responsio: Dicendum quod, sicut supra [91.3] dictum est, praecepta legis naturae hoc modo se habent ad rationem practicae, sicut principia prima demonstrationum se habent ad rationem speculativam: utraque enim sunt quaedam principia per se nota. Dicitur autem aliquid per se notum dupliciter: uno modo, secundum se; alio modo, quoad nos. Secundum se quidem quaelibet propositio dicitur per se nota, cuius praedicatum est de ratione subjecti; contingit tamen quod ignoranti definitionem subjecti talis propositio non erit per se nota. Sicut ista propositio, Homo est rationale, est per se nota secundum sui naturam, quia qui dicit hominem, dicit rationale; et tamen ignoranti quid sit homo, haec propositio non est per se nota. Et inde est quod, sicut Boetius in libro de Hebdomad., quaedam sunt dignitates vel propositiones per se nota communiter omnibus; et hujusmodi sunt illae propositiones quarum termini sunt omnibus noti, ut Omnes totum est maius sui parte, et Quae uni et eadem sunt aequalia, sibi invicem sunt aequalia. Quaedam vero propositiones sunt per se notae solis sapientibus, qui termi-

nos propositionum intelligunt quid significent; sicut intelligenti quod
angelus non est corpus, per se notum est quod non est circumscriptive
in loco, quod non est manifestum rudibus, qui hoc non capiunt.

In his autem quae in apprehensione omnium cadunt, quidam ordo
invenitur. Nam illud quod primo cadit sub apprehensione est ens cuius
intellectus includitur in omnibus quaecumque quis apprendit. Et ideo
primum principium indemonstrabile est quod non est simul affirmare
et negare, quod fundatur supra rationem entis et non entis; et super hoc
principio omnia alia fundantur, ut dicitur in IV *Metaphys*. Sicut autem
ens est primum quod cadit in apprehensione simpliciter, ita bonum est
primum quod cadit in apprehensione practicae rationis, quae ordinatur
ad opus; omne enim agens agit propter finem, qui habent rationem
boni. Et ideo primum principium in ratione practicae est quod fundatur
supra rationem boni, quae est Bonum est quod omnia appetunt. Hoc est
ergo primum praeceptum legis, quod bonum est faciendum et prosequendum, et malum vitandum. Et super hoc fundatur omnia alia praecepta legis naturae; ut scilicet omnia illa facienda vel vitanda pertineant
ad praecepta legis naturae, quae ratio practica naturaliter apprendit
esse bona humana.

Quia vero bonum habet rationem finis, malum autem rationem
contrarii, inde est quod omnia illa ad quae homo habet naturalem inclinationem, ratio naturaliter apprehendit ut bona, et per consequens ut
opere prosequnda, et contraria eorum ut mala et vitanda. Secundum igitur ordinem inclinationum naturalium, est ordo praeceptorum legis
naturae. Inest primo inclinatio homini ad bonum secundum naturam
in qua communicat cum omnibus substantiis; prout scilicet quaelibet
substantia appetat conservationem sui esse secundum suam naturam.
Et secundum hanc inclinationem, pertinent ad legem naturalem ea per
quae vita hominis conservatur, et contrarium impeditur. Secundo inest
homini inclinatio ad aliqua magis specialia, secundum naturam in qua
communicat cum ceteris animalibus. Et secundum hoc, dicuntur ea esse
de legi naturali quae natura omnia animalia docuit, ut est coniunctio
maris et feminae, et educatio liberorum, et similia. Tertio modo inest
homini inclinatio ad bonum secundum naturam rationis, quae est sibi
propria; sicut homo habet naturalem inclinationem spectant; utpote
quod homo ignorantiam vitet, et quod alios non offendat cum quibus
debet conversari, et cetera hiusmodi quae hoc spectant.

C. ST IaIIae.94.4

·WHETHER NATURAL LAW IS THE SAME FOR ALL: . . . *I answer that*,
as was said above [94.2], those things to which humans are naturally in-

clined pertain to natural law; and among them, it is proper to humans to be inclined to act according to reason. And it pertains to reason to proceed from the common to the proper, as is clear from *Physics I*. However, speculative and practical reason are situated differently in this matter. For since speculative reason deals chiefly with the necessary, which cannot be otherwise than it is, truth is found in its proper conclusions without fail, just as it is in its common principles. But practical reason deals with contingent things, among which are human activities. And therefore, even if there is a certain necessity in its common [principles], the more one descends to the proper [conclusions], the more one finds defects. Therefore, in speculative matters, truth is the same for all both in principles and in conclusions, though the truth in conclusions is not known by all but only that in the principles which are called "common conceptions." In the case of actions, however, the truth or rectitude of practice is not the same for all with respect to the proper [conclusions] but only with respect to the common [conceptions]; and even where there is the same rectitude for all in proper conclusions, it is not equally known to all.

It is clear, therefore, that, as regards the common principles of speculative or practical reason, there is the same truth and rectitude for all, and it is equally known. Indeed, with regard to the proper conclusions of speculative reason, truth is the same for all but not equally known to all: it is true for all that the angles of a triangle are equal to two right angles, although this is not known to all. But as to the proper conclusions of practical reason, truth or rectitude is not the same for all, and even among those for whom it is the same, it is not equally known. Thus it is right and true for all that action be carried out according to reason. From this principle it follows, however, as if a proper conclusion, that deposits [i.e., goods held in trust] be returned; and this is true for the most part. But it can happen in some case that it would be ruinous [*damnosum*], and as a result irrational, if the deposit were returned: for example, if someone sought it to fight against [one's] country. And one will find this defect all the more, the more one descends to particulars: for example, if one says that deposits should be returned with such and such guarantee, or something of that sort. For the more particular conditions that are added, the more ways it could fail, so that there may be no right thing to do either in returning or not returning [the deposit].

Therefore, it should be said that natural law, with respect to its first common principles, is the same for all with regard to both rectitude and knowledge. But with regard to certain proper matters, which are, as it were, conclusions from the common principles, it is the same for all for the most part, with regard both to rectitude and knowledge; but in some few cases it can fail: in regard to rectitude because of some particular impediments (just as generable and corruptible natures fail in rare cases because of impediments); and in regard to knowledge because in some, reason is depraved because of passion or evil habits or evil dispositions of nature: e.g., formerly among the Germans theft, although it is expressly against natural law, was not considered wrong, as Ceasar relates.

Utrum lex naturae sit una apud omnes: . . . Responsio: Dicendum quod, sicut supra [94.2] dictum est, ad legem naturae pertinent ea ad quae homo naturaliter inclinatur; inter quae homini proprium est inclinetur ad agendum secundum rationem. Ad rationem autem pertinet ex communibus ad propria procedere, ut patet ex I Physic. Aliter tamen circa hoc se habet ratio speculativa, et aliter ratio practica. Quia enim ratio speculativa praecipue negotiatur circa necessario, quae impossibile est aliter se habere, absque aliquo defectu invenitur veritas in conclusionibus propriis, sicut et in principiis communibus. Sed ratio practica negotiatur circa contingentia, in quibus sunt operationes humanae; et ideo, etsi in communibus sit aliqua necessitas quanto magis ad propria descenditur, tanto magis invenitur defectus. Sic igitur in speculativis est eadem veritas apud omnes tam in principiis quam in conclusionibus, licet veritas non apud omnes cognoscatur in conclusionibus, sed solum in principiis, quae dicuntur communes conceptiones. In operativis autem non est eadem veritas vel rectitudo practica apud omnes quantum ad propria, sed solum quantum ad communia, et apud illos apud quos est eadem rectitudo in propriis non est aequaliter omnibus nota.

Sic igitur patet quod, quantum ad communia principia rationis sive speculativae sive practicae, est eadem veritas seu rectitudo apud omnes, aequaliter nota. Quantum vero ad proprias conclusiones rationis speculativae, est eadem veritas apud omnes, non tamen aequaliter omnibus nota; apud omnes enim verum est quod triangulus habet tres angulos aequales duobus rectis, quamvis hoc non sit omnibus notum. Sed quantum ad proprias conclusiones rationis practicae, nec est eadem veritas seu rectitudo apud omnes; nec etiam apud quos est eadem, est aequaliter nota. Apud omnes enim hoc rectum est et verum ut secundum rationem agatur. Ex hoc autem principio sequitur quasi conclusio propria, quod deposita sint reddenda, et hoc quidem ut in pluribus verum est; sed potest in aliquo casu contingere quod sit damnosum et per consequens irrationabile, si deposita reddantur, puta si aliquis petat ad impugnandam patriam. Et hoc tanto magis invenitur deficere, quando magis ad particularia descenditur, puta si dicatur quod deposita sunt reddenda cum tali cautione, vel tali modo; quanto enim plures conditiones particulares apponuntur, tanto pluribus modis poterit deficere, ut non sit rectum vel in reddendo vel in non reddendo.

Sic igitur dicendum quod lex naturae, quantum ad prima principia communia, est eadem apud omnes et secundum rectitudinem, et secundum notitiam. Sed quantum ad quaedam propria, quae sunt quasi conclusiones principiorum communium, est eadem apud omnes ut in pluribus et secundum rectitudinem et secundum notitiam; sed ut in paucioribus potest deficere et quantum ad rectitudinem, propter aliqua particularia impedimenta (sicut etiam naturae generabiles et corruptibiles deficiunt ut in paucioribus, propter impedimenta), et etiam quantum ad notitiam; et hoc propter hoc quod aliqui habent depravatum rationem ex passione, seu ex mala consuetudine, seu ex mala habitudine naturae; sicut apud Germanos olim latrocinium non reputabatur iniquum, cum tamen sit expresse contra legem naturae, ut refert Iulius Caesar, in libro de Bello Gallico.

Part II. Cases of Mutability

A. The Siege (ST IaIIae.96.6)

WHETHER SOMEONE SUBJECT TO THE LAW MAY RIGHTLY ACT AGAINST THE LETTER OF THE LAW: . . . Since the legislator cannot envisage every individual case, he frames a law according to what happens most of the time, directing his intention to the common welfare. So if a case arises in which observing such a law would be damaging to the common well-being, it is not to be observed. For example, in a city under siege, it may be ordered that the gates be kept closed; and this serves the common welfare most of the time. But it might happen that the enemy is pursuing some citizens through whom the city is maintained; it would be most harmful to the city if the gates were not opened to them. And so in such a case, the gates are to be opened, against the letter of the law, so that the common advantage will be served, which the legislator intended.

Utrum Ei Qui Subditur Legi Liceat Praeter Verba Legis Agere: . . . Quia igitur legislator non potest omnes singulares casus intueri, proponent legem ea quae in pluribus accidunt, ferens intentionem suam ad communem utilitatem. Inde si emergat casus in quo observatio talis legis sit damnosa communi saluti non est observanda: sicut si in civitate obsessa statuatur lex quod portae civitatis maneant clausae, hoc est utile communi saluti ut in pluribus; si tamen contingat casus quod hostes insequantur aliquos cives per quos civitas conservatur, damnosissimun esset civitati nisi eis portae aperirentur. Et ideo in tali casu essent portae aperiendae contra verba legis, ut servaretur utilitas communis quam legislator intendit.

B. The Starving Family (ST IIaIIae.66.7)

WHETHER THEFT IS ALLOWABLE IN CASES OF NECESSITY: ... *On the contrary*, in a condition of necessity, all things are common; and thus it is not a sin if someone takes something of another's which necessity has made common. . . . It is no problem for the division and apportionment of things established by law that human needs be met with those things. And so, according to natural justice, the poor are to be sustained from what some have in superabundance. . . . However, since the needs of those who suffer are many, and it is not possible for all to be served from the same thing, the management of one's property is left to the judgment of each, so that the needs of the suffering can be met. But should there be an urgent and evident need, where it is clear the immediate need must be met from whatever is available—for example, when a person is in imminent danger—and cannot be met otherwise, then one can legitimately supply the need out of someone else's things, either secretly or openly. And this does not really amount to theft or plunder.

Utrum Liceat Alicui Furari Propter Necessitatem? ... Sed contra est quod in necessitate sunt omnia communia, et ita non videtur esse peccatum, si alicuis rem alterius accipiat propter necessitatem sibi factam communem. Responsio . . . Et ideo per rerum divisionem et appropriationem de jure humano procedentem non impeditur quid hominis necessitati sit subveniendum ex huiusmodi rebus. Et ideo res quas aliqui superabundanter habent, ex naturali jure debenter pauperum sustentatione. . . . Sed quia multi sunt necessitatem patientes, et non potest ex eodem re omnibus subverneri, committitur arbitrio uniuscujusque dispensatio propriarum rerum, ut ex eis subveniat necessitatem patientibus. Si tamen adeo sit urgens et evidence necessitas ut manifestum sit instanti necessitati de rebus occurrentibus esse subveniendum, puta cum imminet personae periculum, et aliter subveniri non potest, tunc licite potest aliquis ex rebus alienis suae necessitati subvenire, sive manifeste sive occulte sublatis; nec hoc proprie habet rationem furti vel rapinae.

C. Special Divine Commands

1. WHETHER NATURAL LAW CAN BE CHANGED (*ST* IaIIae.94.5 ad2): [Reply to the second objection:] All men without exception, guilty and innocent alike, have to suffer the sentence of natural death from divine power because of original sin. . . . Consequently, without injustice God's command can inflict death on anyone, guilty or innocent. Similarly, adultery is intercourse with a woman to whom one is not married in accordance with divinely given law; nevertheless, to have intercourse with a woman by divine command is neither adultery nor fornication. And the same idea holds for theft which is the taking of what belongs to another. For what is taken by God's command, who is the lord [or owner] of the universe is not taken against the lord's [or owner's] will, which is [the essence of] theft.

Utrum Lex Naturae mutari possit: Ad secundum dicendum quod naturali morte omnes communitur, tam nocentes quam innocentes; quae quidem naturalis mors divina potestate in ducitur propter peccatum originale. . . . Et ideo absque alia injustitia secundum mandatum Dei potest infligi mors cuicumque homini vel nocenti vel innocenti. Similiter etiam adulterium est concubitus cum uxore aliena, quae quidem est ei deputata secundum legem Dei divinitis traditam: unde ad quamcumque mulierem aliquis accedat ex mandato divino non est adulaterium nec fomicatio. Et eadem ratio est de furto, quod est acceptio rei alienae; quidquid enim accipit aliquid ex mandato Dei, qui est dominus universorum, non accipit absque voluntate domini; quod est furari.

2. WHETHER THE PRECEPTS OF THE DECALOGUE ARE DISPENSABLE (ST IaIIae100.8 ad3):   [Reply to the third objection:] . . . When the children of Israel, by God's command, took the spoils of the Egyptians, it was not theft, because these were due to them by the sentence of God. Likewise, Abraham, in consenting to kill his son, did not commit homicide, since it was right that his son should be put to death by the command of God, the Lord of life and death. For it is God who inflicts the punishment of death on all men, the just as well as unjust, on account of the sin of our first parents; and if a man carries out this sentence on the authority of God, he is no murderer any more than God is. In the same way, Hosea, in taking to wife a harlot or adulteress, was not guilty of adultery or fornication, since she was his by command of God, the author of the institution of marriage.

Utrum Praecepta Decalogi Sint Dispensabilia: Ad tertium . . . quando filii Israel praecepto Dei tulerunt AEgyptiorum spolia, non fuit furtum: quia hoc eis debenatur ex sententia Dei. Similiter etiam Abraham, cum consensit occidere filium, non consentit in homicidium: quia debitum erat eum occidi per mandatum Dei, qui est Dominus vitae et mortis. Ipse enim est qui poenam mortis infligit omnibus hominibus, justis et injustis, pro peccato primi parentis: cujus sententiae si homo sit executor auctoritate divina, non erit homicida, secut nec Deus. Et similiter etiam Osee, accedens uxorem fornicariam, vel ad mulierem adulteram, non est moechatus nec fornicariam: quia accessit ad eam quae sua erat secundum mandatum divinum, qui est auctor institutionis matrimonii.

D. Interpretation

WHETHER THE PRECEPTS OF THE DECALOGUE ARE DISPENSABLE (*ST* IaIIae100.8):   1. [Reply to the fourth objection:] The [decision of the Maccabees] was an interpretation of the precept rather than a dispensation from it. For one is not held to be violating the Sabbath in doing something for human welfare, as the Lord himself shows (Matthew 12:3).

2. [Reply to the third objection:] The Decalogue forbids the taking of human life insofar as it is undue; in this the precept embodies the very nature of justice. Nor can human law permit that a man be lawfully killed when he does not deserve it. But it is no infringement of justice to put to death criminals or the state's enemies. This does not contravene the commandment; nor is it the homicide which is forbidden, as Augustine says [*De libero arbitrio* 1.4]. Likewise, when someone is deprived of what belongs to him, if he deserves to lose it, this is not the theft or robbery which is forbidden by the commandment. . . . Accordingly, the precepts of the Decalogue are immutable insofar as they embody justice in its essence; but as applied to particular acts—as for example, whether they constitute homicide, theft, adultery or not—they admit of change. . . .

Utrum Praecepta Decalogi Sint Dispensabilia: Ad quartum dicendum quod illa excogitatio magis fuit interpretatio praecepti quam dispensatio. Non enim intelligitur violare sabbatum qui facit opus quod est necessarium ad salutem humanam; sicut Dominus probat.

Ad tertium dicendum quod occisio hominis prohibetur in decalogo secundum quod habet rationem indebiti; sic enim praeceptum continet ipsam rationem justitiae. Lex autem humana hoc concedere non potest, quod licite homo indebite occidatur. Sed malefactores occidi, vel hostes reipublicae, hoc non est indebitum. Unde hoc non contrariatur praecepto decalogi: nec talis occisio est homicidum, quod praecepto decalogi prohibetur, ut Augustinus dicit. Et similiter si alicui auferatur quod suum erat, si debitum est quod ipsum amittat, hoc non est furtum vel rapina, quae praecepto decalogi prohibentur. . . . Sic igitur praecepta ipsa decalogi, quantum ad rationem justitiae quam continent, immutabilia sunt. Sed quantum ad aliquam determinationem per applicationem ad singulares actus, ut scilicet hoc vel illud sit homicidium, furtem vel adulterium, aut non, hoc quidem est mutabile. . . .

E. *The Deposit*

[1. See paragraph 4 of *ST* IaIIae.94.4, in Part I, above]

2. WHETHER JUDGING THE EXCEPTIONAL IS A SPECIAL VIRTUE . . . (*ST* IIaIIae.51.4): . . . Cognitive habits are distinguished according to higher and lower principles. For example, in speculative [matters], wisdom considers higher principles than science does, and so is distinguished from it. And it must be the same in [practical matters].

It is clear that those things which are beyond the order of lower principles or causes are sometimes traced back to principles of a higher order: for example as monstrous births of animals are beyond the order of the active power of the seed but still fall under principles of a higher order, such as that of celestial bodies or, ultimately, divine providence. Hence a firm judgment cannot be made about this sort of monstrosity by considering the active power of the seed; although a judgment can be made from a consideration of divine providence.

Now it sometimes happens that something is to be done outside the common rules for action: for example, that a deposit is not to be returned to an enemy of the country, or something else of this sort. And so one has to assess this sort of case in accordance with some higher principles than the common rules with which *synesis* deals. And the higher principles require a higher power of judgment which is called *gnome*, and which implies a certain perspicacity of judgment. [*Synesis* is sound judgment according to the common rules of conduct: *ST* IIaIIae.48.unica. *Gnome* is judgment of the exceptional. See also *epikeia* or equity: *ST* IIaIIae.120.]

Utrum Gnome Sit Specialis Virtus: . . . Dicendum quod habitus cognoscitivi distinguuntur secundum altiora vel inferiora principia; sicut sapientia in speculativis altior principia considerat quam scientia, et ideo ab ea distinguitur; et ita etiam oportet esse in activis.

Manifestum est autem quod illa quae sunt praeter ordinem inferioris principii sive causae reducuntur quandoque in ordinem altioris principii; sicut monstruosi partus animalium sunt praeter ordinem virtutis activae in semine, tamen cadunt sub ordine altioris principii, scilicet celestis coporis, vel ulterius providentiae divinae. Unde ille qui considerat virtutem activum in semine non posset certum judicium ferre de hujusmodi monstris; de quibus tamen potest judicare secundum considerationem divinae providentiae.

Contingit autem quandoque aliquid esse faciendum praeter communes regulas agendorum, puta cum impugnatori patriae non est depositum reddendum vel aliquid aliud hujusmodi. Et ideo oportet de hujusmodi judicare secundum aliqua altiora principia, quam sint regulae communes, secundum quas judicat synesis; et secundum illa altiora principia exigitur altior virtus judicativa, quae vocatur gnome, quae importat quamdam perspicacitatem judicii.

III

&

MORAL THEORY IN PHILOSOPHY OF LANGUAGE AND METAPHYSICS

E. JENNIFER ASHWORTH

ﾞﾑ

Aquinas on Significant Utterance: Interjection, Blasphemy, Prayer

It may seem perverse to turn to Aquinas's moral philosophy for light on his philosophy of language, but I argue that his study of human actions forced him to modify the intellectualism prevalent in much thirteenth-century logic and grammar.[1] This intellectualism had three components. First, it privileged the notion of language as a rational, rule-governed system which could be studied in isolation from context and speaker intention.[2] Second, it focused on propositions as the linguistic units which conveyed the information necessary for *scientia* and rejected other forms of discourse as irrelevant. Third, it described individual words as the signs of concepts and ignored utterances which express passions of one sort and another. These components, particularly the second and third, do indeed characterize Aquinas's considered ap-

---

[1] A note on texts: I have used the Leonine editions for *In DA, In DSS, In NE, In PH,* and *In Po.* I have used the Marietti texts for *In I Cor, In Joh, In PA, QDP, QDV,* and *ST.* I have used the Busa edition for *CA, DRP, In Matt,* and *In Sent.*

[2] For discussion of this approach in the modistae, and for full information about grammarians who adopted an alternative approach, which she has dubbed intentionalist because of its focus on the *intentio proferentis,* see the papers by Irène Rosier cited throughout, all of which contain further references. See esp. Irène Rosier, "La distinction entre actus exercitus et actus significatus dans les sophismes grammaticaux du MS BN lat. 16618 et autres textes apparentés," in *Sophisms in Medieval Logic and Grammar,* ed. Stephen Read (Dordrecht: Kluwer Academic Publishers, 1992), pp. 257–59; and her book (published after this paper was written), *La parole comme acte: Sur la grammaire et la sémantique au xiiie siècle* (Paris: J. Vrin, 1994). Rosier's work is particularly important for its demonstration that the modistic paradigm does not apply to much thirteenth-century grammar. I would like to take this opportunity of thanking Irène Rosier for the generous way in which she has shared her as yet unpublished research with me; this essay owes much to her work.

proach to language as expressed particularly in his commentary on Aristotle's *De interpretatione*. Nonetheless, his recognition that human beings are animals with passions, together with his recognition that utterances are themselves a kind of action subject to moral assessment, forced him to take a different direction in other places.[3]

I proceed as follows. In sections 1 and 2, I set forth the intellectualist components of Aquinas's theory, paying particular attention to the manifestation of truth and to the senses in which conventionally significant utterances could also be said to be naturally significant. In sections 3, 4, and 5, I explore the relationships between animal noises and human utterances, paying particular attention to the role of the imagination and to interjections. In sections 6 and 7, I consider the role of human passions and human intentions in the understanding and production of conventional utterances, especially sinful ones. In sections 8 and 9, I look at two aspects of language production which can serve to mitigate sin: slips of the tongue, and linguistic incontinence, or breaking out into ill-considered words. In the last section, I turn to the situation in which we recite and appropriate the words of others, particularly in prayer. Throughout, I examine not only Aquinas's own doctrines but also those of grammarians and logicians contemporary with him.

1. Words, Concepts, and the Manifestation of Truth

In order to understand the intellectualist approach, we must consider the central semantic notion of signification (*significatio*) as it is presented in Aquinas's commentary on *De interpretatione*, one of the few places where he speaks explicitly as a logician. It is important to recognize that, given the subject matter of *De interpretatione*, the focus is on nouns, verbs, and expressions (*orationes*).[4] I cite only those nouns and verbs that pick

---

[3] Rosier has shown that in his discussion of the sacraments Aquinas was far closer to the intentionalist grammarians than he was to the modistae. See Irène Rosier, "Signes et sacrements: Thomas d'Aquin et la grammaire spéculative," *Revue des sciences philosophiques et théologiques* 74 (1990): 431–32. She writes (p. 394): "Les particularités linguistiques des formules sacramentaires, et du sacrement comme signe non seulement cognitif, mais opératif, l'importance accordée à l'intention du locuteur et du récepteur, la conjonction de ces divers éléments dans un acte à chaque fois singulier, nous situent d'emblée dans la dimension 'pragmatique' du langage, développée, à la même époque, en ce milieu du XIIIe siècle, par les grammairiens 'intentionalistes.'" Both here and later (p. 433) she speaks of the encounter between grammarians and theologians, but she refuses to speculate about whose influence was primary (pp. 432–33).

[4] Aquinas explains this limitation: *In PH* I.1, p. 5, 34 to p. 6, 46.

out nonmental objects and activities, but we must remember that medieval authors were perfectly well aware of the problems presented on the one hand by terms picking out mental, abstract, or fictional entities, and on the other hand by syncategorematic terms such as 'all' and 'not.' We must also remember that a term's signification cannot be taken as equivalent to its meaning.[5] A term can signify both concepts and things, but it does not mean either.

In the thirteenth century there were two not entirely compatible approaches to signification, each based on a sentence from *De interpretatione*. According to the first approach, based on *De interpretatione* 16b19–21, to signify is to generate or establish an understanding.[6] Following the spirit of this phrase, Peter of Spain wrote: "A significative utterance is one that represents something to the hearer, for instance, 'man,' or the groan of an invalid."[7] We should notice two things here. First, the emphasis is placed not on the speaker but on the hearer. Second, given this emphasis, it is possible to regard groans and perhaps also animal sounds as significant. So long as the hearer can acquire some understanding through hearing, the utterance is significant even if the speaker is incapable of rational, abstract thought, and even if the speaker has no intention of conveying a message.

The second approach tied the significative power of an utterance to its being the sign of a concept. The crucial text here is *De interpretatione* 16a3–4: "Spoken words are signs of concepts" (or "Sunt ergo ea que sunt

---

[5] For a much fuller discussion of signification, see E. J. Ashworth, "Signification and Modes of Signifying in Thirteenth-Century Logic: A Preface to Aquinas on Analogy," *Medieval Philosophy and Theology* 1 (1991): 39–67. See also Irène Rosier, "*Res significata* et *modus significandi*: Les implications d'une distinction médiévale," in *Sprachtheorien in Spätantike und Mittelalter*, ed. Sten Ebbesen (Tübingen: Gunther Narr Verlag, 1995), pp. 135–68.

[6] For the translation used by Aquinas, see *In PH*, I.5, p. 25: "Constituit enim qui dicit intellectum, et qui audit quiescit." For use of this formulation, see L. M. de Rijk, *Logica modernorum* (Assen: Van Gorcum, 1962–67), 2.1, pp. 140, 183, 190. See also, e.g., John of Dacia, *Summa gramatica*, in *Johannis Daci opera*, ed. Alfred Otto, Corpus Philosophorum Danicorum Medii Aevi I, pt. 1 (Copenhagen: G. E. C. Gad, 1955), p. 106, 22: "et sic significare est proprie intellectum constituere"; Martin of Dacia, *Quaestiones super librum Perihermeneias*, in *Martini de Dacia opera*, ed. Heinrich Roos, Corpus Philosophorum Danicorum Medii Aevi 2 (Copenhagen: G. E. C. Gad, 1961), p. 243, 25–27. "Primo modo significare est aliquid intellectum repraesentare. Nam significare est intellectum alii constituere," and cf. p. 161, 21–22: "vocem significare nihil aliud est quam intellectum alicuius constituere." For discussion, see Irène Rosier, "Variations médiévales sur l'opposition entre signification 'ad placitum' et signification naturelle," forthcoming in *Acts of the 10th European Symposium on Medieval Logic and Semantics*.

[7] Peter of Spain, *Tractatus, called afterwards Summule logicales*, ed. L. M. de Rijk (Assen: Van Gorcum, 1972), pp. 1–2: "Vox significativa est illa que auditui aliquid representat, ut '*homo*', vel gemitus infirmorum."

in uoce earum que sunt in anima passionum note," as the normal medieval translation has it).[8] A related text, which was very influential in medieval grammar, is found in Priscian, who wrote that a significant utterance (a *vox articulata*, in his terminology) is one that is joined to some sense in the mind of the person speaking ("copulata cum aliquo sensu mentis eius, qui loquitur").[9] Both texts support the view that it is the speaker's intellectual capacity and intentions that are crucial to significant utterance, and this certainly seems to be Aquinas's own view. In his commentary he writes that generating an understanding in the mind of a hearer is a property (*proprium*) that a significant utterance has just because it is the sign of an understanding.[10]

Aquinas recognized that we use words to speak about external objects, but he emphasized that the signification of concepts is immediate, whereas the signification of external objects is mediate.[11] This was a fairly standard view, found in grammarians as well as logicians and theologians. For instance, in Pseudo-Kilwardby's *Commentary on 'Priscianus Maior'* we find the claim "An utterance is instituted to signify an understanding of the mind primarily and per se, and a thing by means of that."[12] An obvious consequence of the view, at least when interpreted rigorously, is that creatures which do not have concepts are not capable of significant utterance. We will see below what modifications were introduced to allow for animal sounds and for those human utterances which do not seem to be subordinated to concepts.

Another consequence of the view is that the significance of an utter-

---

[8] Boethius's translation, cited as it appears in *In PH* I.2, p. 9. For a discussion of this passage, see Norman Kretzmann, "Aristotle on Spoken Sound Significant by Convention," in *Ancient Logic and Its Modern Interpretations*, ed. John Corcoran (Dordrecht: D. Reidel, 1974), pp. 3–21.

[9] Priscian, *Institutionum grammaticarum libri XVIII*, in *Grammatici Latini*, vols. 2–3, ed. Heinrich Keil (Leipzig, 1855: rpt. Hildesheim: Georg Olms, 1981), I.I, p. 5, 6–7. For a logician's use of Priscian, see Nicholas of Paris, *Syncategoremata*, in *The Cambridge Translations of Medieval Philosophical Texts*, vol. 1, *Logic and the Philosophy of Language*, ed. Norman Kretzmann and Eleonore Stump (Cambridge: Cambridge University Press, 1988), p. 179. Aquinas's use of *articulata* is not that of Priscian: see note 75 below.

[10] *In PH* I.5, p. 29, 263–66: "supra dictum est quod uoces significatiue significant intellectus, unde proprium uocis significatiue est quod generet aliquem intellectum in animo audientis."

[11] *In PH* I.2, p.11, 109–12: "ideo necesse fuit Aristotili dicere quod uoces significant intellectus conceptiones inmediate, et eis mediantibus res." See also, e.g., *ST* Ia.13.1: "secundum Philosophum, voces sunt signa intellectuum, et intellectus sunt rerum similitudines. Et sic patet quod voces referuntur ad res significandas, mediante conceptione intellectus."

[12] Pseudo-Kilwardby, *The Commentary on 'Priscianus Maior' Ascribed to Robert Kilwardby*, ed. K. M. Fredborg, N. J. Green-Pedersen, Lauge Nielsen, and Jan Pinborg, Cahiers de l'institut du moyen-âge grec et latin 15 (1975): 67: "Dicendum quod vox instituitur ad significandum primo et per se intellectum mentis et mediante illo rem."

ance is a function of the speaker's cognition. Aquinas constantly emphasizes that we name as we know,[13] and that names conform to our cognition rather than to things as they actually are.[14] Aquinas also tells us over and over again that "the analysis that a name signifies is the definition [ratio quam significat nomen, est definitio, ut dicitur in IV Metaphys.],"[15] or that "the analysis that a name signifies is the intellect's conception of the thing signified by the name [ratio enim quam significat nomen, est conceptio intellectus de re significata per nomen]."[16] To understand the relationship between these two formulations, we must remember both that *definitio* can be taken in more or less strict senses,[17] and that the human cognizer is capable of progression from a confused concept to a full-fledged definition.[18] Aquinas's position is perfectly compatible with the recognition that, for instance, students and teachers have a different grasp of the same realities,[19] and with the fact that there are many things whose natures we do not know and perhaps never will.[20] Indeed, this is why the pagan and the Christian can both use the word 'God' in the same sense, for neither is in a position to know God's essence.[21]

Just as Aquinas focused on nouns and verbs as the basic bearers of signification, so, when it came to expressions (*orationes*) he focused on statements, those sentences capable of being true or false. Following Aristotle, he remarked that the study of other kinds of sentence belongs to rhetoric and poetry.[22] This stance is not peculiar to his commentary on *De interpretatione*, for it relates very closely to his view that the proper

---

[13] *ST* Ia.13.prologue: "unumquodque enim nominatur a nobis, secundum quod ipsum cognoscimus"; *ST* Ia.13.3: "secundum quod apprehendit <sc. intellectus>, ita significat per nomina." Qualifications are also introduced: *ST* Ia.13.6 obj. 1: "Secundum enim quod cognoscimus aliquid, secundum hoc illud nominamus, cum nomina, secundum Philosophum, sint signa intellectuum"; ad1: "obiectio illa procedit quantum ad impositionem nominis"; *ST* Ia.13.8 obj. 2: "secundum hoc aliquid nominatur a nobis, secundum quod cognoscitur."

[14] *ST* Ia.13.9 ad2: "Nomina enim non sequuntur modum essendi qui est in rebus, sed modum essendi secundum quod in cognitione nostra est."

[15] *ST* Ia.13.6; Aristotle, *Metaphysics* 4.7 (1012a24–25). The phrase is frequently cited by Aquinas: see, e.g., *ST* Ia.13.1, Ia.13.8 ad2; Ia.85.2 ad3.

[16] *ST* Ia.13.4. Cf. *ST* Ia.5.2: "Ratio enim significata per nomen, est id quod concipit intellectus de re, et significat illud per vocem."

[17] See *In PA* II.8.484.

[18] *ST* Ia 85.3 ad2, ad3. For discussion of the progression, see Norman Kretzmann, "Infallibility, Error, and Ignorance," in *Aristotle and His Medieval Interpreters*, ed. Richard Bosley and Martin Tweedale, *Canadian Journal of Philosophy, supp. vol.* 17 (1991): 188–90.

[19] See *ST* Ia.106.4.

[20] Kretzmann, "Infallibility, Error, and Ignorance," p. 187.

[21] *ST* Ia.13.10 ad1, ad5.

[22] *In PH*, 1.7, p. 38, 109–27.

function of language is to make known the truth by means of making known our concepts.[23] He claimed that to speak with another is nothing other than to manifest one's concepts to another,[24] a view which received graphic illustration in the twelfth-century grammarian Peter Helias's remark that a locution was like a picture of the understanding.[25] Aquinas's fullest discussion is in *Summa theologiae* Ia.107.2, where he makes it clear that not all manifestation is important but only the manifestation of truths about what is external to us. He explains that since truth is the light of the intellect, and since the rule of all truth is God, the manifestation of what the mind conceives, as it depends on the First Truth, can be called both speech (*locutio*) and enlightenment (*illuminatio*), as when one man says to another, "Heaven is created by God," or "Man is an animal." On the other hand, the manifestation of those things that depend on will is mere speech (*locutio tantum*), as when one person says to another, "I want to learn this, I want to do this or that." Aquinas remarks that it does not pertain to the perfection of my intellect to know what you will or understand. More important, he says a little later that insofar as a manifestation or statement is a moral act (and truth-telling is a moral act), it must depend on the intention of the will.[26]

This notion of speech as a moral act is closely bound up with the question of what is natural to the human being. For Aquinas, what is natural for us is to be explained in terms of our having a certain kind of nature, involving a set of abilities, functions, and ends. Thus it is natural to us to speak in at least three senses. First, we are physical creatures, and so we have the natural ability to make sounds, as indeed do many animals.[27] Second, we are social creatures, and since concepts cannot be revealed without words, speech is needed to fulfil the ends of social life. In particular, it is needed to communicate abstract notions of what is harmful and useful, just and unjust.[28] Third, we are moral creatures who should

---

[23] *ST* IIaIIae.110.1: "virtus veritatis . . . in manifestatione consistit, quae fit per aliqua signa."

[24] *ST* Ia.107.1: "Nihil est enim aliud loqui ad alterum, quam conceptum mentis alteri manifestare." See also, e.g., *ST* IIaIIae.3.1; IIaIIae.91.1; IIIa.60.6.

[25] Peter Helias, *Summa super Priscianum*, ed. Leo Reilly, 2 vols. (Toronto: Pontifical Institute of Mediaeval Studies, 1993), p. 833, 33–34: "Locutio enim simili est picture, quia sicut pictura representat et depingit rem, ita quoque locutio depingit intellectum." On p. 834, 56–57, he remarks: "Non enim dicitur latine loqui / nisi ille cuius locutio aliquem intellectum generat in auditore."

[26] *ST* IIaIIae.110.1: "Inquantum tamen huiusmodi manifestatio sive enuntiatio est actus moralis, oportet quod sit voluntarius et ex intentione voluntatis dependens."

[27] *In PH* I.2, p. 12, 174–75: "uoces autem naturaliter formantur"; *In PH* I.4, p. 20, 47: "uox sit quedam res naturalis."

[28] *In Po* I.1/b, p. A 79, 147–54: "Cum ergo homini datus sit sermo a natura, et sermo ordinetur ad hoc quod homines sibi inuicem communicent in utili et nociuo, iusto et iniusto

act in concordance with right reason, aiming at the ends that are appropriate for us. This involves the manifestation of truth, for one man owes another that without which human society cannot be conserved.[29] Men could not live together if they were unable to believe each other. Lying, then, is basically unnatural, because it violates the rule that utterances are naturally signs of what is in our mind.[30] It can even be compared with bad workmanship, for just as bad workmanship is contrary to art, so lying is contrary to *scientia*.[31] Parenthetically, we may note that even telling the truth is not foolproof, for one can tell the truth unjustly, as when one speaks of another's crime contrary to right order.[32] Neither, for that matter, is remaining silent foolproof, for we may do that simply in order to anger someone.[33]

2. Rational Imposition and Natural Signification

So far, I have said nothing about how our utterances acquire their signification, a question that will lead us to consider further senses of 'natural.' The most obvious sense of 'natural' in the context of language use is the sense in which natural signification is incompatible with conventional signification. Aquinas, like everyone else, did make the distinction between utterances—such as animal noises and human groans—which signify naturally, and utterances which signify *ad placitum*. The former, which I discuss in subsequent sections, are taken to be naturally revelatory not of concepts but of specific passions and sensory states, such as fear and pain. The latter involve conventional signification. Aquinas wrote that, while it is natural to humans to signify their concepts, the determination of the signs is *secundum placitum*,[34] and he explained that *secundum placitum* means according to the institution of human will and reason.[35] The reference to reason is particularly important

---

et alia huiusmodi: sequitur, ex quo natura nichil facit frustra, quod naturaliter homines in hiis sibi communicent. Set communicatio in istis facit domum et ciuitatem; ergo homo est naturaliter animal domesticum et ciuile."

[29] *ST* IIaIIae.109.3 ad1. The same point is made in *ST* IIaIIae.114.2 ad1. See also *In PH* I.2, p. 9, 29 to p. 10, 48.

[30] *ST* IIaIIae.110.3: "cum enim voces sint signa naturaliter intellectuum, innaturale est et indebitum quod aliquis voce significet id quod non habet in mente."

[31] *ST* IaIIae.57.3 ad1.

[32] *ST* IIaIIae.62.2 ad2.

[33] *ST* IIaIIae.72.3 ad3.

[34] *ST* IIaIIae.85.1 ad3: "significare conceptus suos est homini naturale: sed determinatio signorum est secundum humanum placitum."

[35] *In PH* I.6, p. 35, 191–95: "oratio significat *secundum placitum*, id est secundum institutionem humane rationis et uoluntatis, ut supra dictum est, sicut omnia artificialia cau-

here, because one can ask whether the relationship between conventionally significative utterances and concepts is purely arbitrary, or whether there is some way in which even conventionally significative utterances can be said to be appropriate to or revelatory of specific concepts and hence of the things that are mediately signified. Although little attention was paid to the theories discussed in Plato's *Cratylus*, as they could be gleaned from such secondary authors as Ammonius,[36] there was a fair amount of discussion of various ways in which conventionally significative terms could be said to have a natural relationship to what they signify.

We must first note that for most, if not all, thirteenth-century grammarians and logicians the imposition of a term was supposed to involve its endowment not only with a primary signification, but also with a complete set of secondary grammatical significations or *modi significandi*—both essential, such as being a noun, and accidental, such as being of a particular gender. These *modi significandi* were said to be present before a word enters a sentence, and they were not thought to be altered by the role the word plays in a sentence. Peter of Spain, for instance, wrote that the person who imposes a word to signify such-and-such a thing, at the same time imposes it to signify such-and-such a gender and number.[37] In the context of such a theory, one could begin by asking whether there was some agreement between the primary significate of a word and its modes of signifying.[38] Once one has named an object, is there some constraint to put the name in a particular grammatical category (for example, noun), and does it then follow that there are other constraints (such as gender)? Even the answer that there were natural constraints here, however, did not by itself affect the arbitrariness of the original imposition.

santur ex humana uoluntate et ratione." On the general issue of how original imposition could take place, see Pseudo-Kilwardby, *The Commentary on 'Priscianus Maior'*, pp. 49–81.

[36] Ammonius, *Commentaire sur le Peri Hermeneias d'Aristote: Traduction de Guillaume de Moerbeke*, ed. Gérard Verbeke, Corpus Latinum Commentariorum in Aristotelem Graecorum II (Louvain: Publications Universitaires de Louvain; Paris: Editions Béatrice-Nauwelaerts, 1961), pp. 66–72. Aquinas passes over Ammonius's discussion in a few lines: *In PH* I.4, p. 22, 185 to p. 23, 200. Stoic discussions were reported on in Augustine's *De dialectica*, which was used by Henry of Ghent: see discussion and references in E. J. Ashworth, "'Can I Speak More Clearly than I Understand?' A Problem of Religious Language in Henry of Ghent, Duns Scotus, and Ockham," *Historiographia Linguistica* 7 (1980): 31.

[37] Peter of Spain, *Tractatus*, p. 114. Peter excluded case from his remarks, however, since this is indeed given to a word so that it may be ordered in relation to other words: see pp. 108, 114–15.

[38] Irène Rosier, "Mathieu de Bologne et les divers aspects du pré-modisme," in *L'Insegnamento della Logica a Bologna nel XIV Secolo*, ed. Dino Buzzetti, Maurizio Ferriani, and Andrea Tabarroni (Bologna: Presso l'Istituto per la Storia dell'Università, 1992), pp. 75–83.

A related topic had to do with the use of etymology, which Peter Helias defined as the exposition of one word by another word or words. Some etymologies are given in terms of linguistic change, but others are given "in accordance with the property of a thing and the similarity of the letters [secundum rei proprietatem et litterarum similitudinem]."[39] Here he cited Isidore of Seville's claim that a "stone" (*lapis*) is "what hurts the foot" (*quod laedat pedem*),[40] a claim also picked up by the logicians Peter of Spain and Lambert of Lagny[41] and by Martin of Dacia, who used it in his explanation of why *lapis* is masculine.[42] Once more, however, the discussion of this kind of relation between words does not affect the arbitrariness of primary imposition, for it does not take us outside a language which has already been formed. The etymology of *lapis* may depend partly on the prior observation of a stone's foot-hurting properties, but it also depends on the prior existence of the phrase *quod laedat pedem*.

In the middle of the thirteenth century, Pseudo-Kilwardby seems to have been willing to go further. He emphasized that in imposition in general mere chance is not enough, for "institution should be rational and deliberate [institutio debet esse rationalis et a proposito)."[43] There must be a relationship of the signifying utterance to the thing signified or its properties ("exigitur proportio vocis significantis ad rem significatam vel ad eius proprietates"). Moreover, it is not the case that any utterance can signify any understanding; it must be one appropriately formed, as in the case of *lapis*. He added that even if the relevant property of the thing signified is not obvious to us from the utterance, it would have been to the one who instituted the utterance.[44]

Aquinas's own discussion fits very well into this picture of imposition as a rational, deliberate activity, both in the case where imposition is related to an already established language and in the case where the im-

---

[39] Peter Helias, *Summa*, pp. 70–71; the quotation is from p. 70, 88–89. He was followed closely here by Simon of Dacia, *Domus gramatice*, in *Simonis daci opera*, ed. Alfred Otto, Corpus Philosophorum Danicorum Medii Aevi III (Copenhagen: G. E. C. Gad, 1963), pp. 7–8.

[40] Isidore, *Etymologiarvm sive Originvm libri XX*, ed. W. M. Lindsay (Oxford: Clarendon Press, 1911), vol. 2, 16.3.1.

[41] Peter of Spain, *Tractatus*, p. 62; Lambert of Lagny (mistakenly called Lambert of Auxerre), *Logica (Summa Lamberti)*, ed. Franco Alessio (Florence: La Nuova Italia Editrice, 1971), p. 8. Lambert also used Isidore, 11.1.5, "Nam proprie homo ab humo."

[42] Martin of Dacia, *Modi significandi*, in *Opera*, pp. 36–37. He said that *lapis* was masculine because it is connected with *laedens pedem*, which is understood *per modum agentis*. *Petra* is feminine because it is connected with the passive *pede trita*.

[43] Pseudo-Kilwardby, *The Commentary on 'Priscianus Maior'*, p. 76.

[44] John of Dacia, *Summa gramatica*, p. 190, follows Pseudo-Kilwardby very closely on these points.

position is genuinely innovative. I do not go into his handling of the example *lapis* here,[45] though I note that he was careful to distinguish etymology from signification.[46] More interesting is his argument that proper names themselves are drawn from the properties of things.[47] Despite the fact that proper names were a standard example of purely arbitrary imposition,[48] Aquinas claims that they are always taken from some property of the person on whom the name is imposed.[49] A child may be named from the time of its birth (as on a Saint's Day), from blood relationship, from some event, from some quality (for example, "Esau" means "red"), or, in the case of names imposed by God, from some divine gift (see Genesis 17:5).

All these examples depend on the existence of an already established language, but at the very beginning of his discussion Aquinas raises the more fundamental issue of original imposition when he writes that names should correspond to the properties of things, as is obvious from the names of genera and species.[50] This theme of the correspondence between names and things appears in several other places in the context of whether Adam had perfect cognition of natures. In each case, Aquinas puts forward a *sed contra* argument to the effect that Adam must have had such cognition, since he was the original impositor of names, and names must be in conformity with natures.[51] In his commentary on *De interpretatione* he cites the view that names signify naturally in the sense that their signification is in agreement with the natures of things.[52]

[45] See Ashworth, "Signification and Modes of Signifying," pp. 46–50; Rosier, "*Res significata* et *modus significandi*," pp. 140, 153.

[46] *ST* IIaIIae.92.1 ad2: "aliud est etymologia nominis, et aliud est significatio nominis."

[47] *ST* IIIa.37.2: "Utrum convenienter fuerit Christo nomen impositum."

[48] Simon of Dacia, *Domus Gramatice*, p. 8, uses proper names as his example of words imposed "secundum rudem voluntatem nullam similitudinem vocis ad rem attendentem." The main discussion of the arbitrariness of proper names comes from their use as an example of chance equivocals in commentaries on Aristotle's *Categories*. Grammarians were more flexible: Helias, *Summa super Priscianum*, p. 218, 20–21, allows for a "rational sharing" of names, as when a small boy is given his father's name.

[49] *ST* IIIa.37.2: "Nomina autem singularium hominum semper imponuntur ab aliqua proprietate eius cui nomen imponitur."

[50] *ST* IIIa.37.2: "nomina debent proprietatibus rerum respondere. Et hoc patet in nominibus generum et specierum: prout dicitur *IV Metaphys.*: *Ratio enim quam significat nomen est definitio*, quae designat propriam rei naturam."

[51] *In Sent* II.23.2.2 sed contra 1, p. 191a: "nomina imponuntur rebus ex proprietatibus eorum sumpta; quia unaquaeque res nominatur ab eo quod in ipsa est nobilius"; *QDV* 18.4 sed contra 4: "Praeterea, nomina rerum debent esse consona earum proprietatibus"; *ST* Ia.94.3 sed contra: "Nomina autem debent naturis rerum congruere." For a recent article on the issue, see Gilbert Dahan, "Nommer les êtres: Exégèse et théories du langage dans les commentaires médiévaux de *Genèse* 2, 19–20," in Ebbesen, *Sprachtheorien*, pp. 55–74.

[52] *In PH* I.4, p. 22, 188 to p. 23, 196: "Alii uero dixerunt quod nomina omnino naturaliter significant, quasi nomina sint naturales similitudines rerum. Quidam uero dixerunt quod

Unfortunately, he does not explore the issue further in any of the places to which I have referred, but so far as I can see, he has no intention of claiming that the name in itself, viewed just as a sound, exhibits any correspondence with the nature of the thing. Instead, his point is that if we take seriously Aristotle's remark "The analysis that a name signifies is the definition [ratio quam significat nomen, est definitio, ut dicitur in IV Metaphys.],"[53] then what a name signifies by convention must itself capture the nature of a thing. As he put it in his *Commentary on John's Gospel*, "the nature of the thing understood" (*naturam rei intellectae*) is seen in the inner word.[54] The natural relationship obtains between concept and thing, rather than between word and concept or word and thing directly. In other words, the position Aquinas adopted has in the end more to do with epistemology than with language as such.

So far, everything I have said has had to do with utterance as a phenomenon bound up with human rationality and intellectual capacity. The moment we turn to the sense (or senses) of natural signification in which this is incompatible with conventional signification, we can begin to see how Aquinas, like others, was forced to modify his intellectualist stance. In order to explain the significance of such utterances as barking and groaning, I first consider some psychological issues—in particular, the role of the imagination.

3. Utterance and the Imaginative Power

To understand the role of the imagination in utterance, we need to remember Aquinas's insistence that human beings are "at the horizon," intermediate between purely intellectual beings, such as angels, and nonrational animals. When it comes to utterance, however, human beings have more in common with animals than with angels. Although angels do communicate with humans by means of bodies, their communication is only a similitude of speech, since the angelic bodies themselves are only similitudes.[55] Many animals, on the other hand, have the

---

nomina non naturaliter significant quantum ad hoc quod eorum significatio non est a natura, ut Aristotiles hic intendit, quantum uero ad hoc naturaliter significant quod eorum significatio congruit naturis rerum, ut Plato dixit."

[53] *ST* Ia.13.6; Aristotle, *Metaphysics* 4.7 (1012a24–25). The phrase is frequently cited by Aquinas: e.g., *ST* Ia.13.1; Ia.13.8 ad2; Ia.85.2 ad3.

[54] *In Joh* I.1.25.

[55] *QDP* 6.8: "locutio quae attribuitur Angelis in corporibus assumptis, non est vere naturalis locutio, sed quaedam similitudinaria per similitudinem effectus"; *ST* Ia.51.3 ad4: "angeli proprie non loquuntur per corpora assumpta; sed est aliquid simile locutioni, inquantum formant sonos in aere similes vocibus humanis." In *ST* Ia.107.1 Aquinas discusses how angels can speak to each other by revealing their concepts.

same mechanisms for utterance as we do, and this has to be taken into account. Furthermore, Aquinas sees soul in both human beings and animals as involving a complex of powers, including sensory apprehension, imagination, and sensual appetition. In human beings these powers are subordinated to intellect and will, but there is still a strong nonrational component in our activities, especially when we allow passion to overcome reason. This relation between human and animal psychology must have a bearing on the explanation of any human activity, including utterance.

Once more, the appropriate starting point is a text drawn from Aristotle. In *De anima* 420b5–421a7, Aristotle gives an account of utterance (voice, *vox*) as a special kind of sound which is produced by those animals able to breathe. In order to distinguish utterances from such sounds as coughs, he writes (*De anima* 420b31–33): "What produces the impact must have soul in it and must be accompanied by an act of imagination, for voice is a sound with a meaning." [56] In the translation used by Aquinas, this reads: "Set oportet animatum esse uerberans et cum ymaginatione aliqua; significatiuus enim quidam sonus est uox." [57] Both Avicenna and Averroës wrote comments on this passage which were influential in the thirteenth century. [58] Avicenna says that animals make sounds by which others may know the dispositions of their hearts, but that these sounds signify *naturaliter et confuse*. [59] He goes on to argue that the causes of animal activity are not conceptions but instinctive affections, which are *ad modum imaginationis*. [60] In Averroës' commentary on the *De anima* we find the reference to the imagination explained in terms of the *anima ymaginativa et concupiscibilis*, which is the first mover as far as utterance is concerned. [61]

---

[56] *The Complete Works of Aristotle: The Revised Oxford Translation*, ed. Jonathan Barnes (Princeton: Princeton University Press, 1984), 1:670.

[57] I cite William of Moerbeke's Latin translation as found in *In DA*, p. 143.

[58] Rosier has drawn my attention to the importance of the approach to language as a product of intellectual operations, an importance that is obvious in the modistic grammarians, and also to the appropriation of Aristotelian psychology, through the *De anima* and the Arab commentaries on it. See also Irène Rosier, "Interjections et expression des affects dans la sémantique du XIIIe siècle," *Histoire Epistémologie Langage* 14.2 (1992): 69–71, on the influence of Avicenna on linguistic questions.

[59] Avicenna Latinus, *Liber de anima seu sextus de naturalibus IV–V*, ed. Simone Van Riet (Louvain: Editions Orientalistes; Leiden: E. J. Brill, 1968), p. 72.

[60] Ibid., pp. 74–75, esp. p. 75: 79–82: "aliquando autem contingit hoc accidens in natura instinctu insito, sicut amor omnis animalis circa filium suum non ex conceptione aliquo modo, sed ad modum imaginationis."

[61] Averroës, *Averrois Cordvbensis commentarivm magnvm in Aristotelis De anima libros*, ed. F. Stuart Crawford (Cambridge, Mass.: Mediaeval Academy of America, 1953), II.90, p. 268, 28–33: "Et ideo dixit: *animatum et cum ymaginatione*. Innuit enim quod ista actio completur duabus virtutibus anime, quarum una est concupiscibilis et altera ymaginativa. Deinde

The reference to the imagination as a motive power or efficient cause was supplemented by means of reference to images as contents of the imagination. In various works, including those of Albert the Great and Pseudo-Kilwardby, Aristotle's phrase is translated as *cum imagine vocis*.[62] Pseudo-Kilwardby gives a very full account of the issues, which also makes plain the influence of Avicenna and Averroës. He explains that a *sermo* or significant word can exist in the mind in two ways, first as an abstract object of cognition, and second *per affectum et imaginationem*. As such, it is the principle of the sensible exterior *vox*, for the appetitive and imaginative powers concur in the production of the *vox*, as Averroës said. The soul informs the sensible exterior *vox* according to the intention of the *vox* impressed on the appetitive and imaginative power.[63] Later, he makes similar points about the *vox*, as opposed to the *sermo*. The appetitive and imaginative powers produce *voces* in animals. Hence, animals do not take counsel or deliberate, but act by nature rather than imagination. Here Pseudo-Kilwardby refers to Avicenna on natural instinct.[64] He then goes on to speak of the *intentiones et imaginationes* of the *vox* found in the soul along with the similitudes of things. We appeal to these when we are deciding which conventionally significative *vox* to join to which concept.[65] It is clear from this account that imagination's role in utterance is to provide both the motive power for the production of utterances and the exemplars in accordance with which the utterances are formed.

Most logic texts, including the *Summule* of Peter of Spain and Roger Bacon, as well as those edited by L. M. de Rijk in *Logica modernorum*, pay no attention at all to the place of imagination in the definition of utterance. Aquinas, however, makes considerable use of imagination. The first of these uses in his commentary on *De interpretatione* is somewhat

---

dixit: *Vox enim est sonus illius*, etc. Idest, primum enim movens in voce est anima ymaginativa et concupiscibilis."

[62] Albert the Great, *Liber I Perihermenias* II.1, in *Opera omnia* I, ed. Auguste Borgnet (Paris: Vivès, 1890), p. 382A: "vox est sonus ab ore animalis, cum imagine alicujus significationis prolatus." The text of Pseudo-Kilwardby, *The Commentary on 'Priscianus Maior'*, has both versions: "omnis vox est sonus prolatus cum aliqua imagine significandi" (p. 64), and "vox est sonus cum imaginatione significandi prolatus, et imaginatio est vis formativa vocis, ut dicit Averroes" (p. 69). Martin of Dacia, *Quaestiones super librum Perihermeneias*, p. 243, 15–16, cites Aristotle as saying that every *vox* "profertur cum imagine significandi." John of Dacia, *Summa gramatica*, p. 104, 30–31, referring to the definition of *vox* given in *De anima* II, writes: "omnis vox profertur cum imaginatione significandi." Cf. René-Antoine Gauthier, preface to *In PH*, p. 72* n. 5, on the use of *imago* for *imaginatio*.

[63] Pseudo-Kilwardby, *The Commentary on 'Priscianus Maior'*, pp. 10–11.

[64] Ibid., p. 57.

[65] Ibid., p. 58. He remarks of the soul: "cogitat enim apud se quem intellectum per quam vocem debeat significari."

puzzling, as it seems to exclude animal utterances. In his discussion of the word *interpretatio*, Aquinas remarks that it excludes those *voces* which signify naturally rather than "by intent and with an imagination directed toward signifying something [ex proposito aut cum ymaginatione aliquid significandi]," like the *voces* of brute animals.[66] I think the answer is that in this first reference Aquinas is relying on Boethius, who tied *imaginatio* to *significandi* and whose use of the phrase could be thought to imply intention or purpose.[67] When the phrase *cum ymaginatione* next occurs, in his definition of *uox*, Aquinas explicitly refers to the *De anima* as his source.[68] In his commentary he explains that an utterance can signify naturally or *ad placitum*, and that the percussion involved in this kind of sound production comes from the soul, "for animal operations are said to be those which proceed from the imagination."[69] It is clear from the context that nonhuman animals are now definitely included; and that the role of the imagination is causal.[70]

The notion of the image of an utterance does not play a role in Aquinas's commentary on *De interpretatione*, but it plays an important part in his accounts of the threefold word (*verbum*). In each place Aquinas distinguishes between the spoken word, the inner word, which is the *significatio*, and the imagined word, which serves as intermediary. In the *Sentences* commentary[71] he emphasizes the aspect of considering which

---

[66] *In PH* I.1, p. 6, 40–44: "similiter etiam uoces significantes naturaliter, non ex proposito aut cum ymaginatione aliquid significandi, sicut sunt uoces brutorum animalium, interpretationes dici non possunt: qui enim interpretatur, aliquid exponere intendit."

[67] *Anicii Manlii Severini Boetii commentarii in librum Aristotelis* ΠΕΡΙΕΡΜΗΝΕΙΑΣ, ed. Carolus Meiser, 2 vols. (Leipzig, 1877–80), 2d ed., p. 4, 26–29: "illa quoque potest esse definitio vocis, ut eam dicamus sonum esse cum quadam imaginatione significandi. vox namque cum emittitur, significationis alicuius causa profertur." See also p. 5, 24 ("aliqua significandi ratio") and p. 6, 3 ("imaginatione aliqua proferendi").

[68] *In PH* I.4, p. 20, 36–38: "uox est sonus ab ore animalis prolatus cum ymaginatione quadam, ut dicitur in II De anima."

[69] *In DA* 2.18, p. 146, 160–67: "*Oportet* enim, ad hoc quod sit uox, quod *uerberans* aerem sit aliquid *animatum et cum ymaginatione aliqua* intendente ad aliquid significandum; oportet enim quod *uox* sit *sonus quidam significatiuus*, uel naturaliter uel ad placitum, et propter hoc dictum est quod huiusmodi percussio est ab anima: operationes enim animales dicuntur que ex ymaginatione procedunt."

[70] See, e.g., *In PH* I.4, p. 22, 169–84.

[71] *In Sent* I.27.2.1, vol. 1, p. 74b: "invenitur triplex verbum; scilicet cordis, et vocis, et quod habet imaginem vocis; cujus necessitas est, quod cum locutio nostra sit quaedam corporalis operatio, oportet quod ad ipsam concurrant ea quae ad omnem motum corporalem exiguntur. oportet autem ad hoc quod sit motus corporalis hominis, qui scilicet est per deliberationem, quod praecedat deliberatio et judicium in parte intellectiva. sed quia intellectus est universalium, et operationes singularium, ideo, ut dicitur 3 de anima, oportet esse quamdam virtutem particularem quae apprehendit intentionem particularem rei, circa quam est operatio; et tertio oportet quod sequatur motus in corpore per virtutes motivas affixas musculis et nervis; ut quasi videatur esse quidam syllogismus, cujus in parte intellectiva habeatur major universalis, et in parte sensitiva habeatur minor particularis,

utterance will be used to express the intellect's concepts, and in *De veritate* he appeals to the notion of an exemplar.[72] In the *Summa theologiae*, where he uses the phrase *imaginatio vocis* instead of *verbum quod habet imaginem vocis*, he emphasizes the notion of imagination as an efficient cause.[73] Whether or not he read Pseudo-Kilwardby (or vice versa), the two authors seem to be working within the same context.

We will see below what uses Aquinas made of the notion of the imagined word in his accounts of blasphemy and of prayer.

4. Animal Noises and Natural Signification

So far, I have been speaking as if the notion of natural as opposed to conventional signification is not problematic, but in fact a further distinction is needed at this point between the sign as symptom or index and the sign as a symbol which is nonetheless produced naturally. Using a division which is at least hinted at by Augustine in *De doctrina christiana* 2.1–2, and which was made explicit by Roger Bacon in the mid-thirteenth century, one can first divide signs into two groups.[74] The sign as symptom or index is a causal or concomitant effect of the thing signified, and the relationship between the two is an inferential one based on a real causal relation. On seeing smoke, one can infer that there is a fire. To say that smoke is a natural sign of fire is simply to say that causal and hence inferential relations do exist between smoke and fire. The sign as symbol is something, whether utterance or object, which has been intentionally endowed with significance or, at the very least, in-

---

et demum sequatur conclusio operationis particularis, per virtutem motivam imperatam. . . . secundum autem quod est in imaginatione, quando scilicet quis imaginatur voces quibus intellectus conceptum proferre valeat, sic est verbum quod habet imaginem vocis."

[72] *QDV* 4.1, on the three types of *verbum*, the spoken word, the *verbum cordis*, and "*exemplar exterioris verbi, et hoc dicitur verbum interius* quod habet imaginem vocis." In the process of production the *verbum cordis* comes before the exemplar, and that precedes the uttered word. On this aspect, see Mark D. Jordan, *Ordering Wisdom: The Hierarchy of Philosophical Discourses in Aquinas* (Notre Dame, Ind.: University of Notre Dame Press, 1986), pp. 33–34. Jordan writes: "The imagined word is the link between the inner word and the physical production of speech, the pattern for the production of the word-sound. Thus it takes on in Thomas a number of names associated with formal causality" (p. 34).

[73] *ST* Ia.34.1: "vox ex imaginatione procedit, ut in libro *de Anima* dicitur." In the same place he refers to both John Damascene, *De fide orthodoxa* 1.13, and to Augustine *De trinitate* 15.10.19. Claude Panaccio has emphasized to me the importance of Augustine's references to the triple word (cf. *De trinitate* 13.20.26; 14.16.22). Rosier emphasizes the importance of Damascene, who is also used by Pseudo-Kilwardby: see Rosier, *La parole comme acte*, pp. 127–29; cf. pp. 70–73.

[74] For discussion and references, see Rosier, "Variations médiévales." See also Rosier, "La distinction entre actus exercitus et actus significatus," p. 243 n. 46.

tentionally produced in order to point the hearer to whatever it is a symptom of. A further subdivision is now possible. The sign as symbol can be purely conventional, or it can be natural in the sense of being produced naturally and hence being the same for all. A dog can bark in order to show that it is angry, a human being can groan in order to show that he is in pain, but neither the dog nor the human controls the fact that that particular sort of sound is a symptom of anger or pain. As a result, both barks and groans can be naturally significative in two different ways. They can be natural as mere symptoms or indices, or they can be natural as nonconventional but intentionally produced.

Bearing these distinctions in mind, let us consider what Aquinas has to say about animal utterances. One kind, in which the animal itself is in no sense an agent, can be immediately dismissed. Aquinas explains that a demon can make a dog appear to speak by causing it to form a sound which is similar to a writable and articulate utterance (*litterata et articulata vox*),[75] just as an angel caused Baalam's ass to appear to speak. But the dog, unlike a mute who is miraculously cured, still does not have the power of speech (*virtus loquendi*).[76] For one thing, it lacks understanding.[77] Nor, indeed, is the mere potential for understanding a sufficient condition for genuine speech, for demons can also cause human beings to appear to speak.[78]

So far as genuine animal utterances are concerned, Aquinas is at one with the logicians in classifying animal noises along with human groans as an example of sounds that are naturally significative.[79] Their being the same for all is appealed to as a criterion.[80] He is also quite clear about

---

[75] Aquinas, unlike Priscian, uses these terms more or less synonymously. For discussion of senses of *articulata*, see Umberto Eco, Roberto Lambertini, Costantino Marmo, and Andrea Tabarroni, "On Animal Language in the Medieval Classification of Signs," *Versus* 38/39 (1984): 4–6, and Rosier, "Variations médiévales." The *Versus* article is reprinted in *On the Mediaeval Theory of Signs*, ed. Umberto Eco and Costantino Marmo (Amsterdam: John Benjamins, 1989), pp. 3–41.

[76] *QDP* 6.5 ad3.

[77] *In Po* I.1/b, p. A 78, 122–26: "nam etsi quedam animalia locutionem humanam proferant, non tamen proprie loquuntur, quia non intelligunt quid dicunt, set ex usu quodam tales uoces proferunt."

[78] *ST* Ia.115.5: demons can bring it about that "arreptitii loquuntur lingua ignota, quod recitant versus et auctoritates quas nunquam sciverunt."

[79] *In PH* I.4, p. 21, 82–84: "et per hoc differt nomen a uocibus significantibus naturaliter, sicut sunt gemitus infirmorum et uoces brutorum animalium." The typical example is the dog's bark; see Peter of Spain, *Tractatus*, p. 2: "Vox significativa naturaliter est illa que apud omnes idem representat, ut gemitus infirmorum, latratus canum." See De Rijk, *Logica Modernorum* 2.2 for four texts that mention both the dog's bark and the invalid's groan (pp. 78, 149, 179, 463) and one (p. 418) that mentions "latratus canum et similia." For discussion, see Eco et al., "On Animal Language," and Rosier, "Variations médiévales."

[80] *In PH* I.2, p. 12, 181–83: "Voces autem ille que naturaliter significant, sicut gemitus infirmorum et alia huiusmodi, sunt eedem apud nos."

what such utterances are for: they signify such passions as joy and sadness.[81] Indeed, even some of those animals that don't make use of a voice, because they lack lungs, signify their own passions naturally through sounds.[82] What is less clear is whether Aquinas thinks of these utterances as natural only as symptoms or indices, or whether they can also be intentional. He certainly speaks of animals as expressing their passions to each other[83] and as manifesting their feelings.[84] But doing so need not be intended communication; it could instead involve the instinctive interpretation of causal signs, in the way that a sheep reacts to a wolf with fear.[85] In his commentary on *De sensu et sensato*, Aquinas remarks that the utterances of animals naturally signify their inner passions, and that in this way animals can cognize each other's passions from their utterances.[86] Again, in the *Summa theologiae*, Aquinas remarks that even if brute animals manifest some truth, they do not intend the manifestation but by natural instinct do something from which the manifestation follows.[87] Such remarks certainly seem to place the weight on the inferential process rather than on any initial intention to signify. He does not tell us whether the same is true of human groans, but his remarks about interjections suggest that neither groans nor interjections are intentional.

5. Human Passions: Groans and Interjections

Once it has been recognized that humans have utterance in common with animals, it becomes clear that at least some human utterance can

---

[81] *In Po* I.1/b, p. A 79, 128–37: "Nam uox est signum tristitie et delectationis, et per consequens aliarum passionum ut ire et timoris, que omnes ordinantur ad delectationem et tristitiam, ut in II Ethicorum dicitur. Et ideo uox datur aliis animalibus quorum natura usque ad hoc peruenit, quod sentiant suas delectationes et tristitias et hec sibi inuicem significent per aliquas naturales uoces, sicut leo per rugitum et canis per latratum; loco quorum nos habemus interiectiones."

[82] *In PH* I.4, p. 22, 179–81.

[83] *DRP* I.1, vol. 3, p. 595b: "est proprium hominis locutione uti, per quam unus homo aliis suum conceptum totaliter potest exprimere. alia quidem animalia exprimunt mutuo passiones suas in communi, ut canis in latratu iram, et alia animalia passiones suas diversis modis."

[84] *In PH* I.2, p. 9, 38 to p. 10, 40. Aquinas speaks of animals other than man "que per quasdam uoces suas conceptiones inuicem sibi manifestant." (The context makes clear that *conceptio* is not intellectual or abstractive.)

[85] Aquinas insists that any apparent inference made by animals, as when the hunting dog seems to use disjunctive syllogism, is really instinctive: *ST* IaIIae.13.2, obj.3, ad3.

[86] *In DSS* I.1, p. 14, 260 to p. 15, 264: "et ideo uox animalis in quantum huiusmodi naturaliter significat interiorem animalis passionem, sicut latratus canum significat iram ipsorum; et sic perfectiora animalia ex uocibus inuicem cognoscunt interiores passiones."

[87] *ST* IaIIae.110.1.

be explained without reference to concepts. Groans, like tears, are natural ways of showing grief, even if words can also be used,[88] and there is no essential difference between the sick person's groan and the dog's bark. Interjections, however, seem to form a kind of intermediary between the natural and undeliberated expression of affections and the reasoned, deliberated expression of concepts.

So far as medieval grammarians were concerned, the main issues concerning interjections were whether to classify them as parts of speech or not, and how to describe their particular kind of signification.[89] Peter Helias presented material taken from Priscian[90] by means of the distinction between utterances that were significative *ad placitum* and those that were naturally significative.[91] Standard interjections—that is, those that have an adverbial function and are language-specific—are significative *ad placitum*, but those that are the immediate result of passion are naturally significative.[92] Both types signify affects or emotional states such as joy, grief, fear, and admiration, but those that are naturally significative are "interjected by means of an exclamation impelled by some passion."[93]

So far as I can see, Aquinas does not classify interjections into types. In his commentary on Aristotle's *Politics* he merely remarks that whereas animals signify their joys and griefs by natural utterances, such as the lion's roar and the dog's bark, human beings use interjections.[94] A fuller discussion is found in the places where he takes up the use of *Raca* in Matthew 5:22: "But I say unto you, That whosoever is angry with his brother without a cause shall be in danger of the judgment: and whosoever shall say to his brother, Raca, shall be in danger of the council: but whosoever shall say, Thou fool, shall be in danger of hell fire." In the *Summa theologiae*, Aquinas is concerned with Gregory's claim that there are three degrees of anger: without utterance (*sine voce*), with utterance

---

[88] *ST* IaIIae.38.2. When people overcome by sorrow "exterius suam tristitiam manifestant vel fletu aut gemitu, vel etiam verbo, mitigatur tristitia." Hurtful things hurt more if they are shut up, so giving vent to them is bound to help, Aquinas remarks.

[89] See Rosier, "Interjections et expression des affects," pp. 61–84. There is also a long discussion in Rosier, "La distinction entre actus exercitus et actus significatus," pp. 235–49.

[90] Priscian, *Institutionum grammaticarum* 15.40–42, pp. 90–91.

[91] Peter Helias, *Summa*, pp. 805–8.

[92] Priscian and Peter Helias also include a category of interjections that are imitations of unwritable sounds. Cf. Rosier, "La distinction entre actus exercitus et actus significatus," pp. 243–44 n. 47.

[93] Peter Helias, *Summa*, p. 806, 101–5: "sed etiam voces significant illum affectum que non sunt invente ad placitum sed naturaliter, que, scilicet, per exclamationem interiaciuntur, cogente pulsu cuiuscumque passionis animi ut 'ha,' 'hei' et similia." Cf. Priscian, *Institutionum grammaticarum*, p. 90, 13–14: "voces, quae cuiuscumque passionis animi pulsu per exclamationem intericiuntur."

[94] See note 81 above.

(*cum voce*), and explicit words (*cum verbo expresso*).[95] Aquinas explains that these degrees correspond to the course of the human act (*processus humani actus*). First, one becomes angry; second, one manifests this anger by exterior signs; and third, one acts. *Raca*, which is the interjection of an angry man (*interiectio irascentis*), represents the second stage, while "Thou fool" (*Fatue*) represents the third stage, though Aquinas does note that a harm done in words alone is minimal. Thus, *Raca* is the vocal expression of anger without being a full-fledged speech-act. In the *reportatio* of his commentary on Matthew 5:10–22, Aquinas contrasts the case of an utterance which signifies a determinate concept with an interjection which signifies an affect.[96] He cites Augustine in support of this point, as he does in the *Catena aurea*.[97]

6. Human Passions and Conventional Speech

Once attention has been drawn to the passions in relation to human utterance, one can see that these passions can affect our speech in a variety of ways. At the simplest level, Aquinas gives a physiological explanation of why those in pain can hardly refrain from crying out, while those beset by fear keep silent.[98] At a more complex level, he claims that anger can cause taciturnity, either because reason steps in and prevents one from saying what one thinks, or because one is so disturbed that one's tongue simply does not function.[99] Anger can also be shown by the mode of utterance, as when our speech is disordered and confused, and here Aquinas once more uses the example *Raca*. In the same place, Aquinas talks of a second kind of disorderliness produced by anger, that shown in blasphemy and contumely, when we burst into injurious words against God or our neighbor.[100] Indeed, the point that passion affects normal utterance can be generalized, for as Aquinas remarks in his

---

[95] *ST* IIaIIae.158.5 ad3; cf. *ST* IaIIae.46.8 obj. 3.

[96] *In Matt*, vol. 6, p. 363b (this *reportatio* is taken from the unpublished Leonine edition): "racha, secundum quosdam, non est vox significans aliquem determinatum conceptum sed est interiectio irascentis. secundum augustinum, (est) sicut heu interiectio dolentis et significat quemdam affectum; unde iam prorumpit ira exterius non tamen in nocumentum." Aquinas also reports on those who hold that the word does signify a determinate concept.

[97] *CA* 5.13, vol. 5, p. 150b. Aquinas cites Augustine as saying of "Raca": "probabilius autem est non esse vocem significantem aliquid, sed indignantis animi motum exprimentem. Has autem voces grammatici interiectiones vocant, velut cum dicitur a dolente: heu." The reference is to Augustine, *De sermone Domini in monte* I.9, on Matthew 5:20–22.

[98] *ST* IaIIae.44.1 ad2.

[99] *ST* IaIIae.48.4.

[100] *ST* IIaIIae.158.7.

commentary on *De interpretatione*, one's desire to reveal one's concepts to another may be caused by some passion, such as love or hate.[101] Nor need utterance as a result of passion always be harmful. In his defense of spoken prayer, Aquinas cites the fact that vehement affections over-flow into the body and thereby bring about speech.[102]

In the same place, Aquinas speaks of the power of words to excite and move the hearer, whether oneself or another person.[103] Spoken prayers arouse inner devotion, and this is why they are helpful to the person praying.[104] Certainly the words are not needed to transfer any informa-tion to God, the person to whom our prayers are addressed.[105] Aquinas has similar remarks to make in his discussion of praise, another pur-poseful use of speech which goes beyond the mere making of state-ments.[106] We use words to praise other humans, not just to let them know that we have a good opinion of them but to provoke the person praised to better things and to induce others to have a good opinion of him, to reverence and imitate him. When we use words to praise God, the in-formative function of the words disappears, for God knows our hearts, but the function of inducing reverence in ourselves and others remains.

A good example of the ways in which hearers can become involved through speech is found in Aquinas's account of the vow, through which something is promised to God. He explains that making a promise is not a mere intention of the will; it involves directing oneself to do some-thing for another, in the same way that one can ask someone else to do something for oneself by ordering or supplicating.[107] One can make a promise to God without words, but in making a vow we use words both to rouse ourselves up and also to call others to witness.

Just as speech can be used to affect its hearers in various ways, so it can be used to bring about various sacramental effects, such as the conse-cration of bread and wine. This factive aspect of speech, which Aquinas compares to God's use of the Divine Word in creation,[108] together with

[101] *In PH* I.2, p. 11, 127–30: "ex aliqua anime passione prouenit, puta ex amore vel odio, ut homo interiorem conceptum per uocem alteri significare uelit."

[102] *ST* IIaIIae.83.12.

[103] Aquinas is quite happy with the notion that we can speak to ourselves (cf. his re-marks about promising, below), and he even specifies that we can do so without uttered words in *QDV* 4.1 ad5: "quamvis apud nos manifestatio, quae est ad alterum, non fiat nisi per verbum vocale, tamen manifestatio ad seipsum fit etiam per verbum cordis."

[104] *ST* IIaIIae.83.12. His first argument in support of vocal prayer is this: "Primo quidem, ad excitandum interiorem devotionem, qua mens orantis elevetur in Deum. Quia per ex-teriora signa, sive vocum sive etiam aliquorum factorum, movetur mens hominis et se-cundum apprehensionem, et per consequens secundum affectionem."

[105] *ST* IIaIIae.83.12 ad1.

[106] *ST* IIaIIae.91.1.

[107] *ST* IIaIIae.88.1: "promittendo ordinat quid ipse pro alio facere debeat."

[108] E.g., *ST* IIaIIae.76.1; IIIa.78.5.

his admission of the expressive aspect of speech, affects what he has to say about the admissibility of those sentences he refused to consider in his commentary on *De interpretatione.* Although it may be true that the logician is concerned only with assertions, and that non-indicative sentences are more ordered toward the expression of desires and passions than to the interpretation of what is in the intellect,[109] the moralist and the priest have to recognize commands, requests, and performative utterances. In various places Aquinas talks about the causal function of the imperative mood, and the expressive function of the optative mood,[110] but he also recognizes that illocutionary force is to some extent independent of grammatical considerations. Thus one can command another to do something either by using an imperative or by using an indicative sentence of the form "You must do this" ("Hoc est tibi faciendum").[111] More important, one can use indicative sentences *per modum exercentis actum* in order to perform actions, as when one says "I baptize you" or "I confirm you."[112]

The notion that a speaker is performing a particular kind of action brings us to the question of intentions. So far as the sacraments are concerned, the minister's intention was thought to be a crucial element in their proper administration;[113] but in fact virtually any full-fledged utterance can be regarded as a moral act and, as such, must be assessed in terms of the speaker's intention. Truth-telling has already been considered briefly in section 1. Now it is time to consider the ways in which words can be used to sin: by blaspheming, cursing, insulting others, perjuring oneself, and so on.

7. Intentions and Sinful Speech

In order to understand the relationships between our intentions and various kinds of sinful speech-act, it is worth considering one passage in particular: Aquinas's discussion (in *ST* IIaIIae.72) of reviling, or in-

---

[109] *In PH* I.1, p. 6, 52–55: "cetere uero orationes, ut optatiua et inperatiua, magis ordinantur ad exprimendum affectum quam ad interpretandum id quod in intellectu habetur."

[110] E.g., *ST* IIaIIae.76.1; IIIa.78.1.

[111] *ST* IaIIae.17.1.

[112] *ST* IIIa.78.1: "formae aliorum sacramentorum proferuntur ex persona ministri: sive per modum exercentis actum, sicut cum dicitur *Ego te baptizo*, vel, *Ego te confirmo;* sive per modum imperantis, sicut in sacramento ordinis dicitur, *Accipe potestatem*, etc.; sive per modum deprecantis, sicut cum in sacramento extremae unctionis dicitur, *Per istam unctionem et nostram intercessionem*, etc." For discussion, see Rosier, "Signes et sacrements," pp. 410–13.

[113] See Rosier, "Signes et sacrements," pp. 427–32.

sulting and hurtful language. He asks whether reviling consists in words (*verba*) and says that, properly speaking, it does. Nonetheless, words as audible sounds do not injure, except perhaps by being too loud. Rather, they hurt as signs which represent something to another person.[114] He then moves swiftly away from the hearer to the speaker. Words are harmful insofar as they signify something, and this signification proceeds from an interior *affectus*.[115] This is why, where sins of speech are concerned, one must pay the closest possible attention to the speaker's intention.[116] If the words are said for a good motive, such as correction, and not from any desire to dishonor the hearer, then we do not have a case of reviling, except perhaps *per accidens*, insofar as what is uttered could be insulting.[117] We may note here that Aquinas generally seems to place more weight on the speaker's intention than on the hearer's reception, except in the one case of guileful oaths. If the oathtaker deliberately interprets an oath in some abnormal way, then he should be bound by the correct understanding (*sanum intellectum*) of the person to whom the oath was sworn, but in other cases where the two parties disagree, it is the intention of the oathtaker that counts.[118]

Aquinas goes on to consider the kinds of intention which, though they do not totally exonerate, at least excuse. Speaking out of irritation, with no firm intention of dishonoring someone else, is one such excuse.[119] Saying something in fun can also excuse and even exonerate, provided the circumstances are appropriate.[120] As Aquinas remarks elsewhere, a joke is a venial sin if it is not useful, but it is not sinful at all when uttered from a reasonable cause (*ex causa rationabili*).[121] And playfulness

---

[114] *ST* IIaIIae.72.1.corpus and ad1.

[115] The word *affectus* picks out some condition of the soul; it can refer to passions and emotions, to desires, or even to intentions. See the passage quoted in note 117 below; cf. also note 144 below.

[116] Cf. *ST* IIaIIae.73.2: "peccata verborum maxime sunt ex intentione dicentis diiudicanda." Cf. also *ST* IIaIIae.76.3: "peccata verborum maxime ex affectu pensantur."

[117] *ST* IIaIIae.72.2: words are harmful "inquantum significant aliquid. Quae quidem significatio ex interiori affectu procedit. Et ideo *in peccatis verborum maxime considerandum videtur ex quo affectu aliquis verba proferat.* . . . si intentio proferentis ad hoc feratur ut aliquis per verba quae profert honorem alterius auferat, hoc proprie et per se est *dicere convicium vel contumelium.* . . . *Si vero aliquis verbum convicii vel contumeliae alteri dixit, non tamen animo dehonarandi, sed forte propter correctionem vel propter aliquid huiusmodi, non dicit convicium vel contumeliam formaliter et per se, sed per accidens et materialiter,* inquantum scilicet dicit id quod potest esse convicium vel contumelia."

[118] *ST* IIaIIae.89.7 ad4.

[119] *ST* IIaIIae.72.2 ad3: "ex levi ira, absque firmo proposito aliquem dehonestandi."

[120] *ST* IIaIIae.72.2 ad1.

[121] *ST* IIaIIae.43.7 ad5: "verbum iocosum est peccatum veniale quando absque utilitate dicitur; si autem ex causa rationabili proferatur, non est otiosum neque peccatum."

and relaxation do count as reasonable causes.[122] Of course, these remarks apply only to those actions and words which, if sinful, are so
only because of the intention, and not by virtue of any objective feature.[123] Some things ought not to be said, even in fun.[124]

From the point of view of philosophy of language, the most interesting cases arise when there is some discrepancy between the speaker's
intentions and the speaker's words, or when the speaker's awareness of
what he is saying is somehow limited. Consider two such cases: slips of
the tongue, and bursting into speech.

8. Slips of the Tongue

Slips of the tongue can occur in many ways, whether we are reciting
the words of others or using our own. We can add or omit words, use
synonyms or even antonyms, order our sentences wrongly, alter the beginnings or the ends of words, pause where we ought not to pause, and
so on. Such slips can result in sentences which are semantically or syntactically deviant, or they can result in sentences which are, as sentences, perfectly correct but count as insults or blasphemies or false-
hoods where none had been intended. Aquinas's most careful analysis
of errors at the syntactic or semantic level occurs in his discussion of the
sacraments,[125] but as this has been discussed elsewhere, I will not pursue it at length here.[126] The main point to notice is his insistence that although deviant sentences technically lack signification, we are allowed
to treat them as significant,[127] provided that they are not completely
garbled, and provided that the error is a genuine one. If the deviance
is intentional and the minister was not in fact aiming at the correct
utterance, then the sacrament in question may be invalid.

Moral slips of the tongue, those that cause us to perjure ourselves[128]
or engage in detraction[129] without intending to, are not pursued in
such detail, though Aquinas does comment that sins of speech are less

---

[122] *ST* IIaIIae.168.2. It can even be rational to allow reason to be fettered; see *ST* IaIIae.34.1 ad1.

[123] *ST* IIaIIae.168.3 ad1.

[124] See *ST* IIaIIae 98.3 ad2, on perjuring oneself for fun.

[125] *ST* IIIa.60.7 and 8.

[126] For full discussion, see Rosier, "Signes et sacrements," esp. pp. 402–5.

[127] *ST* IIIa.60.7 ad3: "Quamvis enim huiusmodi verba corrupte prolata nihil significent ex virtute impositionis, accipiuntur tamen ut significantia ex accommodatione usus. Et ideo, licet mutetur sonus sensibilis, remanet tamen idem sensus."

[128] *ST* IIaIIae.98.3 ad2.

[129] *ST* IIaIIae.73.2 ad3; IIaIIae.73.3.

weighty than others because they so easily come about through a slip of the tongue, without much premeditation.[130] It seems probable, however, that such slips are more allied with the case of bursting into speech than with the syntactic and semantic deviance discussed in the context of the sacraments.

9. Bursting into Speech: Blasphemy and Perjury

The notion of bursting into speech was neither new nor without its intellectual and moral counterparts.[131] So far as intellect is concerned, Aquinas mentions the sudden movement of unbelief prior to deliberation: for instance, suddenly thinking that the resurrection of the dead is impossible naturally.[132] So far as morality is concerned, we can link bursting into speech with the *fomes*—the mark of original sin and "the unpredictable source of impulses selfish, loutish, lascivious, and perverse"[133]—and also with incontinence in general. As one might expect, the kind of sin involved in bursting into speech can be more or less grave. Sometimes it is the sign of something deeply wrong. Thus the unredeemed sinner who is given over to lust is likely to break out in obscene words, scurrilous words lightly and inconsiderately spoken, and wanton words.[134] Breaking out into words aggravates the sin of blasphemy,[135] and if such bursting forth has an element of deliberation, as when we decide not to control ourselves, it proceeds from the sin of pride.[136] Yet there are many occasions when the words we come out with are signs of something less gravely wrong. Anger in particular may produce injurious words, whether against God, in the form of blasphemy, or one's neighbor, in the form of contumely.[137]

---

[130] *ST* IIaIIae.73.3: "Et secundum hoc *peccata locutionis habent aliquam levitatem*: inquantum de facili ex lapsu linguae proveniunt, absque magna praemeditatione."

[131] Rosier, "La distinction entre actus exercitus et actus significatus," p. 243 n. 42, has an interesting discussion of the history and use of the phrase *prorumpit in vocem*. For use of the phrase *prorumpens in uerba contumeliosa* in an early Dominican confessional manual, see Joseph Goering and Pierre J. Payer, "The 'Summa penitentie Fratrum Predicatorum': A Thirteenth-Century Confessional Formulary," *Mediaeval Studies* 55 (1993): 29.

[132] *ST* IaIIae.74.10.

[133] Norman Kretzmann, "Warring against the Law of My Mind: Aquinas on Romans 7," in *Philosophy and the Christian Faith*, ed. Thomas V. Morris (Notre Dame, Ind.: University of Notre Dame Press, 1988), p. 186.

[134] *ST* IIaIIae.153.5 ad4.

[135] *ST* IIaIIae.13.3.

[136] *ST* IIaIIae.158.7 ad1: "blasphemia in quam aliquis prorumpit deliberata mente, procedit ex superbia hominis contra Deum se erigentis."

[137] *ST* IIaIIae.158.7.corpus and ad1: "Sed blasphemia in quam aliquis prorumpit ex commotione animi, procedit ex ira."

At this point, we need to ask what is going on in the mind of the person who comes out with an undeliberated blasphemy, one that has, as it were, sneaked up on him (that is, it occurs *ex subreptione*). Aquinas suggests that there are two cases here. In the first, we are dealing with *verba imaginata*, whose signification is not considered.[138] That is, the causal story must include reference to those elements found in the imagination which serve as models for the actual utterances. At least so far as articulate and writable utterances are concerned, they cannot be regarded merely as random and spontaneous noises, with no precedent in our experience. Even a parrot can only parrot what it has heard. In the second case, the speaker does consider the significates of the words (*significata verborum*) and is not excused from mortal sin, any more than is the person who, moved by sudden anger, kills someone sitting next to him. The same point about the role of paying attention to what one says comes up in relation to slips of the tongue. Someone who swears falsely as the result of a slip of the tongue is not guilty of perjury unless he notices what he is saying.[139] Perhaps we need to add the detail that the blasphemer and the perjurer, once conscious of their words, do not immediately repudiate them. In any case, one is forced to make a distinction between conventional meaning and speaker meaning. Viewed objectively, the words are blasphemous, and any hearer will understand that. Nonetheless, the speaker may not know or intend what he is saying, at least in the sense of giving it assent once he has said it.

The distinction between speaker meaning and conventional meaning becomes particularly important when the speaker is reciting the words of another. How far does he intend to say what he recites, particularly if he does not understand the words he is uttering?

10. Recitation and Appropriated Words: Prayer

Let us first consider the case of the person who utters sentiments which do not seem to be his own. Aquinas puts forward this case in the context of the question whether reason can be overcome by passion

---

[138] *ST* IIaIIae.13.2 ad3. "blasphemia potest absque deliberatione ex subreptione procedere dupliciter. Uno modo, quod aliquis non advertat hoc quod dicit esse blasphemiam. Quod potest contingere cum aliquis subito ex aliqua passione in verba imaginata prorumpit, quorum significationem non considerat." One can also curse *ex subreptione*; see *ST* IIaIIae.76.3.

[139] *ST* IIaIIae.98.3 ad2: "Ille autem qui ex lapsu linguae falsum iurat, si quidem advertat se iurare et falsum esse quod iurat, non excusatur a peccato mortali, sicut nec a Dei contemptu. Si autem hoc non advertat, non videtur habere intentionem iurandi: et ideo a crimine periurii excusatur."

against its knowledge, and he considers the objection that since words are signs of understandings, when a man in a state of passion says that what he has just chosen is wrong, he must also know that it is wrong. Aquinas replies that such a man is like the drunkard who comes out with profundities, even though he is not, at the time, capable of judging them, and he refers the reader to *Nicomachean Ethics* 1147a17–23.[140] In his commentary on this passage, Aquinas repeats Aristotle's point that the incontinent man is like those who utter scientific proofs and verses by Empedocles while mad or drunk. They are no better than simulators (*simulantes*), and so one could say that they are, as it were, reciting the words of others.[141]

A second type of case occurs when someone intentionally and knowingly utters words without intending to appropriate them for his own use. This is the case of quoting. More than once Aquinas tries to explain Augustine away by claiming that he is reciting, not asserting.[142] Similarly, some apparently false or blasphemous passages in Scripture are the reports of what others thought or said, and not the direct word of the Holy Spirit.[143]

The most important case of recitation is prayer, for here people do appropriate the words of others to their own use, and very often the words appropriated are not understood by the speaker, since they are in Latin. Even for the literate—that is, those who know Latin—attention can be a problem, for the mind wanders with distressing ease. A full account of these issues is found in Reginald of Piperno's *reportatio* of Aquinas's lectures on I Corinthians, as well as in related passages in the *Summa theologiae*.

According to 1 Corinthians 14:13–14, "Anyone who speaks in tongues should pray for the ability to interpret. If I use such language in prayer [si orem lingua], my spirit prays, but my mind is barren." In his com-

---

[140] *ST* IaIIae.77.2 ad5: "sicut ebrius quandoque proferre potest verba significantia profundas sententias, quas tamen mente diiudicare non potest, ebrietate prohibente; ita in passione existens, etsi ore proferat hoc non esse faciendum, tamen interius hoc animo sentit quod sit faciendum, ut dicitur in VII *Ethic.*"

[141] *In NE* II, p. 392, 194–220. Lines 214–20 read: "Et ita est etiam de incontinente; etsi enim dicat: 'Non est mihi bonum nunc persequi tale delectabile,' tamen non ita sentit in corde; unde sic existimandum est quod incontinentes dicant huiusmodi verba quasi simulantes, quia scilicet aliud sentiunt corde et aliud proferunt ore."

[142] *ST* Ia.77.5 ad3: "In multis autem quae ad philosophiam pertinent, Augustinus utitur opinionibus Platonis, non asserendo, sed recitando"; *ST* Ia.89.7 ad2: "Et hanc opinionem . . . Augustinus expresse tangit: licet enim magis recitando quam asserendo tangere videatur." Cf. *ST* Ia.54.5: "Qua opinione frequenter Augustinus in libris suis utitur, licet eam asserere non intendat."

[143] *In Sent* III.38.1.3 ad4, vol. 1, p. 411a. Aquinas uses the phrase "verba alicujus qui in scriptura recitatur loquens."

mentary, Aquinas first remarks that to pray in an unknown tongue is to be like the unlettered person (*idiota*) who says a psalm or *pater noster* without understanding what he is saying. It is more beneficial to pray and understand what is being said than just to utter the words of a prayer.[144] He then discusses the phrase *spiritus meus orat* and canvasses three possibilities. The reference may be to the Holy Spirit, or to my own reason, or to the imaginative power (*virtus imaginativa*). In this third case, the utterances or similitudes of corporeal things are only in the imagination, without being understood by the intellect.[145] He argues that although praying without understanding, or without attention, cannot produce the fruit of spiritual consolation and devotion, it is not entirely fruitless with respect to merit so long as one's end in praying is the right one. Moreover, if total attention were required, many prayers would be without merit, for one can hardly say one *pater noster* without one's mind wandering off to something else.[146] Finally, he discusses the three kinds of attention that are possible: to the words themselves (*ad verba*), to the meaning of the words (*ad sensum verborum*), and to the purpose of the prayer (*ad finem*).[147] Only the last sort of attention, which is possible even for the unlettered, is necessary. The first can be harmful, as can the second to some extent, presumably because it is a kind of meta-activity: if I am too consciously weighing the sense of my words, I may forget that I am worshipping God.

The last case of appropriating the words of another goes beyond making the words one's own, since it involves speaking as if with a double *persona*, whether the second *persona* is that of Christ or of the whole Church. The first situation, speaking for Christ, arises in the context of the Eucharist, when the minister says "This is my body."[148] The words have to be taken significatively in order to make reference to the substance which changes from bread to the body of Christ[149] and also to effect that transubstantiation; yet the minister also says them *recitative*.[150]

---

[144] *In I Cor* XIV.3, n. 837. He says that the person who understands is refreshed "quantum ad affectum et intellectum."

[145] Ibid., n. 838: "virtus imaginativa, orat, inquantum voces seu similitudines corporalium sunt tantum in imaginatione absque hoc quod intelligantur ab intellectu."

[146] Ibid., n. 839: "cum vix unum *Pater noster* potest homo dicere, quin mens ad alia feratur." Cf. *ST* IIaIIae.83.13, on attentiveness and the importance of the original intention.

[147] *In I Cor* XIV.3, n. 840. Cf. *ST* IIaIIae.83.13 on the three kinds of attention.

[148] *ST* IIIa.78.5.

[149] Cf. *ST* IIIa.78.2 ad4: "per hoc pronomen *meum*, quod includit demonstrationem primae personae, quae est persona loquentis, sufficienter exprimitur persona Christi, ex cuius persona haec proferuntur."

[150] *ST* IIIa.78.5: "<haec verba> Quando proferentur a sacerdote, significative, et non tantum materialiter accipiuntur.—Nec obstat quod sacerdos etiam recitative profert quasi a Christo dicta." Cf. IIIa.78.1 ad4, on the problem of leaving out the words prior to the ac-

It is he who recites and Christ who gives significance. The second situation, where the minister speaks for the Church, comes up in the context of whether the minister's intention is required for the validity of the sacrament.[151] Aquinas says that it is enough for the minister to utter words in which the intention of the Church is expressed, unless there is some very specific reason to suppose that the minister has some contrary intention.[152] Curiously, this works even when the minister lacks faith, for he can still intend to do what the Church does, even though he thinks it is all nonsense.[153]

There remains an unresolved tension in Aquinas's writings between his basic intellectualist account of language and his awareness of actual linguistic practice. The intellectualist view implies that significative utterance requires sentences that are neither syntactically nor semantically deviant, whose components are neatly lined up with the speaker's concepts, and whose end is the statement of truth. Yet in practice, people's discourse is fragmented, allusive, and not aimed at mere information. Moreover, people often fail to say precisely what they mean, or fail to mean what they say, or even deliberately use Latin words they do not understand without the occurrence of any basic failure in communication. It is impossible to tell whether Aquinas would have resolved this tension had he set out to provide an explicit account of his philosophy of language, but one can say that his discussion of language in the context of moral philosophy offers considerable grounds for optimism.[154]

---

tual consecration sentence: "si sacerdos sola verba praedicta proferret cum intentione conficiendi hoc sacramentum, perficeretur hoc sacramentum: quia intentio faceret ut haec verba intelligerentur quasi ex persona Christi prolata, etiam si verbis praecedentibus hoc non recitaretur."

[151] *ST* IIIa.64.8.

[152] *ST* IIIa.64.8 ad2: "Et ideo alii melius dicunt quod minister sacramenti agit in persona totius Ecclesiae, cuius est minister; in verbis autem quae proferuntur, exprimitur intentio Ecclesiae; quae sufficit ad perfectionem sacramenti, nisi contrarium exterius exprimatur ex parte ministri et recipientis sacramentum."

[153] *ST* IIIa.64.9 ad1: "non obstante infidelitate, potest intendere facere id quod facit Ecclesia, licet existimet id nihil esse. Et talis intentio sufficit ad sacramentum: quia . . . minister sacramenti agit in persona totius Ecclesiae, ex cuius fide suppletur id quod deest fidei ministro."

[154] I would like to thank Norman Kretzmann for persuading me to read Aquinas on moral and theological matters, and for showing me that one can move beyond the history of logic.

JAN A. AERTSEN

ಎ

Thomas Aquinas on the Good:
The Relation between Metaphysics and Ethics

"It belongs to the wise person to order [*sapientis est ordinare*]." This statement of Aristotle in *Metaphysics* 1.2 (982a18) must have had a strong appeal to Thomas Aquinas, for he begins two of his works with a reference to it. The first chapter of the *Summa contra gentiles* deals with "the office of the wise person," and the opening section of his commentary on the *Nicomachean Ethics* not only cites Aristotle's saying but also provides an explanation of it. Wisdom is the most powerful perfection of reason, whose characteristic it is to know order. Even if the sensitive powers know some things "absolutely," it belongs to reason alone to know the relation of one thing to another and the order of a multiplicity of things to one end.[1] To order is the office of the wise person, because in Thomas's interpretation, order is the basic feature of thought.

In the first lectio of his commentary on the *Ethics*, he uses Aristotle's statement as the point of departure for a classification of the sciences. Order is related to reason in four different ways, to which different sciences correspond. First, there is the order that reason does not make but only examines. This is the order of natural things, with which natural philos-

---

[1] *In NE* I, lec. 1, 1 (Leonine edition): "Sicut Philosophus dicit in principio *Metaphysicae*, sapientis est ordinare. Cuius ratio est quia sapientia est potissima perfectio rationis, cuius proprium est cognoscere ordinem; nam, etsi vires sensitivae cognoscant res aliquas absolute, ordinem tamen unius rei ad aliam cognoscere est solius intellectus aut rationis." *Absolute* means here the opposite of *relative*. In *ST* IIaIIae.58.4 Aquinas provides an example. He argues that the subject of justice is not the sensitive appetite but the will, that is, the rational appetite: "To render to each what is his own cannot proceed from the sensitive appetite: since sense apprehension does not extend to the consideration of the proportion of one to another, but this is proper to reason."

ophy (*philosophia naturalis*) is concerned. But reason in its consideration of things can also produce an order. The order that reason produces in its own acts—for example, the arrangement of its concepts—pertains to rational philosophy (*philosophia rationalis*) , that is, to logic. The order that reason produces in the actions of the will pertains to the consideration of moral philosophy (*moralis philosophia*). Finally, reason can be the rule for the making of external things; the order that reason makes in the production of artifacts belongs to the mechanical arts (*artes mechanicae*).

The aim of Thomas's classification of the sciences is to come to a determination of the subject matter of ethics. He draws the conclusion that "the proper office of moral philosophy, to which our present attention is directed, is to consider human actions insofar as they are ordered to one another and to an end."[2] Ethics has a place and domain of its own in the system of the sciences. The main division in this system is that between theoretical and practical reason. The moral order is not an object of theoretical reflection. Ethics is a practical science.

In modern studies of Aquinas's ethics there is a strong tendency to emphasize the autonomy of moral philosophy. This tendency can refer to Thomas's division of the sciences and fits in a more general trend in philosophy which has been called "the rehabilitation of practical reason." The autonomy of ethics is emphasized especially in opposition to a metaphysical interpretation. Ethics is not founded on the science of being; neither is the principle of morality deduced from metaphysics. Moral philosophy is based first of all on "the actual experience of the moral."[3]

There is, however, something odd about Thomas's classification of the sciences in his commentary on the *Ethics*. He presents four different orders of reason but does not say anything about the order of these orders or the relation between theoretical and practical reason. The classification is based on the Stoic tripartite division of philosophy into rational, natural, and moral philosophy, which was known to the Middle Ages through Augustine, who, in *De civitate Dei* 8.3 and 10, attributed it to the "Platonists." Problematical in this division is the place of metaphysics. When Thomas states that natural philosophy is concerned with the order in natural things that reason does not make but only exam-

---

[2] *In NE* I, lec. 1, 2.

[3] The exponent of this view is Wolfgang Kluxen, whose study of Aquinas's ethics is the most important inquiry of recent decades: *Philosophische Ethik bei Thomas von Aquin* (Mainz: Matthias-Grünewald-Verlag, 1964; 2d ed., Hamburg: Meiner, 1980), esp. pt. 3 (pp. 166–217). See also Kluxen, "Zum Gutsein des Handelns," *Philosophisches Jahrbuch* 87 (1980): 327–39; and Kluxen, "Metaphysik und praktische Vernunft. Über ihre Zuordnung bei Thomas von Aquin, " in *Thomas von Aquin 1274/1974*, ed. Ludger Oeing-Hanhoff (Munich: Kösel-Verlag, 1974), pp. 73–96.

ines, he adds that metaphysics is also included under natural philosophy. But it remains unclear whether this inclusion is compatible with Thomas's conception of metaphysics. For him, metaphysics is a *scientia communis*, for it is concerned with that which is common to all things. Its consideration is not restricted to natural beings but also deals with rational beings and moral beings. The subject of first philosophy is being as being and that which belongs to being as such.[4]

Thomas does not elaborate in his work the order between metaphysics and ethics. In this essay I want to clarify some fundamental aspects of their relation through an analysis of a number of texts. These texts are selected from the perspective of the notion of "good." The fertility of this perspective will have to appear from what follows, but since "good" is a basic concept both in ethics and in metaphysics, we may expect that the analysis of the good somehow reflects the relation between the two sciences.[5]

1. The Notion of "Good" (*In NE* I, lec. 1)

The first lectio of Thomas's commentary on the *Ethics* is also a key text on the notion of "good." After having classified the different sciences, he discusses a definition of the good mentioned by Aristotle. Aristotle begins the *Ethics* with this observation (1094a1–3): "Every art and every inquiry, and similarly every action and decision, is thought to aim at some good." He continues: "For this reason the good has rightly been declared to be that which all things desire." Aristotle's intention is to investigate the good for *human beings*, and therefore he presents in his opening statement a swift inventory of human acts or deeds. The context of the definition of the good, which he cites in passing but does not discuss any further, is human activity.

In his commentary Thomas examines at length the definition "the good is that which all things desire [*bonum est quod omnia appetunt*]" and advances an interpretation of it which goes far beyond the *littera* of the text. First of all, he discusses the peculiar nature of this definition, formally considered. Normally, a definition classifies something into the

---

[4] The main texts for Thomas's conception of metaphysics are *In BDT* 5.4 and *In M* prologue. See Jan A. Aertsen, "Was heißt Metaphysik bei Thomas von Aquin?" in *Scientia und Ars im Hoch- und Spätmittelalter*, ed. Ingrid Craemer-Ruegenberg and Andreas Speer (Berlin: Walter de Gruyter, 1994), pp. 217–39.

[5] For the notion of "good," its ontological and ethical aspects, see Eleonore Stump and Norman Kretzmann, "Being and Goodness," in *Being and Goodness: The Concept of the Good in Metaphysics and Philosophical Theology*, ed. Scott MacDonald (Ithaca: Cornell University Press, 1991), pp. 98–128.

scheme of genera and species: it states what something is by reducing it to something more general, the genus, and by adding to the genus the specific difference. But the definition given of the good is not of this character, nor can it be. Thomas explains the reason: "One must keep in mind that the good is reckoned among the firsts [*prima*] to such a degree according to the Platonists that the good is prior to being. But in reality, good is convertible with being [*bonum cum ente convertitur*]."[6] Neither of these points—the firstness of the good or its convertibility with being— is elaborated in the commentary; rather, they are taken for granted.

That the good is reckoned among the *prima* means that it belongs to the first conceptions of the human intellect. Elsewhere, in *De potentia* 9.7 ad6, Thomas names four *prima*: being, one, true, and good. They are the "first intelligibles," because they are analytically prior to any other conception in the sense that their understanding is included in every- thing a human being apprehends. This cognitive priority stems from their commonness. The *prima* are *communia*; they extend to everything that is. They transcend the special modes of being that Aristotle called "the categories" and are therefore called *transcendentia*.[7] Transcenden- tals are coextensive with being and are accordingly studied by the "common science" of being as being. The doctrine of the transcenden- tals has an anti-Platonic moment. According to the Platonists, the good is first in the sense that it is prior to and more universal than being. Thomas criticizes this view and bases his critique on another aspect of the transcendentals, their convertibility. In his commentary he thus in- terprets the good in a transcendental sense by referring to its firstness and its interchangeability with being.[8]

Because the good belongs to the *prima* and is coextensive with being, it cannot be reduced to something more general and be manifested by something earlier. In the definition cited by Aristotle, the good is there- fore made known by its effect. The proper character of this definition is, according to Thomas, that it is *per posteriora*.[9] Hence the definition does not mean to say that something is good because it is desired but rather

---

[6] *In NE* I, lec. 1, 9.

[7] Transcendentals are to be distinguished from universals, for the latter are restricted to one categorical mode of being, whereas the *communia* extend to everything that exists and are found in all categories.

[8] For a more extensive account of the doctrine of the transcendentals in Aquinas, see Jan A. Aertsen, "Die Transzendentalienlehre bei Thomas von Aquin in ihren historischen Hintergründen und philosophische Motiven," in *Thomas von Aquin: Sein Leben, sein Werk und seine Zeit in der neuesten Forschung*, ed. Albert Zimmermann (Berlin: Walter de Gruyter, 1988), pp. 82–102.

[9] *In NE* I, lec. 1, 9: "Prima autem non possunt notificari per aliqua priora, sed notifican- tur per posteriora, sicut causae per proprios effectus."

the opposite: something is desired because it is good. Through the effect, in this case the appetite, the cause is manifested: that is, the good. The nature of the good is such that it is appetible. The causal influence of the good consists in its attraction. Thus the definition indicates the character of the good as end and final cause.[10]

Thomas also discusses the definition of the good with respect to its substance. One of his remarks is that the definition must not be understood to mean that there is one specific good that all things desire. The good for human beings is different from the good for animals. Every thing desires a good that suits its nature. The definition expresses "the good in general" (*bonum communiter sumptum*).[11] Thomas gives the definition an ontological import. It is for this reason that in his discussion of the transcendentals (for example, in *De veritate* 1.1 and 21.1) he uses the phrase "the good is what all things desire" as the definition of the transcendental good.

In the first lectio of his commentary Thomas seems to follow a twofold strategy. On the one hand, he attributes to moral philosophy a place of its own in the system of the sciences. But from his interpretation of the definition of the good cited in passing by Aristotle, we may infer that Thomas places the beginning of the *Ethics* explicitly in the metaphysical perspective of the transcendentals. Why he does this he does not say, but it seems not improbable that there is a connection with Aristotle's critique, later in the first book of the *Ethics*, of Plato's Idea of the Good.

In chapter 4 Aristotle adduces several objections to Plato's conception of the "general Good." The most important (1096a23–29) is that the Idea of the Good presupposes that in all good things there is one and the same form and nature of "good." But "good is spoken of in as many ways as being is spoken of." The good in the category of substance is god and mind, in that of quality, the virtue; in that of quantity, the measure; in that of relation, the useful; in that of time, the opportune moment. "Hence it is obvious that one common Idea of the Good that is universal does not exist." An important consequence of the diversity of goods for Aristotle is that the study of the good must be undertaken in diverse sciences. Even if there is one good that is commonly predicable, the knowledge of it would be of no use to the carpenter or weaver. The investigation of the good for man is the domain of practical philosophy. This conviction determines the starting point of his *Ethics*.

---

[10] Cf. *In M* I, lec. 11, 179 (Marietti edition): "Bonum enim secundum propriam rationem est causa per modum causae finalis. Quod ex hoc patet, quod bonum est, quod omnia appetunt. Id autem, in quod tendit appetitus, est finis."

[11] *In NE* I, lec. 1, 11.

Thomas does not deny Aristotle's conclusions, but his accent is somewhat different. He is focused not on the categorial diversity of the good but on its transcendentality. If good is found in all categories, then it is convertible with being.[12] The transcendental commonness of the good must be distinguished from the commonness of the Platonic Idea, because it does not presuppose one form or nature of the good. The categorial diversity of the good does not exclude a science that considers the good in general. The transcendental consideration of the good is the domain of the science that deals with being in general, metaphysics. This conviction determines the starting point of Thomas's commentary on the *Ethics*.

2. On the Good in General (*ST* Ia.5.1)

In the *Summa theologiae* I, question 5, Thomas deals with "the good in general." In article 1 he gives a strictly metaphysical account of the thesis of convertibility, which he mentions in his commentary on the *Ethics*. His argument for the ontological connection between being and goodness consists of four steps.

The starting point is the concept (*ratio*) of good. This consists in the good's being "desirable," for the good is the end for appetite. Thomas refers here, of course, to Aristotle's definition at the beginning of the *Ethics*. The second step in the argument is that "desirable" is identified with "perfect" (*perfectum*): "Now it is clear that a thing is desirable insofar as it is perfect, for all things desire their own perfection." In this step the transition is made from the concept of good to the nature of the good.[13] Proper to the good as good is that it is perfect. "Perfect" is that which has attained its end; the notion expresses completeness. The third step is the identification of what is "perfect" with what is "in act" (*in actu*). A thing is not perfect when its potentialities are not yet actualized. It is not completed until it has attained its act. Only then is the thing what it can be. By means of the notion of "act" Thomas is now able to establish the connection between good and being. For to be (*esse*) is the actuality (*actualitas*) of every thing. With this final step Thomas has arrived at the foundation of the thesis that every being is good. "Therefore it is manifest that good and being are really identical."[14]

---

[12] *In NE* I, lec. 6, 81. Cf. *QDM* 1.2 ad4.

[13] Thomas makes this distinction between the *ratio* and the *natura* of the good in *SCG* I.37.

[14] Cf. Jan A. Aertsen, "The Convertibility of Being and Good in St. Thomas Aquinas," *New Scholasticism* 59 (1985): 449–70.

The thesis of the convertibility of being and good is often interpreted in a moral sense and, on the basis of this understanding, sharply criticized. Values, as John F. Crosby argues, are irreducible to being: "The person as substantial and the person as having nobility, excellence, dignity are to all eternity distinct dimensions of the being of the person."[15]

Against this interpretation two things should be noted. First, when being is understood as actuality, no value can be outside of being. No person would have any nobility or dignity if this perfection were not actualized. As Thomas puts it, "Every excellence [*nobilitas*] in a thing belongs to it according to its being."[16] Every being—a natural thing, an action, or a being of reason—*as being* is good. The reduplicative statement expresses the formal point of the thesis of convertibility. It is a metaphysical or metaethical thesis. Second, an often neglected aspect of Thomas's doctrine is that he not only defends the identity of being and goodness but also introduces a difference between the two. Interestingly, the *Summa* (Ia.5.1) presents both moments.

The first objection in this question refers to a statement from Boethius's treatise *De hebdomadibus*: "I perceive that in nature the fact that things are good is one thing, that they are is another." Therefore it seems that being and good differ really. In his reply to this objection Thomas repeats the conclusion of his preceding argument: being and good are really identical. Yet this does not mean that "being" and "good" are synonymous. There is a conceptual difference between the two, for "good" expresses something different from "being." The concept "good" adds something to "being," namely, the aspect of "desirableness." From this conceptual difference another, real difference results: that between being absolutely (*ens simpliciter*), which I call B1, and good absolutely (*bonum simpliciter*), G1. What does Thomas mean by this difference?

The proper meaning of "being" is that something is in act. An act is related to a potency. Therefore, something is called B1 insofar as it is first distinguished from something that is merely in potency. This primary act is the substantial being of each thing. A thing is therefore B1 by its substantial being—for example, human being. By actualities added to the substance, such as white being, a thing is called "being in a certain respect" (*ens secundum quid*), B2, for these actualities belong to something that is already in act.

With respect to the good, the reverse applies. The concept "good" says that something is perfect and has therefore the aspect of being final (*ra-*

---

[15] John F. Crosby, "Are Being and Good Really Convertible: A Phenomenological Inquiry," *New Scholasticism* 57 (1983): 493–94.

[16] SCG I.28.

tionem ultimi). Hence, something is called G1 when it possesses its *ultimate* perfection through actualities added to the substantial being. A thing that has substantial being but not the ultimate perfection it ought to have is called "good in a certain respect," G2, because it has a certain perfection insofar as it is a being. To be a human being is a good, but this is not identical with being a good human being.

Boethius's statement about the nonidentity between being and being good is interpreted by Thomas as a reference to the difference between being absolutely and good absolutely. There appears to be an inverse ordering between the two: what is B1 is only good initially, G2; what is G1 is accidental in an ontological respect, B2.[17] This conclusion leads to an important specification with respect to the interchangeability of being and good. The thesis of convertibility applies to being and to good taken generally. Every being as being, regardless of whether it is B1 or B2, is good. Not considered in this thesis is the question whether this good must be understood as G1 or G2. But when the thesis bears upon "being absolutely" and "good absolutely," it is no longer valid. Good in the primary sense is *not* interchangeable with being in the primary sense. On the contrary, this good divides being.[18] Not every being is good absolutely.

In *Summa theologiae* Ia.5.1 Thomas does not indicate wherein the complete goodness of a thing consists. Elsewhere he argues that this completion concerns the actualization of the powers or faculties of a being in act. The perfection to which the appetite of everything is directed is the operation, because through the activity the powers and faculties inherent in its substance are actualized. In Scholastic philosophy, this actuality is called "the second act." The first act is the specific form whereby a thing has being; the second act is its operation.[19] By its first act, its substantial being, a thing is "being absolutely"; by its second act, its activity, it is "good absolutely." But from the terms "first" and "second" act it appears that the difference between good in a certain respect and good absolutely cannot be described only through the model of an inverse ordering of being and goodness. The first act and the second act are in line: the first act is for the sake of the second act; both are an ac-

---

[17] *ST* Ia.5.1 ad1. Note in particular (Marietti edition): "Secundum primum actum est aliquid ens simpliciter; et secundum ultimum, bonum simpliciter. Et tamen secundum primum actum est quodammodo bonum; et secundum ultimum actum est quodammodo ens."

[18] *QDV* 21.2 ad6 (Leonine edition): "Aliquid potest dici bonum et ex suo esse, et ex aliqua proprietate vel habitudine superaddita. . . . Ratione igitur primae bonitatis ens convertitur cum bono et e converso; sed ratione secundae bonitatis bonum dividit ens."

[19] *In NE* I, lec. 1, 12: "Finale bonum in quod tendit appetitus uniuscuiusque est ultima perfectio eius. Prima autem perfectio se habet per modum formae, secunda autem per modum operationis." Cf. *QDV* 1.10 ad3; *ST* Ia.48.5 and 105.5.

tuality (*actualitas*).[20] Since actuality is always the actualization of being, the absolute goodness of a thing can also be seen as its completed and perfected *being*.

The difference between good in a certain respect and good absolutely holds for every thing, because in each (finite) thing to be and to act are not identical. This non-identity is important to the relation between metaphysics and ethics, for the proper subject matter of the latter science are human actions.

3. On the Good in Human Action (*ST* IaIIae.18.1–4)

Part IaIIae of the *Summa theologiae* is concerned with "a moral consideration of human acts" (question 6, prologue). Human acts (*actus humani*) are to be distinguished from acts of a human being (*actus hominis*). The latter are actions found in human beings but not attributed to them insofar as they are human. Acts as growth or digestion are called "natural" rather than "human." Properly, human acts proceed from reason and will, the faculties proper to a human being.[21] In these voluntary acts the moral good appears, since "the *genus moris* begins where the reign of the will is first found."[22]

Summa theologiae IaIIae.18 deals with the goodness of human acts. Article 1 opens with the statement "We must speak of good and evil in actions as of good and evil in things." Thomas adduces in explanation the correlation between being and acting: "because such as everything is, such is the action it produces." The second act is proportional to the first act of being. Each agent acts insofar as it is in act; its mode of acting follows its mode of being.[23] Yet it is not the intrinsic connection between things and their actions that Thomas investigates in question 18.1–4. Things and actions are treated, as we shall see, as separate orders.

First, Thomas considers the goodness in the order of natural things: "Now in things, each one has as much good as it has being (*esse*), for

---

[20] *QDSC* 11 (Marietti edition): "Sicut autem ipsum esse est actualitas quaedam essentiae, ita operari est actualitas operativae potentiae seu virtutis"; *ST* Ia.54.1.

[21] *ST* IaIIae.1.1. Cf. *In NE* I, lec. 1, 3: "Dico autem operationes humanas quae procedunt a voluntate hominis secundum ordinem rationis; nam, si quae operationes in homine inveniuntur quae non subiacent voluntati et rationi, non dicuntur proprie humanae sed naturales, sicut patet de operationibus animae vegetabilis."

[22] *In Sent* II.24.3.2.

[23] *ST* IaIIae.18.1: "De bono et malo in actionibus oportet loqui sicut de bono et malo in rebus: eo quod unaquaeque res talem actionem producit, qualis ipsa est." Cf. *ST* Ia.89.1: "Cum nihil operetur nisi in quantum est actu, modus operandi uniuscuiusque rei sequitur modum essendi ipsius."

good and being (*ens*) are convertible." For this convertibility he refers to the first part of the *Summa*. In question 5.1 it appeared that there is not only an identity between being and goodness but also a difference. Now Thomas again introduces the difference between good in a certain respect and good absolutely (*ST* IaIIae.18.1), which he here describes not by the inverse ordering of being absolutely and good absolutely but by the term "fullness of being" (*plenitudo essendi*). Created things possess the fullness of being only through a diversity of acts (*secundum diversa*). Hence it is possible that a thing has being but still is lacking in the fullness of its being. Because the fullness of being belongs to the very notion of good, a thing is said to be good absolutely if it has its fullness. If a thing is lacking in its due fullness, it is good only in a certain respect, namely, insofar as it is a being. Thomas next applies the transcendental perspective to the goodness of human actions. Because being and good are convertible, we must say "that every action has goodness insofar as it has being." If, however, a human action is lacking in something that is due to its fullness of being, it is lacking in goodness and is said to be evil.[24]

In articles 2–4 of question 18 Thomas works out the fullness of being—in article 3 also called "the fullness of perfection" and "the fullness of goodness"—with regard to natural things and to actions. Since we are not interested in the details of his analysis, we are limiting ourselves to a brief description of it. The first that belongs to the fullness of being is that which gives a thing its species. That which specifies a natural thing is its form; that which specifies an action is its object. "Therefore, just as the primary goodness of a natural thing is derived from its form, which gives it its species, so the primary goodness of a moral action is derived from its suitable object" (article 2). Yet in natural things the "fullness of perfection" consists not solely in the specific form but also in supervening accidents such as, for example, shape and color in a human being. The same is the case in the operation. The fullness of its goodness also includes its due circumstances of place and time, which are, as it were, its accidents (article 3). Finally, for both the goodness of things and the goodness of human actions, the relation to the end that they depend upon is essential (article 4). As a distinction must be made

---

[24] *ST* IaIIae.18.1, esp.: "In rebus autem unumquodque tantum habet de bono, quantum habet de esse: bonum enim et ens convertuntur, ut in primo dictum est. Solus autem Deus habet plenitudinem sui esse secundum aliquid unum et simplex; unaquaeque vero res alia habet plenitudinem essendi sibi convenientem secundum diversa. Unde in aliquibus contingit, quod quantum ad aliquid habet esse, et tamen aliquid eis deficit ad plenitudinem essendi eis debitam. . . . Sed quia de ratione boni est ipsa plenitudo essendi, si quidem alicui defuerit debita essendi plenitudo, non dicetur simpliciter bonum, sed secundum quid."

between the form and the final end of a thing, so must one be made between the object and the end of an action. When a person gives alms from vainglory, a good action is ordered to an evil end.

At the close of article 4 Thomas summarizes his analysis and reviews the elements of the goodness of human action. This goodness is fourfold: the first concerns the action as such (its genus), the second is derived from the suitable object (its species), the third from the circumstances (its accidents), and the fourth from the end, as from the cause of goodness.

What interests us in question 18.1–4 is the question as to the intention of Thomas's analysis. The conclusion that the goodness of the action is *fourfold* plays an important role in the interpretation of his ethics, emphasizing its autonomy in relation to metaphysics. The fourfold goodness is seen as the expression of the special character of the moral order.[25] This special character, it is argued, becomes obvious through comparison with a text (*ST* Ia.6.3) in which it is said that the perfection of a thing is *threefold*: it consists in the being (*esse*) that a thing possesses through its substantial form, in the accidents that are necessary for the perfect action, and in the attainment of its end.[26] In Thomas's analysis of human action (*ST* IaIIae.18) the first perfection, that of being, is divided into two elements, namely, the act as such and its specification. The act as such is the first, generic goodness, because as act it is a being and therefore possesses a certain goodness. Yet this goodness is not moral in character. Moral good and evil do not occur until the act is specified by its object. This specification must therefore be distinguished from the first goodness of the act, which is the foundation of the moral order, but this order itself cannot be deduced from the first goodness.

The argument that in articulating the fourfold goodness of the human action Thomas intends to express the special character of the moral order is not convincing. It is not based on the comparison with the goodness of things in question 18 but rests entirely on a comparison with *Summa theologiae* Ia.6.3. This comparison seems to me misplaced, because the latter text deals with the perfection of a thing that consists in its ultimate act, the activity. The complete goodness of a thing is the second actuality, which is the accidental completion of the first act of being. In IaIIae.18.1–4, however, things and actions are treated as separate orders. That the action is the ultimate act of the *thing* remains outside of

[25] Kluxen, *Philosophische Ethik*, pp. 184–86.
[26] *ST* Ia.6.3: "Perfectio autem alicujus rei triplex est. Prima quidem, secundum quod in suo esse constituitur. Secunda vero, prout ei aliqua accidentia superadduntur ad suam perfectam operationem necessaria. Tertia vero perfectio alicujus est per hoc quod aliquid aliud attingit sicut finem."

consideration. The accidents mentioned in 18.3, such as color and shape in a human being, are not the accidents that are necessary for the perfect operation. If it had been Thomas's intention in question 18 to show the uniqueness of the moral order, then this must appear from his comparison with the order of things in the first four articles.

What is most striking in Thomas's analysis is precisely the parallelism that he develops between the two orders, in keeping with his starting point: "We must speak of good and evil in actions as of good and evil in things." He discusses both the good of things and the good of actions according to the scheme of genus, species, accidents, and end. The first that belongs to the *fullness* of being of a natural thing is the form which gives it its species. This implies that in things too the specific goodness is preceded by a generic goodness. This goodness consists in this: that as a natural thing it is a being and as such—that is, not yet specified to this or that being—is good. It is this idea that is formulated in 18.1 with reference to the thesis of the convertibility of being and good.[27]

Thomas's intention (in *ST* IaIIae.18.1–4) is not to express the special nature of the moral order in contrast to the order of things but to explain the goodness in human actions by analogy with the goodness in things. In both orders there is a generic goodness whereby something is good in a certain respect, and a specific goodness as the first condition of the fullness of being whereby something is good absolutely. Thomas's procedure in this text is illuminating for his view of the relation between metaphysics and ethics.

He considers two distinct orders, the good of natural things (*bonum naturae*) and the good of human actions (*bonum moris*).[28] The consideration is based on the outcomes of his reflection on the good in general, the convertibility with being and the difference between good in a certain respect, and good absolutely. There is a structure common to both orders, one that is studied by the *scientia communis*: metaphysics. Thomas's analysis in IaIIae.18.1–4 is a concrete application of the analysis of the transcendental good in Ia.5.1, to which he refers. There are, indeed, dif-

---

[27] This interpretation is confirmed by the train of thought in a parallel text, *QDM* 2.4 (Leonine edition). There the goodness of the human act as act, its generic goodness, is put on the same level as the good of an animal as animal that is not yet specified to the proper good for a human being, horse, or cow: "Manifestum est autem quod non est eadem perfectio propria omnium, set diuersa diuersorum. . . . Vnde aliter oportet accipere bonum animalis et bonum hominis, et equi et bouis. . . . Et similiter dicendum est in actibus de bono et malo. Nam alia est consideratio boni et mali in actu secundum quod est actus, et in diuersis specialibus actibus."

[28] Cf. *QDM* 2.5 ad2: "Ens et bonum conuertuntur simpliciter et in quolibet genere. . . . Set uerum est quod ens simpliciter non conuertitur cum bono moris, sicut nec etiam cum bono nature."

ferences between the two texts. In the latter text the non-identity between good in a certain respect and good absolutely is related to the distinction between substantial being and accidental being, in the former text to the distinction between generic being and the fullness of being. That has to do with the fact that IaIIae.18.1–4 deals with human action that itself is an accidental perfection. But the main point is that the order of natural things and the order of human actions, which Thomas had distinguished in the system of the sciences in the commentary on the *Ethics*, are brought together into the transcendental consideration of the good. The meaning of the metaphysical interpretation is to make the structure of the morally good action understandable.

4. "The Good of Man Is to Be in Accordance with Reason" (*ST* IaIIae.18.5)

It is not until article 5 (*ST* IaIIae.18) that Thomas unfolds the specific character of the moral order. He comes back to his exposition in article 2, where he formulated the first condition of the fullness of being and of goodness. Just as the primary goodness of a natural thing is derived from its form, which gives it its species, so the primary goodness of a moral action is derived from its suitable object. It is this specification of an action which Thomas works out in article 5.

When every action derives its species from its object, it follows that a difference of objects causes a diversity of species in human actions. A difference of objects causes a diversity of species in actions only insofar as the objects are essentially referred to one active principle. A difference of objects, which is essential in reference to one active principle (for instance, to know color and to know sound in reference to sense), may be accidental in reference to another active principle (for instance, to the intellect). In human actions good and evil are essentially related to reason, "because the good of man is to be in accordance with reason [*bonum hominis est secundum rationem esse*]." Consequently, the difference of objects, which specifies human actions, is the difference of good and evil in relation to reason. A human action is good *qua* species when its object is in accordance with the order of reason.[29]

Thomas adduces a brief and quite general argument for his view that

[29] *ST* IaIIae.18.5. See also the summary in 18.8: "Actus omnis habet speciem ab objecto, et actus humanus qui dicitur moralis, habet speciem ab objecto relato ad principium actuum humanorum, quod est ratio. Unde si objectum actus includat aliquid quod conveniat ordini rationis, erit actus bonus secundum suam speciem, sicut dare eleemosynam indigenti."

the human good is to be in accordance with reason: "for the good of each thing is that which suits it [*convenit*] according to its form." This points to the intrinsic connection between things and their actions, which remained outside of consideration in question 18.1–4. The specific goodness of a human action is derived from its suitable object. What a *suitable* object of an action is can be understood only in correlation with the substantial form of a thing, for activity is the completion of the first act of being and its goodness. Because the distinctive form of a human being is that which makes him a rational animal, his good is to act in accordance with reason.[30] Reason is therefore the rule and measure of morality ("moralium mensura est ratio").[31]

A distinctive feature of Thomas's ethics which comes to the fore is the correlation between morality and rationality (*ST* IaIIae.18.5). Moral acts are voluntary acts, but the will itself is not the measure of the goodness of an action. In contrast to natural processes in which the rule regulating the action is the natural virtue itself, in voluntary actions the will must be regulated by a principle different from the will. This principle is human reason: "Only insofar as the good is ordered by reason does it pertain to the *genus moris* and cause moral goodness in the act of the will."[32]

A point that requires clarification is the question of the nature of the rationality, expressed in the principle "the good of a human being is to be in accordance with reason." Does this principle mean that the possession of scientific knowledge (*scientia*) makes someone morally good? As has been suggested by Eleonore Stump and Norman Kretzmann, science is the actual exercise of the specifying potentiality for human beings: "Since human beings are essentially rational animals, human moral goodness is coextensive with actualized rationality."[33] Thomas recognizes that scientific knowledge is a good. It is one of the intellectual virtues that Aristotle deals with in the *Ethics*. Yet it is not a virtue in a strict sense, for a virtue is somehow related to the will.[34]

---

[30] *In NE* II, lec. 2, 257: "Bonum cuiuslibet rei est in hoc quod sua operatio sit conveniens suae formae; propria autem forma hominis est secundum quam est animal rationale." *ST* IaIIae.85.2: "Quae quidem convenit homini ex hoc ipso quod rationalis est: ex hoc enim habet quod secundum rationem operetur, quod est agere secundum virtutem."

[31] *SCG* III.9. Cf. *ST* IaIIae.90.1: "Causa et radix humani boni est ratio." On reason as the principle of morality, see the remarkable study by Léonard Lehu, *La raison règle de la moralité d'après saint Thomas* (Paris: J. Gabalda, 1930), pp. 44–77 (on *ST* IaIIae.18.5).

[32] *ST* IaIIae.19.1 ad3. Cf. Carlos Steel, "Natural and Moral Ends according to Thomas Aquinas," in *Finalité et intentionalité: Doctrine thomiste et perspectives modernes*, ed. Jacques Follon and James McEvoy (Paris: Vrin, 1992), pp. 113–26.

[33] Stump and Kretzmann, "Being and Goodness," p. 107. See also pp. 103–5, esp. n. 30.

[34] *QDVC* 12 ad15 (Marietti edition): "Ex hoc autem aliquid morale dicitur, quod se habet aliquo modo ad voluntatem."

Thomas expressly criticizes Greek intellectualism.[35] A human being is called "good absolutely" not in virtue of his intellect but in virtue of his will. The will concerns the whole human person; it commands the acts of all human powers. A human being possessing scientific knowledge—Thomas gives the example of grammar—is good not absolutely but only in a certain respect (*secundum quid*). On the basis of his knowledge such a person has acquired the capacity (*facultas*) for good action, but knowledge of grammar does not guarantee that a person will always speak correctly. An evil will is not opposed to knowledge of truth. A grammarian can voluntarily make a spelling mistake. Yet something is called good absolutely not insofar as it is in potency but insofar as it is in act.[36]

Instructive for the relation between rationality and morality is the first lectio of Thomas's commentary on the *Ethics*. The classification of the sciences is founded on a fourfold relation of order to reason. The order that reason produces in the actions of the will pertains to the consideration of moral philosophy. Moral goodness has a practical character. Consequently, reason that is the ordering principle of human actions is not theoretical but practical, for it is proper to practical reason alone to be directed to action.

5. The Good and Practical Reason (*ST* IaIIae.94.2)

Human reason is not the measure of things but the measure of what is to be done by human beings. In forming its judgments, practical reason is aided by law, defined as "a rule and measure of acts through which someone is led to acting or is held back from it."[37] Thomas's classic exposition of natural law (in *ST* IaIIae.94.2) contains a number of aspects that are of importance for the relation between metaphysics and ethics.[38] I restrict my attention here to just these aspects.

Noteworthy in this text in the first place is that Thomas develops a structure for practical science, parallel to that of theoretical science. The analogy, which is an original element in his ethics, forms the starting point of his argumentation: "The precepts of natural law are to practical reason as [*sicut*] the first principles of demonstrations are to theo-

[35] Cf. his critique of "the opinion of Socrates" in *ST* IaIIae.58.2.

[36] *ST* IaIIae.56.3; *QDVC* 7 and ad 2.

[37] *ST* IaIIae.90.1.

[38] See for this text Germain Grisez, "The First Principle of Practical Reason," in *Aquinas: A Collection of Critical Essays*, ed. Anthony Kenny (Notre Dame: University of Notre Dame Press, 1976), pp. 340–82.

retical reason, for both are self-evident principles [*principia per se nota*]."
Practical and theoretical reason have the same formal structure of rationality. Earlier in his Treatise on Law (*ST* IaIIae.91.3) Thomas had already observed that they follow the same procedure (*processus*): both
proceed from principles to conclusions. As theoretical reason starts from
first principles that are naturally known, so practical reason starts from
first principles—the precepts of natural law.[39] At the same time the domain of practical thought is distinct from that of theoretical thought, for
each has its own first principles. The analogy is therefore an indication
of the autonomy of ethics.

Yet this does not mean that the practical is separated from the theoretical. Theoretical reason and practical reason are not "two branches"
of knowledge. They are not distinct powers but differ only in their ends:
theoretical reason is directed solely to the knowledge of truth, whereas
practical reason directs truth to action. Its end is the operation. Practical reason knows truth, just as theoretical reason does, but regards the
known truth as the norm (*regula*) of action. The striking term through
which Thomas characterizes the relation between theoretical and practical reason is "extension": theoretical reason becomes practical only *per
extensionem*.[40] There is no reason at all to minimize the significance of
this expression. "Extension" implies that human reason is theoretical
prior to its becoming practical. Thomas's analogy between theoretical
and practical reason (in *ST* IaIIae.94.2) must also be understood as a relation between what is prior and what is later. We must see what sense
of priority is meant here.

Both theoretical and practical reason proceed from self-evident first
principles. Thomas discusses the nature of these propositions and introduces a distinction between them. Some propositions are self-evident
only to the learned, who understand the meaning of the terms of such
propositions. Other axioms are universally self-evident because the
terms of these propositions are known to all.[41] Those that are known
to all human beings are those that are most common (*maxime communia*).[42] They are the *prima* to which Thomas refers in the first lectio of his
commentary on the *Ethics*. Thus he enters the domain of the transcen-

---

[39] Cf. *QDV* 16.1.

[40] *ST* Ia.79.11 sed contra; *QDV* 14.4; *In Sent* III 23.2.3.2.

[41] *ST* IaIIae.94.2: "Sicut dicit Boethius, in libro De hebdomadibus, quaedam sunt dignitates vel propositiones per se notae communiter omnibus; et hujusmodi sunt illae propositiones quarum termini sunt omnibus noti. . . . Quaedam vero propositiones sunt per se
notae solis sapientibus, qui terminos propositionum intelligunt quid significent."

[42] *In BDH*, lec. 2, 20.

dentals by reducing the universally self-evident principles to the first intelligibles.

The next part of the argument is focused on the order among the transcendentals. The order is related to the apprehension of the most common notions. That which the intellect first conceives is "being," for its understanding is included in all things whatsoever a human being apprehends.[43] That being is the first known is a central thesis of Thomas's philosophy and his doctrine of the transcendentals.[44] The remarkable thing in his exposition is that he establishes a relation of foundation between the first conception of the human intellect, "being," and the first principle of theoretical reason. The principle of contradiction—"the same thing cannot be affirmed and denied at the same time"—is founded (*fundatur*) on the notions of "being" and "not-being."[45] Thomas gives a transcendental foundation to the principle that Aristotle in *Metaphysics* 4.3 (1005b14) called the *anhypotheton* of human thought.

In the continuation of his argument Thomas makes the transition from theoretical to practical reason, a transition that goes together with a change in what is first known: "As 'being' is the first that falls under the apprehension absolutely [*simpliciter*], so 'good' is the first that falls under the apprehension of practical reason." Being is the first known in the absolute sense, but "good" is the first concept of practical reason, for practical reason is directed to action, and every agent acts for an end, which has the nature of good.[46] The order among the most common notions throws light on the priority of theoretical reason to practical reason. "Being" is analytically prior to any other concept, and since being is the object of theoretical reflection, theoretical reason precedes practical reason. In the "extension" of theoretical to practical reason, the good, which is the last in the order of the transcendentals, becomes the first.

The analogy between theoretical and practical reason enables Thomas to establish a relation of foundation between the notion of "good" and the first principle of practical reason. The *ratio* of good is "that which all

---

[43] *ST* IaIIae.94.2: "In his autem quae in apprehensione omnium cadunt, quidam ordo invenitur. Nam illud quod primo cadit sub apprehensione est ens, cujus intellectus includitur in omnibus quaecumque quis apprehendit."

[44] See his most important text on the transcendentals: *QDV* 1.1.

[45] *ST* IaIIae.94.2: "Et ideo primum principium indemonstrabile est quod non est simul affirmare et negare, quod fundatur supra rationem entis et non entis; et super hoc principio omnia alia fundantur, ut dicit Philosophus in IV *Metaph*." Thomas works out the relation of foundation in *In M* IV, lec. 6, 605.

[46] *ST* IaIIae.94.2: "Sicut autem ens est primum quod cadit in apprehensione simpliciter, ita bonum est primum quod cadit in apprehensione practicae rationis, quae ordinatur ad opus: omne enim agens agit propter finem, qui habet rationem boni."

desire." Hence the first principle of practical reason is "Good is to be done and pursued, and evil avoided."[47] This principle has the same structure as the principle of theoretical reason, insofar as both principles are marked by an opposition.[48] But the first principle of practical reason, based on the notion of the good, has a *normative* character. The principal act of practical reason is to prescribe.[49] Its first principle, "good is to be done," is "the first precept of law" which directs human actions.

Concluding Remarks

The relation between metaphysics and ethics remains unclear in Thomas's classification of the sciences, which was the point of departure of this essay. He distinguishes different orders of reason to which the different sciences correspond but does not indicate whether there is any relation between them, and he includes metaphysics under natural philosophy. The analysis of Thomas's reflection on the good, its relation to being, and its practical character clarifies his view of the relation between metaphysics and ethics in three respects.

1. The good belongs to the transcendentals that are studied by metaphysics because they are common to all things. The transcendentality of the good plays an important role in the key texts I have discussed. Thomas explains the goodness in human actions by a comparison with the goodness in natural things, which is based on the convertibility of good and being and on the difference between good in a certain respect and good absolutely. From this text (*ST* IaIIae.18.1–4) it is apparent that the doctrine of the transcendentals has an *integrating* function: it analyzes the good common to the different orders of natural things and human actions and applies the common structure to the two orders.

2. The good belongs to the first conceptions of the intellect. The cognitive mark of the transcendentals has a *founding* function that comes most clearly to the fore in Thomas's account of natural law. The first principle of theoretical reason, which pertains to the domain of metaphysics, is reduced to "being"; the first principle of practical reason to "good" (*ST* IaIIae.94.2). "Being" and "good" are different *prima* but are not separated. The transcendental foundations of theoretical thought

[47] *ST* IaIIae.94.2: "Et ideo primum principium in ratione practica est quod fundatur supra rationem bonip quae est, bonum est quod omnia appetunt. Hoc est ergo primum praeceptum legis, quod 'bonum est faciendum et prosequendum, et malum vitandum.'"
[48] Cf. *QDM* 10.1.
[49] *ST* IaIIae.47.8.

and morality indicate therefore the connection between metaphysics and ethics. Ethics as science is not based on "the actual experience of the moral"; it requires a reflection on the foundation of praxis.

3. The first principle of practical reason is founded on the transcendental *ratio* of good, "that which all things desire." Consequently, this principle shows both the connection of ethics with metaphysics, which reflects on the good in general, and the autonomy of ethics (it is its first principle). Thomas himself points out that the extension of the theoretical to the practical leads to another understanding of the good. When we consider the good theoretically, we consider it under the aspect of *true*. So we can define "good" and reflect on its *ratio*. When we consider good practically, we consider it insofar as it is the end of an action. Good is then considered *as good* and is manifested in its practical character.[50] The good to be done is the *human* good.[51]

[50] *QDV* 3.3 ad7.

[51] A first draft of this paper was read at the Ninth International Congress of Medieval Philosophy (Ottawa, August 17–22, 1992) in a special session in honor of Norman Kretzmann. I am grateful to Scott MacDonald and Eleonore Stump for their comments on this draft.

PAUL VINCENT SPADE

ða.

Degrees of Being, Degrees of Goodness: Aquinas on Levels of Reality

This essay is unlike others in this volume. Its focus is almost entirely on Aquinas's metaphysical views; the consequences for his moral theory are only indirect. But Aquinas's moral theory is grounded in part in his metaphysics. It should come as no surprise, therefore, that a revised understanding of his metaphysics might well affect our understanding of his moral theory too. Here I propose such a revised view of Aquinas's metaphysics. Its consequences for moral theory I leave mostly undeveloped, although I do make some suggestions along the way and at the very end. I leave their full development to the reader.

1

It is a commonplace that Aquinas accepted the doctrine of the so-called transcendentals. In fact, at the beginning of his *De veritate* he offers a very interesting systematic "deduction" of the other transcendentals from the central notion of *being* (*ens*).[1] There are six such transcendentals discussed in the passage: being, thing, one, something (*aliquid*),[2] good, and true.

One item stands out in this list: good. It is the only one there that in altogether ordinary usage, prior to any special philosophical theory, ad-

---

[1] *QDV* 1.1 resp. See also *ST* Ia.5.1 (on good), Ia.11.1 (on one), and Ia.16.3 (on true). For all texts of Aquinas, I have used the critical Leonine edition (1882–) where it is available. Otherwise, I have used *In M* (Marietti) and *In Sent* (Mandonnet-Moos). All translations are my own.

[2] Read etymologically, as *aliud quid*.

mits of degrees. Few people but philosophers (and not all of them) will talk about levels or degrees of being, unity or truth, and not even philosophers talk about degrees of "thing" or "something."[3] But everyone talks about degrees of goodness; 'good', 'better' and 'best' are in everyone's idiom.

Indeed, in the *Summa theologiae* (Ia.5.1 obj. 3) Aquinas appeals to just this disparity as the basis for an argument against the convertibility of being and good: "Moreover, good admits of more and less. But being (*esse*) does not admit of more and less. Therefore, good is really different from being (*ente*)." In his reply to this objection, Aquinas rejects the conclusion but says nothing to contradict the premise: "Likewise it is to be said to the third [objection] that good is said according to more and less according to a supervening act—for instance, according to knowledge or virtue."[4]

Nevertheless, whether pre-theoretical usage countenances it or not, there are plenty of passages where Aquinas does not hesitate to speak of degrees of truth and being, or degrees of unity.[5] There are many ways of interpreting such passages. But there is in particular one prominent interpretation of Aquinas according to which being, in its most fundamental sense, does *not* admit of degrees. This interpretation may be found, among other places, in an elegant article by Joseph Owens, "Common Nature: A Point of Comparison between Thomistic and Scotistic Metaphysics."[6] The interpretation proposed there is the main focus of this study. I do not want to claim that Owens has misinterpreted the very ample textual evidence he cites to support his interpretation.

---

[3] No doubt this is because the words are grammatically not adjectives or adverbs and so do not admit of comparative forms. Nevertheless, the noun 'thing' (*res*) does have the adjectival form 'real' (*realis*), and one does find authors talking about degrees of "reality."

[4] The reference to knowledge in this reply may at first seem puzzling, more appropriate to true than to good. (See again *QDV* 1.1 resp.) But in fact it is not so difficult. Aquinas is saying that a human being, for instance, is said to be better or worse according to certain actualizations of his distinctive potentialities—perhaps appetitive ones (hence 'virtue' in the quotation) or cognitive ones (hence 'knowledge'). A human being with knowledge is thereby *better* than one without. The point of the response, then, is that the possession of virtue or knowledge is an actualization of a potential. Since Aquinas has just argued (in the reply to obj. 1) that being is linked to actualization, the result is that it is one and the same feature that gives a human being both more goodness (because greater perfection) and more being (because greater actuality). Thus, not only is it proper to speak of degrees of being, but it is proper to speak of them *for the same reason* that it is proper to speak of degrees of goodness. Objection 3 therefore fails. (I am grateful to an anonymous referee for shedding light on this passage.)

[5] For truth and being, see the fourth of the famous "five ways" in *ST* Ia.2.3. For unity, see *ST* Ia.11.4 ad1.

[6] Joseph Owens, "Common Nature: A Point of Comparison between Thomistic and Scotistic Metaphysics," *Mediaeval Studies* 19 (1957): 1–14.

But I do think that if Aquinas held what Owens says he did, then he shouldn't have held it. For there are features of Aquinas's doctrine, ironically some of the very features Owens appeals to, that commit Aquinas to the direct opposite of what Owens attributes to him. Thus, if Owens has correctly interpreted the textual evidence he cites, then Aquinas simply has an inconsistent theory.

On Owens's interpretation, Aquinas is committed to rejecting degrees of being.[7] How can this interpretation be maintained, given the passages where Aquinas explicitly allows gradations in the transcendentals?

Well, a distinction must be drawn. Often when Aquinas speaks of degrees of being, he is ranking things according to their level of perfection.[8] In this sense, the measure of a thing's perfection, and so where it stands in the ranking, depends—to put it roughly—on how much it can do. Thus, inanimate material bodies merely exist; they do little else. Organisms, however, not only exist but are alive; they possess the additional powers of growth and reproduction. Animals do all of that and in addition are able to move about under their own power and to sense the material world around them. Human beings in turn have all these powers plus the additional power of intellectual knowledge.[9] And so on. The resulting hierarchy is of course familiar to anyone conversant with the broad Platonic-Augustinian tradition.

Owens does not deny that Aquinas allowed degrees of reality in this sense but does deny it in another, more basic sense. In the hierarchy just described, things are ordered according to a ranking of their *natures* and the powers built into those natures. But at least as Owens interprets it,

---

[7] A point of clarification: strictly speaking, the question (1) whether there are different *kinds* of being, in the sense relevant to this essay, is distinct from the question (2) whether those different kinds of being are *ranked* in hierarchical order so that one can speak of them in terms of more and less, in terms of "degrees." The second question presupposes an affirmative answer to the first. Owens argues that Aquinas does not admit *kinds* of being in the relevant sense, from which it of course follows that he would not allow their being *ranked* in terms of more and less. I argue, on the contrary, that Aquinas *is* committed to different kinds of being, but it by no means automatically follows that he is also committed to ranking them in a hierarchy. Nevertheless, I do not think ranking is the real issue here; the important question is whether there is anything to be ranked. Given the Avicennian background to the medieval discussion, as described by Owens and as sketched briefly in section 2 below, there is little doubt that Aquinas would have ranked the relevant kinds of being if he had had any reason to admit their distinction in the first place. (I argue that he did have such a reason.) Accordingly, I continue to speak of Aquinas as committed to "degrees" of being, even though my main theoretical task is to argue for an affirmative answer to question (1) above.

[8] This seems to be what is happening in, e.g., the "fourth way" of *ST* Ia.2.3. (Cf. also note 5 above.)

[9] Different parts of this picture may be found in *ST* Ia.4.2 ad3, Ia.76.3 resp., Ia.76.4 ad3; *SCG* I.28, etc.

any *given* nature either exists, in individuals or in the mind as a concept, or else it does not. To the question of existence the answer can only be yes or no; there are no degrees or levels about that.

It is thus a little like a radio for which the on/off switch is separate from the volume control. The volume can be set at different degrees or levels, and the higher it is set the more powerful (metaphorically, the more "perfect") the resulting sound. But wherever the volume is set, the radio as a whole is either on or off. Being on and very loud does not count as being "more on" than does being on but very soft.

It is in this sense, then, that Owens says Aquinas does not allow degrees of being. In this sense, to call prime matter, for example, a being merely "in potency" is not to say it really *is* a kind of being after all—although only a low-grade, undignified, "potential" one—but rather to say it is *not* really any kind of being at all, but only "potentially" a being.

This then is Owens's interpretation. But there is also textual evidence for the view that Aquinas *is* committed to degrees of being in the sense Owens denies. If this is so, then good, which is convertible with being but makes a kind of "oblique reference" to desire or appetite,[10] will admit of more and less not only because some things are simply more *desirable* than others but also because some things simply *are* more than others.

2

As the title of his article suggests, Owens is concerned with the theory of "common natures"—in effect, the problem of universals.[11] He be-

---

[10] See *ST* Ia.5.1 resp.; *QDV* 1.1 resp. The phrase 'oblique reference' is mine, not Aquinas's; in the fourteenth century this kind of reference would be expressed by saying the term "connotes" desire or appetite. But this is not Aquinas's usual vocabulary.

[11] In late medieval usage the expression 'common nature' is often reserved to refer to a universal in the *metaphysical* sense described by Boethius in his second commentary on Porphyry, *In Isagogen Porphyrii commenta*, ed. Samuel Brandt, Corpus Scriptorum Ecclesiasticorum Latinorum, vol. 8 (Vienna: F. Tempsky, 1906), pp. 162.16–163.3: something shared by several things (a) as a whole, (b) simultaneously, and (c) in such a way that it enters into their innermost metaphysical makeup. By contrast, the term 'universal' is often reserved for the *logical* sense described by Aristotle at *De interpretatione* 7 (17a39–40): what is naturally apt to be "predicated of many." Although Aquinas does sometimes use the term 'common nature' (e.g., *In Sent* I.23.1.1), it does not appear to be reserved for use as a technical expression in his vocabulary. Nevertheless, it does emerge as a technical expression later on and is in any case a convenient way to capture a notion that is certainly present in Aquinas, even though he may express it in a variety of ways. I follow Owens and continue to use the term here.

gins by looking to Avicenna for background. For Avicenna, a nature—
for example, *animal*—is neither singular nor universal taken just in itself. It *is* singular—for instance in Fido and Dobbin and Socrates—and
it *is* universal as a concept in the mind, predicated of many things. But
in itself it is neither the one nor the other. Taken in itself, the nature is
neutral on the question of unity.[12] And it is this neutral, indeterminate
nature that came to be called the "common nature."

On the other hand, although the question of unity does not apply to
the common nature all by itself, Avicenna thought there is a kind of reality or being that does belong to the common nature all by itself.[13] It is
not the full-fledged existence the nature has in individuals, to be sure,
and neither is it the kind of being the nature has as a universal concept
in the mind. But it is there nonetheless, a kind of "lesser being" ontologically prior to these distinctions. It is what some Latins would later
call an *esse essentiae* ("being of essence").

When all this is put together, Avicenna leaves us in a curious situation. Common natures have a kind of "lesser" being all their own, prior
to their being in individuals or in the mind, but they have no unity of
their own at all.[14]

By the time Avicenna's texts were in general circulation in Europe,
Latin philosophy was thoroughly committed to the convertibility of the
transcendentals, and in particular to the Augustinian view that being
and unity are equivalent. Obviously then, Avicenna's theory, which allowed a kind of being where there was no unity, could not be accepted
as it stood.

There were two possible ways to go. One could (a) accept the Avicennian view that common natures have a lesser kind of being of their
own and conclude that therefore they have some kind of unity of their
own too, despite Avicenna's arguments that they do not. On this alternative, one would have to distinguish kinds or grades of unity to go

---

[12] See *Logica* III, in Avicenna, *Opera in lucem redacta ac super quantum ars niti potuit per
canonicos emendata* (Venice: Bonetus Locatellus for Octavianus Scotus, 1508), fol. 12ra. See
also his *Metaphysics* V.1, in Avicenna, *Liber de philosophia prima sive scientia divina*, ed. Simone van Riet, 2 vols., Avicenna Latinus (Louvain: E. Peeters, 1977–80), vol. 2, p. 228.31–
36 (= ed. 1508, fol. 86va); p.230.58–70 (= ed. 1508, 86vb); p. 231.74–81 (= ed. 1508, fol.
86vb); pp. 233.36–234.44 (= ed. 1508, fol. 87ra). A sketch of Avicenna's arguments for this
striking conclusion may be found in Owens's article. The arguments are not silly, but they
are far from unproblematic, particularly the argument about singularity. But this is not
the place to dwell on them.

[13] See, e.g., Avicenna *Metaphysics* V.1, vol. 2, pp. 233.36–234.44 (= ed. 1508, fol. 87ra).

[14] Avicenna's doctrine is of course much more nuanced than this quick sketch indicates.
But nothing in this essay rests on the correct interpretation of Avicenna, or even on the
correct interpretation of the way Avicenna was viewed in the Latin Middle Ages. I am
here simply following Owens's own way of setting up his presentation.

along with kinds or grades of being. Or one could (b) accept Avicenna's denial that common natures have any kind of unity of their own and conclude that therefore they have no being of their own either, not even a "lesser" being, despite what Avicenna said to the contrary. According to Owens, Duns Scotus, with his doctrine of "real, less than numerical unity," took the first alternative, Aquinas the second. Both were consciously working in the context of Avicenna's views.

3

For Aquinas, on Owens's interpretation, the *only* kind of being a thing has is its act of existing, its *esse*, or what later would be called its *esse existentiae* ("being of existence"). Aquinas has no room for Avicenna's "lesser being" belonging to natures in their own right. In part, this is because of his theory of essential predication. As Owens explains it:

> Predication requires identity of subject and predicate. It asserts that the one is the other. If the nature to be predicated of the individual had of itself any being whatsoever, it could not actually be predicated, for the required identity would be rendered impossible. *Any being of its own would at once set up the nature as a reality distinct in some real way from the individuating principle, and so would prevent the identity necessary for predication.* Predication requires a genuine identity in reality between nature and individual. Such identity is possible because of the entire lack of being in the essence considered absolutely just in itself and in abstraction from any existence.[15]

The talk of predication here as requiring an identity of subject and predicate (or of their ontological correlates, if we insist on restricting predication to a purely linguistic relation) frequently confounds readers coming at this material from an analytic background. After all, if 'Socrates is a man' is true because Socrates is identical with the common nature *man*, and if 'Plato is a man' is true because Plato is identical with that same common nature *man*, then why can't we conclude that Socrates is Plato, by the transitivity and symmetry of identity? But in fact the idea is not so hard to explain. The common human nature, insofar as it is *common*, is "potential" in the sense of being indeterminate, indefinite. It can be narrowed down, "contracted" or "individuated," either to Socrates or to Plato or to any other human being. To say then that Socrates is identical with the common nature *man* is simply to say that Socrates is *actually* what that common nature is *potentially*. Or, more

---

[15] Owens, "Common Nature," p. 6 (emphasis added).

fully, that Socrates is *actually* identical with *one* of the things (namely, Socrates himself) with which the common nature is *potentially* identical. And so is Plato, for that matter. But it in no way follows from this that Socrates is Plato. In short, Aquinas's theory of predication that Owens is appealing to here is an offspring of the marriage of identity (plain old identity, familiar to any analytic philosopher) with the distinction between potency and act. The latter distinction is a notoriously difficult one, but it is not especially a difficulty about the notion of identity.

Nevertheless, I find Owens's argument in the foregoing passage obscure. Why *should* attributing being to the nature like this get in the way of the identity needed for predication? Is the idea simply that, as the italicized portion of the quotation seems to suggest, Socrates cannot be identical with something distinct from himself? But if we understand predication in the way just described, it does not appear that attributing being to the nature all by itself *does* make it distinct from Socrates in any way that threatens the required identity. In short, there seems to be something missing from the argument.

Let us therefore look more closely at what Aquinas has to say about common natures.

4

The following discussion can be regarded as in effect a partial and very selective commentary on the notion of "form" in Aquinas's *De ente et essentia* 2–3. Aquinas of course discusses common natures in many other places too, but this will suffice to make the point I want to present.

First, a distinction, one half of which can be disregarded. Aquinas mentions (*DEE* 2.285) what he calls the "form of the whole" (*forma totius*).[16] This is to be distinguished from the "form of the part" (*forma partis*).[17] The latter term is not used in *De ente et essentia*, but Aquinas does use it elsewhere.[18] The form of the part is what Aristotle called τὸ τί ἦν εἶναι and εἶδος and identified as the substantial form of a material substance, excluding the matter.[19] The exclusion of matter is what makes

[16] On this locution, see Armand Maurer, trans., *Thomas Aquinas: On Being and Essence*, 2d rev. ed. (Toronto: Pontifical Institute of Mediaeval Studies, 1968), p. 31 n. 7.

[17] The genitives in 'form *of* the whole' and 'form *of* the part' are "genitives of apposition," as in 'the city *of* Chicago'—that is, the city that *is* Chicago. For 'the form of the whole,' see the explanation at *DEE* 2.284–91.

[18] For example, *In M* VII.9.1467–69. See also *SCG* IV.81.

[19] On the Greek equivalents, see Armand Maurer, "Form and Essence in the Philosophy of St. Thomas," *Mediaeval Studies* 13 (1951): 165–76.

it "partial" for Aquinas; for him the whole essence includes not only the substantial form but matter as well.[20] In the case of a human being, the form of the part is the rational soul, the form of the body.

The form of the whole, on the other hand, is the whole essence, including both the substantial form *and* the matter. It is what Aristotle called the τὸ τί ἔστιν.[21] In the case of a human being, the form of the whole is *man*, or *humanity*. (The distinction between the concrete and abstract forms of the noun is significant, as we shall see later in this section.) Terminologically, it is perhaps a bit confusing to call the entire essence here a "form," since it includes matter as well, but that is what Aquinas does call it.[22] In an immaterial substance, of course, the distinction between the form of the part and the form of the whole breaks down. The substantial form in that case just *is* the essence; there is no matter involved. Henceforth, we are concerned only with a material substance's form of the whole, the entire essence, Avicenna's common nature.[23] I mention the form of the part only to set it aside.

In *De ente et essentia* Aquinas speaks of the form of the whole, the essence or common nature, as being "taken," "expressed," "signified," or "considered" in various ways. These locutions are puzzling. One wants to know whether they reflect ontological distinctions, purely psychological or verbal distinctions, or what. Let us begin with two distinctions:

First, Aquinas sometimes speaks of certain features as "belonging" to an essence "as such." For example: "In this sense, nothing is true of it [a

---

[20] At *DEE* 2.67–84, Aquinas anticipates an objection: "But because matter is the principle of individuation, perhaps it would seem to follow from this that an essence, which embraces in itself matter together with form, is particular only, and not universal." In response, he introduces a distinction between what he calls "designated matter" and "undesignated matter." The former is the principle of individuation; the latter is what is mentioned in the definition of man, which signifies the essence. The nuances of Aquinas's theory of designated matter are notoriously complex, and in fact he seems to have changed his theory over the course of his career. For an informative study, see M.-D. Roland-Gosselin "Le principe de l'individualité," in his *Le "De ente et essentia" de s. Thomas d'Aquin* (Paris: J. Vrin, 1948), pp. 51–134, esp. chap. 11, pp. 104–26.

[21] Again, on the Greek equivalents, see Maurer, "Form and Essence."

[22] For his reason for the terminology, see *DEE* 1.34–35, and the explanation in Maurer, *On Being and Essence*, p. 31 nn. 7–8.

[23] Avicenna does not use the term 'form of the whole' but does explicitly say that the essences of composite substances consist of both form and matter. See his *Metaphysics* V.5, vol. 2, p. 275.62–75 (= ed. 1508, fol. 90ra). Aquinas himself draws the terminological connection between Avicenna's doctrine of essence and what Aquinas calls the "form of the whole." See *In M* VII.9.1467–69, where Avicenna's view is contrasted with that of Averroës, for whom the essence is what Aquinas calls the "form of the part." See also Aquinas, *In Sent* I.8.5.2; *In Sent* IV.44.1.1 sol. 2 ad2. For a discussion, see Maurer, "Form and Essence."

nature or essence] except what belongs to it (*convenit sibi*) as such. . . . For example, to man insofar as he is man there belongs 'rational,' 'animal,' and the other things included in his definition."[24]

As the quotation's second sentence suggests, what "belongs" to an essence "as such" seems to be just what is mentioned in the definition of that essence. Now if "rational" is one of the things that "belongs" to the essence of man "as such," then presumably "irrational" is by the same token "ruled out" by the essence of man "as such." Just as anything having the essence of man is rational ("by nature," as we say), so too anything having the essence of man is by nature *not* irrational. I shall import some terminology from logic and say that what "belongs" in this sense to an essence "as such" is *entailed* by that essence, and that what is "ruled out" by an essence "as such" is *inconsistent* with that essence.[25]

For the first distinction, then, we want to consider (a) what is entailed by an essence, (b) what is inconsistent with it, and (c) everything else.[26]

The second distinction recognizes that Aquinas speaks of essences as being "taken," "expressed," "signified," or "considered" in different ways. Let *e* be an essence and let *w* be one of the "ways" Aquinas recognizes of taking it. What exactly are we saying about something *x* by predicating of it the essence *e* taken in way *w*? We shall say that, with respect to *w*, *e* "includes" a feature φ if and only if to predicate of *x* the essence *e* taken in way *w* is to say that *x* has feature φ.[27] Likewise, we shall say that with respect to *w*, *e* "excludes" feature φ if and only if to

---

[24] *DEE* 3.29–34. Aquinas is here discussing the essence "considered as whole and absolutely"; see (2a) below. But for the present that refinement does not matter; I only wish to call attention to the notion of what "belongs" to an essence "as such."

[25] This may seem like a needless multiplication of terminology, since we already have the locutions 'belongs to' and 'is ruled out by.' But I want terminology that *looks* like technical vocabulary, so that the reader is warned when it occurs and will know to read it in the sense just described. 'Belongs to' and 'is ruled out by' are too plain for that purpose.

[26] "Tall" and "red-haired," for example, are neither entailed by "man" nor inconsistent with it.

[27] Notice how I put this. I do *not* say "if *e* taken in way *w* is truly predicated of *x*, then *x* has feature φ." The latter will be trivially true if *e* taken in way *w* cannot be truly predicated of anything at all. But we shall be talking about ways of taking an essence so that it *cannot* be truly predicated of anything, and in such cases we do not want the essence to "include" absolutely *everything* by default. What I intend here, therefore, is more a matter of a "meaning" relationship. If it were not for this complication, I would have said simply that with respect to way *w*, "*e* includes a feature φ if and only if, if *e* taken in way *w* is truly predicated of *x*, then *x* has feature φ," and bypassed the awkward notion of what it is "to say" that *x* has φ. Note also that in order to avoid uncontrollable complications, I am confining myself to the "ways" of taking *e* that Aquinas explicitly discusses in *DEE* 2–3, as described below. I do not intend to include "ways" in a more general sense such as various *metaphorical* ways of taking things. (I am grateful to Eleonore Stump, who called my attention to this potential complication in an earlier draft.)

predicate of x the essence e taken in way w is to say that x does *not* have feature φ. Otherwise, we shall say that e taken in way w neither includes nor excludes φ.

Combining these two distinctions, let us now ask which of the kinds of things listed in (a)–(c) above is included and which is excluded by various essences taken in the various ways Aquinas discusses.

The semiformal machinery is of course not Aquinas's own way of doing things. But I do not think it distorts what he does do, and it will serve, I hope, to organize and clarify his very diffuse discussion.

The form of the whole or essence, Aquinas says, can be considered either *as* a part or *as* a whole.[28] The difference lies in whether the essence is signified with or without "precision." To signify an essence with precision is to *exclude* what is not entailed by the essence; to signify it without precision is simply to leave what is not entailed by the essence out of account, without positively excluding it.[29] Thus:

(1) Considered as a *part*, the essence is signified *with precision* from all other ingredients of the individual in which it is found. Aquinas gives as an example the term 'body' (*DEE* 2.105–50), which can be used not only in the sense in which we say Socrates is a man—that is, a rational animal, and therefore a rational sensate living *body*—but also in the sense in which we say Socrates is a *composite* of body and soul, so that body is just one part of him.[30] It is in the latter sense that body is considered as a part. Thus:

> Therefore, the noun 'body' can signify a certain thing that has a form such that the possibility of designating three dimensions *with precision* in [that thing] follows from [the form]—that is, so that no further perfection follows from the form. Rather, if anything else is added on, it is beyond the signification of 'body' said in this way. In this sense, the body will be an integral and material part of an animal, because in this way the soul will be

---

[28] *DEE* 2.242–308.

[29] See Maurer, *On Being and Essence*, p. 39 n. 15. Medieval authors did not use the word 'precise' and its related forms loosely. The word comes from *praescindere*, "to cut off."

[30] The example is a notoriously difficult one, but it is Aquinas's own. There are conflicting ways to interpret the passage, but as I understand it, at least part of the point rests on the fact that in Latin (as in English) the *same* term 'body' (*corpus*)—not just related terms, such as 'body' and 'bodiliness'—can be taken in both ways, both as signifying the essence with precision and as signifying it without precision. 'Body' is a rather unusual word in this respect. In Latin as in English there are not many terms that can play this dual role, and it is therefore all the more instructive to ask why Aquinas picked it for his example. In my view, Aquinas means to contrast this case with other concrete nouns, such as 'animal,' which normally signify the essence only without precision, and therefore to reinforce the semantic distinction he generally observes between concrete and abstract nouns. See the discussion below.

beyond what is the significate of the noun 'body,' and it will come in addition to the body, so that the animal will be constituted out of these two [factors]—body and soul—as out of parts.[31]

More often, however, Aquinas uses the grammatically abstract form of the noun to signal the essence or common nature considered as a part. In the case of human nature, it is 'humanity.' In the terminology introduced above, we can say then that humanity

(α) *includes* just exactly what is entailed by the essence (by human nature), and
(β) *excludes* everything else.

Thus:

If on the other hand the nature of the species is signified with precision from designated matter, which is the principle of individuation, then it will stand in the manner of a part. It is signified in this way by the name 'humanity.' For 'humanity' signifies that whereby a man is a man. . . . Since, therefore, humanity *includes* in the understanding of it only the factors whereby a man has it that he is a man, it is plain that designated matter is *excluded* or prescinded from by [its] signification.[32]

(2) The essence or common nature considered as a *whole*, on the other hand, is signified *without precision* from everything else. The other ingredients of the individual in which it is found are left out of account but not positively ruled out. The term Aquinas uses to signify the essence considered in this way is grammatically the concrete form of the noun;[33] in the case of human nature, it is just 'man.'[34]

The essence considered as a whole (that is, without precision) can in turn be taken in various ways.[35]

(2a) *Absolutely*. Aquinas doesn't have any special terminology to express every occurrence of this notion, but when it occurs in *subject* position, he often uses so-called "reduplicative" expressions, 'as-' or '*qua-*' locutions. In

[31] *DEE* 2.123–34.

[32] *DEE* 2.254–65.

[33] But terminology is not an infallible guide here. We just saw that the concrete term 'body' could be used also for the nature considered as a *part*.

[34] This is why, as promised above, the distinction between the concrete and abstract forms of the noun is significant.

[35] *DEE* 3.26–72.

the case of human nature, we have 'man as man,' 'man *qua* man,' or 'man as such.' The essence or form of the whole considered in this way

(a) *includes* exactly what is entailed by the essence, and
(b) *excludes* only what is incompatible with the essence.[36]

(2b) "According to the being (*esse*) it has in this or in that [individual]."[37] And this in turn admits of two subcases:

(2b.i) "In singulars," which here means *material* individual things.
(2b.ii) "In the soul," as a concept in the mind.[38]

This is at first obscure. "According to the being" *what* has in this or in that individual? It is clear from the context that it is the "essence" that is here said to have being in this or in that individual. But it is also clear that this is supposed to be one of the ways of considering the essence "*as a whole*." Now metaphysically speaking, the essence as a whole is just the *whole individual*.[39] We signify it without bringing out all its individual features explicitly, to be sure, but it is the whole individual that is signified, nothing else. Thus, "For the noun 'man' signifies it [the essence] as a whole—that is, insofar as it does not prescind from the designation of matter but rather contains it implicitly and indistinctly. . . . And therefore the name 'man' is predicated of individuals. . . . *For this reason the name 'essence' is sometimes found predicated of a thing. For we say that Socrates is a certain essence.*"[40]

So when Aquinas says we are going to consider the essence "as a whole" according to the being it has in this or in that individual, this is strictly speaking incoherent. It amounts to saying we are going to consider an *individual*, or perhaps several individuals, according to the being they have *in* this or that individual. But of course individuals do not have being *in* individuals.[41] Aquinas goes on: "And in this way something is predicated of [the nature or essence] accidentally by reason of

[36] What is neither entailed by nor incompatible with the essence is neither included nor excluded by the essence taken in this way. See above on the notions of inclusion and exclusion as used here.

[37] *DEE* 3.46–47.

[38] *DEE* 3.52–72.

[39] Otherwise it could not be predicated of the individual. I am taking seriously Owens's account of Aquinas's theory of predication, as described in section 3 above. See also the explicit statement in the passage quoted at the end of this paragraph.

[40] *DEE* 2.294–306, emphasis added.

[41] Aquinas does say that individual accidents have being *in* individual substances. But that is not what we are talking about here. We are asking about the relation between an

what it is in, as it is said that man is white because Socrates is white, although this does not belong to man insofar as he is man."[42]

The first part of this passage is just as obscure as what went before. What we are talking about is the essence taken as the whole *individual*. But individuals do not exist in individuals.

Nevertheless, despite the wording, the example Aquinas gives clarifies his intention. We say man is white ('a man is white' is better in English, but Latin does not have the article) because Socrates is white, and in doing so we are considering the essence as a whole "according to the being it has" in Socrates.

In terms of predication, what is going on here is clear enough. We are taking the indefinite and indeterminate word 'man,' which signifies the essence as a whole, indefinitely but without precision, and are then predicating of it a predicate ('white') that picks out one of the features we did not take into account by using the word 'man' but did not prescind from either. When we do this we *continue* to signify the essence by the word 'man' in such a way that we leave that feature out of account without prescinding from it, since if we were *not* leaving it out of account, the predicate would not *have* to be added separately, and if we *were* prescinding from it, it *could* not be added.

In this sense, then, man is white, Greek, snub-nosed, running, and so on, insofar as Socrates is white, Greek, snub-nosed, and running. On the other hand, insofar as man exists as a concept in the mind, it is universal, predicated of many, immaterial, and so on. Thus, taken according to (2b), man

(α) *includes* whatever is true of the material individual or of the concept under consideration, and
(β) *excludes* everything else.

5

For Aquinas, the essence or nature taken in sense (1) does not exist. The term 'humanity,' for instance, is simply a non-denoting term. Although he never, as far as I know, makes this striking claim outright, it nevertheless follows quite straightforwardly. If the nature considered

---

essence and the individuals of which it *is* the essence; in short, we are talking about an essential, not an accidental, relation.

[42] *DEE* 3.47–51.

as a part *prescinds* from—that is, *excludes*—what is not included in the essence of man, then it prescinds from or excludes existence or *esse*, which is included only in the essence of God.[43]

Humanity, then, does not exist for Aquinas. What does exist is a *composite* of humanity plus other factors—"individuating conditions," accidents, plus an act of existing or *esse* that actualizes the whole complex structure. But the resulting composite is not an existing *humanity*: it is an existing *individual*—say, Socrates.

Note that this conclusion commits us to the odd view that an existing whole can have a *non*-existing part—indeed a non-existing *essential* part. If Owens's interpretation of Aquinas is right, we cannot weasel out of this oddity by allowing that although this essential part, the nature, doesn't really *exist*, it is still "out there" with at least some minimal kind of "lesser" reality. No, if Owens is right, it has no reality *at all*.[44] We will return to this metaphysical oddity below.

Again, for Aquinas the essence or nature in sense (1) cannot be what is predicated of existing things. Given the theory of predication in terms of identity (as described in section 3 above), the common nature, in the sense in which it is predicated of existing things, must be taken in some way that doesn't positively *exclude* existence. Hence, "because a part is not predicated of the whole, thus it is that humanity is predicated neither of man nor of Socrates."[45]

In order to be predicated, then, the common nature must be taken not as a part but "as a whole"—that is, in some form of (2) above. But as *which* whole? If as the whole that is Socrates, that cannot be predicated of Plato. And if as the whole that is Plato, that cannot be predicated of

---

[43] Here is another argument for the same conclusion: It conforms to standard medieval logical usage to say x is non-φ if and only if x exists and x is *not* φ. That is, negative *predicates* can be truly affirmed only of things that exist (whereas negative *propositions* can be truly said also about things that do not exist). Now since neither being snub-nosed nor being non-snub-nosed is entailed by human nature (some people are the one, some are the other), both are *excluded* from human nature considered as a part. Hence humanity is not snub-nosed and yet humanity is not *non*-snub-nosed either. If humanity existed, therefore, then in virtue of the foregoing equivalence, it would be both not snub-nosed and not non-snub-nosed and so, by double negation, both not snub-nosed and yet also snub-nosed. Since this is a contradiction, it follows by *reductio* that humanity does not exist.

[44] Note that a similar situation arises for accidents. What exists is an individual substance *with* its accident; the accident itself has no reality of its own. Nevertheless, in this case Aquinas is willing to say that the accident has an "accidental being" (*DEE* 6.11–13). If Owens is right, this "accidental being" must be interpreted as we have just done for humanity, as a matter of *adding* something extra. What is added is not the being of the accident itself (except in a derivative sense) but rather the being of the composite; the accident does not have and never gets any being of its own.

[45] *DEE* 2.265–67.

Socrates. Similarly, if as the whole that is the concept in the mind, that cannot be predicated of either Socrates or Plato.[46]

In order to be predicated *of many*, therefore, the nature must not be taken in a sense that includes this or that *esse*, either (2b.i) in a material individual or (2b.ii) in the mind; that would preclude its being predicated of anything else. Only sense (2a) remains, and it is the nature taken in that sense that is "predicated of many" for Aquinas: "And this nature so considered is what is predicated of all individuals."[47] To put it another way, the nature taken in sense (1) cannot be predicated of many because it *excludes* too much. Taken in sense (2b.i) or (2b.ii) it cannot be predicated of many because it *includes* too much. Only in sense (2a) is the nature taken with the neutrality needed in order to be predicated of many.

But although the common nature taken as a whole absolutely is what is predicated of many, it cannot *exist* any more than can the common nature taken as a part. There exists no such thing as "man as such," although of course there exist individual men and there exists the concept "man." To say there exists no such thing as "man as such" is to say there exists nothing that is *completely* and correctly described by a term expressing the nature taken in sense (2a).

Let us put this another way. Although human nature in sense (2a) can be predicated of many, when it *is* predicated in this sense of something *x*, all we are saying about *x* is that it has the features entailed by human nature.[48] We are saying nothing at all about any other features *x* might or might not have. Something *completely* and correctly described by a term expressing human nature taken in sense (2a) would thus be something that had *exactly* the features entailed by human nature, and *no other features*. In short, it would just be *humanity* all over again and could not exist any more than the latter can, for exactly the same reasons.[49]

As before, if we accept Owens's interpretation of Aquinas, we can-

---

[46] Do not be confused. The concept *is* predicated of both Socrates and Plato. Insofar as predication is a *mental* act, the common nature can be predicated only if it is thought of or conceived. In that sense it is the conceived nature, the concept, that is predicated of Socrates and Plato. But it is not predicated *as* a concept—that is, in sense (2b.ii). Otherwise, since it is immaterial, when it is predicated of Socrates, it would follow that Socrates is immaterial too.

[47] *DEE* 3.70–72.

[48] See section 4 above.

[49] The fact that if "man as such" existed it would be identical with humanity should come as no surprise. When we talk about the nature considered as a whole absolutely and when we talk about the nature considered as a part, we are after all talking about the same thing, the nature. We are just "considering it" in different ways. Ontologically, it is all the same. Considered as a whole absolutely, it can be predicated of many; considered as a part, it cannot be predicated at all. In neither case does it exist.

not temper the ontological significance of this by allowing that what is predicated of many nevertheless has some lesser degree of reality all its own, a reality falling short of full existence but nevertheless enough to carry with it some minimal ontological dignity. No, if Owens is right, there are no degrees of reality for Aquinas.

Although Aquinas is silent about the ontological status of the nature considered as a part, he is more explicit about the nature considered as a whole and absolutely: "It is plain therefore that the nature of man absolutely considered, *abstracts from every being* (*esse*), yet in such a way that there is no precision from any of them."[50]

The crucial word here is the 'every.' Owens takes this passage, particularly the words 'abstracts from every being,' and argues that the nature so taken abstracts not only from the kind of being it has in material individuals or in the mind as a concept but from *every* kind of being; it has *no* being of its own at all, contrary to Avicenna.[51]

6

Owens's interpretation is an influential one. Many people have accepted it, both as the correct *interpretation* of Aquinas, and as the correct *theory* in its own right. Nevertheless, I think there are insuperable philosophical objections to it as a theory. In particular, I think there are two distinct but related problems.

First, how is this theory ever going to account for the *community*, the "commonness," of the common nature? For Aquinas, if Owens is right, the nature taken in sense (2a) is what is predicated of and so what is somehow metaphysically in both Socrates and Plato, and for that matter also in the mind as a concept. On the other hand, we are told, there is nothing metaphysically out there that *answers* to the nature so taken—nothing at all! From this standpoint, then, it looks as if Aquinas is heading straight for nominalism: there is *nothing* really common to many. This is not yet an objection,[52] but it is the beginning of one, as we shall see.

Second, there is an altogether similar situation with the Aristotelian theory of knowledge, which Aquinas by and large accepts. (He accepts

---

[50] *DEE* 3.68–70.

[51] Owens, "Common Nature," p. 6.

[52] At least it is not for those who, like me, do not think nominalism is automatically a philosophically objectionable position.

enough of it to generate *this* problem.) If the nature in the mind is not somehow *the same* as the nature in the thing, then how can our theory ground the objective certainty of knowledge? One of the main claims of the Aristotelian approach to epistemology is that the knower in a very real sense mentally "takes on" the form of the known object. Because it is *the same* form, no dubious inference is required, as it is for Descartes, from what is going on in the knower's mind to what is going on in the external world. But on Owens's interpretation, what is *the same* here is a complete nonentity; what is common to the known object and to the concept in the mind has no common *reality* at all, so that it is hard to see how it could be "the same."[53]

Let me develop these points more fully. As Owens has it, Aquinas seems to be unable to make up his mind. Sometimes he sounds like a nominalist, sometimes like a realist. If we stress the claim that knowledge and common predication are grounded in the common nature, then he sounds like a realist. But if we then add the claim that the common nature, taken in the only way in which it can do all this, *does not have any kind of reality at all*, then he certainly sounds like a nominalist.

On this reading, although Aquinas does not want to grant any reality to the common nature in the only sense in which it is common, he nevertheless wants it to do work for him. He refuses to give it any metaphysical rights yet demands that it take on epistemological and predicational duties. It is supposed to ground the objectivity of knowledge; it is supposed to be the justification for the fact that we predicate the same term 'man' of Socrates and Plato without being arbitrary about it. These are not trivial theoretical tasks. And yet we are asked to entrust them to a complete nonentity!

7

Let me introduce a basic philosophical principle that Aquinas appears to be violating, on Owens's interpretation. I call it the "Principle of Philosophical Fair Play." The idea is that if, in your philosophical thinking, you appeal to something to do a certain theoretical task for you, then it is only "fair" to grant that something some kind of "on-

---

[53] This problem is not avoided by interpreting Aquinas as saying only that when the knower "takes on" the form of the known object, the form in the mind is not strictly *identical* with the form in the object but only a kind of representation (literally, a "re-presentation") of it. The problem is precisely how the *same* thing can be "presented" twice, unless there is some unity between the two presentations, and therefore some being they share. But this shared being is just what Owens denies.

tological status" in your theory. After all, if it is not even there, it can hardly do any serious work, solve any philosophical problems for you. In short, the basic idea is *no pay, no work.*

I called this a "basic philosophical principle," but of course that does not mean it is certainly true, or that all serious philosophers have to agree on it. But it is at least initially plausible if one approaches things in a certain way.

For example—and this is *only* an example, not a theory I would recommend—consider thoughts. Thoughts, one might plausibly suppose, are distinguished from one another by what they are about, by their objects. Now thinking about a golden mountain is certainly quite different from thinking about a round square and from thinking about the present king of France. Hence those thoughts, it follows, are distinguished by their objects—that is, by golden mountains, round squares, and the present king of France. But those objects do not exist (and, in the second case, *cannot* exist).

In situations like this, some philosophers—for example, Meinong— found the Principle of Philosophical Fair Play to be so persuasive that they felt compelled to grant a certain kind of ontological reality to golden mountains, round squares, and present kings of France. Such things do not exist, of course, at least not in the familiar sense in which tables and trees do, but they must have *some* kind of reality or other, or else they could not do the jobs required of them.[54]

Thus, if we follow this line of reasoning, we begin to make distinctions among kinds of reality. The exact terminology does not matter, and in fact the "ranking" of the various kinds of reality does not matter[55]—so long as *everything* we are ever going to appeal to in our philosophy ends up being awarded some kind of reality or other.

On the other hand, one can imagine philosophers who do not find this "principle" to be persuasive, who are willing to reject it and to appeal to some things to play certain important theoretical roles for them, all the while denying that those things have any kind of reality at all. If Owens is right, Aquinas was just such a philosopher.

[54] Alexius Meinong, "The Theory of Objects," trans. Isaac Levi, D. B. Terrell, and Roderick M. Chisholm, in *Realism and the Background of Phenomenology,* ed. Roderick M. Chisholm (Glencoe, Ill.: Free Press, 1960; rpt. Atascadero, Calif.: Ridgeview, n.d.), pp. 76–117. The motivations behind Meinong's theory are of course much more sophisticated than my simple example about distinguishing thoughts. But the point stands: Meinong distinguishes his various kinds of being because he needs things of those various kinds to do theoretical work for him.

[55] That is, it does not matter whether one's theory awards familiar existing objects the "fullest" kind of reality or the least kind.

The reader may find the idea of appealing in this way to complete nonentities to do philosophical work a very strange idea indeed. But feelings of strangeness do not by themselves count as legitimate philosophical arguments. The Principle of Philosophical Fair Play, then, seems to me to be an open question about which reasonable philosophers can disagree. Nevertheless, it *is* clear that there are situations where one has to make a choice: either to *deny* the principle or to start distinguishing *kinds of reality*. Thinking about nonexistent objects, for example, may be one such situation (if we agree that thoughts are distinguished by their objects). Common natures are certainly another.

Aquinas appeals to the common nature in his account of predication and in his theory of knowledge. Hence either he is to have to grant it some kind of reality, or else he is going to have to deny the Principle of Philosophical Fair Play. According to Owens, Aquinas chose the latter alternative. Being is being, and that is all there is to it. It does not come in kinds or levels. The common nature has no being of its own at all; the only being it has is the *esse* or existence of the individuals in which the nature is found, or else the *esse* it has as a concept in the mind.

Nevertheless, if that *is* Aquinas's view, he has got himself into a hopeless fix. For even if he does in this sense deny the Principle of Philosophical Fair Play, there are other features of his doctrine that commit him to *accepting* it, at least for common natures. That is, the particular kinds of jobs Aquinas asks the common nature to do for him are jobs that *on his own grounds* cannot be done without granting it a being of its own.

What are those jobs? They are *unifying* jobs. Consider the first of the two problems raised in section 6 above. The nature in Socrates and the nature in Plato must somehow be *the same* nature, or else there is no real, non-arbitrary basis for Socrates' and Plato's both being called "men." Or, to put it in terms of predication, the nature in sense (2a) that is predicated of Socrates and the nature in sense (2a) that is predicated of Plato must be *the same* nature. If they were not, if what is predicated of Socrates were *not* the same as what is predicated of Plato, then each would be predicated of one thing only, and there would be nothing "predicated of many."

On the other hand, to say it is *the same* thing that is predicated in both cases is to say it is *one* thing.[56] And to say it is *one* is just to say it does have being after all, on the basis of the traditional equivalence of being and unity, which Aquinas certainly accepted. To say *the same one* com-

---

[56] On the link between sameness (*identitas*, identity) and oneness, see Aristotle, *Metaphysics* 5.9 (1018a8–9), and Aquinas, *In M* V.11.911–12.

mon nature considered as a whole and absolutely is what is predicated of many and then to say that *this same one* common nature has no being at all is to *deny* the equation of being and unity, not to uphold it in the face of Avicenna's theory, as Owens makes that theory out to be.

Similarly, consider the second problem I raised in section 6 above. If there is no sense whatever in which we can say that the nature existing mentally in cognition and the nature existing externally in Socrates and Plato are *the same one* nature, then the entire Aristotelian account of knowledge collapses, and with it the Aristotelian strategy for guaranteeing the objective certainty of our knowledge. That strategy depended crucially on our being able to say there is no inference needed to be sure our concepts match reality, since our concepts are formally identical with—that is, the same as, one with—the objects known. But if we say they are the same, then we are committed, on the basis of the equation of being and unity, to saying they have some degree of being too, contrary to Owens's account.

Notice that it does no good to say that, yes, the common nature does have being: (1) it has one (mental) being in the mind, but this is not the being it has in Socrates or Plato; (2) it has another being in Socrates, but this is not the being it has in Plato or in the mind; and (3) it has yet a third being in Plato, but this is not the being it has in Socrates or in the mind. Now we have *three* beings, and so three unities. But none of them is what we need. The being the nature has in Socrates will make the nature there the same as *itself*, but it will not make it the same as the nature in Plato or in the mind. For that we need a kind of being the nature has *in all three locales*. The only way to have that and simultaneously to preserve the convertibility of being and unity is to give the nature a kind of being all its own, a being the nature carries with it wherever it is found. And that is why I think Owens's reading of Aquinas, although it may accurately reflect one strand of Aquinas's thought, it at best only part of the story. Aquinas is committed to degrees of being whether he likes it or not.

If this conclusion is correct, then Aquinas's metaphysical commitments are much closer to those of Duns Scotus than has generally been thought. To be sure, these commitments are not stated as explicitly or in as much detail by Aquinas as they are by Scotus, but they are there. The convertibility of the transcendentals, together with Avicenna's granting of a lesser being but no unity at all to the common nature taken in itself, meant, as Owens says, that later Latin authors had to make a choice— the choice described at the end of section 2 above: either to allow degrees of unity corresponding to degrees of being, or to allow neither one. But, contrary to Owens, it does not appear that Scotus took the former path and Aquinas the latter. Rather Aquinas and Scotus together took the former path; the latter was left to thoroughgoing nominalists such as William of Ockham.

8

Although the discussion has so far proceeded entirely in terms of common natures, note that exactly the same situation arises with prime matter. If prime matter is going to do its job of providing the element of continuity in substantial change,[57] then the prime matter in the substance before the change occurs must be somehow *the same* as the prime matter in the substance that results from the change. But if it is the same, it is one, and if it is one, it is a being, in virtue of the convertibility of being and unity. Hence, like the common nature, if prime matter is going to be able to do its job, it must—on Aquinas's own grounds—be granted some kind of reality or being of its own, in addition to the reality or being it gets from the material substances in which it is found.[58]

This conclusion, like the conclusion about the being of common natures, seems to fly in the face of some of Aquinas's texts. For instance, "For matter by itself neither has being nor is knowable" (*ST* Ia.15.3 ad3). Again, "Being itself is not the proper act of the matter but of the whole substance. For being is the act of what we say *is*. But being is not predicated of the matter but of the whole" (*SCG* II.54). Yet again, "Matter is 'what according to itself' (that is, considered according to its essence) is 'neither a what' (that is, neither a substance) 'nor a quality,' nor anything in the other genera 'by which being' is divided or 'determined'" (*In M* VII.2.1285).[59]

On the other hand (*SCG* II.43), "For matter is only in potency." Likewise (*DPN* 2.117–18), prime matter "is in potency only." Again (*DPN* 1.31–32), prime matter "by itself . . . has an incomplete being (*esse*)." As in section 1 above, existing "in potency only" or "having an incomplete being" can be taken either as a lesser way of existing or else as not a way

[57] That is, if prime matter is going to be what is responsible for substantial change's being a *change*, not merely a *succession* whereby one substance is annihilated and is followed by another. If I die and someone else is born, we do not say I have *changed into* that other person unless there is something common to us both (as a theory of transmigration, e.g., would hold).

[58] Of course, it does *not* follow from this that prime matter can ever be *found* by itself, on its own, outside all material substances. That is quite another question, just as it is for the common nature.

[59] Aquinas is commenting phrase by phrase on *Metaphysics* 7.3 (1029a20–21).

of existing at all but only as "potentially" or "incompletely" existing. Owens is committed to the latter, I to the former.

Aquinas, it seems, tends to use the term 'being' (*esse*) to mean being in the *fullest* sense of the word, because that kind of being has a special role to play in his philosophy. He doesn't seem to have any term for the kind of "lesser" reality his theory commits him to, the "common" reality of common natures and of prime matter. But he is committed to it nonetheless.

9

The metaphysical conclusion derived above, that Aquinas is committed to kinds or degrees of being in the sense described, is the result of combining two themes in his philosophy: (a) the convertibility of the transcendentals, of being and unity in particular, and (b) the unifying tasks Aquinas calls on common natures and prime matter to perform. A second application of the convertibility of the transcendentals ensures that this metaphysical result will affect the theory of the good, and indeed of all the other transcendentals as well.

Thus, if common natures have a degree of being and unity of their own, apart from the being and unity they have in individuals, then—and not otherwise—they will have a degree of goodness of their own as well, apart from the goodness of the individuals partaking of those natures. As goods of their own, they can serve as ends and be desired in their own right. (The same result will hold for prime matter.) It is a legitimate question to ask how, as possible ends in themselves, desirable on their own, they are to be incorporated into moral theory. But I will not pursue that story here.

Norman Kretzmann's Publications on Aquinas

"Eternity" (with Eleonore Stump). *Journal of Philosophy* 78 (1981): 429–58; reprinted several times.

"Goodness, Knowledge, and Indeterminacy in the Philosophy of Thomas Aquinas." *Journal of Philosophy* 80 (1983): 631–49.

"Abraham, Isaac, and Euthyphro: God and the Basis of Morality." In *Hamartia: The Concept of Error in the Western Tradition*, ed. D. V. Stump et al., 27–50. New York: Edwin Mellen Press, 1984.

"Absolute Simplicity" (with Eleonore Stump). *Faith and Philosophy* 2 (1985): 353–82.

"Atemporal Duration: A Reply to Fitzgerald" (with Eleonore Stump). *Journal of Philosophy* 84 (1987): 214–19.

"Simplicity Made Plainer: A Reply to Ross" (with Eleonore Stump). *Faith and Philosophy* 4 (1987): 198–201.

"Being and Goodness" (with Eleonore Stump). In *Divine and Human Action*, ed. Thomas V. Morris, 281–312. Ithaca: Cornell University Press, 1988.

"God among the Causes of Moral Evil: Hardening of Hearts and Spiritual Blinding." *Philosophical Topics* 16 (1988): 189–214.

"*Lex iniusta non est lex*: Laws on Trial in Aquinas' Court of Conscience." *American Journal of Jurisprudence* 33 (1988): 99–122.

"Warring against the Law of My Mind: Aquinas on Romans 7." In *Philosophy and the Christian Faith*, ed. Thomas V. Morris, 172–95. Notre Dame, Ind.: University of Notre Dame Press, 1988.

"Trinity and Transcendentals." In *Trinity, Incarnation, and Atonement*, ed. Ronald J. Feenstra and Cornelius Plantinga Jr., 79–109. Notre Dame, Ind.: University of Notre Dame Press, 1989.

"Being and Goodness in Aquinas" (with Eleonore Stump). In *Knowledge and the Sciences in Medieval Philosophy*, vol. 3, ed. Reijo Työrinoja et al., 288–98. Helsinki, 1990.

"Reason in Mystery." In *The Philosophy in Christianity*, ed. Godfrey Vesey, 15–39. Cambridge: Cambridge University Press, 1990.

"A General Problem of Creation: Why Would God Create Anything at All?" in *Being and Goodness: The Concept of the Good in Metaphysics and Philosophical Theology*, ed. Scott MacDonald, 208–28. Ithaca: Cornell University Press, 1991.

"A Particular Problem of Creation: Why Would God Create This World?" In *Being and Goodness: The Concept of the Good in Metaphysics and Philosophical Theology*, ed. Scott MacDonald, 229–49. Ithaca: Cornell University Press, 1991.

"Prophecy, Past Truth, and Eternity" (with Eleonore Stump). In *Philosophical Perspectives, 5: Philosophy of Religion, 1991*, ed. J. W. Tomberlin, 395–424. Atascadero, Calif.: Ridgeview, 1991.

"Aquinas's Philosophy of Mind." In *Medieval Philosophy*, special issue of *Philosophical Topics* (Fall 1992): 77–101.

"Eternity, Awareness, and Action" (with Eleonore Stump). *Faith and Philosophy* 9 (1992): 463–82.

"Infallibility, Error, and Ignorance." In *Aristotle and His Medieval Interpreters*, ed. Martin Tweedale and Richard Bosley, *Canadian Journal of Philosophy*, suppl. vol. 17 (1992): 159–94.

Cambridge Companion to Aquinas, edited (with Eleonore Stump). Cambridge: Cambridge University Press, 1993.

"Philosophy of Mind." In *Cambridge Companion to Aquinas*, ed. Norman Kretzmann and Eleonore Stump, 128–57. Cambridge: Cambridge University Press, 1993.

"Aquinas on God's Joy, Love, and Liberality." *Modern Schoolman* 72 (1995): 125–48.

"God's Knowledge and Its Causal Efficacy" (with Eleonore Stump). In *The Rationality of Belief and the Plurality of Faith*, ed. Thomas Senor, 94–124. Ithaca: Cornell University Press, 1995.

"Aquinas's Disguised Cosmological Argument." In *Faith, Freedom, and Rationality*, ed. Jeff Jordan and Daniel Howard-Snyder, 185–204. London: Rowman & Littlefield, 1996.

"Creation Without Creationism." *Midwest Studies in Philosophy* 21 (1997): 118–44.

The Metaphysics of Theism: Aquinas's Natural Theology in Summa contra gentiles I. Oxford: Clarendon Press, 1997.

"Aquinas, Thomas" (with Eleonore Stump). In *The Routledge Encyclopedia of Philosophy*, vol. 1, 326–50. London: Routledge, 1998.
The Metaphysics of Creation: Aquinas's Natural Theology in Summa contra gentiles II. Oxford: Clarendon Press, 1998.

Norman Kretzmann died while working on *The Metaphysics of Providence: Aquinas's Natural Theology in* Summa contra gentiles III, the final volume of his trilogy on Aquinas's natural theology. Sadly, that project will remain forever incomplete. The chapters that Kretzmann was able to finish will be published in *Medieval Philosophy and Theology* 9 (2000).

Contributors

JAN A. AERTSEN is Professor of Philosophy at the University of Cologne and Director of the Thomas Institute.

E. JENNIFER ASHWORTH is Professor of Philosophy at the University of Waterloo.

JOHN BOLER is Professor of Philosophy, Emeritus, at the University of Washington.

MARK D. JORDAN is Professor in the Medieval Institute at the University of Notre Dame.

SIR ANTHONY KENNY is Warden of Rhodes House, Oxford.

PETER KING is Professor of Philosophy and Adjunct Professor of Classics at the Ohio State University.

SCOTT MACDONALD is Professor of Philosophy and the Norma K. Regan Professor in Christian Studies at Cornell University.

GARETH B. MATTHEWS is Professor of Philosophy at the University of Massachusetts at Amherst.

PAUL VINCENT SPADE is Professor of Philosophy at Indiana University.

ELEONORE STUMP is the Robert J. Henle Professor of Philosophy at St. Louis University.

References to Aquinas's Works

(Page numbers appear after the colon in each entry. Note numbers appear in parentheses after the page numbers.)

Index of Names

Ackerman, John, 10
Aertsen, Jan A., 8, 10, 237n, 238n, 240n
Albert the Great, 81n, 87, 89–90, 219
Alessio, Franco, 215n
Alfanus of Salerno, 85n
Alston, William, 34, 37n, 40–41, 45n, 62n
Ammonius, 214n
Anscombe, G. E. M., 134n, 135n, 140, 190n
Arendt, Hannah, 62
Aristotle, 15–27, 47, 72, 83–85, 87–90, 101,
   104n, 122n, 125, 130, 133, 135–37, 141–
   42, 162n, 164n, 188, 190n, 191n, 192,
   208, 210n, 211, 216n, 217–19, 232, 235,
   237–40, 248, 251, 257n, 260–61, 272n
Armstrong, R. A., 162n, 167n, 189n
Ashworth, E. Jennifer, 8, 209n, 214n, 216n
Audet, Th.-André, 84n
Augustine, 10, 47n, 73–74, 83, 88–89, 96n,
   159n, 182, 214n, 221, 225n, 232, 236
Averroës, 218–19, 261n
Avicenna, 85, 218–19, 258–59, 261n, 269

Bacon, Roger, 219, 221
Barnes, Jonathan, 136n, 218n
Bartholomaeus Anglicus, 85
Baur, Ludwig, 81n
Beaty, Michael, 31
Bennett, Jonathan, 35n
Bernstein, Richard, 62n
Berti, Enrico, 164n
Bezwinska, Jadwiga, 55n
Bloomfield, Morton W., 91n
Blund, John, 85

Boethius, 10, 97, 167, 210n, 219, 241–42,
   249n, 257n
Boler, John, 7, 159n
Borgnet, Auguste, 219n
Bosley, Richard, 211n
Boyle, Joseph M., Jr., 5, 72–74
Brady, Ignatius, 90n
Brandt, Samuel, 257n
Bunyan, John, 59n
Burgundio of Pisa, 85n
Burnyeat, Miles, 164n
Buzzetti, Dino, 214n

Cajetan, 73–74
Callus, D. A., 85n
Chisholm, Roderick M., 34, 271n
Cicero, 83, 89n
Clifford, W. K., 34
Constantine the African, 85n
Corcoran, John, 210n
Craemer-Ruegenberg, Ingrid, 81n, 237n
Crawford, F. Stuart, 218n
Crosby, John F., 241
Crowe, M. B., 161n, 162n
Czech, Danuta, 55n

Dahan, Gilbert, 216n
D'Arcy, Eric, 102n
Descartes, René, 112, 131, 270
Donagan, Alan, 5, 70–71, 137–38, 142,
   144–47, 155–57, 167n, 175n, 191n
Donceel, Joseph F., 65n
Dugauquier, Jean-Albert, 92n